# FOLLOWING THE
# Still Small Voice

READY WRITER
P R E S S

Published in the UK in 2022 by Ready Writer Press

Paperback ISBN 978-1-7396463-0-1
eBook ISBN 978-1-7396463-1-8

Cover design by SpiffingCovers.com

# FOLLOWING THE
# Still Small Voice
# Voice

David Robinson

# A Word of Thanks

I do wish to place on record my sincere and grateful thanks to two special people who have done so much to prepare my word processed manuscript for publication.

Our son in law, Mark Wooffindin has checked and formatted the manuscript into a form which is easier for a publisher to work with. Our granddaughter, Emma Wooffindin has painstakingly read the formatted manuscript checking it for errors before checking it again!. Many hours of work has been invested on my behalf and I am so grateful.

# Contents

# Foreword

It is fair to say, I have known of David Robinson for more years than I care to remember, but over the last 20 years I have had the privilege of getting to know him. In that time, I have had the honour of working with him in the areas of church leadership, charity work and governance.

I would describe David as gentle but tenacious, as I have seen first-hand his pastoral heart and determination for justice being brought to bear on behalf of those whose circumstances would define them as vulnerable and in need.

Another consistent trait over the years has been David's ability to recall and relate a good story, which has often brought some helpful insight for a particular challenge we may have been facing at the time.

The book you are holding is full of such stories from David's many years of working in commercial, charity and church environments. If you want to know how a person's faith can help navigate those three worlds well, this book is worth a read. You will see that simple belief and reliance in a God who guides, provides and intervenes has been evident throughout his life.

With the support of Edith, his family and friends, David has been instrumental in bringing about much needed transformation in the lives of countless individuals, has had the opportunity to influence government policy, and spoken to international audiences. I think he would readily acknowledge, in the words of Nehemiah, "The gracious hand of the Lord has been upon us."

Read, enjoy, laugh and cry as the anecdotes keep coming. Be ready to be inspired and challenged and brace yourself for a tale of adventure with God that can be your experience too.

David Jones.
(Chairman of the Board of Trustees, Christian Action and Resource Enterprise Ltd)
February 2022.

# I become the Man from the Prudential

The black bonnet of the old Morris Minor had never shone so much before. True, there were rust holes around the headlamps, but I had really worked on the bonnet and polished it to perfection. Now like a mirror, it reflected the blue early December sky. The stark bare branches of the overhanging trees formed a perfect picture in the deep black paint of the faithful little car's bonnet. I was excited as I drove out to the old grey stone market town of Holmfirth to begin a new job. This was not just a new job, it was to be the start of a whole new career with the promise of a new and brighter future for Edith my wife and Joy our nine months old daughter.

Waiting to welcome me, scrutinise me, and hopefully teach me all that I needed to know, was Walter Slater. He was to meet me outside the post office, and would be my superintendent and immediate boss. Mr Slater, (I did not dare call him by his Christian name) had worked for the Prudential Assurance Company for more years than I had lived, and my first glimpse of him filled me with foreboding. I was not sure what to make of him, he did not look the type of man who could be trifled with. I guess he must have looked at me with similar uncertainty.

I was thirty five years younger than him, with none of the self assured confident air he exuded. In fact, I was not too sure of myself, and was rather self conscious at being two stones overweight. I did not have the money to dress as expensively as Walter Slater. He was an expensive dresser, everything he wore spoke quietly of tasteful quality. Compared with him, I felt shoddy and conspicuously cheap and nasty. My clothes were fresh, clean and well cared for, but had the well used well cared for look, which announced that limited money compelled everything to last as long as possible, and then a little longer still! I remember that morning, the smartest thing about me was the pair of shoes I had worn on our wedding day. They were the most expensive pair I had ever owned, and I had polished away at the toe caps until I could see my face in them.

Because I was of a comfortably rounded shape, my clothes did not seem to hang on me just right. I was not an extrovert, in fact I would soon learn that when, in the course of my duties, I knocked on a strange door for the first time, I would keep my fingers crossed hoping there would be no-one in. I had to overcome that fear before Walter Slater had any chance of transforming me into a super salesman.

How different Walter Slater was. He was a bespectacled, six foot, fifty eight years old success story. He had been with the Company almost all his adult life, and was now within two years of retirement. He was a kindly man, but there was a core of steel within him, creating a gentlemanly, no nonsense quiet firmness, which always seemed to be saying, "Challenge me if you dare!"

He had four married daughters and often talked about them, his wife and his grandchildren. On such occasions his face would light up with genuine pleasure. He had a very gentle smile, and when he had something harsh to say, the smile would soften it and make it acceptable. When the smile was absent, it was time to beware.

I never saw him in casual clothes, and even today, many later, whenever I think of him, I see him as one of nature's gentlemen. He always appears in the photograph album of my mind, in his plain medium grey three piece suit, very dapper with smart waistcoat, blue and white striped shirt, official Company tie, grey socks, and as always, those "K" shoes, gleaming like patent leather, putting the finishing touches to his immaculate appearance.

In those days, "Gannex" overcoats were very fashionable. Harold Wilson, the Prime Minister always seemed to wear one, and perhaps he had a hand in making them popular. Harold Wilson was a personal friend of Lord Kagan, who made the material for the waterproof coats at one of his factories twenty or thirty miles away. Walter Slater wore a "Gannex". It did something for him, it certainly made him look even more like a professional insurance man. I decided that I must have one too. Upon discovering the price, I had to make do with a second hand fawn gaberdine mac purchased at a local charity shop. The colour was right, but there the similarity and the effect ended. The coat was very loose fitting, covering my ample proportions like a huge tent. It fluttered around me announcing my impending arrival. I felt safe and comfortable in it and wore it for years. I was so attached to it that I would sweat my way through my duties in the hot sun with it draped around me. One day an elderly lady greeted me "Hello, I knew it was you coming along the street, I recognised the mac", this was perhaps the first way in which I tried to emulate Walter Slater's appearance.

I stood in awe of him, he looked every inch what I was hoping to become, a success story. There was nothing showy or flamboyant about him,. He had an unassuming air which somehow breathed self confidence and success. I had struggled for long enough and wanted to be as successful as Walter Slater, and I was prepared to work hard and long and honestly to achieve this ambition. I did not appreciate him fully in those early days, often thinking that he was hard and inflexible. I now know how good he was for me, and that without his gentle firmness I probably would not have made it in my new career.

It was the first Friday in December 1965, and an ideal day to be shown round my country agency and introduced to the Yorkshire folk who would soon become part of my life. There had been a hint of frost, but now the sun was shining brightly from a clear blue sky. The brightness threw into sharp focus the sheer beauty of the Pennines upon which Holmfirth nestled, beauty which I had never appreciated before.

I had been born and bred at Wakefield a busy engineering and textile city only twenty miles away and had grown up in the grime associated with the Yorkshire coal field. My first sight upon opening my bedroom curtains each morning for over twenty years had been the local colliery slag heap. As a  family we had occasionally visited Holmfirth and picnicked on the moors with the sheep for companions.  My youthful perception of Holmfirth was that it was a place to visit only in the summer. I imagined that in the winter months it would be the most inhospitable place on earth. My mind's eye saw Holmfirth gripped by swirling evil mists, shrouded in freezing winter fog and cut off by huge snow drifts.  How different the local canvas looked today. The cerulean blue sky smiled down upon the hazy blue distant peaks and the winter sun illuminated the variegated greens of the fells and fields. The stone cottages and terraces of  houses gratefully bathed in the spring like freshness of the morning.  Holmfirth was welcoming me and celebrating with me the start of my new life. The doors of the cottages seemed to be smiling a welcome, the distant peaks beckoned from the horizon inviting me to explore their secrets. I would discover before too long just how hostile and foreboding those hills could be during the long dark winter days.

I was twenty three, we had been married two years and had not found it easy to set up home, pay our mortgage and find enough money for all the necessities. Now we had a beautiful little daughter, Joy, and my previous job as a "commission only" insurance salesman had been a disaster for more than one reason.

I had little or no previous experience and did not know the area I had worked in. Consequently I had no nucleus of friends and acquaintances amongst whom I could begin to sell my products. Also in hindsight, I guess I did not have the self discipline in those early days to stick at it when disappointments came along and when not closely supervised. True, I had learned by experience many things which would be a great strength to me in years to come. Right now though, I was as poor as a church mouse and a steady income and security were high priorities.

My new career as "The Man from the Prudential" held promise of all this security. Little did I realise as I drove out to Holmfirth that I was entering into a new adventure, into a new lifestyle which would bring tremendous fulfilment. It would also bring me into close contact with so many colourful characters, tragic and humorous situations which would fill the rest of my life with a store of rich memories.

However, as I eagerly raced the little car round the tight bends on the Holmfirth Road, my thoughts were not just taken up with what was likely to happen to me on that first day. My mind sped back to an unhappy event which occurred when I was nineteen. It was a sad experience for Edith not long after we had become engaged, and which resulted in me vowing that if the Prudential Assurance Company were the last company under the sun, I would never work for them. Strange isn't it, how many rash words and hasty promises have to be taken back as the future unfolds.

Edith and I were engaged and saving every penny we could. I worked in the offices of a family owned motor body builders just on the outskirts of Wakefield in the tiny village of Alverthorpe. The company built tipping lorries, travelling libraries, mobile shops, bread vans, huge removal vans as well as carrying out accident repairs and spray painting and sign-writing, a walk through the large workshops was a fascinating experience. I never ceased to marvel at the craftsmanship I witnessed daily and the team work needed to create a pantechnicon van complete with beautiful bright paint and hand painted letters. My own role within the company was tedious and humdrum. I did not find much job satisfaction in sending out monthly accounts, costing up the price of a finished job, preparing wages and helping keep stock control records. I was so bored that to alleviate the monotony

I used to munch ginger biscuits constantly. Terry, the accountant and I would sit facing each other across his desk checking columns of figures, and I was aware that he put up with my endless crunching of biscuits under great sufferance only because it helped my concentration. Terry's patience was stretched to breaking point one day when I coughed whilst reading out a list of figures to him. I peppered his paperwork with moist partly chewed ginger biscuit particles. Terry exploded, "Say it, don't spray it!" I dissolved into fits of laughter but from that day on I was banished to sit at a separate desk whilst working with him.

The managing director had a chocolate brown Rolls Royce, and the highlight of my day was when he would let me take it to collect his children from the local school. Although only nineteen, I felt very grown up when he threw me his keys and said "David, take the Roller and pick up the kids from school." There I sat, cosseted in the soft white leather seat, driving through the village in opulence and style. I would wave at the locals and pip the horn as I silently cruised past them. A couple of hours later I would ring my bicycle bell at these same good folk and wave to them from my rock hard cycle seat. After the luxury of the Rolls my humble pedal cycle seat seemed purpose built to give an instant hernia each time the wheels hit a hole in the road.

Two to three years into our marriage, Edith had problems with me scrunching ginger biscuits in bed and put her foot down when the aggressive grinding noise began to keep her awake. She hid the biscuits so effectively that I was compelled to become an addictive cheese eater instead, finding that I could consume cheese in bed without being molested..

During the time I was still deafening the accountant with my biscuit chomping, Edith was working as typist in the offices of a local woollen mill in Wakefield. She enjoyed the work but the wages were small and she was eager for a better paid job. Her parents were customers of the Prudential Assurance Company, and their local representative told them that his manager was looking for a secretary. He thought that Edith would be an ideal candidate for the position and offered to recommend her to his manager. The salary was so good that Edith could not afford to miss the opportunity. She applied for the position and was invited to attend for an interview with Mr Dawson the branch manager.

This is when things began to go sadly wrong. Edith attended the interview, discovering to her surprise that some girls she knew from her typing pool were also there, hoping to land the same job. The first section of the interview was a communal affair. All the girls were together in one room and had to take dictation and complete mental arithmetic tests. Those unfortunate enough to fail at this hurdle were thanked and sent home.

Edith had done well and was one of the girls to be given a personal interview in private whilst the remaining girls sat outside chewing their finger nails whilst they waited for their turn.

Finally Mr Dawson appeared from the inner sanctum having completed all the interviews, and beamed at Edith before making his announcement, "I have decided to offer Edith the position, the remainder of you can now leave, and thank you for your interest."

Of course Edith was delighted to accept her new post, but when she arrived at her desk next morning, the word had already spread, "Have you heard about Edith, she has got a new job at the Prudential Assurance Company, she will be giving her notice in to start there next week." But give her notice in, Edith most certainly did not. What our Mr Dawson had failed to tell Edith that she must pass a stringent medical examination" because of the generous pension scheme."

Poor Edith, she was better at taking dictation that passing medical examinations. Due to the residual effect of a childhood illness she failed the medical examination and no longer qualified for the position. Her employers, although not wanting her to leave, knew that she was considering looking elsewhere for a job and this placed Edith in an embarrassing position.

I was usually quite a calm sort of fellow. In fact Edith's mum always said that I was as placid as a cow in a field, but I was not placid this time. I thought that the mighty Prudential Assurance Company had mishandled the whole affair and conducted its business in a most unprofessional way. I sat down and vented my feelings in a strong but courteous letter to their Chief General Manager at their Holborn Bars office in London. Immediately I had posted the letter I felt better.

I don't think I actually expected a reply, but my letter had put the proverbial cat amongst the Chief Office pigeons, and none other but their

Chief General Manager wrote me an apologetic letter. He signed off by informing me that Mr Dawson would be getting in touch with me so that I could make my feelings known to him in person. It was hoped that a mutual discussion would clear the air. True to his word, not many days later the postman brought another letter in a Prudential envelope. This letter summoned me to meet Mr Dawson in the privacy of his office so that my official complaint to his superiors could be chatted through.

I don't know whether you have ever undertaken a mission and then when it is too late to back out asked yourself, "How did I get into this mess?" I asked myself that question a hundred times as I cycled from Alverthorpe to Westgate, in Wakefield to keep my five thirty appointment with Mr Dawson. I decided to be brave, not to be intimated, to stick to my guns and give Mr Unprofessional Dawson a piece of my mind.

He kept me waiting(no doubt a ploy to play on my nerves and give him the advantage) and he looked very serious when he called me into his office. The room was large and heavily furnished with old dark oak furniture. Mr Dawson sat behind a huge oak desk, reminding me of a bank manager about to turn down a request for an overdraft. I looked at him across the massive desk top and all my firm resolve evaporated. Before I knew it I was apologising to him, I was telling him that I regretted writing my letter of complaint, that I was sure it was just a misunderstanding. I heard myself mumbling that in the cold light of day my actions seemed hasty. Notwithstanding the fact that Edith had been badly treated and difficulties had been caused due to his bad handling of the matter.

To my utter amazement Mr Dawson agreed with me, thanked me for my letter, which he said was an excellent letter which had showed them a basic flaw in their interview structure. He went on to apologise at an even greater length than I did. Finally, the last few ounces of his apology having been wrung from him, he told me that he liked me, that he thought that I would make a good insurance agent, and promptly offered me a good job as the local "Man from the Prudential".

I am afraid that I told him where to put his job (very politely of course) and left his office with the parting shot, "Mr Dawson, if I was desperate for a job, and if the Prudential was the only company under the sun, I would never work for them after seeing how they have treated my Edith."

Ah well, a lot of water has flowed under the bridge since then. Here I am, four years later and twenty miles away, driving out to Holmfirth to become "THE MAN FROM THE PRUDENTIAL."

# Lavatory Seat or Personal Effect!

The first day with Walter Slater was fairly uneventful, being really just a getting to know each other session. He showed me the geography of my agency as he introduced me to some of the clients and began to instruct me in the easier routine duties. I guessed that he was weighing me up and deciding how best to handle me in initiating me into the many skills, and technical knowledge needed before I could look after my policyholders and begin to sell the companies products. Slater enthused over the beauty of the area, reminding me how fortunate I was in being able to spend my working life enjoying my twenty two square miles of territory, centring on the little stone built market town of Holmfirth.

The shallow River Holme ran through the centre, splashing and sporting over its stony bed. The mills upstream discharged their effluent into the river which changed colour almost daily as the different coloured dyes were emptied into it. The river always smelled of methylated spirits and on a mild day, the scent from the heather and pine trees always seemed to be tainted with a hint of meths. Even today, years later, I find the smell of methylated spirits very evocative of those days back in Holmfirth.

I realised that first day, just how fortunate I was to be working daily in such a beautiful area. Just two or three miles away from the bustling market place was some of the most magnificent scenery imaginable. Forests of pine, lush fields where sheep grazed, desolate acres of wild moorland, featureless and mysterious, deep secret lakes and reservoirs, all set against the back cloth of the looming heights of the Pennines. From the highest visible peak rose the mighty television mast, like a giant steel finger, pointing skywards as though reminding us Who had created all this beauty.

Mr Slater took me to the home of my predecessor, Norman Peace, who had just retired after spending forty years on the same territory. Norman was a household name in the locality, He was well respected and enjoyed a certain prestige as the local "man from the Prudential." He had served the company and its clients well and was now able to sit back and enjoy his well earned pension. Norman had the advantage of being a local lad, being born and educated in Holmfirth. When he became the "man from the Prudential" he was viewed entirely without suspicion, was he not one of them? Many of Norman's school friends became his clients. He had so much in common with them, he knew their families, their customs, he spoke their language, and his harsh nasal accent  proclaimed that he was not a "comer in" to the Holme Valley, as I indeed was. The vast amount of goodwill Norman had generated over forty long years was to become part of my stock in trade, if that was not enough, Norman gave me an open invitation to "call and pick his brains " whenever I needed help.

As we sat in the lounge of his bungalow, looking across the  valley which he knew so well, he gave me a piece of advice which I have never forgotten. Placing his coffee mug on the carpet beside his feet, he cautioned me,

"David, you will get this job round your neck unless you learn one simple thing.  Your motto must always be SERVICE to customers, and not SERVITUDE to customers. Get the difference between these two methods of operation into perspective, otherwise you will not last forty years as I have done."

I learned that Norman only had  sight in one eye, and for this reason he had never trusted himself to learn to drive a car. For forty long summers and even longer winters he had walked the twenty two square miles of his "parish". The endless trekking up hill and down dale had kept him superbly fit. Once a week, when he donned his salesman's hat and went out canvassing for new business, he condescended to hire a taxi for the evening. The driver, a local man, was sworn to confidentiality concerning the clients he transported Norman and his huge briefcase to.

Norman laughed as he reminisced, "I never had any bother closing a sale David, if clients began dithering and shilly shallying, I just reminded them that the taxi meter was ticking away and I could not afford a huge bill."

Norman was as straight as they come and always the model of discretion. There were hundreds of stories circulating about him which his former clients loved to recount to me with great relish.  One white haired eighty years old lady told me about the retired gentleman who lived right at the end of her terrace, who had died suddenly in his sleep.  Two or three days after  the funeral, on a hot sultry afternoon, Norman walked along the back of the terrace, on his way to the widow's back door. Being such a hot day, the folk were sitting out on their back steps, chatting over the fence to the neighbours. As Norman strode passed the garden gates, one curious old man, rasped in his harsh broad Yorkshire,

"Na then Norman mi lad, ow ista? Thou'll be on thi way to see Mrs Batty to sort art er usband's policies?"

"I might be, then again I might not be" responded Norman, tight lipped and looking straight ahead.

A second old man had a go,

"Na then Norman, we all know that ole Joe Batty wor insured bi thy company. We ave all sin thee going to t'ouse for years, he wor hobviously reight well insured, worn't he?"

Norman, his six foot frame still hurrying along retorted,

"I don't know what you are talking about."

A third inquisitive neighbour was not going to be fobbed off quite so easily, and throwing caution to the wind he was more direct. He rose from his seat on his back door step, and rushed into the footpath to stop Norman in his tracks. He looked Norman in the eye, with a desperate pleading expression, and after hesitating a moment, burst out,

"Nay, look 'ere lad, lets be knowin', were owd man Batty reight well insured or not?"

A hidden fire began to rise in Norman's face, but the inquisition continued,

"It's not that we want to know ought, its that we need to know like. If tha can tell us 'ow much brass t'owd lass 'as to come, then we'll know like 'ow much 'elp she might need from 'us, being good neighbours like."

Norman, visibly angry at the impertinence, raised his voice so that the whole terrace could hear, and thrusting a finger defiantly under the old man's nose, retorted,

"Sam, if you tell me every intimate detail of your private affairs, I might just tell you mine, but my clients affairs are my business and are nowt to do with you nor any other busybody. Now let me pass if you don't mind."

Yes, that first meeting I had with Norman made me realise that over the coming years I would be able to learn much from him. I often called in to see him at Pennine View during the first twelve months and he felt needed when I brought him some of my little problems. Occasionally he would put on his coat and squeeze his huge frame into the tiny Morris Minor to accompany me on some of my calls. He would make us both laugh as he remembered and recounted stories about his former clients and showed me short cuts and warned me about all the dangerous dogs.

One afternoon we were together in the car at the extreme tip of my area, in the village of Holme lying under the shadow of the great television mast. As I pulled the car to a halt beside the village green Norman picked up my collecting book and cradled it under his arm. "Please David" he pleaded, "just wait in the car, and for old time's sake let me walk into these homes again. I would give anything just to open the doors and see the looks on their faces."

"Go on then, but on one condition Norman, if anyone makes you a drink, come back and fetch me!"

It did not seem long before Norman was back beside me in the car, as he counted out the money into my hands he was aglow,

"Oh that was marvellous, just like the old times, you must let me do it again sometime."

I had every intention of letting Norman loose again, but tragically, almost on the first anniversary of his retirement, Mrs Peace got in touch with me to inform me of Norman's death. It seemed that switching off after leading so active a life had been more than his system could cope with. Lack of exercise had provoked a massive heart attack, and his loss was felt by the whole community. I knew that I had lost a good friend and a treasure trove of help and advice.

I still had Walter Slater, who was a man of great resources. He too knew his job inside out and really gave me a first class grounding into the basics needed. It was he who put down a solid foundation upon which I built my future. For the first six months he practically lived with me, not allowing me to perform a single task for the first time, apart from routine collecting, unless he was with me. His on the job training was augmented by a weekly visit to the companies training school in Leeds. This weekly day out took me away from routine duties, but placed added pressure on the rest of the working week. Les Jackson the training officer made it all so worthwhile. Les was the brains behind the Leeds Training Centre and saw the huge benefit in getting new recruits away from their duties for a day each week, to share experiences with colleagues from other areas who were also rookies. The training was intense and a great deal of information had to be retained, but Les was a master in the art of communication, his face lit up, his eyes sparkled, his whole personality became enthused and animated as he illustrated his lectures with plentiful amusing or sad stories from his own years in the field.

Walter Slater obviously realised that I would be able to cope far better with a car than Norman had done on foot, suggesting that provided I stick exactly to Norman's routine for the first six months. I would then be free to arrange my routine in any way I wished. At the end of the first six months I had to be subjected to a confirmatory audit, and if Slater was happy with the state of my work and with the financial accounting, then I would be offered a permanent contract. I felt uneasy at being on approval for six months, but felt sure that the combined efforts of Les Jackson and Walter Slater would successfully groom me for a permanent job.

Slater had one concern about me, and over a flask of coffee in his car he voiced it,

"David, never forget that the local folk regard you as a "comer in" and if you are on this patch as long as Norman was, you will still be a "Comer in" and will be treated as a foreigner. The locals are a tight knit community and if they don't like you, they will close ranks and starve you out. If they like you, they will want to know all your private business, and will appear to take a genuine interest in you. As soon as they have found out all they want to know, they will drop you, so be careful."

His general assessment of these folk was very astute being built upon his own long experience with them. I found that time and time again the Holmfirth community ran true to Slater's assessment of them.

Two or three weeks before my audit was due, Mr Slater explained at length what the procedure involved. He would personally spend four whole weeks with me and visit every policyholder's home to enable him to compare their records with mine. Whilst he was doing this, he would be on the lookout for the way in which the customers related with me. These Yorkshire folk gave a lot away by the manner in which they received their agent when his superintendent was with him. Every penny I had collected in the six months had to be accounted for, and my selling skills, clerical ability and all the other hundred and one skills would be scrutinised. Following the audit, Slater would make his recommendation to the District Manager Redfearn Rogers, who would decide whether to dismiss me or confirm my appointment.

Slater reminisced concerning Norman's final audit some six months previously in November, heavy snow had made the audit an absolute nightmare. Some of the farm tracks were blocked, drifting snow made some roads and lanes impassable. One farmer's wife loaned him and Norman a clothes prop each so that they could feel their way through the drifts back to the main road. To get to one isolated farm house they had both walked on top of a dry stone wall as the track was blocked.

"You don't know what real snow is David," grinned Slater, "wait until you have seen one of our winters, they are a culture shock to you townies."

Suddenly he looked relieved, "At least there won't be any snow around when I do your audit in May, it will be a doddle after the last one."

He confided that my audit may possibly be the last one he would do, as he intended to retire within twelve months. When I felt a twinge of sadness as this remark, I knew that deep down I really liked Slater, and would be sorry to see him go.

May came, and with it the commencement of my "investigation". We were just two days into the audit and were concluding the Friday night collections on a tiny council estate in Hinchliffe Mill, when quite suddenly it became dark, the wind changed direction, and we were chilled to the bone. As we hurried along, Slater explained to me that Hinchliffe had been a mill owner a hundred years ago, and he provided small terraced houses for his workers. They were built in a cluster along the main road, and the community became known as Hinchliffe Mill. In more recent times the local council had expanded the "village" by building a small council estate of thirty or forty properties, with open views across the Holme Valley below.

The cold became more intense and we were glad to get back into the warmth of Slater's Hillman Super Minx. Moving the heating control to maximum, he pointed the car in the direction of my home and began to compliment me on his findings so far. Soon we were opposite the Town Hall, and I glanced across the road at the welcoming light in the front room of our little home.

"Off you go David and get round the fire. I will pick you up at nine o'clock in the morning."

The next morning I woke up to a complete silence. We lived on the main road leading into the town, and there was always a steady flow of traffic and pedestrians. Why was it so quiet? Perhaps I had woken far too early. A quick glance at the clock assured me that it was eight o'clock, but why was it so quiet? Pulling aside the bedroom curtain I looked at onto the Huddersfield Road. There was a foot of snow! Snow was still falling and the snowflakes were the size of potato crisps. A solitary lady was trying to push her pram but the snow was so deep that it covered all four wheels making the job almost impossible. Slater could not get through, his village, only four miles away was cut off. The snow blizzard brought down over two thousand telephone wires and crippled communications. Cars were abandoned at crazy angles on street corners and all roads into Holmfirth were closed.

By Monday morning there was not a trace of snow in the town, but it lingered on the "tops" and on the fells for weeks, giving me my first taste of the suddenness and harshness of the Holmfirth winters. Slater was relieved that the inclement weather did not really hinder my audit, which went without a hitch.

I signed my permanent contact in May 1966 and Slater acted as witness. It was the last audit he conducted and the last employment contract he witnessed, as true to his word, a little over a year later he retired. The completion of my audit brought a change in Slater's manner and attitude. He became more relaxed, he did not feel my collar to the same degree, and I began to enjoy breathing space. Although he still worked with me one day each week, it was mainly to help me obtain sales. He had begun to let go of his grip on the reins, he trusted me to run things my way .

During my first six months I had compared notes with colleagues who covered adjoining territories, and was surprised to find that none of them collected on Thursdays and Saturdays. I asked Slater why these two days were necessary, as they were proving to be a nuisance. Thursday was a good day for canvassing, and working on a Saturday spoiled our weekend.

"Oh those two days are essential " insisted Slater, "There are so many people working shifts in the mills that Saturday is the only time you can catch them in"

"But what about Thursdays?"

"As long as I can remember this agency has had Thursday collections. If you try and break it, you will lose goodwill and lose customers."

"But you said that I could reorganise after six months and do it my way."

"Yes, but that does not include cutting out Thursday and Saturday collections."

I checked out with Norman Peace, "Norman, are the Thursday and Saturday collecting days essential?"

"Good heavens no, David, get rid of them as quick as you can."

"But why did you always do Thursday and Saturday collections.?"

"Aw that were nowt to do with the customers."

"No, really!"

"No lad, I always collected Thursday because it got me out of shopping with the wife, and I always collected Saturdays because it got me out of gardening and cleaning the house."

Needless to say, within a few weeks I had completely rescheduled my work arrangements, and integrated Thursdays and Saturdays into the rest of the week. I don't think Slater ever completely forgave me for it. I discovered later that he often used to work with Norman on a Saturday. Perhaps it was his escape from gardening too!

During the six moths on "intensive" training, Slater always insisted on showing me how to perform each new duty which arose. One evening when he was working with me, he insisted on showing me how to handle a claim on a household contents policy. Mrs Hobson had phoned asking me to call with a claim form, so Slater took the lead, all I had to do was sit and watch how to do it.

Mrs Hobson was a short, rounded, large bosomed lady with an immaculate little terrace home. She directed us with a stubby finger to take a seat on the expensive looking gold moquette settee, and then sitting opposite us in the easy chair, brushing bread crumbs from her ample bosom with the back of her hand, she opened the interview demurely.

"I have broken the lavatory seat, and would like to claim for a new one."

"I am very sorry to hear that" Slater sympathised, "How did it happen?"

Mrs Hobson, slightly embarrassed, continued,

"I was sitting on it, just took the weight off my legs I did, and it cracked. Made a noise like a gun it did. Frightened me to death, nearly fell off the seat I did!"

I was on the verge of laughing, but Slater's serious tones warned me off, as he continued,

"I am ever so sorry Mrs Hobson, but that kind of damage does not constitute a claim under the terms of your contract of insurance."

"Not a claim" she exploded, "I assure you that you would think it a claim if you had to sit on it. Can't relax at all on it, if I do not balance just right on the broken seat, the crack opens up and nips my er, my bottom. Have you ever had your bottom nipped by a cracked lavatory seat? Obviously not! Or you would not be saying that it is not a claim. I could show you the bruises on my bottom, the crack in the seat bites me as soon as I take the weight off my legs. What do you mean by telling me it is not a claim, of course it's a claim."

Walter Slater, solemn as an undertaker, assured her that he did not doubt her for one minute, and that he did not need to see the tell tale marks on her private parts. That was not in question. The point at issue is that for accidental damage to be covered by the insurance, the damage must be to a bath, wash basin or sanitary pan.

There followed a discourse from Mrs Hobson on the legalities of the expression "sanitary pan" and when she felt that she had more than proved her point she made a defiant thrust.

"Of course it's a sanitary pan which has become broken!"

"No, no madam, it is the lid which has sustained damage" countered my superintendent.

Mrs Hobson, getting redder by the minute exploded,

"Lid! isn't the lid a part of the privy then? Without a lid you cant sit on the lav. Would you like to sit on a cold pot seat in the middle of winter? Of course you wouldn't!"

"Madam, one moment" began a flustered Slater.

"Don't you madam me" threatened Mrs Hobson, trembling with emotion, "am I going to get a new seat for my privy or not?"

"You may certainly have a new seat for your toilet madam, if you pay for it yourself."

"If I pay for it myself! What do you think I pay insurance for?"

Mr Slater, showing me how to do it, continued.,

"You pay insurance madam to protect your valuable personal effects, not to cover items like toilet seats."

"Isn't a toilet seat a personal effect then? I think it's a very personal effect."

Mrs Hobson was beginning to enjoy this, and I was not sure how much longer this demonstration in "how to do it" could go on. Every ounce of meaning had been wrung out of the term "sanitary pan", now Slater and Mrs Hobson were at loggerheads over the legal meaning of "personal effects" and I realized that Slater was rapidly losing ground.

Whilst the debate had been proceeding I had been reading Mrs Hobson's insurance policy and so I broke in,

"Mrs Hobson, exactly how much will a new toilet seat cost you?"

"Fifteen shillings young man"

"Then I am very sorry that on this occasion we cannot help you. You will see from your policy that you must pay the first five pounds of any claim. As this claim is less than five pounds I regret that you do not have a claim."

Mrs Hobson relaxed, and completely wound down. She picked up her policy, read the paragraph I pointed out to her, and putting back into its envelope smiled at me,

"Thank you Mr Robinson, I do understand, you have put it so simply. Why couldn't your boss explain it as simply as that!"

# Holmfirth Town

Holmfirth town sprawled far beneath me in the valley bottom, like a model village. A few minutes ago I had crawled my way along the congested main street, queuing in my little car in the steady stream of lorries and coaches, coughing as the diesel fumes were drawn into the car. Now, a mile or two out of the town, I was in a different world, the only scent was the rich blend of heather, lush grass and pine. The only sounds were the wind, moaning high above me, punctuated by the bleating of the sheep, and the excited shrill chattering of the birds. I looked down the side of the valley to Holmfirth, nestling in the bottom of the basin, it was so near, yet seemed so unreal and distant. Its grimy stone walls, grey blue slate roofs, ribbons of streets and twisting roads seemed vague and dreamlike, like an industrial mirage painted onto a backcloth rich in greenery.

The blue grey smoke from a hundred chimneys struggled upwards, vainly trying to compete with the black belching billows from the mill chimneys. Their united pall hung like a shroud over the little town, softening the sharp contrasts, and like a canopy, prevented the thousand noises rising from the town. I looked down at the death silent township whose only signs of life were the thread of motor vehicles and the pulsating smoke, spiralling and rising, before settling like a vague semi transparent umbrella over the stone buildings.

I had to get out of the car and savour the scene beneath me. This was the first time the awesome beauty of the place had taken a hold on me. An unseen lark was singing above me, then two or three fields away, a tractor slowly made its way down the track towards a lonely farmstead, marking its progress with a thin blue feather of smoke. The sign post proclaimed that Holmfirth was two miles away. It was worlds away! This was a different land, another universe where time stood still and where man and his problems seemed so trivial. Everywhere I looked spoke of the artistry and design of some great Architect. The vastness of the rolling fells, the looming indistinct heights of the Pennines, the broad breast of England, proclaimed that its Artist did everything on a grand scale, unhindered by space and lack of raw materials. Here was a grand airiness, here was space, here was room to move and time to think.

I could not believe my good fortune, that I would soon by moving to live amidst these beautiful hills and valleys. Walter Slater was pressing me to find a suitable house quickly. Many of my clients were calling into the local office in Huddersfield for service as I was not easily accessible, living about fourteen miles away. Their visits to the office were putting extra work onto the staff, especially Walter, as he always dealt with my clients if he was in the office.

I had lost count of the number of times he had reminded me, as he left me at the end of a busy day,

"David, get moved over here as soon as you can. You will find the job a heck of a lot easier, and you will sell a lot more business when the folk see that you are living amongst them. It will be a lot easier for the poor office staff in Huddersfield too!"

I was only too anxious to move into this idyllic setting, but as yet my income was not high, and there were not many properties on the market within our modest price range. Ah well, something will turn up. Until it does I shall just have to travel backwards and forwards, and the office will just have to cope with the extra work.

I took a photograph of the panorama before driving towards my next call. It was my first visit to a couple who managed a small kennels, and the husband was busy with his hose pipe, swilling out the concrete compound when I parked on the rough grass beside their detached stone house. He came towards me, pointing the hose behind him and grinned an acknowledgement when I explained that I was Norman Peace's successor. I enquired whether he ran boarding kennels or whether he was a breeder.

"Neither" he grated in his rough Yorkshire dialect, "t'missus and me look after t'kennels for t'Holme Valley Beagles. All t'dogs 'ere are 'ounds used for beagling. I 'ave a full time job in t'mill, but t'wife works full time for t'hunt. I just 'elp 'er out when I 'ave some free time."

He showed me around the outbuildings and the yard, the dogs, friendly and curious were barking excitedly as they pawed at the heavy wire cage doors. They seemed gentle enough, but I guessed it would be a different story when they were in full cry on the scent of a fox. In my ignorance I asked my host, Roy, where the stables were for the horses.

"Osses !" he laughed, "there aint no 'osses 'ere. This is beagling and in beagling the 'untsmen run on foot behind t'ounds, and we don't 'unt foxes, we 'unt 'ares. Redfearn Rogers your District Manager is t'president of 'Holmfirth Valley Beagles. He looks a swell figure in 'is bright red jacket and white trousers. It certainly keeps 'im fit too. You will 'ave to watch your step, he will be trying to get you to join us, it will get some o'that flab off" he laughed as he gently slapped me in the stomach.

"Redfearn Rogers, running behind the hounds! I don't believe it." I laughed, "he must be nearly sixty!"

"Aye 'e is" confirmed Roy, "but 'e 'ad a bit of an 'ealth problem, went to seed sitting be'ind that desk all day. His doctor told 'im to get some 'ealthy outdoor exercise, so 'e took up beagling. You would be amazed to see just who does follow t'ounds. In fact James Mason, t'actor allus follows t'ounds when 'e 'is not away on 'is trips. He was up ere last week at our social do."

"What about Walter Slater?" I laughed, "does he run behind the hounds too? I don't think I can imagine Walter in tight white trousers and a bright red jacket!"

Roy grinned, "Oh 'eck lad, tha'll never see Walter Slater dressed up like that. Too prim an proper is our Walter. The only road Walter would follow t'ounds would be from t'driving seat of his precious car wearing 'is posh city suit. Even then I don't think we could tempt 'im to join us, 'ave you ever known Walter drive that precious car of 'is any where is some muck."

Laughing together, we turned away from the pens, and the cry from the dogs subsided. Roy apologised for the dirty state he was in, and informed me that Sheila, his wife would normally be in, but she had nipped into Holmfirth in the Land Rover.

"Just go into t'kitchen, you will find your money on t'worktop. There is only Charlie in, just speak to 'im and he won't harm you." With that Roy went back to his hose pipe and started mucking out the yard.

I stepped up the well worn stone steps and pushed the stout door open. It had been grained and varnished years ago, now the surface was cracked and uneven. I wondered who Charlie was, and felt a little apprehensive at Roy's warning. What would Charlie do to me if I did not speak to him? I stepped into the kitchen which was typical of so many of the local farm houses. Eggs and egg boxes were everywhere. Wellington boots standing on a newspaper in the doorway. The hook on the back door was piled high with jackets and scarves. There was a wooden notice board on the far wall, with cheaply printed notices of forthcoming events pinned in glorious disarray. A whole carton of dog meat was pushed out of the way under the old kitchen table, but no sign of Charlie.

I coughed loudly, hoping that if Charlie was in the other room he would hear me and come through so that I could speak to him and ensure my safety. I listened for Charlie's footsteps, half expecting a hunch-backed dwarf to shuffle through, or perhaps a huge barrel-chested chap with violent tendencies, who would stare at me with an insane leer before trotting away without molesting me when I had told him who I was. I marked the premium receipt books, rattled the coins in my pocket, shuffled my feet, coughed and coughed again, but no Charlie. I left the kitchen , closing the door behind me and descended the stone steps, coming face to face with Roy who quizzed,

"Did Charlie bother ye then?"

"No, never saw anyone, there was nobody in the kitchen, he must have slipped out in the Land Rover with Sheila."

Roy turned off the hose pipe and swore quietly as the last few drops of water soaked the front of his trousers.

"Nay, Charlie never goes out in the daylight, allus waits until it's well and truly dark. He is in there now alright, he would be watching you while you took the money and signed the books."

"Really, well I never saw him, where was he?"

"Oh where he allus is, sitting on the 'ot water pipe near t'kitchen ceiling."

"On the hot water pipe! Who is Charlie then?"

"Thou 'ad better go back in and meet 'im" invited Roy.

I climbed back up the stone steps rather uncertainly, sure that I could hear Roy laughing gently behind me. I stood in the centre of the kitchen and looked up for the hot water pipes. There was the shiny copper pipe, my eye ran along its length, and there, in the corner, looking at me out of one eye, sat the biggest owl I had ever seen. It was so large and so close to me that at first I felt afraid, until I remembered Roy's words, "Speak to Charlie and he won't harm you".

"Hello Charlie" I croaked.

I swear that Charlie winked at me before closing both eyes. Then, ignoring me he began rocking gently backwards and forwards on his centrally heated perch.

I was still smiling as I drove away from the kennels. In the years ahead Charlie was always there at the same vantage point. He wisely scrutinised my every move when I entered Roy and Sheila's kitchen on my frequent visits.  Charlie had been caught and injured by one of the dogs when he was hardly strong enough to fend for himself. Roy and Sheila had brought him up, feeding him milk through a fountain pen , and tearing meat into small enough pieces  for him to digest. A bond developed between them, and Charlie had no inclination to return to the wild.  Even though he could be self sufficient and free he chose to remain in the kitchen, and sallied forth after dark for long enough to catch the occasional tasty morsel to supplement the "fast food" served him by Roy and Sheila.

Edith and Joy and I still lived fourteen miles away in the next town.  It was too far from my work. It was also a condition of my appointment that I move to live on my "patch" at the earliest opportunity, and at the latest, within six months of commencing duty.  As I drove around Holsmby and the surrounding countryside, I had an eye open for a suitable house.  The criteria was quite simple. The property had to be relatively cheap as I was not yet established. It must not need a lot of restoration as I was a do it yourself idiot. It had to be smart enough to receive Prudential clients on business, and must have an image in fitting with the regulatory brass plate which must be fixed at exactly the right height beside the front door so that all could clearly read " Agent for The Prudential Assurance Co Ltd. The available properties fell into two categories, they were either cheap and nasty or expensive and well beyond our reach.

When Edith and I married, we moved into a flat above the shoe shop which Edith's father managed.  It was a fairly large modern flat, well maintained but not decorated to our taste.  I decided to prove my skills at painting and decorating, and wondered why it was taking me so long to paint the ceiling with emulsion paint.  It took me a few hours to realise that if I were to change my 2" brush for a proper  ceiling brush, the whole process could be speeded up! I then ran out of paint and decided to mix the paint together from two odd cans to avoid the expense of buying a new can. The effect on the ceiling was dramatic! The first section of the lounge ceiling shone with its brilliant white sheen, the remainder was a faded shade of khaki. It took a valiant rescue act by Edith's dad to "improve" my work and get rid of the two tone ceiling.

Discovering that I was a failure at painting ceilings, I decided to gloss the lounge door. Edith wanted it light grey, I bought a tin of what I thought was light grey paint. Miraculously the light grey paint reacted to the light when I opened the can and turned bright pink! " Too late now" I thought, " the shops are closed, Edith will not notice the difference" But she did! But that was the least of my problems, when I proudly ushered Edith into the room next day to display my handiwork, I found to my horror that the beautiful gloss paint had dried with a corrugated iron effect, and huge trickles of paint had run down the door and formed pools on the plastic tiled floor.

True to form, Edith's dad came to the rescue. He rubbed off all the paint I had applied before completing the job professionally in the correct colour. Neither of our parents trusted me with paint or brushes again, and together they joined forces and with their help we soon made our little flat into a comfortable home. It was ideally situated right in the centre of Wakefield a large West Riding City, and our front garden was the traffic island, resplendent with lush grass, and colourful flowers, we even had a team of council gardeners who tended our plot for us. This had one disadvantage, it removed the opportunity to demonstrate my gardening skills!

When Edith and I celebrated our silver wedding, her dad, in his speech, enlightened the amused audience concerning my prowess as a decorator all those years ago.

So, the house had to be ready to move into, but such properties seemed few and far between. It was my good fortune though after leaving the kennels, to make a business call at the little estate agents in the centre of Holmfirth. One of the partners, Mr Vernon had a car insurance due for renewal, I needed to pop in and collect his cheque. As he rummaged for his cheque book, I glanced around his office. It was like scene from Dickens, it would not have surprised me if Mr Pickwick had walked in. There were no modern amenities, the typewriters were ancient, the ladies who operated them looked like they too belonged in a museum! I expected Mr Vernon to sign his cheque with a quill pen, he puffed away at his pipe as he laboriously signed his cheque with an extra large fountain pen.

"I don't suppose you have a house on your books which would suit my modest finances" I asked. He asked what my requirements were, and I was delighted when he assured me that he had just the right property, which would be ideal for Edith, Joy and I. He showed me details of a three storey terraced house, with stone walls two feet thick and a large cellar. It had two large bedrooms, was situated on Huddersfield Road, right in the centre of Holmfirth, just opposite the Town Hall, and the main shopping street was only two minutes walk away. He kept the best news until last. It had been the home of two spinster sisters, who had always had professional decorators to keep the house spick and span. They had just moved out into a small cottage, and their former home was ready to move straight into. As they wanted a quick sale, it could be ours for only fifteen hundred pounds.

We looked round the house, decided that it would be an admirable place to live. We sorted out a mortgage, and sold our little bungalow and prepared to move. We had moved house before, from the little flat where Edith and I began our married life, into our little bungalow. We decided to employ the same removal contractors again to move us into Holmfirth. I thought that the owner would be delighted to do business with us again but when I phoned to ask for a quotation his attitude surprised me.

"Robinson! I know that name. Have we moved you before?"

"Yes you moved us from our flat in Wakefield into our bungalow."

"Oh no, you're not the  chap with the huge great piano"

"Yes that's us. You remember the pianola do you?"

"Remember it! How the Dickens can I ever forget that great huge brute! Moving it last time nearly broke our backs and our necks. We deserve a medal for hoisting that great ancient monument! They shouldn't be allowed to make furniture as big and as heavy as that. Your piano is a removal man's nightmare! Apart from it being almost impossible lift it is pinafore and a half wide. There aren't many doors wide enough to get anything that wide through without skinning your knuckles.

"Oh really. We were so pleased with you last time that we were hoping you would move us again."

By now I was almost pleading with the man,

"It is not a long journey to Holmfirth, only about 15 miles."

"Tell you what mate, you sell the piano or give it away or leave it behind or set fire to it or something. Then we will move you to Holmfirth." Then he began to chuckle softly as he continued.

"Of course we will move you to Holmfirth. Your piano might be dreadful but your money and your coffee are good. When do you want to move?"

We agreed a date and Edith began the process of packing. She had never tried to pack before with an eighteen months old daughter trying to help. Joy's enquiring mind and busy fingers were into everything and much of the work had to be done after Joy had gone to bed.

The pianola certainly did dominate our living room. I did not know a note of music, but what music I could play on it! It looked just like a normal piano but was slightly larger and two or three times heavier. Sliding one lever opened up two doors just behind where the music normally rested. Sliding another lever opened another door at the bottom of the instrument, and down dropped a pair of harmonium type pedals.. It was the work of just two or three seconds to pop in a roller containing a long length of paper perforated with holes. In response to operating the two foot pedals, the paper was rolled across the surface of what really looked like the mouthpiece of a large mouth organ. As the holes in the paper coincided with the holes on the "mouthpiece" so different notes were played.

We had rolls with stirring military marches, the Hallelujah Chorus from Handel's Messiah and some of Strauss's waltzes. Even a musical ignoramus like me could pull out all the stops and produce beautiful music without a finger touching the keys!

I smiled as I remembered my school-days and the confidence trick I once played on a group of classmates. We lived on a busy main road in Wakefield and the front door of my parents little terraced house opened straight onto the street. Passers by literally walked within two or three feet of the window of the front room. One day as I was walking home from school with a group of friends, I excused myself saying that I must rush ahead to begin my piano practice.

I knew that within a few minutes these friends would walk past our window. I must make sure that as they walked past they were able to hear me blasting away loud enough to really impress them. I ran home, opened up the pianola, popped on a paper roll containing one of Sousa's marches and blasted away. I was aware that my friends were outside the window, so I thought that I would really astonish them. I leaned from side to side like a concert pianist running my fingers up and down the motionless keys, when I paused, I could hear comments. "Blimey just listen to David playing the piano." "Cor that's terrific." "Had no idea he could play like that!"

The joke very nearly backfired on me at school a few weeks later. We had just finished morning assembly and Miss Markland the music teacher had closed the piano lid when one of my friends dropped me right in it.

"Miss, have you heard David play the piano? He's brilliant. He plays better than you. We know we have heard him having his practice!"

"Really David, I had no idea you were a concert pianist" said Miss Markland as she re-opened the piano lid. "You must give us a demonstration of your virtuosity. I dreamed up some excuse about being late for maths and babbled on about obliging at some other time. I had to use an awful lot of ingenuity to ensure that I avoided any more potentially embarrassing situations with Miss Markland.

The day finally came when it was time for us to launch ourselves onto the unsuspecting people of Huddersfield Road Holmfirth. We led the way proudly in our Morris Minor, the roof rack stacked up with assorted boxes. Behind us trundled the bright blue furniture van with our pianola safely strapped down. There were muffled oaths breathed by our two contractors as they lifted the instrument onto the van.

On arriving at Huddersfield Road the beefy removal men dropped down the tail gate of the van and swore again as they saw the piano challenging them to move it. One of them ran up our footpath and measured the width of the front door.

"It's just over a pinafore and a half wide" he yelled back to his mate as he smoothed his crumpled apron. His boss appeared to ignore him as he rushed into the middle of Huddersfield Road. Standing there, feet planted firmly on the tarmac, arms outstretched, he yelled at an approaching Land –Rover,

"Stop!"

With a screech of brakes the vehicle came to an abrupt halt, the driver wearing a puzzled expression climbed out and ambled over to our strong man.

"What's up mate?"

"Nowt's up yet but if you don't give us a hand to get this piano into this house, I will let your tires down!"

"That's an offer I can't refuse" grinned our anonymous friend, "I'll go and get my mate to give us a hand!"

So that is how our massive pianola found its way into its new home in Holmfirth. A few hours later, aching in every limb and desperate for a cup of coffee, we too were well and truly moved into our new home.

The "Man from the Prudential Assurance Company", wife child and dog were in residence.

# The Brass Plaque

For a novice 'Do it yourself man'. I did not consider that I had done a bad job. There on the stone wall alongside our front door shone the brass plate bearing the proud inscription "AGENT FOR PRUDENTIAL ASSURANCE CO. LTD."  I rubbed my hands in anticipation at the amount of enquiries this discreet publicity would bring me I had also rubbed the brass plate with gallons of brass polish until it shone brightly vying for the attention of each passer-by.

I felt rather proud that our little terrace home was exactly in the right situation.  As soon as my brass plate was noticed vast amounts of business would come rolling in. Noticed it was sure to be, how could it not be seen by everyone? They had to pass our door when they went to the market, or the dentist, or the town hall, or the high street where most of the shops were.

Directly opposite our house was the Town Hall, and every Tuesday lunchtime the local Round Table had their meeting and lunch there. Then there were the wedding receptions held there, almost every Saturday, with the occasional posh high society wedding during the week. As the bride and groom posed on the town hall steps for their photographs, they would be sure to see my brass plate and say to each other, "We will go across there after our honeymoon and sort out some life assurance."

Then of course, next door to me was the local dentist's surgery, they too had a brass plate announcing that Brian and Bridget Heaney conducted their practice there. Alongside the Heaney's surgery, was a short steep street which led to the open space known locally as "Bottoms" where two days a week, the market traders set up their stalls and tried to out cry each other as they called out their wares. The many hundreds of shoppers who passed my door each week would be sure to visit me for life assurance.

Even if all the visitors to the town hall, dentist and the market did not see my brass plate, there was always the local pub, three doors away from us. The steady stream of drinkers and socialisers would pass my door in their hundreds too, all of them eagerly looking for an insurance man.  I really had it made!

I backed away, to observe the plate from a distance. It was ever so slightly tilted in a different direction to the horizontal but it would take a good eye to spot this. I polished my finger prints away with my handkerchief, and retired into the house to await developments. My parents were coming over to see us on the Saturday, and we expected them sometime mid morning; we were looking forward to showing them round our new home, and Edith went to a great deal of trouble to make sure that everything was just right for their visit. There was a loud ringing of the door bell, and we knew that mum and dad had arrived because we heard the door open, and the sound of footsteps on the lino in the long entrance passage.

The living room door opened and dad appeared in the doorway. He put their suitcase down in the hallway and looked at me questioningly.

"Nay lad what the heck?"

"What's wrong?" I asked.

"Who put the brass plate up on the wall?"

"I did Dad" I beamed, proudly.

"Nay, what the heck lad, it can't stay like that, it's a mile out of being straight."

"Oh it's fine, you have to look really close before you notice it's not level, it's good enough."

It was not good enough for dad, and the first thing he did after lunch was remove my handiwork, and refit it. This time it was absolutely straight and true. Sure to be noticed now and bring in the customers I thought.

I knew that although I lived only two or three hundred yards from the high street, which was the boundary of my agency, I was technically living on another agent's patch, and that he had the right to object to me living on his territory. Walter Slater had discussed this with me, and warned me that the local man was Harold Dobby, quite a character, and that he had not been too sure about having me living right on his agency. Slater had "smoothed him over" and assured me that there would be no problems.

I answered a loud ringing on the doorbell one morning, and found a pleasantly rounded little lady with a bright friendly face looking up at me from the door step.

"I'm awfully sorry to bother you, but are you the new agent for the Prudential?"

My heart missed a beat, this was a real live enquiry for some business, the brass plate has done its job. "Yes, I'm David Robinson, how can I help you?"

She hesitated a little, as though getting her words together, and then dropped her voice almost to a whisper,

"It's a little bit difficult, but I have called on behalf of a few Prudential policyholders who live on Huddersfield Road. We want to ask you a big favour," she continued, seeming rather ill at ease.

"You see we, that is my neighbours and I, have been with your Insurance Company for years but none of us like Harold Dobby the local agent. We want you to take over our business and collect from us, you seem such a nice young man."

Flattered, I quizzed her to try and find out what was wrong with Harold Dobby, and the refined little lady did not need much encouragement to open up and tell me exactly now her and her neighbours felt about their Mr Dobby.

"Oh, he is downright rude" she volunteered, "nothing is private when Harold Dobby is in the house. Just before Christmas, he came for my money and began picking up the Christmas cards off the mantel shelf. He looked at them to see who they were from, then began asking me where the friends lived who had sent the cards. Told him it was no business of his, and he got quite unpleasant. Then he picked up an envelope, looked at the post mark and asked who was writing to me from York."

"Really, I am surprised"

Before I could continue, the middle aged lady became more direct stating the reason for her visit.

"You see it's like this. None of us want Harold Dobby in our homes ever again, and we want you to ask him not to call, and get him to transfer all our insurances to you, you seem such a nice young man."

I sympathised with her, and explained that much as I would like to help her and her neighbours, it was not ethical for me to get involved. They would have to put up with Harold Dobby, or make a formal application through the office to have me as their agent.

I had almost forgotten this incident, when two or three weeks later, there was a continuously loud ringing on the door bell. I swung the door open to find a well dressed gentleman of about sixty years of age greeting me on the doorstep. He raised his brown trilby, to reveal a shiny bald head streaked with a few strands of silver hair. He peered at me vaguely through gold rimmed spectacles, his hand still held high in the air, holding the hat a foot above his shiny head.

There was a sarcasm in his expression, as he questioned me softly.

"David Robinson I presume. Agent for the Prudential Assurance Company Ltd?"

"Yes that's me, how can I help you?"

He swept down the trilby hat from above his head, and with a wide flourish, positioned it above his heart. Then bowing gracefully, he said very solemnly, with mock humility.

" Harold Dobby at your service  I want you to know that I have never harmed anybody in my life."

Before I could invite him in or think how to answer him, he waved the trilby again, much like a matador waves his cloak at the bull, and with a servile "Goodbye" he was gone. I watched him climb into his red Renault car and stayed at the door until he disappeared towards the town centre. Although I often saw his car parked in Holmfirth, I never again actually saw Harold Dobby from that day even though I worked in the area for another five years.

Walter Slater did confide in me that Harold Dobby was a very successful salesman for the Prudential. He suspected though that Mr Dobby was so unpopular that his clients signed up for a new policy just to get rid of him.

Two to three hundred yards from our home, the High Street lined with very old-fashioned shops, many of them family businesses, entered the main Huddersfield Road. From this junction, going out of Holmfirth in the opposite direction to our home, the terraced houses became rather smaller. It was one of these small terraced houses which I noticed one day had become empty. Its windows were bereft of curtains. Swirls of dirt and paper nestled under the door step, speaking of neglect and desertion. Its walls were of stone, and must have been two feet thick, its woodwork was in desperate need of painting. For several weeks the condition of the house remained unchanged, but one Thursday morning, as I walked past, I had to take a second look for there was something different about it. The windows had been cleaned, inside and out, and they shone like expectant eyes from the drab stone walls.. The accumulation of dust, grit, cigarette packets and fish and chip wrappers, had all gone. The footpath traversing the front of the house was swept and washed clean. I glanced through the still bare window, the room was empty, but obviously someone had bought the little house, and was preparing to move in.

I kept a careful watch on the little home, and often, in an evening, it was ablaze with lights. It became clear that a young couple were working inside. I caught a glimpse of a shock of ginger hair as a young man passed the window carrying a pair of wooden steps. He looked very young, and I guessed that he and his young lady were preparing their first home before they got married. There was a motor cycle standing proudly beside the door a few evenings later, and there beside the front door, neatly displayed on the wall, was a brand new wooden house name plate, bearing the name "Bethany" in black copperplate style lettering.

Bethany of course is the little village where Jesus used to visit his friends Mary and Martha, and their brother Lazarus, and seemed to have a special place in the affections of Jesus. It was to Bethany that He led the disciples after His resurrection, and from there that He ascended on a cloud, back to His Father. In my imagination, I had already decided that the young couple were probably members of the local Methodist Church. If this was so, then we may have a lot in common.

Over the next few weeks, furnishings and carpets were delivered to "Bethany" and I waited until the young couple had moved in before deciding it was time to knock on the door and introduce myself.

Timidly, but expectantly, I lifted the heavy letter box flap two or three times, and let it beat out its message on the stout wooden door. The door swung wide open, and there stood my ginger haired good Christian, member of the Methodist Church, who I hoped would also be a prospect for life assurance.

"Sorry to disturb you" I began, "Here is my card, I am David Robinson, the local agent for the Prudential Assurance Company. I see that you have called your house "Bethany" and wonder whether you are practising Christians?"

The young man's face creased up into a genuine smile of welcome. Accepting my card he chuckled, "Flipping heck, we have only been back from honeymoon for a few days. Here we are already being harassed for life assurance. Come in mate and meet the wife!"

I was impressed by the cosiness and homeliness of the little cottage. It was shining like a new pin, and had the smell of new carpets, new paint, and the excitement that it was their first home. They introduced themselves as Douglas and Mary Marlow, and sat me down to enjoy a mug of hot coffee.

"Flipping heck" began Douglas, I soon was to realize that his Christian heritage prevented the use of any stronger language than these two words which  made up quite a large part of any conversation.

"Fancy you flipping well twigging on that we are Christians.  Flipping heck, it's because we have called the flipping house flipping Bethany.  Never flipping well thought that any flipping body would know what flipping Bethany is."

Doug hardly paused for breath before continuing,  "We are both flipping members of Holmfirth Methodist Church. Mary teaches a Sunday School class and I play the flipping organ most flipping Sundays.  Which flipping church do you go to?"

I had to confess that we did not belong to any church in the Holmfirth area. Edith and I had been part of a large Pentecostal Church twenty or so miles away, and there was nothing like we were used to in Holmfirth. Some Sundays we travelled back to this church, but were hoping to settle into a local church where we could feel at home and be part of its work in the community.

Douglas explained that he worked at a local coal mine, eight or nine miles away, and that he was studying to become a deputy manager. Mary worked in the offices of a local textile mill. Her parents, as well as Doug's mother were strict Methodists. Doug's father had passed away a few years before. He too had been a strict Methodist.

After feeling that we had got to know each other quite well I arranged for Mary and Douglas to come and meet Edith and Joy. Then I got down to the business of life assurance. Doug warmed to the thought of insuring himself for Mary's benefit. I soon learned that Mary's very deeply entrenched Methodist background, viewed life assurance with the same disdain as gambling. Mary refused to discuss the subject and Doug wisely saw that to proceed into a commitment would displease Mary. So the subject was dropped. However, Doug produced an old Prudential Life Policy for the grand sum of one penny per week premium, explaining that his mum had taken it out when he was born, and handed it over to him now that he was married. Mary wanted Doug to cash it in but with a characteristic "Flipping heck" Doug produced a few coins and paid up to the year end.

Later that week, we had the pleasure of a visit from Doug and Mary and found that we had quite a lot in common. Douglas and I shared the same taste in music, and we loaned each other records of George Beverly Shea, The London Crusader Choir, Black Dyke Mills Silver Band, and of course "Sankey's favourites", played on the piano by Jack Ward an Anglican clergyman.

A few mornings later, our door bell loudly announced that someone was at the door. It was Doug with his ginger hair glinting in the weak early morning sunlight. He was returning some of my records, which were safely pinioned under his arm.

"Flipping heck David, your bell is like a flipping fire alarm. Frightened me to death it flipping well did, I have brought some of your flipping records back. Flipping heck, that one of the Black Dyke Mills Bank playing Deep Harmony is flipping good. I have played that one a flipping lot. Hope I have not flipping well worn the flipping thing out."

Doug came in for a coffee, and obviously had something on his mind. Thoughtfully, between sips, he began to confide,

"David, I'm flipping worried about Mary. She is not in good health you know.".

"Really Doug, I had no idea, she looks a picture of rude health."

"Oh she looks flipping good David, but she is far from well. She has flipping epileptic fits. Have you ever seen someone having a flipping fit? It's flipping awful. Mary is not as bad as she used to be, thought at one time she was flipping cured, but she isn't. We had just signed up to buy Bethany, when she had a flipping bad fit. She was frying some chips when she took a fit, ended up in hospital. I tell you, I was flipping frightened."

I sympathised with Doug,

"I am sorry to hear all this Doug, I have seen people in an epileptic fit, it is quite frightening. I hope that Mary's burns have healed OK."

Doug was visibly near to tears,

"She will be scarred for life David, it just a flipping good thing that it was her arms and not her face. She can keep her arms covered with flipping long sleeves."

Sensing my sympathetic response, Doug continued,

"This is the thing that flipping worries me David. I worry myself sick when I think of how Mary would cope if she lost me. I don't intend dying yet for a flipping long time, but you know, if I died suddenly, well the shock could increase Mary's fits, and she may not be able to flipping well work and support herself."

I topped up Doug's coffee as he continued,

"You know David, Mary is so against life assurance. Thinks it is gambling. Somehow she has got the flipping idea that insurance is a trap of the flipping devil. Oh I don't know David, but without some decent life assurance on me, Mary would struggle if anything flipping happened to me."

I could tell that Doug was struggling with his conscience.

"David, would it be wrong for me to insure myself for a flipping worth while amount without flipping well telling Mary?"

We discussed this at length, and I did not have any conscience about setting up a substantial life assurance on Doug with all the benefits under a trust deed for Mary. It was 1966, and a life assurance with a lump sum of £2500 payable on death, doubled should death occur by accident, and followed by a tax free income of £1000 per year for 25 years, was a large amount in those days. The premium was just over £5 every three months. Doug paid me the first premium and he agreed to bring future premiums to my home. We agreed to keep our secret from Mary for a while. As Doug said "Good bye" he grinned back at me,

"Flipping heck David, I only came to bring your flipping records back, now I am worth more dead than alive. But every-time I passed by and saw your brass plate it made me think about insuring myself.

As Doug disappeared down the road, I wiped the dust from my brass plate with my best handkerchief.

"Thanks, that's the first flipping business you have brought me!"

# Doug & Mary

I was on the last lap of my late afternoon calls, there were just two or three more visits to make before I slipped home for a quick sandwich and a few minutes rest before beginning the evening calls. I was starving, and the smell of cooking which assaulted my nostrils in the little cottages in Hinchcliffe Mill was making me hungrier by the minute.

Doug Marlow had spent the morning with me, he was at a loose end, due to his shift not commencing until mid afternoon, and his wife was of course working all day. I was always pleased when Doug appeared at the door on a collecting day, asking whether he could spend the morning or the evening with me in the car. His conversation was witty, he always had some new amusing story, his descriptive powers, and the way he punctuated every sentence with a scattered assortment of "flipping hecks" always kept me smiling. He had a gift for seeing the amusing in every circumstance, and was a great mimic. Between calls, he brightened the time spent driving with his clever impersonations, and there were no dull moments when Doug was in the car.

Doug and Mary had been over to the large Pentecostal Church in Wakefield with Edith and I the previous evening. The church had been fortunate in having a visit from David Newington, an extraordinary missionary who ran Emmanuel Press, a Christian missionary printing press in the Transvaal. David was a tremendous communicator, and held the audience spellbound for over an hour, as he dramatically and skilfully told story after story of the miraculous intervention and provision of God. He thrilled the audience with stories of how he hired an aeroplane, and dropped a huge sack of Christian literature into the exercise yard of a massive prison. Within weeks, hundreds of prisoners, some of them murderers, had become committed Christians, and were completing Bible Study correspondence courses with Emmanuel Press.

David Newington's experiences and commitment had somehow got through to Doug, and his main topic that morning was the fact that he was doing so little by way of Christian service, compared with David Newington, who had given up all to be obedient to the call of God. Doug had been fired, enthused, and as he talked on, I began to think that the challenge he had received whilst listening to David Newington could well change the direction and purpose of his whole life. Doug had stayed with me all morning, we had enjoyed each other's company, but now I was alone again. It had been a day which did not fit the season, it was still winter, but this afternoon had been mild with a bright watery sun bathing the hundred years old stone walls of the little terraced houses in mellow warmth. There was a hardness in those stone walls, built to last the savagery of the Pennine winters for a thousand years. Today, the sun brought out their warmth and beauty, and lent a mature attractiveness to their usually black grimy façades.

There were four well worn stone steps leading up to the Crowther's front door, flanked on each side by a heavy black wrought iron handrail, freshly painted and shining in the fading sunlight. The freshness of the paint contrasted with the aged steps, thousands of pairs of feet had taken their toll, hollowing out a smooth depression in the centre of the old stones. In a freezing winter, ascending those steps was a nightmare. I had found out to my cost that when snow or ice covered the surface, the only safe way of reaching the front door was to haul oneself up a step at a time, using the stout handrail as a hoist. The first time I had tried to conquer that six foot ascent when sleet and slush squelched on the steps, I had scorned at the thought of me, a young chap, using the handrail, handrails were for lesser mortals. Needless to say, on the second step my feet went from under me, and I tumbled base over apex, finding myself sitting on the snow covered pavement, looking up at two smiling ladies watching me from the relative safety of the adjacent bus stop.

Today was a different story, it has been a pleasure to be out, winter had relaxed its evil grip, and today's sunny smile was apologising for the hideous ill humour which had recently been displayed as winter had wrung every bit of warmth and pleasantness out of the short days. Winter, which had mocked people, howling and blowing at them as they darted out of their homes to the corner shop, was today reminding us that spring was not far away, that better things were in store.

I had met the Crowther's briefly on my previous monthly visits to their little stone terrace home, they were local folk, born and bred in the Holme Valley, and both worked in the local textile mills. The textile industry was reeling from the devastating effect of cheap foreign imports, and usually the workers were finished by lunch time on a Friday. Always cheerful, and always welcoming, this was one home I looked forward to calling at. In response to my rattling on the door knocker, the door opened, but instead of Mrs Crowther's matronly form, another picture appeared. The young lady must be her daughter, the same smile, the same black hair, the same good humour, the same Yorkshire accent, and mother's orange premium book held towards me, a five pound note between its pages.

"Mum and dad 'ave gone away fot'weekend. Am looking after thouse till they get 'ome. Mum has left t'brass inside t'book, 'ave you any change?"

Yes I had the right change, and as I fumbled for it in my pocket I quizzed,

"When is your baby due?"

The black curls shook, as she laughed in reply,

"Oh, there's two months to wait yet, and I feel like a puddin' already, 1 have to dash, cos the tea is about done, bye!"

Pleasant girl, I thought as I hurried away, but soon forgot about her as on future visits, her mother or father were always home. How quickly those Friday afternoons sped by. It was three of four months later when I was signing Mrs Crowther's book, that she broke into my concentration,

"You met Audrey our less a few months ago when we were away."

"Yes, indeed, a very pleasant young lady, how is she, has she had her baby yet?"

Mrs Crowther, now a proud grandmother, laughed,

"Oh she's all reight, an' they 'eve a luvly babby, they want to see thee some time when you ' eve a minute. Want to tek out some insurance fo't babby. Just drop in when your passin"

"I certainly will Mrs Crowther, thanks very much, does Audrey still live here?"

"Nay, they live just down t' road, in t'terrace where t'pub is, ah don't know t'number, just look for t' blue door."

Thanking her, I hurried away and scribbled a note in my diary to remind me to see Audrey and Dave. This was just what I needed, another sales prospect to visit with Mr Slater when he next worked with me. It was not always easy finding fresh prospects to sell to, the main industry, textiles, was in recession, and many of my clients were only working part time. We could not fail to acquire some business with Audrey and Dave though, they had actually asked us to call, this was an insurance salesman's dream. I worked on the assumption that if I have been asked to call and arrange insurance, there is a good chance that no other insurance agent calls there, and if this is the case, the door is wide open for a whole range of insurance related products.

I decided to keep this call for Walter Slater's next visit, it would be a pleasant and productive call for him. The atmosphere had been strained between us of late, and he seemed to enjoy finding little things which he could criticise me for. Whenever I displeased him, he would say very seriously, "You will never mek owt in this job." This made me doubt my own ability and feel very insecure with him. The strange thing was that Redfearn Rogers, the branch manager. who was Walter Slater's immediate boss, always seemed happy with me and talked as though he had every confidence in my abilities. I knew of course that Slater and Redfearn obviously discussed me from time to time, and in spite of this I always found Mr Redfearn's manner and attitude very encouraging.

I think the decline in relationships between Slater and myself was for two reasons. Whilst at one of the training seminars run by Les Jackson at Leeds, I had made the discovery that a business practice 1 had inherited when I took over the agency from Norman was in contravention of company regulations, and if discovered, could be dealt with very severely. It was nothing criminal, just that a client who had a policy with premiums due only once a year, was paying me a twelfth of the annual premium each month when I called, and expecting me to refund him all the money once a year so that he could pay the yearly amount when it fell due. Les Jackson frightened us all to death, when he spelled out the implications of this and warned any who were carrying out this practice, to stop it immediately.

When I next called upon the clients, I told them the position, and immediately, under protest, refunded their money, informing them that 1 could no longer continue in breach of company regulations, they were not happy, saying that Walter Slater had suggested they do it that way. They in turn phoned him up to complain, and he instructed me to continue the practice, which I refused to do. The clients took their complaint to Redfearn Rogers, who interviewed me, and finding me to be in the clear, carpeted Walter Slater. Just a few weeks after this, Slater discovered that in the reorganising of my duties, I had cut out Saturday morning collections entirely, absorbing them into the week. He resented this, and was angry at the thought of my taking Saturday mornings off. When he voiced his feelings to Redfearn Rogers expecting support, he supported me, feeling that as I was working every evening, it was not unreasonable to take Saturday mornings off. As my work had not suffered in any way, he gave me his blessing to continue finishing duties on a Friday evening, so that at least I could enjoy a longer weekend with Edith and Joy.

All this did not create a happy working relationship between Slater and I, and so I was anxious not to give him further cause for complaint. If we could have a successful sales stint each time he worked with me, then it would make for a peaceful existence.

Walter's visit came round again all too soon, and it was a most unpleasant evening when we he picked me up. He seemed out of sorts and was very touchy. Maybe it was because he had just bought a brand new Hillman Super Minx, and did not want to take it out on such a filthy evening. May be it was because he did not really like working with me, he was almost retiring age, and perhaps he had had enough. Perhaps he had no time for the younger generation, especially me. Perhaps my rust holed Morris Minor fell short of his standards, perhaps as an individual, I fell short of his standards, but that evening, I heard his phrase, "You will never mek owt in this job" more than I had heard it for a long time.

As the evening progressed I realised that not a lot was happening to put me back into favour with Walter. Some of my appointments fell through, the clients having forgotten had gone out. Some people took one look at us, and seeing how wet and muddy we were, would not let us in. Walter did not seem to like it when unshaven labourers opened the door to him, and answered his polite "Good evening, we are from the Prudential Assurance Company." With "Op it mate, I am watching the television".

By eight o'clock, we had not made a single sale, and it looked like being a blank night. I was getting more and more embarrassed, and Walter getting more and more impatient. It was my fault people would not let us in, it was my fault folk had forgotten and gone out. If the entire population of Holmsby moved away overnight, leaving a town of empty houses, it would still be my fault if sales did not keep rolling in. Tonight looked like being an absolute disaster, and of course it will be my fault again. Suddenly I saw a glimmer of hope, of course, what about Audrey and Dave. Audrey the smiling lass, and Dave the husband I had never met, were waiting in a lovely warm house just wondering when we were going to descend on them to sell them some insurance. With a sense of relief I asked Walter to drive into Hinchcliffe Mill and pull up at the blue door near the pub. As the car sloshed through the water filled roads, I gave him the details of the call, and explained who the couple were and why we were calling. The car cruised effortlessly towards the blue door, the windscreen wipers hardly able to shift all the water which was belting down. We peered through the screen. I was anxiously looking for my blue door. when Walter cleared his throat and gloated in triumph,secretly glad that I had done it again,

"Every door in the terrace is blue"

"That's alright," I replied, unabashed, we just can't go wrong, Mrs Crowther said it was the blue door near the pub, just stop here next to the pub, and leave it to me, I will get us into the house."

We stood at the door step trying to push back our wet hair from our eyes whilst waiting for our loud knocking to be answered. After a few moments the blue door opened, and there stood a young man 1 had never seen before. Anxious to redeem myself in Walter's eyes, 1 cleared by throat and asked,

"Is is Dave?"

"It certainly is" was the warm reply. My confidence growing by the second, I continued,

"Good evening Dave, I am David Robinson, and this is Mr Slater my boss, we are from The Prudential Assurance Company. Your mother in law has asked us to pop in and see you."

The young man grinned "If mother in law has asked you to call then you had better come in.  I thought it would not be long before we had a visit from some insurance men.

We followed him into the warm comfortable, living room a lively coal fire was dancing in the hearth lighting up the obvious newness of the decorations and the furnishings. Walter and I sat next to each other in adjacent easy chairs Dave sat opposite us on the settee. No smiling Audrey though, she was obviously upstairs putting baby to bed. Mr Slater, eager to show what a distinguished and smooth salesman he was, made the first thrust,

"I believe that congratulations are in order then lad!"

Dave beamed his reply

"Yes, thanks very much."

"I'm very pleased for you both, it will have been a stressful time and you will both be glad it's all over. you can relax now that it has worked out so well,"

"Aw aye" grinned Dave, and just as he was going to continue Walter Slater came straight back,

"Just at this moment lad, you will be thinking that once is enough, but you take my advice lad, spread your wings a bit, dont make it a one off job do it again like I have done. I have gone through it four times, it's just as worrying each time lad just as stressful, but well worth it, so don't you stop at once, do it all again,"

Dave, looking bemused and confused managed to mumble,

"Yes" but he obviously had something else to say, but no, my superintendent with his advice and wisdom interrupted him.

"Well lad, one thing is certain now you'll not know what it is to get a good night' s sleep. You'll be up and down, up and down all night long and when you get to work in a morning you will be bleary eyed and tired, and all your work mates will laugh and pull your leg about not getting any sleep.

Dave began to look uncomfortable, but my boss was in full flow and there was no stopping him, he went through it all again, the sleepless nights, the being up and down all night long, the encouragement to do it all again, like he had done.

I thought, perhaps it is what he has done four times which has turned him into the crusty ill tempered individual he is tonight. Then, I heard a sound, ah, footsteps on the stairs, and getting closer. Here comes smiling Audrey, soon that mass of black curls will shake its way through the door and Audrey will make us a cup of hot coffee. The door opened, a young lady made her entrance, it was not smiling Audrey, it was a girl I had never seen before. Like a flash, I worked out what was happening, Audrey was still upstairs putting baby to bed, this was just a relative who has been giving Audrey a little bit of help.

The young lady sat down beside Dave, he put his arm round her shoulder, and said quite simply, "This is my wife" Before he could tell us her name, and before I could say anything, Mr Slater had put the same record on again. Oh no, here it all comes again, but with renewed vigour and freshness. His previous two recitals had been mere rehearsals compared to this one, Lawrence Olivier had never put such fire and enthusiasm into his Shakespearian roles. Out came the references to the sleepless nights, the being up and down all night, the bleary eyes, the workmates laughing at Dave, the encouragement to go through it, all four, times, like he has done. I sat there, the words washing over me, and when the impassioned speech was played out, Walter continued,

Well let's get down to business, we are not the Mighty Prudential for nothing, we believe in being quick off the mark, we have come to insure this baby you have been having

The atmosphere, which had been getting a little uneasy, exploded. Dave and his young wife leapt up from the settee together,

"Blimey" cried Dave, "summat's wrong, we only got married yesterday."

I tapped my confused boss on the ankle with my foot, as he looked at me. I could only huskily whisper to him,

"I think we are in the wrong house,"

It was a simple statement, it was not laden with hidden malice, it was not said in a clever insubordinate way, but he exploded at me. He lost his dignity, and as he leapt to his feet in the centre of the little room he bellowed at me,

"Wrong house, wrong house" then turning to Dave and his pretty young wife he softened his accents as he continued,

"Please forgive my ignorant friend here, wrong house indeed, now he tells me! Please accept my humble apologies. Everything I have just said has been filled with double meanings."

He pawed the ground like a demented horse, the coal fire glinting in his mirror finish "K" shoes as he pawed the carpet like an impatient horse pawing on the cobbled street. He turned his attention back to me,

"And I'll deal with you Mr Robinson when I get you back into the car, wrong house indeed, now he tells me." Ever the opportunist, I grabbed the occasion, "I am sorry that we are in the wrong house, we wanted Dave and Audrey, and you did say your name was Dave. You see, Audrey and Dave's house has a blue door, and they are all blue doors along here." I was beginning to babble, " please accept our apologies, and please accept our congratulations upon your marriage. You must admit, our timing is good, we ought to sit down again and talk to you about life assurance."

But no, my boss was in full flow again. He had put another disc in the player, "There is a time and place for everything Mr Robinson, and this is neither, I will deal with you when I get you in the car." We left the house as gracefully as we could, and sitting in the grey Super Minx I began to laugh softly. Sir Walter Slater began to be angry, not softly at all. I had done it again, I had spoiled his evening, what would that nice couple think of him, and of course he ended his tirade with the regulation words, "You'll never mek owt in this job." There is a sequel to this true story. Two years later, Walter had retired, and I had a new superintendent, David Hodge, only thirty two years old, and we got on famously, we were both on the same wavelength. One night I was out with David, when I saw nappies blowing on the line outside Dave's little house. I led my new boss up the path, knocked on the door, and was pleased to see the same Dave standing there. With a smile I greeted him,

"We are not the Mighty Prudential for nothing, we have come to insure this baby you have been having!" Dave grinned as he replied,

"Aw, last time you was twelve months too soon, this time you're twelve months too late, we have done it with the Pearl." Ah well, Walter always said I would never mek owt!

This behaviour was completely out of character for Walter Slater. I shared the story with another member of Mr Slater's team, and he threw some light upon why my boss had reacted as he had. It seems that only a few weeks prior to my incident with him, he had been taken by one of his agents to discuss savings for a new born baby. When Walter Slater said to the young couple, "Congratulations on the birth of your baby, I am so happy for you both" their reply caught him completely off guard. "Oh thank you, but our baby died and we buried her yesterday." He blamed his staff member for not having done his homework correctly and hoped that he would never be faced with a similar situation again. Upon discovering that I had taken him into the wrong house he had some sort of a throw back to the dead baby incident, thus reacting in an uncharacteristic way. It is a pity Mr Slater did not tell me this at the time, I would have understood his actions better.

# The Accordion

Leaving the main road at Hinchcliffe Mill, I turned down the steep lane which wound down to the little cluster of stone cottages known as Waterside. Six or seven slate roofed cottages, with unusually small windows peering out from the mellow stone walls, looked across the mill dam. Adjacent to the dam, the narrow river tumbled its way along the valley. Though only a mile from the town centre, it seemed impatient to reach its wider bed underneath the stone bridge on the High Street, where it sported and tumbled on its way past the busy shoppers.

I braked to stop the little car running away down the steep slope. There were no pavements, the front doors of the little cottages opened up straight onto the street. Some of the front doors had tiny porches enclosing them, but mostly the door step led straight down onto the tarmac road. I guessed that these dwellings had been built in the days before planning permission was needed. A careless person, stepping straight out of the front door onto the road was a real hazard, and I had no desire on a peaceful Friday afternoon, to entangle my front bumper bar with old Joe Booth's shapeless cord trousers.

Oh no, here comes Joe Booth, ambling down the middle of the little lane, puffing out great clouds of blue cigarette smoke, I think he must go to bed in his faded brown gaberdine mac, tweed check flat cap and shapeless fawn cord trousers. Judging by the thickness of his spectacles he needs a white stick. Normal folk wave their hand or touch their hat as a greeting, why does he always brandish his thick walking stick round his head like a demented helicopter propeller. And who is Joe Booth anyway? Everyone seems to know him, he must be in his seventies, and seems to spend much of his time ambling aimlessly round the streets, mostly in the middle of them. Perhaps he has a kamikaze determination to be Holmfirth's first martyr to suffer death at the hands, or should I say, the wheels of the modern motor car!

Joe always assumes that every vehicle in sight will stop in its tracks just for him, and that everybody he meets on the street has nothing to do but stand and chat with him. As I drove past him, he peered at me through his jam jar bottoms, in a valiant effort to recognise me. I gave him a cheery wave as I passed by, but he had no idea who I was, he reminded me of a friendly dog, searching out anyone who has the time to stop and offer a friendly pat on the head.

Between the dry stone walls surrounding the dam, and the row of cottages, was an eight foot earth track, with a worn grass verge alongside. I pulled the car as close to the wall as I could, and as the engine coughed to a halt, glanced in my collecting book to see where my next call was.

"Mrs Newton, Waterside" was the clear address staring at me in Norman Peace's nicely rounded letters This was a lady I had not visited before who paid such a small amount in insurance premiums that we only called on her two or three times a year. I knew from the net curtains and the aspidistra plant in the window, that Mrs Newton was possibly quite old. Strange how some of the oldest people put the young ones to shame when it comes to caring for their houses. Her windows gleamed, the brown grained front door was fresh and shiny. The stone window sills were scrubbed and shone with a mellow yellow glow in the afternoon sun. Ten or twelve feet from the front door, in the same terrace, was another matching brown grained door, held closed with a padlock and strong chain.

There were no windows near this door, obviously it was the outside toilet. It had been a cultural shock to me when a client in the village told me proudly that he was a "night soil man." I thought he was a gardener on night shift until he explained that a great many folk in the community did not have water closets. Their outside toilets were reached by ascending five or six stone steps, and beneath their wooden toilet seat was the "long drop," a six foot drop down to an enclosed stone ledge where all the waste matter collected. The council employed "night soil men" to come at dead of night when decent folk were asleep, and empty the offensive cargo from the primitive toilets. Each toilet was emptied about twice a year, so they were not places where you would sit long enough to complete the Daily Telegraph Crossword.

I could not believe my eyes one day when I visited one of these working relics from a bygone age to spend a penny. The toilet had a long wooden seat about six feet long, with three round holes, about fifteen inches in diameter, side by side. Visiting the loo in Victorian days was obviously a family or social occasion. I was relieved to find that I was the only occupant that day.

The most common "long drop" toilets were nothing more than a two storey outhouse, the basement being the department where all the waste accumulated. The wooden toilet seat was in effect, perched on the top of a sort of wide "chimney" down which everything dropped. The really "modern" type had a metal tub, precisely balanced on a metal shaft, positioned just beneath the seat. The effluent was allowed to build up in the drum until the drum was almost full. The drum was now almost top heavy, and only needed a bucket of water pouring into it, to overturn it, and make it deposit its contents down into the depths below, to await the "night soil" man's infrequent visit.

I smiled as I remembered Dick and Sandra, some young clients with a young family, who had a primitive outside toilet with a difference. Visiting their loo involved crossing the main road, and entering into a building which for size and shape, resembled a ramshackle punch and Judy theatre. Dick and Sandra were so embarrassed at going to their loo in daylight that they tried to avoid giving in to calls of nature until after dark. Unfortunately, the children did not have such strong and disciplined bowels and bladders, and "for the children's use only" a plastic bucket was kept under the bedroom stairs.

One evening Dick was baby sitting alone whilst Sandra was out working. After drinking several coffees, I enquired whether I could spend a penny. Dick promptly disappeared under the bedroom stairs, to emerge holding forth the plastic bucket. He grinned as he held out the receptacle.

"You do it while I hold it."

I must confess that discretion took the better part, and the desire to use the makeshift loo left me quite suddenly.

Dick was sheepishly crossing the road one evening to empty the receptacle, when a speeding car suddenly appeared. In his effort to dash back into the house before the car driver spotted him, he tripped and fell into the road, emptying the contents of the bucket all over him.

Mrs Newton's toilet was at ground level, and not at the top of a flight of steps, presiding over the "long drop." So I assumed that at least, she had a modern water closet. Her little home did not appear to have been modernised though. Ah well, we will soon see whether my detective work is right.

The door opened and a homely, elderly lady, with a gentle, refined, smiling face greeted me, she had the most spotless luxuriant head of white hair I have ever seen, and her long hair tumbled onto her shoulders. Mrs Newton was a widow, and in her seventies. She lived alone in her rented, unmodernised house. It was old fashioned, but spotlessly clean and homely. The front door opened straight from the street into her living room. An old fashioned coal fire spluttered in the black leaded grate.

The oven door swung open above the hearth. Beside the fireplace, in the alcove between the chimney and the window, stood the white pot sink and wooden draining board, neatly housed behind wooden doors, painted with high gloss magnolia paint, which seemed to be the "in" colour in the Holme Valley.

On the large wooden table was a rich green chenille table cloth, with tassels around the edge. It matched the green chenille drape, also with tassels which decorated the wooden mantel shelf. An old wooden clock, every bit as old as its owner, loudly ticked away the minutes.

On the table was a newspaper, and an old black leather-bound Bible, and two or three hymn books. A curtained aperture led through to a smaller sitting room, and I could just see in the corner, an old pedal powered harmonium, with an open hymn book on the music stand, and family photographs proudly displayed on the lid.

The grand old lady pointed me to a leather covered easy chair, pulled up near the fire, opened the doors which hid the sink from view, filled the kettle, and enquired in a very kindly way, whether I would prefer tea or coffee, and then, whilst the kettle was boiling, cut a few slices of very rich fruit cake, which she placed on a china plate with an assortment of biscuits.

Her accent was not the broad nasal Yorkshire dialect, in fact there was no noticeable accent. All her words were softly and well spoken, her gentle manner, her almost regal bearing and disposition were quite different from the rough and ready manners of the people around her. I would not have been surprised to discover that she had at some time lived in a society far removed from her present status, and that her mean little cottage and present lifestyle were much humbler than the standards she was accustomed to.

Mrs Newton had lived alone since her husband passed away, paying a small rent for her cottage. She knew many of the local people, because when they had been experiencing hard times, perhaps nursing a sick child or husband she had offered to help in any way that she could. She was a woman of great Christian charity, with a loving attitude towards everyone. She was entirely free from malicious gossip, and was a very private person, keeping her own affairs to herself, and never prying into other people's affairs. This alone made her so different from the local folk, who seemed to thrive on scandal and hurtful small talk about their neighbours' private lives.

I was surprised to hear that although a lifelong chapel member, she did not actually attend a place of worship. She had been involved in chapel life when she first moved into the village, but had great difficulty accepting some of the practices and lifestyles which the chapels and churches condoned. She did not see the character and nature of Jesus at work in the churches ministry, and opted out. I felt that she was wrong, and that there was a place for her to try and change the status quo. But no, she chose to worship God at home, but she put many church-goers to shame with her Christian spirit and practical life.

She was a woman I would have gladly confided in during any time of personal hardship or difficulty, because anything passed on to her was retained in absolute confidence. A secret shared with her, remained a secret, a private problem shared with her, remained a private problem. She was a woman of great wisdom, and had a great calming effect; her peace seemed to rub off onto you as you conversed with her. I did not realize during my first meeting with her, that she was to become a close friend of Edith and me. That she would be almost the only visitor Edith ever saw, and that she would soon share a week's holiday with us in North Wales, and that in later years, when we had left the Holmfirth area, we would still travel back from time to time to visit her and take her gifts at Christmas and Easter time.

I scraped together the last few crumbs of the fruit cake, and washing them down with the remains of the coffee, glanced at the old harmonium in the other room,

"Mrs Newton, why don't you play something for me on the harmonium?"

"Oh, you don't want to hear an old lady playing, I don't play well now. I used to be a good musician, but now I only play for my own pleasure."

We stepped through into the sitting room, which was quite small and rather dark; its small window was overshadowed by a terrace of houses just a few yards to the rear of Mrs Newton's house, and I quickly realised that this room would see very little sun. Sitting at the keyboard, she thumbed through the old Methodist Hymn Book, and selecting one of Wesley's good hymns, began to pump some air into the leaking bellows as she firmly pushed away on the pedals. She paused for a few moments until she was satisfied that there was sufficient air in the lungs of the old instrument, before she began to fondly and skilfully ripple her fingers up and down the yellowing keyboard.

It was a dark, damp smelling, depressing little room, but the moment the sweet music began to swell from the old pipes, it seemed as though the little room became suddenly brighter. She threw back her head, tossed the white locks of hair aside, and began to sing Wesley's majestic words. Here was a lady who not only knew the words of the old musical poem, but she knew the God who was the theme of the words, and with deep feeling and sincerity, she filled the little house with her song of praise.

Pausing to search for another old hymn, she gently invited me to join in with her,

"You look as though you have a good pair of lungs, why don't you sing along with me?"

Embarrassed, I made a stumbling apology,

"Oh, I really can't sing, never have been able to, ever since the school choir master refused to have me in the choir, because I was a grunter and not a singer, I have never been much of a one for singing."

"Nonsense," smiled Mrs Newton firmly, "if you are going to be a regular visitor here, I shall be looking forward to the day when I will be able to teach you how to sing!"

Much to my shame, I have to confess that I always chickened out when she lifted the old lid and began to play. As we turned from the old harmonium, I noticed a piano accordion in the corner, and enquired,

"Do you play the accordion? That's an instrument I really love to hear, come on, let's have a tune on it."

"Oh I don't play the accordion, it's my granddaughter's. I tried to get her interested in music and bought it for her a few months ago, but she has not shown any interest in it, it's a shame to see it there gathering dust."

As she was talking, she had picked up the lovely instrument, adjusted the straps to accommodate my generous proportions, and soon the accordion was across my chest, its keyboard at my right hand, and the top of the instrument was tucked under my chin. Obedient to her encouragement, I clumsily opened and closed the bellows, whilst pressing the keys on the right hand keyboard. Fingering one note at a time, I managed to go up and down the scale, but was completely lost when she pointed out that snuggled under the fingers of my left hand were one hundred and twenty buttons just waiting for understanding fingers to coax them into life. The noise I made was rather different to the music she had just played on the harmonium. I just did not have a clue what I was doing, and only succeeded in creating a discord of wheezing and screeching howls like a mad dog in pain.

As she helped me take off the heavy instrument she quizzed,

"Why don't you take it home with you and try it out properly. I can tell that you love music. If you find that you have an aptitude for it, you can have it for eight pounds, which is rather less than I paid for it a few months ago."

I had always fancied myself as Yorkshire's rival to Jimmy Shand, and needed no encouragement to take my prize and stow it safely away in the car boot. In my excitement I never even gave a thought to what Edith would have to say when she saw my new toy.

I locked the car boot, and slipped back to Mrs Newton's to collect my briefcase; as I was locking the accordion in the boot, old Joe Booth appeared again, he sauntered over the little bridge over the river, clouds of blue smoke billowing behind him. Seeing me, he brandished his walking stick above his head as he ambled past. I just had to know who Joe Booth was, perhaps Mrs Newton would know.

"By the way Mrs Newton, who is that gentleman walking up the lane? I understand his name is Joe Booth, just who is he? He seems to be a local character."

"Oh, he lives in the little row of houses just behind my house. His wife won't allow him to smoke in the house. It seems that smoking is his only pleasure, so he spends nearly all his time roaming the streets. At least he can smoke there. There is a large stone detached house further up the hill owned by Clifford and Catherine Mellor, Catherine is Joe Booth's daughter. They are not short of money, she owns a baby wear shop in the town, and Clifford is manager of one of the local mills. Joe does all the gardening for them, but they won't allow him in the house. If the weather is bad, he sits in their garden shed, at least he can smoke in there."

"Thanks, you are a mine of information, and thanks for the coffee and the musical interlude. I'll let you know about the accordion."

As I turned toward my car, Mrs Newton caught hold of my arm,

"Just one thing Mr Robinson, Norman Peace used to call at Nellie Borthwick's, two or three doors from me, I am not gossiping, but you really need to be wary of their family. I don't want to say any more, but they used to give Norman Peace a hard time. Be very careful in any business dealings with them. Goodbye."

# Fire!

Nellie Borthwick's husband, Wilf, tried very hard to speak like a gentleman. Not being of gentle and noble pedigree, his efforts failed to convince anyone that he was anything else but an extremely rough and ready builder's labourer. He did try so hard to put the aitches where there should be an aitch, but his valiant efforts failed miserably, and his resultant speech was a strange mongrel mixed breed of words and pronunciations, which I had to try very hard not to smile at.

"If you would care to step inside, I will hask my good lady to mek you an 'ot drink Mr Robinson."

"Thank you Mr Borthwick, a warm drink will be most welcome."

He pointed to Mrs Borthwick, who was just rising out of her fireside chair on her way into the kitchen to put on the kettle,

"This is my good lady wife, Mrs Borthwick," turning to her, he muttered,

"Say ello to Mr Robinson our new Prudential agent, Nellie."

Mrs Borthwick nodded a greeting as she shuffled off into the dirty looking kitchen. As she left the room, I began to ask her husband a little about himself.

"I am a civil hengineer, and hi build roads and motorways. You will obviously appreciate that in my line of business, I am in demand hall over the country, so I am hoften away from 'ome for weeks on end." I was struck by his resemblance to a wizened up little rat. His eyes were close together and tiny, his ears long and pointed, and his skin was parchment colour which was not all sunburn! He was in need of a good wash. His grubby shirt collar was several sizes too large, and as he kept giving me little darting looks, seeming quite unable to look me in the eye, I formed the opinion that here was a man I could not trust. He spoke and moved silently. There was a furtiveness about the way he walked which reminded me of a timid little rat who had arrived late for a funeral, and was tip toeing down the aisle in an effort to arrive without being seen!

The little front room was well and truly lived in. There were four or five children watching the very noisy television, I guessed that the youngest of them were probably his grandchildren. They looked just as unkempt and unwashed as grandfather. Their thick woollen jumpers were washed out of shape, and their noses certainly needed a good wipe. The room smelled of unwashed bodies, and stale clothing. Everywhere were piles of newspapers and tangled assortments of clothes which seemed to have lost their way to the washing machine. Two ashtrays were overflowing with ash and cigarette stubs, the furniture was cheap and gaudy, and the carpets and curtains were certainly not colour coordinated to match the greasy looking lounge suite.

I am usually a good judge of character, and even if Nora Newton had not warned me about the Borthwicks, I would have been on my guard. Mr Borthwick had been busy clearing away piles of jumbled up washing to create me a little space to sit down in whilst I had been busy taking in the atmosphere of the home. He turned to me with a condescending glance from his furtive little eyes as he quizzed,

"And 'ow long do you think you will last in this job, boy."

I really resented his use of the word boy, and had difficulty not showing my offence.

"A long time I hope. Norman Peace lasted just over forty years, I hope to make my career with the Prudential."

"Well, I suppose someone 'as to do the job, It is not everybody's cup of tea collecting door to door. But then, not all people is as highly skilled as what I ham. I 'ope that a proper job turns up before long for you."

Pompous, objectionable, dirty, scruffy, self-opinionated little individual, I thought. I have a good mind to give you an idea of just how good a job this is. I ought to tell you that a clergyman, a leather merchant, a surveyor, a surgeon and an auctioneer, under the Chairmanship of Mr George Harrison started the Prudential Assurance Company in May 1848. I ought to tell you that by 1905 The Prudential had issued 25 million insurance policies. I ought to tell you that The Prudential was the only insurance company which volunteered to honour all the life assurance policies for the men killed in the 1914-1918 war even though during wartime their liability was legally restricted to making only a return of premiums. I ought to tell you that during the 1914-18 war, the Prudential made a dramatic contribution to the British economy when it placed its total dollar securities valued at £8.75 million at the government's disposal just because the government needed dollars. I ought to tell you just how committed the Prudential Assurance Company is to the highest levels of customer service and satisfaction. Proper job indeed! I ought to tell you that the Prudential agents are regular visitors to over five million homes in the UK I ought to have told you all this. Discretion prevailed however, and I just smiled benignly as his wife handed me a mug of hot coffee.

I studied Nellie Borthwick as I sipped my coffee. She had a pleasant enough face when she smiled, but she had the same shifty look as her husband. She was quite obviously frightened of her husband, and seemed anxious that he should approve of everything she said and did. She reminded me of a puppy who has done wrong, and is expecting a smack from its master. Her black hair was greasy and her skin sallow and yellowing. I quickly summed them up as a couple who knew how to live off their wits, widely experienced in spinning sob stories and giving very plausible reasons for not being able to pay their way. I judged that they would know every trick in the book, they were not the type of people I would want to buy a second hand car from!

The television was blasting away in the corner making normal conversation impossible. I remembered a little trick Walter Slater had passed on to me, so instead of raising my voice to compete with the horse race commentary, I dropped my voice to almost whisper level. For a few moments Mr Borthwick struggled to hear me, and I resisted the temptation to speak loudly. After a while he rose silently to his feet and tip toed across to turn down the television. It was then possible to talk sensibly until the protesting voices of the children reached crescendo level complaining that they could not hear the television.

Borthwick fingered his premium book thoughtfully before casting a shifty look in his wife's direction, then with his little darting eyes avoiding mine, and with a nervous twitch of his thin lips, he questioned me,

"Which office processes fire claims might hi ask? Is it Calcutta or Khartoum? Rising silently he poked soundlessly at the fire, and as he placed the bent poker back onto the hearth continued.

"And 'ow does your, Company send its clients their money? Do they use carrier pigeons or stage coach? I think they must do judging by the time they are taking to settle my claim."

"Exactly what are you referring to,'" I asked as I placed my empty coffee cup on the greasy carpet beside my chair

"I have had the misfortune to have an accident. It was of course only a trivial little thing. Hi dropped a burning coal on the rug and unfortunately slight damage ensued. It was nothink, and the value of the rug was not the point, but hi decided that as we are insured with your Company for fire, it was only right to send in a claim. It is now three weeks since I posted the claim form, and to date I ave heard nothink. Now Mr Robinson, we are not short of money, but purely as a matter of principle, hi 'ave decided not to pay you my monthly premium until your Company ave fulfilled their obligation to me and paid my claim in full."

I quietly reasoned with him, but there was to be no shifting him from his decision. I formed the opinion that he was in fact hard up and to press him would lead nowhere and only cause embarrassment.

Incidentally, I did check with claims department, in an effort to speed up Mr Borthwick's claim. The claim was purely fictional, they had no knowledge of it. The following month when I visited the Borthwicks, he produced his book and two months' premiums. As I rummaged in my pocket for his change I quizzed him,

"Oh, I hope that your fire claim was paid satisfactorily!"

Mr Borthwick smiled uneasily, fixed his eyes on something at the other side of the street, and almost in a whisper, pronounced solemnly,

"The carrier pigeon delivered my cheque safely thank you, and that is the only reason hi ham paying you today. I am a man of principles Mr Robinson. "

The door closed quietly and he was gone.

Later that afternoon I made a business call at the little greengrocery and general store in Hinchcliffe Mill, owned by the Hinchcliffes. The husband was always out travelling the countryside in his mobile shop, leaving his very capable and jovial wife to run the busy little shop. She would often give me a large juicy apple or pear, or the occasional ice-cream when I called. Then whilst I ate them, she chatted to me about the local news; she was often my first source of information of local deaths, fires, accidents, family feuds, and husbands who had walked out on their wives.

As she was checking that I had receipted her book correctly, she began to probe, gently and in a good natured way,

"Have I seen you coming out of Wilf and Nellie Borthwick's house? You know, in that little terrace overlooking the dam."

"Yes, I do call there Mrs Hinchcliffe, why do you ask?"

"Oh I don't know how well you know the family, did you know that Pat Jenkins a couple of doors away from me is their daughter"

"Really, I had no idea." But somehow the information did not surprise me, Pat was of the same strange shifty breed as the Borthwicks and her little house seemed to be run on similar lines, with piles of washing and sweaty grubby children in plentiful supply. Come to think of it, I always had the utmost difficulty collecting from Pat, and I had marvelled more than once at the great lengths she went to weave elaborate stories which all had the same unhappy ending. She had no money, but it was always due to an unbelievable sequence of events, and always involved me in another, weary visit two or three days later. How slow I was in not realizing who her tutor had been!

Mrs Hinchcliffe broke into my reverie as she popped her book under the bank notes in the till before slamming it shut.

"I am not one to pry, you know me better than that, it's just that the fire engine was at Pat Jenkins's last night at midnight, and she, well she owes me some money which she says she will pay me when she gets the insurance money for clothing which was burned last night in the fire. Would it be expecting too much to ask you to let me know when you are paying her so that I can call round and get my share of it?"

"Well Mrs Hinchcliffe, I am not supposed to discuss my clients' business with anyone, all I can say is that officially I have not been notified of a fire claim yet, I will of course take a claim form with me, and you will just have to be satisfied with the knowledge that I call at Pat's every Friday at about three o'clock. There is no reason why you should not watch for me calling at Pat's and then popping in yourself a few minutes later, but I cannot help you more than that. By the way, how much does Pat owe you?"

"Oh it's just about eight pounds but I have about given up hope of getting it."

My basic salary in those days was eleven pounds weekly and petrol was about five shillings a gallon, so Mrs Hinchcliffe's eight pounds was too much to just write off. I knew that Pat Jenkins owed money to various tradesmen. Her Prudential Book was always two months in arrears, and this was the only reason I called every week in a valiant effort to keep the arrears within the company rules. I did know that she owed money to the coal man, the newspaper boy, and her husband had not kept his payments on their car up to date as I had often spoken to a well-dressed gentleman in a trilby hat who seemed to be either just arriving at Pat's as I was leaving, or just leaving as I was arriving. He had told me more than once that if I got paid, he didn't, I suppose that when she could not pay me it was because she had just paid the man in the trilby.

I crossed over the road to get a fire claim form from my car as I knew that Pat had fire insurance with my company, and then climbed the three or four stone steps to Pat's front door. The house was built of stone and the door had a small glass pane which looked directly into the little front room, and through which I could see Pat approaching the door in answer to my knock.

Pat never looked pleased to see me, but today she positively radiated the warmth of genuine welcome. She radiated other things too, the same odour which the Borthwick's house effused, the same shifty almost servile manner, the same attempt as Wilf Borthwick to speak correctly. I could really see now just how strong the family resemblance was.

"Mr Robinson, you 'ave no idea 'ow pleased I ham to see you. Last night we suffered the misfortune to hexperience a fire. It was awful Mr Robinson, it his a good job the firemen harrived so quickly"

I had stepped into the grimy little room which smelled of various unsavoury concoctions, but the strongest smell today was the pungent smell of smoke still lingering from the previous night. Pat's husband had built a stone fireplace with a wooden mantel shelf, and the evidence of fire was plain to see. The wood was charred and the grey stones were soiled with the smoke.

Pat went on the explain that a wooden clothes airer had been standing in front of the fire containing a whole week's washing, which she was drying ready for the weekend. You name it, it was there, denim jeans, shirts dresses, nylon fur coats belonging to the children, pyjamas, nightdresses, socks, blouses, handkerchiefs, and various other unmentionable articles.

The dog had brushed against the flimsy structure and toppled it onto the hearth, the blazing coal fire had soon ignited the washing and it was a miracle the whole house did not burn down.

Her eyes lit up in anticipation as she breathlessly enquired whether she could make a claim on her insurance for the unfortunate loss, she even convinced me that the insurance company were indeed fortunate not to be paying out vast sums of money on her and her husband's deaths, as they had been only minutes away from being burned alive.

"Where are the damaged clothes Pat?" I asked as I pulled the claim form and a pen out of my jacket pocket.

"Oh the kind firemen took them away with them, they were making the 'ouse smell so awful, they offered to dispose of them has we 'ad nowhere 'ere to keep them."

"You do realize Pat that I am supposed to inspect the salvage, how do I know that you have lost so many items?"

Pat was mortally offended that I should doubt her honesty. Had she not been within inches of death, was it not common gossip in the street that the fire engine had been there at midnight. There was the evidence before my very eyes, the charred mantel shelf and the smoke blackened fire place. What about the smell of fire still lingering and spoiling her beautiful home. Was it fair that I should reward her by doubting her honesty just because those kind firemen took away the burnt clothing to prevent it making the house smell.

I had at first an uneasy feeling about all this. But was I being fair to her, had I allowed my suspicions towards this family colour my judgement in this time of need. Suddenly tears began to swell in Pat's eyes and I heard myself muttering,

"That's fine Pat, let's make a list of every item and all the prices, and I will put a note on the claim form explaining why I have not been able to inspect the damaged items. It will be OK I will have the money for you by next Friday."

The value of the damaged clothing came to thirty three pounds, and I crossed the road immediately to pop the form into the post so that I would have the authority to pay Pat by the following Friday. There was still a niggling little doubt at the back of my mind, something was telling me that all was not well, but I pushed the matter to the back of my mind and got on with my work.

During the next few days, my path seemed to cross Pat Jenkins' path almost daily. When I walked past the bus stop, she would greet me with a smile from the bus queue. She was just behind me in the village post office when I went in to buy stamps. Walking home down the hill past Pat's front door, I would see her on the step ladder giving her windows a well overdue clean. Whenever I saw her, she beamed at me, and then quickly turned away, as though at a loss to know what to do or say next.

Leeds office did not let me down, sure enough on the following Friday I had the paperwork necessary for me to pay Pat the thirty three pounds out of my collections. It was then that things began to go wrong!

A lady at the bus stop stopped me, asking me whether I was Pat Jenkins' insurance man.

"Why do you ask?"

"Let me just say that if you are her insurance man, you need to be careful, that's all."

Then a little later I was in the Off Licence collecting Mr O'Reilly's car insurance premium. He was a man who normally had very few words, but as I handed him his receipt, he confided in a whisper,

"Mr Robinson, if you are Pat Jenkins' insurance man, be careful, I don't want to see you lose your job."

"What's going on Mr O'Reilly?" I bought a packet of crisps and a Mars Bar, hoping to play for time and extract more information from him. That was as much as he was going to say, and he dismissed me by turning to serve a customer who had just walked into his shop.

Several more times that morning, clients and folk who I did not really know, gave me similar cryptic warnings. There was no real reason given, as to why I should be careful. They obviously knew more than I did about Mrs Pat Jenkins, but all they were prepared to offer me were veiled warnings.

I thought about the strange events of the morning whilst enjoying my lunch break. "What was really going on?" I decided that I would ask Mrs Watson when I called on her that afternoon, she knew everything that went on in the village, and I sometimes had difficulty getting away from her once she got into top gear with her local gossip.

Mrs Watson never ceased to amaze me at the talent she displayed. She could walk across the room without her feet actually leaving the carpet, she always shuffled toward me in baggy carpet slippers. Week by week I watched the feet approaching, trying to exercise my will over the force of gravity which held those feet down as though glued to the carpet.

She had marvellous control over her cigarette too. False teeth were not essential to her whilst she was in the house. So her cigarette was always gripped between toothless gums which ground together in a peculiar motion which raised and lowered the cigarette as she crossed the room. I watched week by week with bated breath, hoping, I must confess, that I would be present when she set the end of her nose on fire

Her coordination would have been the envy of many skilled exponents of the art of the "one man band." She could shuffle across the room, grinding her jaws, moving the cigarette up and down with great precision, whilst emitting a cavernous belch and breaking wind most noisily together with split second timing, and all at the same time as trotting out a string of local gossip.

I waited until she paused for breath, and trying to catch her by surprise asked,

"Mrs Watson, do you know Pat Jenkins?"

"I do lad."

"Have you heard any gossip, er anything about her this week'?"

"I 'ave lad."

"What have you heard?"

"I 'ave eard that she is pullin' a fast 'on the insurance agent and getting thirty odd pounds out of him by false means."

"Mrs Watson, I am Pat's insurance man, can you tell me more please?"

"Naw, that's all I eard, but I could try and find out a bit more by next Friday for thee."

"Thanks Mrs Watson, leave it with me, you are a gem, you have been a great help."

I walked along Hinchcliffe Mill main street not quite knowing what to do. I was due at Pat's that afternoon to pay her, should I be paying her anything at all when there was obviously fraud being perpetrated?

I decided to call at Will and Nellie Borthwicks, Pat's parents. They were in arrears anyway, and I might be able to find something out from them. I had always shown a talent for weeding out information, and I was determined that this case would be no exception.

Nellie performed a small miracle by actually paying me some money, and just as I was about to leave, I dropped on her, as though an unimportant afterthought,

"I am sorry to hear about Pat's adventure with the fire brigade the other night. I am ever so glad there was no damage done.

Nellie, completely unaware of my baited trap played right into my hands, "Oh Mr Robinson, Hi will never know why er usband Tony piled up all that old wallpaper on the fire like that. They was strippin orf the back bedroom wall paper, and he came downstairs and piled it all up on the fire. Then without thinking Mr Robinson, he went back upstairs to do some more wall paper stripping."

"You don't say."

"Hi do say Mr Robinson, silly hidiot should 'ave known e would set the chimney on fire. Had to send for the fire brigade to die the fire out in the chimney."

"They were lucky not to sustain any damage."

"Aye that's right, they will learn, cheerio now."

I scampered back up the hill towards Pat's, almost rubbing my hands together with glee. So that was it, what did she take me for? I just won't pay her. There was a convenient phone box just outside O'Reilly's shop, and I rang Redfearn Rogers my branch manager to acquaint him with the case, asking for his permission not to pay the claim.

I could hear him tapping the mouth piece of his telephone as he decided what to do,

"David, pay the claim, it's gone too far now to back out, but we now know to be very careful of her in the future."

I was seething as I climbed the steps to Pat Jenkins door and rattled on the glass pane in the door. Usually Pat took a long time to answer, but today she could not get to the door quick enough.

Her black deceitful eyes smiled mockingly as she asked,

"Ave you got my thirty three pounds?"

"Yes." I replied, without warmth or enthusiasm, "I have it with me, but first I need some money from you to keep your book up to date."

I closed the front door and Pat went upstairs to find her premium book. It was then that I heard a tap on the door, and I saw the trilby through the glass.

"Pat "I called upstairs to her, "there is someone knocking at the door, shall I let him in?"

"No there is nobody there, it was just me banging about upstairs."

"Sorry Pat, I can see his trilby though the glass, I had better let him in before he goes away."

"Trilby! Ho no, let 'im go away."

"Too late Pat, I am opening the door."

Our trilby clad visitor stood beside me and opened his account book,

"It's like getting blood out of a stone here, she never has any money, I hope you have more luck than me."

"Really, how much do you need?"

"Twenty five pounds or we repossess the car."

"Hang about mate and watch me, when I have gone you will get your money.

Pat entered the room, I had her money ready, and the receipt for her to sign.

"If you would just like to sign here Pat, I will give you your thirty three pounds. '

She signed the receipt, willing me to shut up, willing me to take her into the other room so that this intruder in the trilby would not hear and see her private business. Willing me to stop counting out the bank notes into her hand one by one. Twenty nine, thirty, thirty one, thirty two, thirty three, there you are Pat, " I raised my voice, "thirty three pounds exactly, see you next Friday, bye."

If Pat could have struck me dead with her icy cold stare, she would have done, but I was on my way out, fast,

As I turned the door handle to leave, I heard Trilby say, very forcefully,

"I will have twenty five pounds out of that thirty three pounds Mrs Jenkins, NOW if you don't mind,"

I glanced back, Pat knew she was defeated, and was silently handing the money over to him.

I escaped up the hill, laughing gently, wondering if Mrs Hinchcliffe was on her way to claim the other eight pounds.

# Denby Dale

It was a bright but cold Sunday morning in late spring when Edith, Joy and I piled into the little Morris Minor. We drove out of the grime of Holmfirth centre taking the open road out towards Wakefield. We had heard that just outside the tiny village of Denby Dale was a small evangelical church and we had decided to drop in on the Sunday morning service.

We were used to the freedom and life of the large Pentecostal Church in Wakefield and had not been able to find such a church community in Holmfirth. We were finding that the round trip of forty miles from Holmfirth to Wakefield and back was getting tedious. We also felt that it was important to belong to a local church, and a church 20 miles away could by no stretch of the imagination be considered as "local". Then Albert Mellors, our minister at Wakefield who had married Edith and I a few years before, suggested that we try the little "mission" church at Denby Dale which was only about 8 miles from Holmfirth.

Albert knew Ernest Turfrey the minister at Denby Dale. Apparently Ernest was a "bit of a builder" by profession and was the lay pastor of the little church. Albert had mentioned Edith and I to Ernest and intimated that we would be paying them a visit one Sunday morning.

The scenery became flatter and less interesting as we drove away from Holmfirth. We left the lush green fields as we entered the built up area which was Denby Dale. One or two grimy stone mills, a couple of corner shops, the bridge over the canal, an Anglican Church, a coal mine and terraces of stone built houses welcomed us.

We knew very little about Denby Dale. Doug Marlow worked there in the coal mine. Denby Dale's unusual claim to fame is that it is the home of the huge Denby Dale Pie. The village claimed a world record on the 4th August 1928 when it created and baked the world's largest pie. This gigantic culinary delight was sixteen feet long, five feet wide and fifteen inches deep, it was baked by the villagers and floated down the canal in a huge metal dish in an ambitious attempt to raise funds for the local hospital. Over a thousand folk invaded the village that day and the pie became the centre of much festivities and revelry. There was a slice of pie each, liquid refreshment and music and dancing until the early hours of the morning. We knew that on special occasions the Denby Dale pie was baked again and floated down the canal to await its grand reception in the centre of the village. To be honest though that was the sum total of our knowledge of the village.

We knew that Pastor Turfrey was a builder by profession although we were not sure exactly what Albert's descriptive expression "bit of a builder" meant. Maybe Ernest only had one arm, or one leg or in some strange way was incomplete as a person. Maybe he only spent a bit of his time building, or maybe he only built bits of buildings. No doubt we would soon find out!

Ernest had commenced church services in the village and had gathered a little flock together. Aided by his wife Ivy, he cared for his congregation visiting them in their sickness, supporting them through their problems, preaching to them and teaching them from the Bible Sunday after Sunday. Being a builder, he was always able to undertake the occasional repairs and maintenance of the church building and the homes of his congregation where he was always a welcome visitor. They were fiercely loyal to Ernest and his wife.

We found the little chapel without difficulty. The first person we enquired of told us that the church was next door to the public house. When we arrived it was obvious from the sound of the singing that the service had already begun. If it had not been for the slightly lopsided notice board with the proud  words "DENBY DALE PENTECOSTAL CHURCH " MINISTER ERNEST TURFREY. We could have been forgiven for thinking that the church was actually a pre-fabricated bungalow.

We parked on the rough land between the chapel and the pub, and unsure what to expect pushed the door hesitantly. The door led into a small vestibule carpeted with a remnant of domestic carpet and sported  a colourful floral pattern. In the corner was a table with a neat pile of red hymn books and one or two Bibles which  had seen better days. Among the old magazines and Christian leaflets stood a cardboard shoe box full of old spectacles resplendently tangled together in glorious disarray. I rummaged through the pile of old glasses trying to find a pair which suited me. This seemed so typical  of what we had heard about Ernest. He cared for his flock so much that he provided a supply of spectacles for the convenience of those who had lost or forgotten their own. I looked in vain for a similar box of assorted false teeth but if there was one it had been carefully hidden away.  It would take a brave man indeed to enter church wearing a deceased person's dentures!

A notice board on the wall was crammed full of announcements of local church events.  Photographs of missionaries smiled down from their newsletters brim full of news of their activities in Central Africa, India or China.  England and its problems were not forgotten.  There were letters and reports from Christian societies involved in helping drug addicts, unmarried mothers, homeless people and those with drink problems.  It seemed that here was a little church whose windows opened out onto the whole world, so wide were their interests.

My eyes scanned the other walls of this little reception area and from some of the pictures on the wall I deduced that the average age of the congregation was quite old.  Old embroidered texts proclaimed that "GOD IS LOVE" and old pictures of the Last Supper and of Christ with a shining halo around his head hung proudly in their allotted positions.

The sound of the hymn singing was louder now that we were inside the building.  There was a rich blend of voices and what was lacking in technical expertise and sweetness was more than compensated by the sheer enthusiasm and exuberance of their singing.  The piano hammered out the accompaniment as we entered the little meeting room to be greeted by the loud chorus,

"And crow ow ow ow own Him Lord of all,
and crow ow ow ow own Him Lord of all
and crow ow ow ow own Him Lord of all
and crown Him Lord of all"

On the platform at the front stood a short, rounded little man looking uncomfortable in dark suit and  white shirt which strained dangerously at every button. His brick red face, framed with twisted black rimmed spectacles was aglow as he directed the singing.  Ernest beamed solid goodness and goodwill as in a shaky reedy tenor voice he began to sing again, encouraging the congregation to follow,

"By and by we'll see the King,

by and by we'll see the King,
by and by we'll see the King
and crown Him Lord of all"

Edith and I stood at the back of the hall deciding where to sit, the congregation, mainly elderly, looked round at us and smiled. They all seemed delighted that visitors were present.  The singing came to an uncertain raggy end but before the good folk could sit down, Pastor Turfrey, clean shaved Sunday morning face aglow  began to sing again. This time he was setting a slower more reverent style, as with arms raised and head pointing heavenward, he burst forth,

"Bring forth the royal diadem,
and crown Him Lord of all,
and crown Him Lord of all
and crown Him Lord of all."

The congregation put down their hymn-books and eagerly took up the refrain. There were more discordant notes than harmonious ones and there was an occasional faux pas from the aged white haired lady sitting at the piano, but as we walked to our seats I had the distinct feeling that God was enjoying this and was beaming encouragement upon these good sincere people.  I just sensed that He wanted to hear them sing it all over again.  Why?  Because here was a small company of people who were full of genuine love for God and who with thankful hearts were expressing their praise and worship.  Here was a group of people who had a meaningful relationship with God and were enjoying His grace and favour.

No sooner had we taken our seats among them, the singing stopped and a loud coughing began.  The bouts of wheezing and spluttering started amongst the people sitting closest to the cast iron coke stove.  I glanced across to see what the trouble was but the area surrounding the ancient coke stove was surrounded by clouds of thick blue-black smoke.  In a few seconds the smoke had billowed across the room and was rolling its evil way onto the platform where the still beaming Ernest was about to commence his sermon. It was obvious that only divine intervention would prevent Ernest being swallowed  up by the swirling cloud.

Ernest, grinning from ear to ear, pulled out a large white handkerchief from his pocket and waved it at the approaching cloud of noxious gas which was threatening to swallow him up. He thrust his handkerchief at the smoke like a matador fending off an angry bull, as with running eyes, he prepared to make an announcement. With raised hands as though preparing to give a papal blessing and with a very serious expression he intoned,

"Never heed friends, never heed. There's a bit of a puther on this morning, the old stove's playing up again but that must not put us off from listening to the Word of God. You will find my text in..."

So Ernest carried on with his preaching as though nothing was happening but how he kept to his point I shall never know. There is nothing more off-putting to a preacher than seeing half of his congregation tittering behind their handkerchiefs and nudging each other. Ernest certainly displayed great sense of purpose, nothing was going to prevent him delivering his Sunday morning sermon.

By the time Ernest concluded his sermon the old stove was behaving itself and none of the congregation seemed at all surprised by the antics of the primitive heating system. He came down from the lectern on the curtained platform and headed straight for Edith and I. Ernest looked even jollier at close range, though how he could see through his spectacles was a minor miracle. The lenses were coated with specks of white paint, liberal applications of dust and grease and smudged with finger prints. He extended a hand towards us in welcome.

His handshake was a thing to experience, he pumped my arm up and down with vigour as though he was trying to draw water from a well! My feet almost left the ground with each upward sweep of his arm. There was no doubt, we were welcome.

"You must be brother and sister Robinson. Albert told us to expect you. He speaks very highly of you both. We all hope that you will join our little flock here at Denby Dale. We certainly need folk like you to help us here in our work"

He quizzed us concerning where we were living, what kind of house we had bought, and how my job was working out. After his genuine expression of interest I guess that there was not much he did not know about us.

"You will come again tonight to our Gospel service" he encouraged as he beckoned several members of the congregation over to meet us. After a few minutes of greetings from our new friends, Ernest resumed his pulpit voice and as he tried to clean his spectacles he addressed us all,

"I have been thinking for a while that it is time we ripped out the old coke stove, well we all saw how it behaved again this morning. The main problem though is next Thursday night when we have Tom Woods with us and the hall will be packed out with people. We will get a few more in if we rip out the coke stove and clear a bit more floor space. What do you all think?"

"Oh I don't think that would be a good idea Ernest, at least not just yet. It is only April and I can remember snow in June."

"Snow in June Sykes!" beamed Ernest, "when did we have jolly snow in jolly June?"

Sykes knew exactly when there had been jolly snow in jolly June and he was ready with his response. Serious as a judge he continued,

"Nineteen twenty three Ernest. Nineteen twenty three. It snowed in the last week in June"

Ernest could not believe his ears,

"Nineteen jolly twenty three! But its jolly 1966. Nineteen jolly twenty three is forty three jolly years ago! I shall take out the stove this week, we will need the extra space."

They were a very warm and friendly group and before we left them, we promised that at least I would be back that evening and we set off for home where the chicken was cooking in the oven.

After lunch I took Nora Newton's piano accordion out of its case. After a few minutes brisk polishing, the mother of pearl finish looked as good as new. I decided to try out a few simple hymn tunes. I strapped the heavy instrument across my chest after I had extended the straps to their maximum length opened and closed the bellows just to get the feel of it.

When I tried to press the keys in some sort of musical sequence I made an interesting discovery. I quickly learned that because my chin was hard pressed against the top of the instrument, I could not move my head downwards to actually look at the keys before I pressed them. This no doubt had some bearing on the strange discordant groans and sighs which the instrument produced when I heaved the bellows open and closed and pressed the keys I could not actually see.

I soon solved this problem by standing in front of the mirror. Now at least I could see which keys I was pressing. Another vital discovery was awaiting me, whilst I was so busy watching which keys to press with my right hand, I could not fathom the 120 buttons beneath my left hand. They all looked the same and none of them had any names or labels on them. I found that one button did have a small indentation in the centre but I did not have a clue why.

I was disappointed to discover that I had great difficulty finding a button with my left hand which produced a sound which did not clash violently with the note produced when I pressed a key with my right hand.

I decided to compromise. I would completely ignore the buttons on the left and just concentrate on the piano keys at my right hand. In this way I found that I could use one finger of my right hand and just by pressing one key at a time could produce something resembling a recognisable tune. Why did I need one hundred and twenty confusing buttons when I could manage a tune using only my right hand?

I had cracked it, success was just round the corner. An hour later my first flush of success was beginning to disappear. The one or two tunes I could manage had one common characteristic, they were boring. They had no depth, they lacked lustre and whatever I did I could not emulate the lovely music produced by Jimmy Shand.

Then to make matters worse, Sandy our terrier cross who had chosen not to remain in the same room and had slunk away into the kitchen, now began to protest. She sat and stared at me with mournful eyes and howled and howled, she was willing me to stop.

Then I had a brilliant idea. How did I actually know that the accordion was any good. It could be out of tune, it could be damaged, if so then it would be impossible even for Jimmy Shand to play it well. I would take the instrument to church that evening and ask Mrs Wood the pianist to check it over. She would certainly be able to advise me whether it was in tune or not. Yes, that is what I would do.

After an early tea I set off for the evening service at Denby Dale. Edith and I were affectionately referring to the Denby Dale church as "Turfrey's Tabernacle." I don't know what Ernest would have thought about this. I guess that he never found out.

On the way I was planning my strategy. I would take the accordion into the service with me. It would be safer there than in the car. Then at the end of the service I would speak with Mrs Wood the elderly pianist and ask her to check the accordion over for me.

The service had just commenced when I arrived, so I tiptoed into the little hall as quietly as I could and placed the instrument at the back of the room. Stealthily I made my way to my seat and then stood to join in the singing. Ernest was leading the singing but the piano was strangely silent. It did not take me long to see why, the piano stool was empty, Mrs Wood was not there. Suddenly Ernest beamed down at me as he brought the singing to a halt mid-way through a verse. I could not believe what I was hearing,

"Praise the Lord" proclaimed Ernest, "He has provided for us in our time of need. The good Lord knew that Mrs Wood our pianist was going to be ill tonight, but isn't God good! He has supplied a musician. Our brother David has brought his accordion, he will stand in for Mrs Wood"

I pretended I had not heard but there was a murmur of approval and an air of expectancy from the congregation. Ernest was still beaming an invitation to me to take my accordion up onto the platform.

"I am sorry Ernest, I can't really play, er you see…"

"Our brother David is being modest" smiled Ernest, "don't be modest brother, there is no need to be shy. We won't take no for an answer. Come up here and play the hymns"

I shall never know what possessed me. I should have refused and let that be the end. But I didn't refuse and within a few seconds I was on the platform and Ernest was helping me put the heavy instrument across my chest. There was no mirror in front of me, but Ernest plonked a hymn book in front of me on the lectern.

That was bad enough, but then Ernest really excelled himself. Excitedly he invited the congregation to choose their favourite hymns and they did with great enthusiasm.

The next few minutes were amongst the most embarrassing moments of my entire life. I was sinking fast. One finger exercises at home in front of the mirror are one thing but this was something for which neither I nor the congregation were prepared. They all thought that I was Yorkshire's answer to Jimmy Shand, they would soon find out that I was a joke.

I picked out a one finger tune but the congregation were not singing along, they were staring at me with open mouths. Sykes Wood broke in as he shouted to me,

"Brother, you are playing in a key which is far too high, can you lower it a bit?"

Now I did know that there were eight notes in an octave, so it was obvious that if I just counted eight notes down the keyboard and started again, everything would be fine. It was not fine. Everyone had to sing down in their boots and I soon ran out of sufficient keys.

"Brother, you are far too low, can you lift it up a bit?"

"Easy I just moved four notes higher up the keyboard and started again before making an important discovery. There was no way I could play this tune without straying onto the black notes and there was no way I was going to risk exploring that unknown territory.

The congregation took it all in their stride. They were a bright lot. It did not take them long to discover that I could not play. They actually seemed to like me for having a go. But I was still embarrassed, even at the end of the service. Ah well, we all attempt something we make a mess of, even Ernest Turfrey!

Nora Newton looked after Joy on the Thursday night so that Edith and I could travel to the special service with Tom Woods. "Turfrey's Tabernacle" was packed out with a capacity crowd. During Tom's inspiring sermon I realised that my chair was on uneven ground. Two legs seemed to be a couple of inches higher that the other two.

Looking down to see what was causing this I realised that Ernest had in fact removed the old stove but he had left the concrete base in place. Two of my chair legs were on the base, two were on the wooden floorboards.

As the sermon continued my mind began to stray. I remembered that on Sunday morning I had noticed that the smoke was meant to escape up the wide cast iron chimney leading from the top of the stove to the roof of the meeting room.

I glanced up to see what Ernest had done with the chimney. I was horrified to see that he had smashed the chimney off several inches below the plaster board ceiling and tied a plastic bag tightly round the open end to catch any rain water. The plastic bag was directly above my head was threatening to discharge its evil collection of water onto my head.

I remembered how Albert, our pastor at Wakefield had described Ernest. He is a "bit of a builder"` Albert had said. Now I knew what he meant. Ernest glanced down at me from the platform, and seeing the mirth on my face thought that I was really enjoying Tom Woods preaching. My eyes directed Ernest to look up at the ceiling, languishing there was the real source of my amusement. Ernest's brick red face became noticeably redder as though he had been sprayed with liquid embarrassment.

Last Sunday evening it had been my turn to be embarrassed. Now it was Ernest's turn. We felt that we had found our new church family. We were amongst friends. We understood each other. We were going to be happy here. We had come home!

# Death

My job kept me very busy during the week but I tried to keep Saturdays and Sundays as free from interruption as possible. There was always some emergency to attend to and I did not mind handling the real emergency regardless of the day or hour. People could be distressed and part of the job was to reassure them and sometimes to pour oil on troubled waters.

There were genuine emergencies, and there were matters certain clients considered to be an emergency. I did not hesitate to respond to the former, but hated the latter.

It was Christmas Day when there was a violent ringing of the door bell. We were in the middle of Christmas dinner and had family with us.   I answered the door in a bright paper party hat and with knife and fork in my hand.   I imagined that even the most insensitive of clients would realise the error of their ways when they saw my visual aid of Christmas.

I opened the door to a grinning Dennis Garlick. Dennis worked for the local water board and was responsible for maintenance on the reservoir two or three miles up the valley and for helping run the water treatment and pumping station half a mile away.

"How can I help you Dennis?"

"I have just been round the reservoir checking the water level and the banks and am on my way home for Christmas Dinner. Just thought I would call and ask you for a few sample motor car quotes. Think I am changing my car in the New Year."

Needless to say, Dennis did not get his motor quotes until a more suitable time.

In my early days with the Prudential Assurance Company I found that dealing with a death claim could be extremely difficult. I quickly realised that it was kinder and easier to see the bereaved as soon as possible after the death. It became my practice to see the claimant before the funeral and there were huge benefits in this.

I usually found it easier on the bereaved, as between the death and the funeral it was important that they kept themselves occupied. I was also able to give some indication of how much money would be paid out on the policies. There was usually far more than the claimant expected and this information often brought them peace of mind when they realised that there would be enough money to cover funeral costs. It was important that I allow plenty of time when visiting the bereaved to complete the death claim. Almost without exception, the bereaved wished to talk at length about their loved one and their character, strengths and how much they loved them. I often listened to a grieving relative extolling the virtues of their departed loved one and wondered whether they had taken the trouble to let their loved one know just what they felt about them!

There was a bicycle shop just along the road from our home in Holmfirth. The owner was a very jolly portly gentleman known by all the local children as Uncle Joe, I can still visualise him working on a cycle which was suspended in front of him on a frame. If Joe dropped anything onto the shop floor he had great difficulty picking it up as his huge girth prevented him bending down. I was in his shop one day sorting out one of his insurances when the local doctor paused as he was passing the door. He called out with a smile,

"Still digging your grave with your teeth Joe?"

Joe seemed impervious to this remark but I sensed that comments like this hurt him, and I wondered how many times he had tried to lose weight only to immediately put it back again. Joe lived in his little flat above the shop with Susan his unmarried daughter, a quiet, pleasant sensitive young lady who was devoted to her dad and did her best to look after him and their home. Joe did have a married son Josh who lived about a mile away, and I collected premiums regularly from him and his wife.

I answered the doorbell just before six o'clock one evening to find a very distressed looking Susan and Josh on our doorstep. Josh managed to tell me that their father Joe had just died following a heart attack, and he was lying in the little workshop of his cycle shop.

"I just need to call at the undertakers to ask him to take dad away and sort everything out. It would be better if Susan does not go with me, please can I leave her here with you for about half an hour?"

Feeling so sorry for Susan who was obviously in shock, we welcomed her in and Josh set off on his sad mission. Susan was not a very communicative young lady at the best of times, tonight she was too upset to enter into conversation. We tried to break the ice and make her feel at home but it was hard work. The hours ticked by, seven o'clock, eight o'clock, nine o'clock, ten o'clock, eleven o'clock and still no Josh and still not much rapport between Susan and I. It was midnight when Josh appeared, worse for drink and it was a relief to us when he took Susan away, hopefully to spend the night with him and his family. I did not judge Josh harshly for leaving Susan with us for those difficult six hours, he was dealing with his grief in his own way, we were happy to have a played a small part in helping him and Susan cope at a distressing time. Joe was insured by The Prudential and I was soon able to get the death claim sorted out. I was not surprised to see that the death certificate stated that the cause of Joe's death was "extreme obesity".

Poor Joe had dug his early grave with his teeth, and I wondered how his doctor felt when he signed the death certificate. He was also our doctor and he was too nice a man to think,

"Don't say I didn't warn you Joe?"

A death could bring out the worst or the best from the bereaved, people cope with grief in different ways. A hospital chaplain told me that he was expressing his condolences to a lady whose husband had just died.

"How long were you married?" asked the chaplain.

"Sixty years sir."

"That is wonderful; you have sixty years of blessed memories to look back on my dear"

"Rubbish, I have sixty years of hell to remember. I'm glad he has gone!"

A vicar shared with me an unusual experience he went through whilst conducting a service at the crematorium. Right at the end of the service as the coffin was disappearing behind the curtain, and as the vicar was reciting the words,

"We commit his body to the flames" the widow screamed at her husband in his coffin,

"Burn you bastard, burn!"

There are also humorous incidents connected with a death. One of my colleagues was asked by Mr and Mrs Smith to arrange holiday insurance for their holiday in Spain. Two or three weeks later he knew that they would have returned and so called at their home to collect the monthly premiums. Mrs Smith, tears in her eyes, greeted him,

"Come in. I have bad news for you. Mr Smith died suddenly yesterday. He is laid out in the front room. You must come and pay your respects."

Reluctantly my young colleague allowed himself to be led into the front room and stood waiting as Mrs Smith lifted the white cover from her husband's face.

At such a time words do not come to mind easily, especially if this is the first time you have seen a dead person. My young friend's first impression was that the deceased was very sun burnt.

"Doesn't he look well" he blurted out to the widow who replied "Yes, the holiday in Spain did him a world of good!"

I heard of a young Prudential agent, only 22 years of age who had a very unusual experience. One of his policyholders greeted him with very red tear filled eyes. Not entirely sure what to say to her, her young insurance agent simply said,

"What's up?"

He was totally unprepared for her reply,

"My husband's dead."

"Oh heck, when did he die?"

"About two hours ago. I couldn't wake him, he must have died in his sleep." She was beginning to ramble, "I have phoned the doctor and he says there is nothing he can do, but he will come immediately after surgery and certify his death."

"Oh I am so sorry, at least he did not suffer."

"Yes that is one way to look at it. You must come upstairs and have a look at him, he looks so peaceful."

Our young friend tried to use the age-old excuse that he would rather remember the deceased as he was, but he lost his ground and found himself being led up the steep stairs and into the front bedroom. The deceased was laying on the bed with a white handkerchief over his face. The newly widowed lady removed the white covering from her late husband's face replacing it gently when the young man had once again expressed his deepest sympathy.

"I can't submit a death claim without the death certificate but I could have a look at your policies and give you an idea of just how much will be payable to you..."

The grieving widow nodded in approval before finding all their policies in a box in the wardrobe. I still smile as I imagine the scene. The bedroom curtains are closed as a sign of respect to the deceased, however they are not heavy blackout curtains so the morning sunlight filters through illuminating the three figures in the room. The young Prudential agent, anxious and insecure in his first experience of death at close quarters, the weeping wife, with red moist eyes handing the life assurance policies over for scrutiny and the motionless departed husband, lying on the bed, the sunlight dancing across the white sheet concealing his face.

Suddenly there is a loud yawn, the corpse raises a hand and as he pulls the handkerchief from his face sits bolt upright in bed. Seeing his wife and the insurance man standing beside the bed with insurance policies in their hands he shouts,

"What the heck is going on?"

His startled wife responds  "I thought you were dead."

"Thought I was dead, thought I was dead!  It has not taken you long to get the insurance man to come!  What time is it?"

His wife glances at the bedside clock before informing him,

"It's just after ten o'clock."

"Blimey, I'm late for work" cried the corpse as he leaped out of bed, "you should not have let me sleep in."

The "widow" had to phone the doctors to explain that her "dead" husband had simply been asleep, and that he had been resurrected and just set off late for work.

I collected regularly from a sweet old lady, Mrs Smart, who lived alone and was quite frail. Her neighbours did all they could to help look after her. This involved cutting her grass and keeping her garden tidy, checking on her each day to make sure she was OK. Although she did her own cooking and housework the neighbours did bring her the occasional welcome hot meal. I asked one of her neighbours whether she had any family, "Oh yes, she has a daughter who lives two miles away but she never puts in an appearance here, it is at least three years since she came to see her mum."

I remember replying, "That is so sad, but when Mrs Smart dies her daughter will soon be here to see what's in it for her."

Not many months later I was in the bath one Sunday afternoon when Edith called up to me that a lady had come to see me regarding a death claim. I appeared a few minutes later, hair still wet, to find the lady sitting waiting in our lounge.

"How can I help you?" I quizzed rather sympathetically as I was under the impression that she had just been bereaved.

"I am Mrs Smart's daughter, I wonder if you are able to work out for me how much money is due of her policies?"

"Oh I am so sorry to hear that Mrs Smart has passed away, she was a lovely lady and I will miss her" I replied gently.

"Oh she is not dead, but she is old and I am her only relative so I am entitled to know how much I will get when she has gone."

Feeling very annoyed I replied, "I am so glad to hear that Mrs Smart is still alive and well. I am not prepared to discuss her business with you until she has actually died, and I sincerely hope that she lives for many more years. Now if you will excuse me my tea is ready."

As I was ushering her out of the door she retorted rather nastily, "Oh she won't live for ever, so I will be back."

Sadly she did come back only a few weeks later. A neighbour had found Mrs Smart dead in her arm chair. Mrs Smart's daughter was only interested in one thing that was how much money would be left over after payment of the funeral costs. I was thankful that I did not have to deal with many clients like her.

Nothing winds up an insurance agent more than being referred to as "the insurance collector". In truth collecting the premiums was only a small but important part of the job. Collections took up about three working days each week, but involved unsocial hours. Time off in the afternoon was often small compensation for working until late evening. In the Holme Valley many families were out at work all day. Some did find very imaginative places to leave their premium books and money in order to save me having to call in the evening.

Many of the homes had an outside toilet which was a favourite place to hide the money. This was a double blessing for an insurance agent with a weak bladder! Especially when many clients plied me with hot coffee. Some clients even hid the door key in a plant pot so that I could enter their home to pick up their money from the telephone table in the entrance hall. I was continually amazed at the trust placed in me. This trust was hard earned and guarded closely when won. Part of the process involved becoming regarded as a family friend and counsellor.

Collecting several thousand pounds each month took an enormous amount of skill, planning and commitment. People expected their collection to be made on the same day and at the same time, yet people wanted to talk, to confide, to ask advice on a hundred and one issues. They expected that their insurance agent would at all times be a model of professional integrity. Confidences must be kept, and people confided the most intimate family matters. Having the time to spend with people meant a lot to them and was an important part of my job. However my workload was heavy and a healthy balance between socialising and getting on with the job had to be maintained.

In addition to the socialising I never knew what extra duties I would be called upon to perform when I arrived at a person's home. There were motor car claims to attend to, and completing all the details onto a claim form could take a long time, especially when the victim of the accident wanted to describe the incident blow by blow in minute details. Then people changed their motor car or motor cycle and needed a cover note and perhaps a quotation of the premium. Then there were the dreaded burst pipes, and there seemed to be many of those. Holmfirth was a cold, God forsaken place in mid winter. We never got through a winter without struggling through deep snow and huge drifts. It was not unusual for my car to be snowed in for days on end. In the winter I always carried a sack of potatoes in my car boot to help give me a better grip on the ice and snow.

I have lost count of the number of times I have been greeted with the spine chilling words,

"Me pipes have froz and bust!"

Such a message made my spirit sink into the pits. I knew that more often than not the pipe which had frozen and burst was in the loft. Sometimes the ceiling had collapsed and always there was damage to carpets and furniture. At such times huge amounts of tact and diplomacy were needed, especially when the client was distressed or was expecting us to replace a thread-bare worn out carpet with a brand new one!

So collecting was always well punctuated by interruptions, some were emergencies and had to be dealt with immediately. Of course a friendly attitude was essential as it was essential to be well liked and popular. A lot of new business came to me because people recommended me to their friends. Clients have sent me to see a friend of theirs who needed motor car insurance which I arranged. When delivering the new policy two or three weeks later sometimes the new client has exclaimed,

"Oh I did not realise you work for the Prudential Assurance Company!"

This happened quite often and proved that it was the man and not his company that people preferred to deal with.

I was always glad when my weekly collection routine was over. Some weeks the collecting pattern commenced on the Thursday and ended late Monday evening. Other weeks, the collection routine began on the Friday and would end late on Tuesday evening. That final evening of collecting was always hectic. In addition to the regular collections due on that evening, there was the additional workload of catching up on all the people who had been out at the time of my regular visit. Control of arrears was a vital part of the collecting duties, and I was always glad that another week was over and I could relax a little.

So it was home for a late tea before I cleared the kitchen table and began balancing my books and completing my accounts for the week. It was often 9-00pm when I was able to commence the book-keeping and I would not go to bed until I knew that everything balanced.

If the books did not balance I would sit up sometimes until two or three o'clock in the morning searching for the reason. I knew that if I went to bed leaving unbalanced books I would find it extremely difficult to get to sleep. This was especially true if my money was short.

I am convinced that the sub-conscious mind ponders things during sleep. On more than one occasion I have laid awake until the early hours pondering why I was twenty, thirty or forty pounds short. I just did not have a clue and could not work it out. Strange that the first thought on waking next morning has pin pointed exactly where my error is and within a few minutes the problem has been solved.

Once the books were balanced and all the monies accounted for and banked, I then had to change identity and switch into salesman mode until the regular collecting stint began again. The regular collecting duties gave me the opportunity to gently speak with the clients and create an interest in some new product or in increasing the business they already had. Sometimes it took months before their appetite was whetted enough to actually allow me to suggest that I call one evening and give them full details. It was always good to close a sale at that first session, but more often than not people needed to talk it over and I always respected that and gave them time to consider. High pressure salesmen soon burn out, the public get to know them and resist them with their foot in the door methods. It was always my intention to leave a client in such a way that if they saw me walking up their path a few weeks later, they were pleased to see me and welcomed me back into their homes. Business sold in that way, based on goodwill and respect, was always good sound business. When people signed up to something under pressure, they nearly always changed their mind and cancelled when they had really thought it over.

The real core of the work of the Prudential Agent was selling. The best collector in the world would be a failure unless he could sell additional business to existing clients and attract new clients to the Company.

Selling the Prudential products had to be done responsibly. We had to find exactly what the client needed and match that need. So the product had to be the right one and the cost had to be within the client's budget. A vast amount of technical knowledge was needed but we could always call upon the services of a specialist if we felt the need. I always took advantage of this specialist knowledge if asked to insure a factory or to set up a company pension scheme for the employees of a small business. It was so important that we got it right first time.

I had to get it right because if there was a claim under the policy, I had to deal with it. There is nothing more soul-destroying that telling a client that his new policy does not cover him properly and therefore he cannot claim. It is embarrassing for me and it is expensive for the client to discover that his policy does not include damage to his factory roof which has been completely wrecked in the gales.

So, collecting from hundreds of people each month had to be performed to a regular schedule. Some people were literally waiting to go out but delayed until after I had called. Some policyholders answered the door with the greeting, "Hello, I can nearly set the clock by you." This was good as it showed that I had established a regular pattern. Yet there were emergencies, unexpected circumstances which I could not just walk away from because Mrs Brown was expecting me in two minutes time. Thankfully if an emergency had delayed me, no long explanation was needed. It was sufficient to simply say,

"So sorry I am a bit late but something cropped up which needed my immediate attention, but I won't have a coffee with you today if you don't mind."

One of those situations which I could not walk away from arose when I was working alone as Section Superintendent. The Prudential agent I should have been working with was having to do his collections as the deputy collector was ill. That was fine, he had given me his list of appointments and I would visit them on my own. I did have an appointment of my own which I needed to fit in that evening, so when I saw that I would have an opportunity at about five pm, I rang and made my appointment. She was a young mum whose husband had recently left her. I needed her signature in order to finalise one of the attendant issues, and she was looking forward to seeing me at five pm.

Promptly at the allotted time I rang the doorbell of her smart bungalow. One of her children answered the door, she was a bright little girl of about seven years of age.

"Hello" I smiled, "your mum is expecting me."

She looked anxiously at me as she told me that her mum was in the bedroom, and that there seemed to be some blood on the bedclothes. I asked her to wait in the kitchen for me as I tapped on the bedroom door.

"Sally are you there, are you alone, I am coming in" Sally was sitting up in bed with her hands and arms hidden under the bedclothes. There were blood stains on the sheets and on the wallpaper beside the bed.

"Put the form under the bed sheets for me and I will sign it."

"No way Sally, "I have to sign that I have witnessed your signature, we will have it signed openly please."

Reluctantly Sally lifted her hands from under the bed sheets. She had obviously cut her wrists. It is amazing how quickly the mind works at such a time. She was expecting me at five o'clock, she has cut her wrists just before I would be calling, and she has not cut them very deeply!

"Aren't you ashamed of yourself Sally? You are a qualified nurse and can't cut deeper than that, what are you trying to achieve?"

I asked who I could call for help and waited until her friend arrived. Many years later Sally who is now retired, and her daughter who is a social worker, are among my Face Book friends. Being a little late at the remainder of that evenings appointments was a small price to pay for taking time to try and deal with a sad situation.

# Retirement

Walter Slater had set a date for his well earned retirement and was now in the last six months of his forty years of service with the Prudential Assurance Company. He viewed his retirement with mixed feelings. The job which had been a way of life for forty years was coming to an end leaving an enormous gap to fill as during his working life he had been too busy to cultivate any hobbies. Walter was not the type to sit at home in carpet slippers. In fact I could not imagine him being able to relax and unwind enough to enjoy his leisure time. He certainly would not have any financial worries, his pension as a retired superintendent would be more than I was earning so he would not need to take any part time work.

Would he be able to switch off? How would he cope when pressure and challenge of heavy responsibilities were laid down. Could he handle a new life devoid of all the business habits and structures with which he had been so familiar for almost twice as many years as I had lived.

However, changes did become noticeable in Walter in his last few months, changes which I felt were for the better and may ease him into his retirement. He became much more relaxed in his approach to his duties. This is not to say that he worked less efficiently but he seemed able to delegate more, to trust other people more and to be a great deal more laid back. He seemed to achieve the same success but it seemed to need less effort. It occurred to me that the realisation had dawned on him that he could always have worked like this. His less intense manner suited him and brought a new freshness and a greater enjoyment of his work. He was not as driven, having more time for a chat and a joke, more time to share some of the amusing incidents he had experienced over the years. The firm disposition gave way to more approachability; he smiled and laughed, and mellowed. During the last six months of working life I felt that I had got to know him and like him more than in the previous eighteen months since that first day I met him outside Holmfirth Post Office.

One evening Walter called to accompany me on my sales appointments and for once I was actually more eager to make a start than he was. We sat in our lounge drinking coffee and whereas he was usually wound up for action, tonight he just wanted to sit and chat with Edith and me.

As he reminisced about the past he suddenly turned to his future becoming very animated.   He and his wife had found a bungalow on the outskirts of Holmfirth and they intended moving in quite soon. The property was ideal for them and he shared that they had been looking for a bungalow for eighteen months, and this was the only one they had really fallen in love with.  There were two problems.  First of all they had not yet sold their semi detached house situated half way between Holmfirth and Huddersfield. Walter, without any pride or boasting said quite simply,

"It does not matter; we will pay cash for the bungalow and sell the house at leisure."

 I was mightily impressed that he enjoyed such a standard of living. At that time replacing a worn out car battery was a major financial outlay for Edith and I.  The other problem was that the bungalow did not have a garage and Walter was not prepared to leave his new car parked by the roadside.  The property stood on an elevated landscaped plot and one of its lawns sloped steeply down to the retaining wall at the edge of the pavement.

Walter showed us photographs of the bungalow and began to enthuse about its potential. True there were between twenty and thirty steps to negotiate from the pavement to the front door, but the real advantage was that there was room to excavate into the sloping garden and build a garage. They had researched the project well; he produced architects plans for the construction of the garage which would greatly enhance the value and desirability of the property.

Constructing the garage would be a mammoth task as twenty or thirty tons of soil would have to be removed, but everything was meticulously planned, they even knew where they would put all the excavated soil.  The more Walter talked about the project, the more excited he became and the less inclined to actually go out and start work!

Walter was walking on air; there was buoyancy about him and an air of inoffensiveness.  In his newly found attitude to life, it seemed inconceivable that he could become offended or upset.  But I was soon to see how wrong that assumption was.  It was during these few final months that Walter accompanied me of what was until then, the most tragic and distressing business appointment of my short career.  It was an interview which had its beginnings several weeks before on a fateful Thursday morning when Mrs Roberts, the deputy collector was collecting for me as I was away in Leeds on a morning seminar. That evening I called at Mrs Roberts home for the cash and any messages. I had my notebook open and was recording some of the details, when, as though thinking aloud, she said,

"And I think there is something wrong at Bethany, you know, at Doug and Mary Marlow's home. I am not sure what is going on but I think it is serious"

"Really, what makes you think that?"

"Well, I called this morning to collect the few pence due on that small policy they have. There was no-one in though"

"I wouldn't worry about that, Mary works regular days and Doug works shifts. He may have been in bed."

"Well, his motorcycle was not there beside the front door, but that's not what is worrying me. You see I did manage to catch Mrs Smart in, their neighbour. Whilst I was there, a male and a female police officer knocked on the Marlow's door. When they discovered there was no-one in, they called at Mrs Smart's to enquire whether she knew where Mary could be contacted urgently."

"Did the police officer say when he wanted Mary?"

"No, but he looked very serious. Mrs Smart told him where Mary works and they said they would go there immediately to see her. Whatever was wrong though, he was keeping very close to his chest."

As I drove home I could not help wondering why the police were trying to contact Mary. It was probably nothing to worry about but I had a sickly feeling that there was real trouble there. My fears increased as I passed Doug and Mary's house for there was a police car parked outside and two or three other cars. A small group of women were grouped on the corner in very serious conversation. When I noticed that they kept looking towards the Marlows's house I decided to park up and have a word with them.

I managed to find a parking space near the cycle shop, and walked briskly towards the group. Recognising one of them as a Prudential client of mine, I quizzed her,

"You are all looking very serious, is anything wrong Mrs Batty?"

She was obviously thrilled at being the first person to acquaint me with some hot news, nodding her head seriously and speaking in an important tone she responded,

"You mean that you have not heard about the ginger haired young man from Bethany, you know, he rides a motor bike and works down the mine at Denby Dale."

"Yes, I know Doug Marlow really well Mrs Batty, we are close friends. What is wrong?"

"Oh he set off for work as usual this morning, you know, on that great big motor bike, I saw his wife waving to him as he set off."

"But is Doug alright Mrs Batty?"

"He's been killed, he was only two or three hundred yards away from where he works when he put his motor bike under a lorry and was killed instantly. The police are in there now with his wife, she is not a strong person you know. We can't imagine how shocked she will be. Its awful Mr Robinson, isn't it?"

I got back into the car numb with shock. Doug Marlow dead, I just could not believe it. He was always so full of life and vitality, so full of fun and humour. So young too, only twenty one years old. What about Mary, how would she stand the shock? Would it bring on the epileptic seizures again? Oh no, this could destroy her!

Edith could not believe the news when I broke it to her, putting it gently was not easy. I did not want to believe it. Edith poured me a cup of coffee saying,

"David you will have to call and see her tonight."

"I know but what will I say, what can I do, you know I am not very good at handling this sort of thing. I am not very good with words."

"It's not what you say; it's just being there that will help Mary. Just letting her know that we are both here for her anytime she needs us will mean a lot to her."

We had finished our tea and I was helping Edith wash the dishes when the door bell rang.

"I'll get it" volunteered Edith leaving me with the dishes.

I heard muffled voices in the hall; there was a woman's voice and a man's voice. Suddenly Edith was back in the kitchen followed by Mary Marlow and her father. I had never seen anyone as white and shaken as Mary who was moving and speaking in a detached robotic manner. Her father held her arm as she spoke,

"Doug is dead. He was killed this morning on his way to work."

Mary's dad took over from her,

"Doug's motor bike went straight under a lorry which pulled out of a side road right into his path. He was killed instantly."

"Yes we know, we had already heard and I intended calling to see Mary tonight. What can we say? We are extremely sorry" Before I could summon up something more profound to say, Mary continued,

"I have called with Doug's life insurance policy. Dad thought that I should see you immediately with it. Can you tell me what to do with it?"

"Yes of course I can Mary, but which policy have you brought?"

"There is only one for about fifty pounds. You know David; it is the one Doug's parents took out on him when he was a baby. Doug paid a penny a week premium."

I suddenly realised that Doug had not told Mary about the large insurance I had arranged on his life. I struggled for a few moments trying to decide whether it was the right time to gently inform Mary that Doug had loved her so much that he gone against her wishes. He just wanted to cushion Mary financially against just such a crushing blow she was now facing.

I decided that Mary needed to know now. I gently told her that Doug had taken out a life assurance policy in trust for her. She would get five thousand pounds up front followed by one thousand pounds a year for twenty five years. Mary's response to the information I gave her was quite simply,

"I see."

Within a few moments I was ushering Mary and her father towards our door as they said they had other business to attend to.

There was nothing I could do to process Doug's death claim until a death certificate was issued, and this was delayed until after the inquest into Doug's death.  I promised Mary that I would notify the Prudential about Doug's death and then call and complete the paperwork as soon as Mary advised me that the death certificate was available.  It was obvious to me that the initial discussion with Mary had been easy, she had been in shock and the truth of the awful tragedy had not really hit her.  At no time had she become distressed or shown any emotion.  Possibly she had been given a sedative by her doctor.  I knew that when I completed the documentation in several weeks' time the full impact of her loss would have taken hold of her.  The inquest would also have opened wounds which were slowly beginning to heal.  I was afraid too that I was too personally involved with Doug and Mary to be able to sort out the claim without emotional involvement on my own part.

 That is why I decided to take Walter Slater with me.  He would help me through what I knew would be a personal ordeal   Walter's sympathetic and dignified handling of the interview with Mary is one of the lasting recollections I have of him.   It is so easy to say too much on occasions like this and by an unnecessary word cause needless hurts.  The opposite is also true, too little can be said thus projecting a hard, couldn't care less attitude.  Walter took the responsibility from my shoulders and handled the business in an exemplary way.  I shall never forget the great restraint and respect he displayed even when Mary hurt him deeply.

Mary had not really realised just how much money would be paid to her, she expressed the fact that even if she used some of the proceeds to pay off her mortgage, she will still have more money than she would know what to do with.  Five thousand pounds in cash followed by one thousand pounds per year for twenty five years was a lot of money compared with the fact that my annual income was about twelve hundred pounds.

Doug had only paid just over twenty two pounds in premiums.  I was glad that I had been a willing party to Doug's conspiracy to take financial care of Mary in the event of his untimely death.

"I don't know what to do with it all" observed Mary.

Walter, gently and without any hint of pressure or manipulation made a suggestion to Mary.

"Why don't you invest some it where it came from, and lay up a good investment for your own later years?"

Mary's response staggered us both,

"But Mr Slater, I don't believe in life assurance, it is gambling and is totally against my principles. I am not prepared to discuss any investment with an insurance company."

As we drove away, Walter gave vent to his innermost feelings,

"David, you have done a blooming good job for her. She believes in life insurance enough to accept the money though, doesn't she?"

Mary's attitude had hurt Mr Slater more deeply that it showed. He was not a church goer and was enough of a gentleman not to try and convince someone to act against their principles. Having strong principles of his own, he did admire them in others. But he had enormous difficulty with "flexible" principles or with principles which were cheaper than self gain.

Within a few days, "principles" was an in word in Mr Slater's vocabulary. He and his wife had kept an appointment with their solicitor to sign the contract to purchase their dream bungalow. The partner handling their deal broke the news to them that earlier that morning the bungalow had been taken off the market and consequently their deal had fallen through. He was obviously in a difficult position, but suggested unofficially that Mr Slater and his wife should contact the lady who had been selling her bungalow to them. Possibly she could throw some light on the sudden withdrawal of the property.

The vendor feeling very guilty about the whole affair confided to Mr Slater that her own solicitor had phoned her that morning with a very large cash offer, so good that she could not really refuse it. Her own solicitor had been looking out for a bungalow for his own mother, and knowing that Mr Slater had obtained planning permission to build a garage suddenly made his client's bungalow a "must have" for his own mother. He had therefore made an offer he knew she would not refuse

All this was a profound shock to Walter's sense of honesty and decency. He would never stoop to such underhand ways of doing business, and he did not expect to find this character flaw in others. Simply because he had not signed the contract he seemed powerless to take any action. He did take legal advice but it was discovered that the solicitor who had taken advantage of Walter had covered his tracks so well that it was questionable whether a court would have found that there was a cast iron case against him.

As a gesture of goodwill though, Walter was offered an amount of money sufficient to reimburse his expenses incurred in the drawing up of the plans for the garage and for the costs of the planning application. Walter and his wife never did move into their dream retirement home.

Redfearn Rogers, our District Manager arranged one of his famous pea and pie suppers to help give Walter a good send off into retirement. It was a harsh winter night and the howling wind hurled the stinging rain full into our faces as we crossed the car park to seek sanctuary in the warmth of the local hostelry. The log fire blazed in the hearth and the atmosphere was warm and convivial.

We all had the opportunity to reminisce with Walter and to thank him for his help and friendship. Whenever insurance men get together humorous anecdotes abound and tonight was no different. The hot pies and the mushy peas were especially good but it was soon time for Redfearn Rogers to call us all to attention as he presented a suitable gift to Walter. Redfearn rose to the occasion displaying marvellous Yorkshire wit and humour whilst retaining his full dignity as our respected District Manager.

All too soon it was time to button up our overcoats, dash across the Siberian car park and in the warmth of our cars make our way home. I sat for a few moments waiting for my little Morris Minor engine to warm up and for the screen to demist. Walter appeared at the back door of the pub, his bespectacled six foot frame still youthfully erect. He stooped into his Hillman Super Minx, I heard the engine roar into life, and suddenly he was driving off into the dark.

This man who had entered my life eighteen short months ago and filled me with such awe and admiration as I considered his stature and success had now earned my affection and respect. As he drove out of my life forever a wave of sadness washed over me. This tender hearted Yorkshire man had sometimes deliberately been harsh with me. I now knew that his motives had been right and I was beginning to realise just how much I owed to him and beginning to regret some of the problems I had caused him.

I had an overwhelming regret. I wished that just once I had plucked up the courage to ask him whether he really meant it when he said,

"You will never mek owt in this job"

Not long after Walter Slater's retirement there was another sad event at Bethany, the Marlow house. The same policeman who visited Mary Marlow at the place of her employment to break the news that Doug had been killed, paid her another visit. This time to break the news that the brakes of a heavy goods vehicle had failed and the cab of the vehicle had embedded itself in the front room of her house. The driver 's body was trapped in the cab. The house was propped up and boarded up for months and I believe that when we moved away from the area it was still in the same state.

# The Kitchen Sink

I was gazing down into the unexplored depths of Ernest Turfrey's navel when the loud ringing of the doorbell broke into my reverie.

Ernest had been described to us as a "bit of a builder" now we were sampling his workmanship. When we decided to have the old porcelain sink removed from the alcove beside the fireplace and have a new sink unit fitted under the window, we thought that Ernest was our man..

The property was solid stone and the walls were almost 2 feet thick. The previous weekend we had friends, Herby and Irene staying with us, and Herby was a civil engineer. Hearing about our proposals for the change round in the kitchen, Herby offered to put the hole for the waste pipe through the wall to save Ernest a job.

He had a car boot full of tools and it did not take him long to get started. Half way into the job Herby hit his thumb with the hammer and staggered into the middle of the room muttering "I'm going, I'm going" and emitting a strange rattling sound before passing out onto the kitchen floor.

Herby's wife, Irene seemed quite undisturbed, "Don't worry" she smiled, "he often does this, it's something to do with his pain threshold."

"Are you sure he is OK?"

"Yes, just leave him. He'll come round in a bit and be OK."

Sure enough, a few minutes later Herby struggled to his feet, squeezing his thumb before retrieving his hammer and chisel so that he could have another go.

"We were worried about you"

"Yes the chaps were worried to death about me when it happened for the first time at work. As I came round I heard one of the chaps saying that he had only heard that rattling sound once before and the guy doing it died"

For a while Herby attended to the job in hand, sweat pouring off him. Wiping his forehead he broke off for a few minutes rest.

"The first time I passed out like that was whilst I was still at school. We stood to attention as the teacher came in. Before she told us to sit down the kid next to me placed a pencil on my chair point up. I sat on it and it went right where the sun doesn't shine.. I passed out and made the same rattling noises then. There was panic. But I am used to it now"

It took Herby the best part of the day to finish off the hole for the drainage pipes. He cleaned up and said,

"That'll save you a few bob off Ernest's bill. That's the hardest part of the job, done for him. He ought to be pleased!"

But pleased Ernest was not. Herby and Irene had gone home after their weekend visit when Ernest turned up to do our job on the Monday..

"Who put that jolly hole there? That's no good, it's in the wrong jolly place." He spent a few frantic minutes measuring up before reluctantly agreeing that the hole was in fact in the right place after all.

I had my own work to do with Prudential clients to visit and Monday was always a busy day. I managed to get home at tea time and it was already dark.

Ernest was lying on his back under the new sink unit, his quarry like navel exposed to the world. My reverie started, I was back in my school days and although wrestling with vital problems of geography, mathematics and physics there was a huge unresolved question perplexing us young school lads. No one could tell us the answer.

"Why, when a fellow wears a white vest and pants does he accumulate blue fluff in his belly button?"

This problem took on huge proportions. It became almost an eighth wonder of the world. I lost count of the number of times I heard the question at lunch time, in the showers after the cross country run.

"How does the belly button collect blue fluff when the underclothes are white?"

Gazing down at Ernest's dark abyss brought to memory the old quest for a serious answer. I realised that as a married man I still did not know the answer. I was wondering whether to pluck up courage and ask Ernest if he knew when the doorbell clanged.

It was the local policeman at the door, he smiled as he asked, "Is that van parked outside your front door anything to do with you?"

"It certainly is, we have a chappie in doing some work for us. It's his van"

"Do you think you could ask him to move it? It is parked without lights, and its on a main road facing the wrong way"

"Sure, leave it with me. I'll sort it."

Ernest was still sweating and groaning when I stood over him again.

"Ernest, the police have asked that you move your van. It's parked without lights and it's facing the wrong way."

"Don't worry, it'll jolly well be alright. I'll just leave it."

"Ernest, you can't leave it. We don't want the police back again. Just give me the keys and I'll put it on the car park round the corner."

"I don't have a jolly key. It's not jolly locked. Don't worry just jolly well leave it"

I dashed out to move the van before the local bobby called again. It was an aged Hillman and I noticed that there was no key hole or lock in the driver's door. There was a circular hole where many years ago a lock may have resided, but that was in the misty days of yore..

There was a handle, which I took hold of and pulled. The door opened slowly but it felt as though someone was inside the van trying to hold it shut. When the door was 18 inches ajar, I let go to see what would happen. It snapped shut with a vicious thud.

Trying again, I opened it almost fully before I let go. There was a vicious snatch and the door clashed shut, pulled by a mysterious hand.

At my next attempt I determined not to let go. I intended getting the upper hand by surprising the sinister door closer. Then beneath the glow of the street lamp all was revealed. There was no mysterious person sitting in the car wrestling with the door.

There was in fact nothing more sinister than a long strip of rubber inner tube, one end tied around the steering column, the other end screwed onto the inside of the door. In the absence of a "proper" lock this was Ernest's jolly substitute. Typical Ernest.

The next hardship was actually getting into the van and sitting in the driver's seat. This involved circumnavigating the legs and body around the threatening rubber, which seemed poised to amputate various parts of my unprotected anatomy.

At last I was in. How do I start the engine without a key? Good question. I soon found the answer. Where the ignition key should be there was, yes you have guessed! Another hole, this time in the metal dashboard. The ignition switch had been amputated at some time but hanging beneath the dash board were two wires, their bare ends protected with black electrical tape. I was quick to pick up on the clues. These were live wires. If I pulled back the black tape and touched them together something would happen.

As I hesitatingly made contact, there was a spark and the engine coughed into life. We had lift off. I slipped the van into gear and drove round the block onto the car park. Reaching down I found the handbrake and tugged, to my horror I discovered that the handbrake lever was not attached to the floor and it came away in my hands. The best I could do was leave the van in gear before returning to the house to pull Ernest's leg about his "company" vehicle.

"But it's got a topping little engine" Ernest volunteered. "I could go anywhere in it. It has never jolly well let me down."

I remembered Ernest's wife telling me that Ernest paid five pounds for a second hand car and a few days later they drove it from Yorkshire to Minehead in Somerset. She used the same expression as Ernest, "It had a topping little engine in it."

From his recumbent position lying under the sink, Ernest recounted an experience he had with the police when he had owned his previous "company van" which apparently must have borne an uncanny resemblance to his present vehicle.

"I was at the jolly builders merchants buying some copper pipe and other bits and pieces. I came out of the merchants and tied a load of copper pipes onto the jolly roof rack and then just popped back into the shop for the other bits and bobs. When I came out there is a jolly policeman walking round my van with his jolly notebook in his hand.."

"Oh dear, that sounds bad Ernest"

"Oh they don't bother me, I know how to talk to them! I wished him a good morning and said that I hoped he was having a jolly good day before asking him if there was anything wrong"

Ernest screwed his face up as he exerted pressure on his wrench before continuing,

"Do you know what he had to the jolly cheek to say to me?"

"I could have a good guess Ernest!"

"Opening his notebook, he asked whether I was the owner of this heap of scrap, whereupon I said that I was and asked whether anything was wrong."

"Wrong" said the policeman, "Wrong! Just walk round your van with me and show me anything that's right about it. Look at these tyres. Look at the huge holes in the bodywork, look at the cracks in the windscreen, look at…."

"Before he could say any more I stopped him" smiled Ernest. "I said, ah but she's got a topping little engine, she goes like a dream"

"Ah but can you stop it quickly when she gets up to speed" asked the amused policeman.

I think that most police officers would have wanted to test the brakes, and the steering, and the lights, and the indicators and throw the book at Ernest, but not this one. Somehow beguiled by Ernest's naïve innocence, he simply smiled and said,

"Don't let me see this vehicle parked anywhere near here ever again" before putting his notebook away.

Ernest's stock in trade was that he was so likeable, he had the appearance of a transparent innocent benign person, incapable of even a bad thought. So solidly good through and through, that to even suggest that something about him was not quite right was an outrageous supposition.

He was not just our tradesman for those few days, he was also our church minister, a part time unpaid role he faithfully executed. He was a great shepherd of his adoring faithful little flock.

# The Morris Minor

I was on my way to Upperthong, a little village nestling on the hillside above Holmfirth.  It was such a steep climb that I was pleased to be in the car and not on foot. The door of some of the houses opened directly onto the narrow little lane, so great care was needed when leaving a house. As though to compensate for lack of a front garden, many of the homes had a large garden at the rear but flat ornamental lawns were a rarity.  Due to the incline of the terrain, many of the gardens were terraced and had several levels.

The hill was so steep that it was better to stay in 2nd gear and avoid stopping and restarting as much as possible.  For this reason I tended to drive directly to the highest part of the village leaving the stopping and starting for the journey back down the steep hill. In very many years of motoring I have only needed a replacement clutch in one car. That was when I lived and worked in Holmfirth!

I passed St John's Church wondering how a church came to be built on such a steep hill and how long it took the worshippers to get back their breath after the service had started. Long after I had left the area, Bill Owen and Peter Sallis (Compo and Clegg in Last of the Summer Wine) would both be buried in St John's churchyard.  They became the best of friends during so many years of filming that they decided to share their last resting place.  It was during a break in filming that Bill Owen and Peter Sallis visited St John's graveyard. Bill was reading some of the inscriptions on the grave stones when he said wistfully, "What do you think they will put on my grave ?" Without hesitation, Peter Sallis in true Last of the Summer Wine spirit responded "Something heavy I hope".

Upperthong is where my weekly collecting routine began on a Friday morning, it was a pleasant village and my clients there were all most loyal to "Prudential Assurance Co".   Norman Peace who had been the "Prudential"  agent there for forty years lived in the village in a very tidy stone built bungalow with its name on a slate, "Pennine View" and it had a superb view over the moors from the rear windows.  I was a frequent visitor there to visit Norman until his untimely death just twelve months after his retirement.

I was at the highest part of the village making my first visit to a Mr Batty. On the gravel beside the stone built cottage sat a three and a half litre Rover car, obviously someone's pride and joy. The immaculate condition of the car suggested that Mr Batty was most likely to be a dapper white collar worker and I expected a dignified well dressed man to open the door to me.

A portly man, almost as round as he was tall, stood filling the doorway. He was dressed in a long khaki smock, the type which shop keepers often wore, as he removed a surgical type face mask he looked at me quizzically before asking,

"Can I help you?"

"Good morning Mr Batty, I'm David Robinson your Prudential Assurance agent, your motor insurance is due for renewal soon and I have the papers with me."

"Thou had better come in lad but I am painting the living room ceiling so there is a bit of a pong" In a few seconds I had scanned the room and was amazed to see hens scurrying away from me to hide under the table. On the carpet were dishes of water and chicken food and the table and the chairs were littered with piles of newspapers, magazines and discarded clothes. He was using a spray gun to paint his ceiling which is why there was a heavy fog swirling around the room. The buttons on Mr Batty's smock were straining at the button holes. I remember thinking that the smock was almost large enough to make a tent.

"I can't get away wi a poking little brush to do me ceiling tha knows, it's a lot quicker to spray it but it makes a bit of a puther."

"Yes I can see that Mr Batty, but don't you think you should cover everything up before you let the spray gun loose'?

"Nay lad, there's nowt in ere that's very special, any road nobody sees owt inside me house except me, and I'm not a proud chap"

I smiled as he rooted about for his cheque book, " How much dost tha want for t car insurance? It's a big powerful car tha knows, it's a great big Rover, all brute force and nice leather seats"

Mr Batty wrote me a cheque and as I was signing and checking his papers he explained to me why he needed such a big powerful car,

"I work at an old folk's 'ome and I like to tek some of the old ladies out into the countryside for a drive, they don't get out much and they feel special in the Rover. I 'olds the door open for them to get in and out and sometimes a wear a peaked chauffeurs cap, it does mek them feel special."

"You are very good to them Mr Batty.  If I end up in an old folk's home I hope you will be as good to me..."

"Nay lad, I'll be long gone by then, but I bet the Rover will still be going strong.  Do you know I hardly ever have to change gear on these steep hills, like I said, its sheer brute force, she just keeps going and going, uses a drop of petrol though.  But I'm not married and a man needs an interest don't you think?"

As I was leaving Mr Batty was "tuning up" his paint sprayer and as I gently closed his door I could hear that he was back in action, spraying his ceiling.

"Salt of the earth" I thought as I was walking back to my little Morris I000. I passed a largish stone detached house where I was not due to visit today. I smiled though as I remembered Norman Peace telling me about the butcher who lived there.  He was a big fat man, apparently much larger than Mr Batty.  He had staff who ran his butchers shop and he spent much of his working day delivering across quite a large number of villages.  One morning he set off in the delivery van but by the time he reached his first customer seven or eight miles away, he had munched his way through 6 kilos of raw tripe. He had to phone the shop and get one of his staff to bring more tripe out to him.  He was so broad across the upper part of his body that he had to drive with the door window open and could often be seen with his shoulder and arm exposed to the elements.

He was a very demanding man, and expected his hot meal to be on the table as soon as he came in at tea time.  If his homely and long-suffering little wife was late serving up his meal, he, depending how hungry he was, was quite likely to pick up a kitchen chair and hurl it through the picture window.  There was always a pane of glass cut to size ready to be delivered and fitted by the local glass merchant.

Most of the homes in the village were spotless, but Norman Peace had warned me about one.

"David, when you visit there you need to wipe your feet when you come out!"

I thought that he was exaggerating but I soon discovered that he had not painted the whole picture! The smell was overpowering making me want to hold my breath whilst in the house, the odour lingered on my clothes afterwards and I did not want subsequent clients to think that I was dirty and carried my own atmosphere with me. So I hatched a cunning plan! I would simply shout

"It's the Prudential, but I won't come in, I am just enjoying the lovely view!"

I did not know how to respond one Friday morning when the whole village was obscured in dense fog. I had proffered my usual greeting,

"I won't come in, I am just enjoying the lovely view"

The reply came immediately,

"What view, ye can't see owt for the fog."

Further along the lane I had a client who refused to divulge his Christian names to me. He was a plasterer and the signage on his van proudly proclaimed Y N GLADWELL  PLASTERER

"What would you like me to call you "I asked, "Many of my clients like me to use their Christian name but I don't know yours"  this was an attempt to be friendly but also to satisfy my curiosity. I just could not think of a man's name beginning with the letter Y.

"Just call me Gladwell" was his bluff response, "that's what everybody calls me. Not Mr Gladwell, just Gladwell will be fine."

His initial Y became one of the little mysteries I would love to solve. In those days we did not have a computer produced index of our clients' records. Never mind. My time will come!

A few months later my doorbell rang, it was Gladwell.

"Hello Mr Robinson, I have had a minor accident in my van, can you sort a claim out for me?"

Delighted, not because of the accident, but because here was the moment of truth.

"I need your full names please Gladwell."

Very quickly Gladwell almost spat out his Christian names.

"Young Nipper Gladwell."

"Pardon, did you say Young Nipper

In a most matter of fact way he nodded his agreement. I tried not to smile before he volunteered the origin of his names,

"Dad was so relieved and overjoyed when I was born that he went on a bender and was not quite sober when he went to register my birth.

As he took a seat at the desk he told the registrar that he had come to register the young nipper. After the usual congratulations the registrar asked for full details of the babies names. It seems that dad thought that Young Nipper Gladwell had a certain uniqueness, no-one else will be called that, and it sounds awfully good. So that was it, I was registered as YOUNG NIPPER GLADWELL."

The next time I visited Mr Gladwell I greeted him with the words,

Good morning Young Nipper." Which earned the friendly rebuke,

"I'm Gladwell if you don't mind!"

A few months after Mr Batty ( I had discovered that the local children called him Fatty Batty) had renewed his insurance for his Rover car, he visited me one Saturday morning. I was pleased to see him as he was such a cheerful character. We lived on the main Huddersfield Road opposite the Town Hall just two or three minutes' walk from the town centre where there was a garage who were main dealers for Austin and Morris and Rover.

"What can I do for you Mr Batty?" I enquired

"I'd like a cover note please lad, I have just traded the Rover in for a second hand Morris 1000 just like yours. It will do a lot more miles to the gallon and I can still take the old ladies out for drives. I have walked along from the garage to get a cover note from you, then I can walk back and pick up my new car."

The paperwork was soon completed and he surrendered his insurance certificate for the Rover before making his way back to pick up his new car. I had just completed all my paperwork for the week and was about to walk along to the post office to send it to Leeds office, so I naturally enclosed all the paperwork just completed for Mr Batty.

Less than an hour later Mr Batty returned looking embarrassed, "I hope you have not sent any of my paperwork off David. I need the certificate of insurance back for the Rover and here is the cover note you have just made out for the Morris I000. I have taken the Morris back and am sticking with the Rover."

I explained that there was no problem, but the papers had already been sent off so I would need to issue a cover note for the Rover.

"By the way Mr Batty, Leeds office will no doubt want to know the reason for the "temporary" changes to your cover. Could you please write a short note to explain?"

I handed Mr Batty pen and paper, and he wrote quite laboriously,

To The Prudential Assurance Company,

Dear Sirs,

You want to know why I have cancelled the insurance for the Morris I000 after only one hour. It is because I cannot turn the steering wheel as my belly gets in the way.

Sincerely

J Batty.

# Cherith

Life in Holmfirth was quite lonely for Edith.  Although we had our little daughter Joy, we had no relatives or friends in the area.   Edith's parents were living in Lincolnshire in a beautiful little market town and we visited them as often as we could and stayed the weekend.   Compared to Holmfirth, the climate there was so gentle.   Even the winters seemed balmy compared to the harsh weather we had to endure.  My own parents were twenty miles away and we tried to get over to see them every Tuesday.  On more than one occasion we rang them to say that we were snowed in and would not be able to visit them.   They were completely surprised at our news because they had not seen a single flake of snow in Wakefield.

I had my work and interaction with my clients so I was protected from some of the loneliness Edith felt.   One of my clients, Derek, worked for the local council and in the harsh winters he drove the snow blower trying to keep the roads into Holmfirth and across the moors open.  His wife Molly had felt very lonely when they moved to Holmfirth and she guessed how Edith would be feeling.  She kindly offered to visit Edith and a good friendship developed.   Molly had a heart of gold and a very loud voice.   One morning Walter Slater and I were sitting in our front room discussing Prudential business when Molly rang the doorbell, pushed the door open and shouted "Hello!"  Pausing mid-sentence, Mr Slater said "I think that your coal man has just arrived."

We appreciated Molly's friendship and Edith and Joy our little daughter would in turn visit Molly who lived at the top of a very steep hill overlooking the town.  Molly and Nora Newton became a lifeline to Edith and helped us settle amongst a people who were suspicious of us because we had not been born there.   Walter Slater warned me that many of the locals would offer signs of friendship to us until they had discovered all our business, then they would lose interest in us and gossip our affairs all over the area.  Not so with Molly and Mrs Nelson, they were genuine to the core.

Nora Newton visited us in our three storey stone built terraced house opposite the Town Hall.   She asked whether we would be interested in moving into a modern bungalow in Holmbridge just two or three miles away.   She had friends there who lived in a new bungalow but due to a reduction in income they were needing to move down-market. We thought that there was no harm in checking out the bungalow, so introductions were made and we viewed each other's homes. The couple were Sheila and Billy and they had a daughter Christine. So combing their names they had named their bungalow CHRISHELBY. In fact, on the ordnance survey map the bungalow was shown as Chrishelby, it did not have a house number. They fell in love with our terraced home and bought it from us for the same £1500 we had paid for it about a year before. We bought Chrishelby for £3000 assisted with a staff mortgage from Prudential.

Chrishelby had a very small front garden but a huge steeply sloping rear garden which led down to a lovely stream at the bottom which fed into the River Holme a few hundred yards away. There were magnificent views over the moors to the Holme Moss television mast which stood proudly pointing to the sky just two or three miles away. What a wonderful place to live. Visitors were often transfixed with the view remarking that it was like living in Switzerland. We discovered that the large stone built house next door to us had cost £10,000 when it was built three or four years before. That was a lot of money in the mid 1960's. Furthermore, Joe Booth's daughter, Cath Mellor and her husband Cliff lived there. They really were affluent people, Cliff was the manager of a local mill and Cath owned a bay wear shop in the town. Joe Booth was seen almost daily pottering about in their garden and sitting in the shed smoking.

To a city dweller like myself, whose schoolboy hobby had been angling, having a stream at the bottom of the garden was like a dream come true. It was only about six feet wide so I built a dam using the local stone and created a pool about ten or twelve feet wide. A pair of ducks nested in our garden, raised their young there and they all swam in our pool. I occasionally saw small trout there. If I am honest, I think that the stream was one of the main attractions to me, and it was the stream which made us think about renaming the bungalow. CHRISHELBY was fine for Christine Sheila and Billy but not for us There was not a lot we could do with David Edith and Joy! We needed to think of something more relevant.

Edith and I quickly decided to rename our bungalow CHERITH. Cherith was the brook where Elijah hid during days of great national famine. It was there, according to the record in I Kings chapter 17 that God sent ravens to take bread and meat to Elijah each morning and evening and the brook Cherith satisfied Elijah's need for water. To Elijah the brook became a place of protection safety and provision, and what more could we want! So the name sign Chrishelby was replaced with a brand new one bearing the name CHERITH.

I did not need to display the brass Prudential Assurance Company sign here. Redfearn Rogers my District Manager agreed with me that the bungalow was too isolated to risk advertising that there could be money in the property. Cliff and Cath Mellor did not have much to do with us, at least until the fateful night when I cleaned our chimney! We had decided to have gas fire fitted replacing the coal fire in the lounge. Les Heywood the plumber popped in to let us know that he would be staring the installation work in two days' time. He hoped that there would be enough time for us to have the chimney swept before he fitted the gas fire.

"That doesn't give us much time to find a chimney sweep Les."

"Oh don't worry David, my dad has a chimney sweep kit, I am sure he will lend it to you. I will get it and drop it in for you."

"Wow, thanks Les, I used to watch the sweep cleaning my parents chimney, there is nothing to it, it's as good as done."

A few hours later Les popped in with his dad's chimney sweeps brush and rods. As he laid them down beside our door he smiled and informed us,

"Dad lives in a three storey house David, there are enough rods to go right up from the cellar up to the chimney on the roof, so you won't be short of rods."

I thought that it would be better to wait until dark before cleaning our chimney. I don't really know why I felt that way, it just seemed a good idea. We had our tea and I found an old bed sheet which I taped across the fire place. I cut a hole in the sheet to push the rods through after I had shoved one rod and the brush into the bottom of the chimney. I began attaching rods and shoving for all I was worth. I popped outside to check whether the brush had appeared out of the chimney, but no sign of it. Back into the bungalow, more rods attached and more pushing and shoving. Outside once again to look for the brush. Still no brush. Back inside, more rods and more pushing and shoving, but still no brush visible. Thinking that our chimney must be deceptively high I hastily attached all the remaining rods and shoved and pushed again.

It was when Edith made a profound statement that I realised something must be wrong.

"David" she said, "don't you remember Les saying that there are enough rods to sweep a three storey chimney."

"Yes I do"

"Well where are all the rods then, because you have used them all and we live in a bungalow!"

"Oh no, summat's up" I responded lapsing into my Yorkshire dialect. "Let's both go out and see where the brush is."

We stood in the dark gazing up romantically at our beautiful chimney pot. There was no sign of the sweep's brush but there was something else, slender and curved and appearing out of our chimney. Suddenly I heard the gentle purring of Cliff Mellor's Ford Cortina as he slowly swung into his drive. His headlights scanned his immaculate front lawn. Oh no, there in the middle of his lawn was our sweep's brush, the rods attached, like a black, slim, sooty rainbow forming a perfect arch from his lawn until they disappeared down our chimney.

"Quick Edith get inside" but it was too late. Cliff Mellor was out of his car and addressing me in his managerial voice,

"Excuse me but what's that on my lawn?"

"Er, it looks like a sweep's brush Mr Mellor"

"It is a sweep's brush and it appears to have come out of your chimney."

"That's because I am sweeping our chimney Mr Mellor so that we can have…" but before I could continue Mr Mellor cut in

"You are not trying to come up your chimney and down mine are you. Two for the price of one? And what happens if our little white poodle rolls in the soot on our lawn?"

Then he began to laugh gently. We apologised before escaping as quickly as we could. The ice was broken, a somewhat unusual introduction had been made. The Mellors were quite friendly after that, and he greeted me one morning with the question,

"Hello, have you swept any good chimneys recently?"

Cherith was in a lovely situation with views to die for out of the rear windows. It was elevated on a hillside and we looked down on the main road where I could see many of my policyholders' homes. There were drawbacks though, I was sorting some papers out in a client's home when he quizzed, "Did you enjoy the wrestling on TV last night. We saw your TV and lights go out when it finished. Frequently I was informed that a client had watched Edith putting the washing out the previous day. At least we were beginning to feel part of the community.

A short drive from Cherith and I was at the side of Digley reservoir, a quiet picturesque spot, with lush grass pine trees and bird song. I was still practising with the accordion I had now bought from Nora Newton and was able to read simple music tunes. It was a lovely day and I knew that if I rushed through my afternoon collecting duties I would be able to spend half an hour beside the reservoir so I popped the accordion in the car boot.

It was about 4 pm when I parked at a deserted spot overlooking the water. I took the accordion and a Sankey's hymn book, knelt on one of my car mats and spread the hymn book in front of me on a log. For half an hour it was sheer heaven. No wife and children to disturb with the noise, no dog to show her disapproval by howling. There was no need to play quietly so I got lots of air into the bellows and gave it a good blasting, pausing only to thumb through the hymn book. At last after half an hour, feeling pleased with my efforts and completely de-stressed, it was time to return to the car which was about twenty yards behind me. I turned to face the car and could not believe my eyes. There in my path, sitting on the grass eating their picnic teas were about twenty school children with their teacher. Feeling completely embarrassed and wondering how long they had been listening, I tip toed through the middle of them sheepishly acknowledging their hearty applause.

As I gently placed my instrument back into the car boot I said to myself, "David lad, your playing must have improved. You got no applause when you played the hymns at Turfrey's tabernacle."

# Life at Cherith

Life in our terraced house opposite the Town Hall had been relatively quiet. The only visitors we had were Molly who came to see Edith, Nora Newton came to see us both and I would collect her in the car and take her home after her visit. Then of course Mr Slater spent time with me every week for the first six months of my career with the Prudential. It was very rare for him to call unexpectedly, he usually arranged at each visit when he would next see me. As I needed less and less supervision his visits began to take the form of an evening's sales session. He would call for me about six pm and I would exchange riding in my humble Morris 1000 for a ride in the leather luxury of his Wolseley 1500, later replaced with a new Hillman Super Minx. During my regular collecting duties I would chat to people about any product which I felt would interest them and try and make an appointment for me to take Walter Slater along to chat it through with them.

I never had any difficulty in making appointments for Mr Slater and me. I cannot remember anyone saying "Oh don't bring him with you." Or "Don't bring your superintendent here." He had been Norman Peace's superintendent for many years and was well known. He had a pleasant user friendly approach and policyholders felt at ease with him knowing that he would not try and put pressure on them to invest more money with Prudential. Not all superintendents were like that, but I was fortunate that when Mr Slater retired, his successor, David Hodge, proved to be similar in his non-threatening approach as he endeavoured to sell the company products.

My parents came over regularly from Wakefield to see us, and Edith's parents would come from Lincolnshire and spend the occasional weekend with us. Otherwise most visitors we had, had called to see me on insurance business. Moving to Cherith heralded a more hectic, interesting and for certain periods a far less lonely existence. It was also a very fruitful season of our married life.

Some good things, really good things happened whilst living at Cherith. It was whilst there that Edith and I applied to a London-based adoption society in the hope of adopting a baby, a brother or sister for Joy. The Society, rejoicing in the long name "The Mission of Hope and F B Meyer homeless children's aid and adoption society" The Society was based in Croydon and we were interviewed there in a very homely and friendly atmosphere. We were informed that there were more children available for adoption that prospective adoptive parents. It was therefore possible to specify the preferred age of the child you hoped to adopt. We wanted a new born baby, and got through the interview process. The referees we had provided were all satisfactory so the next step was a home visit from one of the adoption society's staff.

This was arranged fairly quickly and I had the pleasant task of meeting the lady at the nearest railway station and driving her out to Cherith. She was a refined gentle lady, probably around retiring age and was a member of an Anglican Church in London. She shared with us an amazing story of God's wonderful provision for a church family at a time of dire need. It was obvious that she was not just a Christian in name, and that she lived a Godly life of faith in The Lord Jesus. She made a big impression on Edith and me. We must have made a good impression on her, because we heard quite soon that we had been accepted and that we were on the waiting list for a baby.

It was during our time at Cherith that we both felt the need for a lively evangelical church to be opened in Holmfirth. We felt part of the church family at Denby Dale and were really happy with Ernest Turfrey as our pastor and shepherd. However the round trip to church and back was 20 miles so we were driving 40 miles each Sunday and in the winter driving conditions were frequently difficult.

We contacted the Home Missions department of Assemblies of God which was the denomination which Edith and I had both grown up in. We told them that we would like to see an Assembly of God church in Holmfirth as there was no lively evangelical church in the area. Their response was a visit from Keith Monument who was then the movement's Home Missions Secretary. Keith was a visionary with a consuming passion to see the Gospel preached though a network of lively healthy local churches across the UK. Keith originally came from Darlington area and had never lost his local accent. He was a human dynamo, driving thousands and thousands of miles each year planting new churches and supporting their ministers. Keith was a gifted and unique preacher too and was a very popular and challenging speaker for church anniversaries etc. He always wore a grey Burtons Director suit and always seemed to carry a tea bag in the breast pocket.

Keith picked up our enthusiasm and promised to place our proposals before the Home Missions Council. Their response was good, they too felt that the time was right and they left it to Keith to make plans for an evangelistic crusade as a basis for starting a new church.

A few weeks later Keith was sitting in our lounge again, this time he had Eric Dando with him. Eric was a member of the executive council of Assemblies of God and was the pastor of a large church in Wales. Eric was a silver tongued preacher himself and he too was in demand in the UK and across the pond as a preacher and teacher. Pastor Dando had been invited to be the evangelist at the proposed Holmfirth Crusade and had come to see the area and look at suitable halls which could accommodate enough people at the crusade meetings. The favourite venue was the Town Hall opposite where we used to live, and I took Keith and Eric into the building to view the facilities.

As I followed Eric and Keith up the steps onto the stage in the Town Hall I was beginning to feel excited. Eric faced the empty hall, assumed his preaching voice and cried out the words of a Bible text to his imaginary audience. The acoustics were good and the hall met with his approval. I could not believe that Holmfirth would have the opportunity to hear this great man preaching for fourteen nights . The majority of his hearers would never have heard preaching like it. Sadly it was not to be as the availability of the Town Hall did not fit in with Pastor Dando's extremely busy schedule

So Keith returned to visit us again accompanied by Ron Hicklin a successful well proven evangelist with the Assemblies of God churches, and himself pastor of a church in Staffordshire. Ron was available, the Town Hall was booked and a hundred and one, or maybe one thousand and one preparatory jobs were commenced. A team of young people known as Heralds were needed in the weeks before the crusade to knock on doors handing out invitations and creating public awareness of the event. Musicians were needed for the crusade to play the Hammond organ. Guest soloists needed to be booked. A gifted children's communicator to do a children's spot in the crusade meetings, interviews on local radio, press releases, literature to design and print. The list seemed endless. One of the guest soloists was William Hunter, sadly the printer made a mistake on the handbills and large posters. WILLIAM HUNTER-BASS was to be the soloist. One of the heralds rang the printer to inform them that William Hunter is not a BASS singer, he is a TENOR. The printer got it wrong again and supplied replacement posters proudly proclaiming that WILLIAM HUNTER BASS-TENOR would be singing.

Cherith became the crusade office, Keith Monument had a key and could come in with his tea bag any time. We had two Heralds sleeping on the kitchen floor one night with our mongrel dog lying between them, one of the Heralds was a lovely young man from Louth, Lincolnshire. His name was John Cox and he had taken a year out from his job at W H Smith's in Grimsby, to serve God and the church with no pay. Whilst John was staying with us he helped me lay a new lawn at Cherith. Sadly soon after returning to his secular job in Grimsby, John and one of his brothers were killed when their car crashed whilst on their way to a football match in Grimsby. I had taken John back home to his parents Kate and Granville when his time in Holmfirth came to an end. Later we were to move into Lincolnshire and were friends of Kate and Granville for many years. Keith Monument was a regular overnight guest. On the morning of the first occasion he was staying the night with us I went into the loft to put some boxes out of the way. I slipped off a joist and my whole leg from foot to groin smashed its way through the bedroom ceiling immediately above the bed. Fortunately one of my policyholders, Wilf Eggletone was an ornamental plasterer and he came at short notice to fix the hole in the ceiling after Keith had slept below it for one night!

Cherith was throbbing with life and visitors. A letter introducing the crusade had gone to every home in Holmfirth and Cherith was shown as the crusade office. One afternoon, David Hodge my Prudential superintendent called unexpectedly.

"Just want you to know that a letter of complaint has been sent in about you. I have just been to investigate and deal with it."

"What kind of complaint David?"

"Oh a lady at the bottom of the lane called Nellie Borthwick has written to the Prudential office complaining. She says she thought that you were supposed to be working for the Prudential not the church and she felt that something should be done about it."

"Oh that's bad David, I'm really sorry."

"Don't be sorry David, I have left her with a flea in her ear. I told her that if you were not doing your job properly I would be the first one to know. As it is I am delighted with how you are doing your job so it's no concern of hers."

Not many weeks later I left my car parked near the Borthwick's house and when I returned it had been badly scratched with a coin or a key. I had no evidence but I was fairly sure who was responsible.

Edith and I did not want an Assemblies of God church in Holmfirth primarily as a church for us to attend. There did not seem to be any real spiritual life in the local churches. When one of my Prudential clients dropped dead whilst doing the washing up, his wife was obviously in a state of shock and grief. The vicar of the established church performed the funeral service, and the widow, looking for answers questioned the vicar,

"My husband died so suddenly that there was no time to prepare for death. Where has he gone, is there life after death and if so what can I do to make sure that I am prepared?"

The vicar's reply left her feeling completely bewildered and empty, he said quite plainly,

"Mrs Briers, some people believe that when you are dead you are done with. If that is any help I suggest that you just believe that." His parish must have been ripe for some Biblical evangelical preaching.

Many years before Holmfirth had been blessed by the preaching of one of their Methodist ministers, the Rev Joseph Dryden Blinco. Doug Marlow had pointed out to me the church where Jo Blinco had been the minister for a while. Jo Blinco was born in Whitehaven in Cumberland in 1912. Reared in poverty in a godless, mining home, his mother's dramatic conversion to Christianity brought about a spiritual awakening. Spending a formative period at the Methodist Cliff College, Jo Blinco was retained as a staff evangelist and his gifts were so marked that Methodist Conference appointed him to minister in run down churches which probably faced closure. Under his preaching and pastoral care the causes revived and he brought many excellent schemes to fruition. He assisted in the organisation of the memorable Billy Graham 1954 Haringey Crusade.

Twelve months later, Jo Blinco joined the Billy Graham team as an associate evangelist. Thrilling years followed and he developed into one of the best known evangelical preachers in the world. His beautiful life (in which were blended a fine mind, quick wit, exuberant, lovable nature, and a prayerful concern for others) was consistent with his powerful spoken advocacy. It inspired the writing of George Beverly Shea's gospel song, "The wonder of it all." In the summer of 1966 he became Director of the Forest Home Churches Conference Centre in California. A promising beginning was marred by the discovery that he was suffering from an incurable disease. Yet never did his faith shine more brightly. Dr Billy Graham said on his last visit, "Joe, I'll see you in the morning just inside the Eastern Gate." "Praise The Lord," came the reply, "I'll be there." (The forgoing is an extract from Jo Blinco's obituary from the Minutes of the Methodist Conference 1969)

Joe Blinco passed away triumphantly at 4-00 am on Sunday 9th June 1968 in his 56th year and in the 28th year of his Christian ministry.

"Some people believe that when you are dead you are done with, if that's any help I suggest that you believe that."

"Praise The Lord I'll be there." These two statements from Christian ministers are poles apart. We felt that Holmfirth once again needed some sound Biblical teaching and needed to hear the hope brought by the Christian gospel.

For 14 nights the same Gospel preached by Jo Blinco and by the Billy Graham team was proclaimed in the Town Hall in Holmfirth. There were good congregations of people there to hear. Ron Hicklin preached his heart out night after night. He believed that as a sign that the truth of the gospel had been preached, God would heal the sick and night after night the sick were prayed for and there were testimonies of healings having taken place. At the end of the crusade there was a nucleus of people happy to belong to a new church, some had expressed faith in Christ for the first time and others were re-affirming the faith they had embraced but had fallen away from. So the pioneer Assemblies of God Church was launched in Holmfirth, initially in a smaller hall in the Town Hall. One of the local Anglican Ministers came to some of the Crusade meetings and it was obvious that the preaching met with his approval.

Ron Hicklin had his own church to look after in Brownhills, so at the end of the Crusade he had to leave. The Home Missions Council appointed John Carter, a young man from Grimsby as the follow up worker. John played the accordion (properly!) so we were never short of a musician. The folk liked him and supported him and he became the loving shepherd of the new flock.

John lived with us at Cherith for several months. It was to Cherith that he invited a young lady for coffee. She had become part of the infant church and after a slow and hesitant courtship they became engaged. We were guests at their marriage in Grimsby. Many, many years later they are still happily married and occasionally come to stay in our home with us. The name of the young lady John invited to Cherith that evening is Bernice, and she is the sister of Doug Marlow, the young man who had been tragically killed in that motor cycle accident!!

Another romance began during the time Ron Hicklin stayed with us at Cherith. His daughter Barbara met Edith's brother, Ian at Cherith. A romance followed and we attended their wedding too. Ian and Barbara had a long and extremely happy married life, adopting two children Paul and Sarah. Sadly Barbara was diagnosed with a brain tumour and passed away in 2016. Their Christian faith was strong throughout. Ian has written a very moving chronicle of their life and his loss of Barbara, it shines with the hope of the gospel. The book is available and is called "By a departing light" by Rev Ian Jennings.

The time came for John Carter to move on to other things. Home Missions Department appointed David Playle as the new pastor, David was a draughtsman by profession, as was Ron Hicklin. David and his wife Rosemary and their children moved to Holmfirth from Basildon. They were not used to seeing houses whose front door opened directly onto the street. It was a novelty for a while. They too were frequent visitors at Cherith and when Keith Monument came to Holmfirth to see them he would also pop in to see us with his tea bag handy!

David and Rosemary nurtured and cared for the infant church. We met in hired premises at first but under David's leadership were able to take out a mortgage through Assemblies of God Property Trust to purchase our own building. In addition to a meeting hall and offices there was living accommodation on site. It certainly was not up to the standard David and Rosemary were used to, but they settled there graciously.

In one of the church services we were singing a Wesley hymn with the words, "No condemnation now I dread." One of Pastor Playle's children said to his dad,

"Dad, that's what we have running down our walls!"

"No" said David, "we have CONDENSATION running down our walls. The Playle's made a great sacrifice in coming to Holmfirth. They knew that God had called them and made huge sacrifices to pursue their calling.

In arranging publicity for the church crusade I had met the editor of the local Holmfirth Express

I called in to see him one day to thank him for the wide range of interests catered for in his weekly newspaper. There were articles for gardeners, footballers, cricketers, darts players, cyclists, and anglers etc. The list was impressive, however his paper lacked something, and it did not have anything with a Christian theme. He looked at me across his desk and said gently, "Well why don't you write something!"

Plunging my hand in my jacket pocket I pulled out an article I had written in anticipation, it bore the title, "The Social Results of the Gospel" and he read it with interest. "It's excellent David, I will publish it, and will you do a regular monthly column?" I thought it better to use a pen name so we settled on the name Torchbearer before the editor shared with me that he was a Methodist and was happy to include some Christian themes into the "Express".

So on Saturday August 10th 1968"The Social Results of the Gospel" appeared in the Holmfirth Express. My typewriter clicked away at Cherith producing columns headed "The light in the valley", "The great mistake" "Through outer space" "Man's shorn God" "Under new management" "The greatest victory in the world" "Not done in a corner" "Heaven's cure for earth's care" "God and the sparrow" "The Divine dilemma" "Not such an old fogey" "The printers theology" "Without help" "Good will" "Wit's end corner"

I had popped into the "Express" office one morning to drop in another article when the editor invited me to have a coffee with him.

"David" he smiled, "your articles have stirred up a hornet's nest. The

Anglican vicar from one of the village churches has been in to see me demanding to know who is writing the Christian columns for the Express. He has checked out with all the local clergy and none of them are writing them. He therefore assumes that the writer must be a layman. It is not the responsibility of a lay person to be enjoying a public platform through the newspaper. He therefore wants your articles banned because he will ensure that the local clergy submit a suitable article each month"

"Really" I commented between sips of coffee, "at least someone is reading my column! What are you going to do about it?"

"Oh I have told him that the clergy are welcome to submit their material to me and I will consider it for publication, but their articles will not be instead of yours but in addition to yours. You see your own articles are being well received and will continue"

Not long after, I called at Nora Newton's and she broke into our conversation by handing me several of my own articles which had been cut from the Holmfirth Express.

"Please have a look at these, they are excellent. My sister has cut them out of the paper and passed them to me. She lives two or three miles away and she showed them to her vicar who was angry and forbade her to read them. He told her that the Bible is not intended to be interpreted that way"

I asked Mrs Newton the name of her sister's vicar, and immediately knew who had complained to the newspaper about me. He had only recently been inducted into that church and the Holmfirth Express had marked his arrival with a large picture of him on the front page. He was holding a bottle of whisky aloft in one hand, and with the other holding a glass of whisky to his lips. The caption beneath the picture bore the comment "Whisky drinking parson hits Holmfirth" I began to see what the editor really thought about him!

I confessed to Mrs Newton that I had written the articles and asked her to keep it to herself. As far as I was aware no-one else apart from the leaders of the little church knew the identity of Torchbearer.

It was whilst John Carter was still leading the church that I drove past the area's largest working men's club one Sunday night and was amazed how many cars were parked outside. I made enquiries and found that the relatively newly constructed building "Burn Lea WMC" had an auditorium which seated 400 people. I felt the same pressure which had prompted me to write articles for the local paper, the urge to somehow get the message of the Gospel to the people attending the Burn Lea concerts each Sunday evening. I had a word with John Carter and shared with him my intention. He was in favour of my making some kind of approach to seek the opportunity of some kind of Christian witness during the crowded Sunday evenings. A few Sunday evenings later I strode into the club, amazed at the size of the audience. An entertainer was midway through his act as I asked to see the concert secretary.

He took me to a quiet corner before asking how he could help me. I introduced myself saying that I was there on behalf of the Assemblies of God Church, and that possibly we could help him by providing a free act for the club. Our church were looking forward to a visit from Pastor David Philips in a few weeks' time. David was the pastor of Wakefield Pentecostal church twenty miles away, he was an extremely talented musician, playing the piano and the accordion, but he also had a lovely tenor voice. When he sang hymns and gospel songs he radiated the love and joy of God. If we could get David into the club to do a session the audience would have an unforgettable taste of what real Christianity is like.

The concert secretary gladly agreed to allow David to sing but on the condition that no preaching would be allowed.

"Oh that's fine" I responded," David would not dream of trying to do that whilst he is a guest here. All he will do is sing some gospel songs and explain what they mean."

That seemed perfectly acceptable and I promised to check out whether David Philips would be available and promised to confirm details later. So a few Sunday evenings later two or three of us took David to "Burn Lea" after our church service, and wished him all the best as he left us to go backstage.

There was a twenty minute interval so that drinks could be enjoyed and then David was "on". He had a very flexible expressive face and a unique sense of humour, I imagined David on stage, behind the curtain waiting to be introduced. Suddenly the curtains began to twitch and a small gap appeared through which David's neck and beaming face appeared.

He beamed at the audience before one of his hands thrust his accordion through another gap in the curtains. Suddenly an unseen hand pulled him back to be hidden behind the heavy stage curtains.

There was a drum roll as the concert secretary walked onto the stage saying "Ladies and gentlemen, please welcome David Philips." Then the curtains opened and David was standing there, still beaming and still holding his accordion.

Grinning at the audience and pointing at the concert secretary, he said "Don't blame me, it's all his fault. He told me to go and stand in front of the curtain. He should have told me to stand behind the curtain, he really needs sorting out" The audience loved it, he was "in" and they hung onto his every word. Four hundred people felt a Presence they had probably never felt before in a working men's club.

We were invited back to the club and we obtained a spot for Paul Lowe who was the organist at David Philip's church in Wakefield. Paul was an absolute genius on the Hammond organ and he often played at the Assemblies of God conferences which attracted several thousand people each May at Butlins Minehead. The Burn Lea resident organist had just done his spot when he came and sat next to his wife immediately in front of me in the audience. He leaned towards his wife and said very patronisingly, " We are in for a good laugh. Paul Lowe is a Hammond organ man, he is not used to playing a Wurlitzer. He asked me to familiarise him with all the controls. I told him that he reckons to be a good organist so he can sort it out for himself." He then settled back waiting for Paul to make a fool of himself.

Paul excelled himself. During "Roll Jordan roll" we could hear the water lapping against the river bank, we could hear the wind whistling in the reeds, we could almost see the water surface disturbed by the squalls of wind. During "The gospel train is coming" we could hear the wheels clicking over the gaps in the steel track, we could hear the train whistle gradually becoming louder as the train approached. We could almost smell the steam and the smoke. The sheer entertainment value of Paul's musicianship made the audience eager to listen as he explained what each song meant to him.

So there were several very profitable visits to the working men's club. We felt privileged to be able to take the witness of the church right into the heart of the hard working community, we treasured the opportunities and would never have acted in a way which would have spoiled our position of trust. However events beyond our control brought these visits to an end. We had the opportunity to visit another working men's club in the town. This was not as modern as Burn Lea and the members were all seated at tables enjoying their drinks as the entertainers performed. The tables accommodated either four or six people and it contributed to a less formal atmosphere. Tonight was their Harvest Festival Special and the produce donated by the members was auctioned off for charity. Then David had the freedom of the stage having been asked to perform for about 45 minutes. Because of the occasion, David began with a powerful rendition of "Great is Thy faithfulness" before delivering a song called "A tent or a cottage" which was a lovely reminder that the Christian can look forward to a glorious future life.

David began to sing a lovely song with Swedish origins, "How great Thou art" There was a radiance emanating from him as he sang his way through the verses.

Oh Lord my God, when I in awesome wonder,
Consider all the worlds Thy hands have made.
I see the stars, I hear the rolling thunder,
Thy power throughout the universe displayed.
Then sings my soul my Saviour God to Thee,
How great Thou art, how great Thou art.
Then sings my soul, my Saviour God to Thee,
How great Thou art, how great Thou art.
When through the woods and forest glades I wander,
And hear the birds sing sweetly in the trees,
When I look down from lofty mountain grandeur
And see the brook and feel the gently breeze.
Then sings my soul etc.
And when I think that God His Son not sparing,
Sent him to die, I scarce can take it in
That on the cross my burden gladly bearing,
He bled and died to take away my sin.
Then sings my soul etc.
When Christ shall come with shout of acclamation,
And take me home, what joy shall fill my heart,

Then I shall bow in humble adoration, and then proclaim.
My God how great Thou art.

Then sings my soul etc.

David Playle and I were standing at the back of the club with our backs leaning against the wall when there was a dramatic change in the atmosphere in the hall. As David was singing about God's son dying on the cross, I felt that a hand had brushed upwards at the back of my head disturbing my hair. Suddenly I had the powerful feeling that every hair was standing on end and I began trembling. Pastor Playle turned to me asking,

"Do you feel as though all your hairs are standing on end?" I nodded my reply before whispering to him, "Look at the audience, what's happening?"

Some powerful Dynamic had entered the room. At every table mature, hard-working unemotional working men and women were weeping. They were wiping their eyes, they had their handkerchiefs to their faces and some were sobbing could not control their feelings. David and I knew that the Holy Spirit was working powerfully in the room.

Sam, the club president strode up to me and as he pointed at David Philips who was still singing, he said "Stop him, the audience has had enough. It's getting late and they want to go home"

In obedience to Sam I strode onto the stage to speak to David, "David, Sam wants you to stop. He says they have had enough." David smiled at me and replied, "Sam is no longer in control here tonight, and come to think of it neither am I. I could give a Billy Graham style appeal tonight and people would come forward."

I had carried Sam's message to the stage so returned to the back of the hall. David, still with his fingers on the accordion keys beamed at the audience as he said,

"Well, that's it. That's your lot. I was asked to sing for 45 minutes, I have sung for about 10 minutes but Sam says you have had enough, and Sam is the boss!"

The audience began shouting "Sing some more, sing some more."

David glanced at Sam and beamed at him. Sam trying to keep his dignity and trying to show that he was in charge replied, "Oh, OK just sing one verse of another song to finish."

The audience were not content with Sam's demand and began to shout, "Sing it all, sing every verse."

So David sang another song in its entirety before closing down our visit. Somehow we all felt that there would be no more opportunities to visit the clubs. The presence of God had descended upon the audience. They had been touched moved and impacted but they had demonstrated that they still wanted more. As we left the building I reflected upon similar incidents recorded in the gospels when the common people (the working class people) heard Jesus gladly, but those who thought that they were in authority tried to restrict and resist what Jesus was doing.

Life at Cherith was hectic and demanding, my work with The Prudential was full time with unsocial working hours. We had lots of visitors, some unexpected. Edith had the marvellous gift of always being on top of everything. It did not seem to matter how many unexpected visitors arrived, before long there was a great meal for them. Edith was unflappable, and had the gift of making everyone feel so welcome. She has been my rock for very many happy years.

Life at Cherith was about to become busier! We had a phone call from the adoption society in London. They had a six weeks old baby girl available for us to adopt. We were invited to their offices to see her and discuss how we felt once we had seen the little baby girl. Keith Monument kindly offered to meet us at King's Cross Station and drive us to the Mission of Hope. We drove to Lincolnshire and spent the night at Edith's parents before leaving our car at Grantham station next morning and boarding the train for London. It was the Christmas period and Keith took us to a Chinese Restaurant in Croydon and Edith, Joy, myself and Keith enjoyed a lovely Christmas meal before Keith drove us to the adoption centre. The short time we spend there is one of the highlights of our married life. The adoption secretary wanted Joy to be the first to see the tiny baby. We heard later that had the staff seen any sign of rejection in Joy's face, we would not have been allowed to bring the baby girl away with us. So Joy was taken to see the baby, and then came back to lead us into the room where baby Deborah was lying in her carry cot. We were smitten and once the paperwork had been cleared, we were proudly leaving the building, no longer a family of three but a proud family of four. Keith saw baby Deborah before our parents saw her, and for very many years showed an interest in Joy and Deborah's welfare. Road traffic was bad and Keith was not sure that he could get us back to King's Cross in time for our train so he took us to the underground where we scurried along , me learning again how to carry a young baby safely.

A few days after receiving the life changing phone call from the adoption society we were back at Cherith with the added responsibility of a new baby, and with another family member to love and cherish. Joy felt special because she had met Deborah before we did, and she helped mother the addition to our family. Deborah brought us nothing but joy and happiness.

Keith had seen my articles in the Holmfirth Express and I believe that he showed one to the editor of Redemption Tidings, the official weekly magazine of the Assemblies of God Churches. The editor, Aaron Linford asked me to consider writing a weekly article for a year under the general heading "Minute Message.", Some of the articles used in the Holmfirth Express appeared in Redemption Tidings, but in the main complete new material had to be written. The typewriter had to be silent too when Deborah was asleep!

Life was very fulfilling at Cherith, such a lot happened in four short years. However the sun was already beginning to set over our sojourn there.

# Moving On

Whilst living in Holmfirth we had been building two lives. Edith's parents lived in a sleepy Lincolnshire market town, where we were frequent visitors... We loved the place, we loved the area, we loved the almost balmy climate, we loved the people, we loved the little church which we were a part of during our frequent forays into "yellow belly" territory. When we came home from a winter visit to Lincolnshire, we always felt cold and had the real feeling that the Holmfirth climate was being hostile to us. So we spent as much time in Lincolnshire as we could.

I had always enjoyed good health, unlike Edith who had coped with a heart condition from childhood. Since moving to Holmfirth I had felt really ill most winters. It was the damp cold atmosphere. It was a breeding ground for bronchitis and chest diseases. When the area was in the grip of an especially cold and damp spell I struggled with breathlessness and severe headaches. I remember days when simply walking on the stone pavement was painful. Each time I planted my foot on the ground there was a heavy thumping in my head as though I was being beaten by a lump of wood.

Doctor Finney was rolling up his stethoscope as he pronounced, "Mr Robinson, you will not reach retirement age unless you leave this area." I remembered hearing him say to the overweight Uncle Joe, "I see you are still digging your grave with your teeth Jo." And he died shortly after! At that moment the smiling corn fields of Lincolnshire where there was perpetual sunshine beckoned even more insistently.

Edith and I decided that I would ask the Prudential to transfer me to Lincolnshire, to the very same town where Edith's parents were living. I was not looking forward to telling Redfearn Rogers, my manager, that I wanted to move to Lincolnshire, but I made an appointment to see him and put my request before him.

"David" he smiled, "I fully understand your reasons but can you wait until after I have retired? I will leave the way open for you to move then."

"I am sorry Mr Rogers, but our minds are made up, we want to go as soon as possible and I don't want to spend another winter here if it can be avoided."

"OK David, leave it with me. I will do it officially and ask our Divisional Office at Leeds to approach Lincolnshire's Divisional Office which is in Nottingham. I am sure you will be hearing from me."

The days passed into weeks and the weeks into months and there was no news. We were in Lincolnshire taking a week's holiday there and had gone shopping to Grantham. Seeing the Prudential office on the High Street I decided to call in and speak with the manager. His secretary beamed at me as she pointed to the manager's office door and said "Mr Hill will see you now sir"

Mr Hill made me feel so much at home and I explained the purpose of my visit. "That's right, you want to live and work in the Sleaford area which comes under my office here in Grantham. The strange thing is this David, I have had two vacancies and they have both been offered to you through the official channels but I was informed each time that you were not interested so someone else was offered the position."

"Really! I knew nothing about that, at no time have I been informed that you had offered a vacancy to me."

Mr Hill expressed surprise at my news before continuing "I would really like to have you as one of my staff, the problem is that we don't get many vacancies and it may be a long time before another opportunity arises."

I really liked Mr Hill and felt that here was a manager I could work well with, it was a pity that such a chance had been denied me.

We had a mid-week meeting at the little Sleaford church on the Wednesday night, and I shared my experience with Jim, one of the members. Jim happened to be the branch manager of a rival insurance company and he was also based in Grantham. He just happened to have a vacancy there in Sleaford.

"Come and work for me David "he pleaded. "And within three or four years you could be a branch manager earning so many thousand pounds a year."

"Why would I want your branch manager's salary in three or four years Jim, I am earning that kind of money now!!"

A cunning plan was brewing however. I completed an application form for employment with Jim's company and was formally offered the position. I then applied to the Halifax Building Society for a mortgage to buy a house in Sleaford giving Redfearn Rogers as the person to write to for confirmation of earnings. Then I waited

We had concluded our holiday and I was back at my duties in Holmfirth when Redfearn Rogers rang.

"David, I can't understand what's going on. I have received a letter from The Halifax Building Society asking for a reference. It appears that you are buying a house in Sleaford. How can you live in Sleaford and continue to work here?"

"I can't Mr Rogers. I have applied for a job with the Royal Liver, they have a vacancy in Sleaford."

Mr Rogers conceded defeat, "David, if you are going to Sleaford with or without the Prudential, I will make sure that it is the Prudential that you go with. Leave it to me".

I declined the offer of employment with the Royal Liver and cancelled the Halifax mortgage application. Within a few weeks Reg Hill rang me from Grantham "David, this is out of the blue but we have a vacancy actually in Sleaford. The Prudential agent there has decided to become a self-employed insurance broker, you can have his agency if you are still interested. The next step needs to be an interview with Mr Robberts, the Divisional Manager in Nottingham. He is very particular who he allows to transfer into his Division."

"That's great Mr Hill, what's the next step?"

Mr Hill told me to speak to my own branch manager who would make all the arrangements. Within a few days I was being interviewed by Mr Robberts in Nottingham. He concluded the interview by saying "Welcome to my Division. You will find it a lot different to Holmfirth. I am putting you under a personal obligation to me not to let me down."

Five years later I was sitting in the same office again being congratulated by Mr Robberts as he promoted me to Section Superintendent in Cleethorpes.

The sun was setting quickly! We needed to sell Cherith and property was taking a long time to sell in the area. I could not believe what Redfearn Rogers was telling me when he rang me a couple of days later. One of the Section Superintendents in the District was unhappy in his job and wanted to revert to being a Prudential agent. He wanted to buy Cherith and take over my area from me.

At a difficult time to sell property, we sold within days and without the cost of an estate agent. We sold for £3300 which was £300 more than we had paid for Cherith.

To conclude my five years in Holmfirth a process of auditing every policyholder's premium receipt books was necessary. David Hodge my Section Superintendent would work with me for two to three full weeks in order to conduct the audit. The presence of a superior checking up on me could set the local jungle drums beating out the message that something was wrong, especially as within a few weeks I would have left! So I prepared by informing selected clients that I had successfully applied for a transfer to Lincolnshire and that David would be carrying out my final audit. I knew the folk, and knew full well that merely by telling a selected number of people that I was moving on, the word would spread. Years later when I was a Superintendent with the Prudential, my District manager mentioned one of my team to me by name and informed me how to use him. "David "he smiled, "if there is anything you want making public but don't want to do it yourself, just tell him in confidence. The whole District will then know within twenty four hours."

I can't remember ever taking advantage of the team gossip in this way, although if I wanted to know what was going on, I asked him and was never disappointed at the level of information he gave.

So when I arrived with David Hodge at what was to be my final visit to those homes, the people were forewarned. Some of them were forearmed too. One gentleman handed me a five pound note as he said, "Thank you David for all you have done for us these last five years. Have a drink on us."

"Oh that's very kind" I responded, "but I am afraid that I can't accept your kind gift. If you look in your premium receipt book you will find that Prudential representatives are not allowed to accept any financial reward for services rendered."

Quick as a flash, David Hodge interjected, "Yes that's right. However there is nothing to prevent you dropping the five pounds note on the floor so that Mr Robinson can pick it up on his way out!" So a few minutes later I was five pounds better off.

It was surprising how many policyholders handed me a farewell gift, usually wrapped in a paper bag. The majority of the gifts were candles of all colours and fragrances. Laughingly I remarked to David Hodge, "Do they all think that I am going to darkest Africa David? We are only going to Lincolnshire." A few days later I regretted that remark when David and his wife Dorothy handed me a gift they had bought for me. They had invited me to their home for coffee and as David handed me my leaving present he said, "It's OK to open it now David"

Imagine my surprise when inside the wrapping was a high powered torch. David added, " We thought it would be useful if you get lost in a twenty acre field." Before leaving the area I discovered the source of the candles I had received as gifts. There were some candle making classes being held in Holmfirth and a great many of the ladies were attending.

My final audit went like a dream. A few months after commencing duties in Sleaford the UK changed to decimal currency. I received a lovely letter from Redfearn Rogers letting me know that due to my excellent preparations and accurate accounting, decimalisation of my Holmfirth agency had been very straightforward.

Once my transfer to Sleaford was confirmed I made yet another call to the removal company who had already moved us twice. "Hello, it's me again, the man with the pianola. Will you move us again, to Lincolnshire?"

So the sun was setting on our life in Holmfirth. It would soon rise upon us as we enjoyed the balmy climate of Lincolnshire.

# Sleaford

Slightly more than five years had passed since meeting Walter Slater on my very first day with the Prudential Assurance Company. Now I am driving out to a Lincolnshire village to meet my new Superintendent, Jim Adams who would be my immediate boss. I was counting my blessings as I considered the circumstances of the opportunity I had stepped into. One Prudential agent had held the territory for very many years and two years ago he had retired. A young man took over the agency but after only two years decided to become a self-employed insurance broker. This created a vacancy in the exact area we wished to live in. Then another blessing was the generosity of Edith's parents who had suggested that we live with them until we had found and bought a suitable house. So our furnishings were in storage we were enjoying temporary accommodation so that I could commence duties immediately and then begin looking for a house.

This should also have been a day when Mr Adams counted his blessings, he was introducing to the policyholders a new agent who would not need any training. Had I been a Section Superintendent at that time and within two or three years of retirement, the last thing I would want was the challenge of teaching the job to a raw recruit. Here was I, already with five years successful service under my belt, raring to go without the need for a great deal of investment in management time. If Jim was pleased, he did not show it. He had a completely different attitude to Walter Slater who in spite of being a disciplinarian had a soft core and a user friendly aura. To use a Prudential expression, Walter was a boss I could take anywhere. He was at home in a humble cottage, he was at ease with a company director, he was comfortable discussing Prudential business with a research chemist. His approach and attitude was such that he was accepted and welcomed by all, high and low. If he had failed to make a sale he still held his cool.

One of the first things I discovered about Jim was that I could not take him everywhere. He could be a gentleman, but he could have a sharp arrogant edge which did not endear him to my clients. I took him one evening to an appointment I had made to discuss an endowment policy which was maturing. A brass plate beside the front door of the immaculate bungalow informed us who we were visiting, "Squadron Leader Kenneth Gibson. (Retired)"

The door opened and a pleasant middle aged gentleman smiled at us as he was about to invite us in. Jim greeted him "Good evening Mr Gibson."

The exchange of greetings completely took me by surprise, our client barked, "Squadron Leader Gibson if you don't mind!"

Jim responded hotly, "I have news for you Mr Gibson, I am not in the RAF so you are not my squadron leader, and you are not in the RAF either, you have retired. You are just a common erk like anyone else, so as far as I am concerned you are just Mr Gibson"

Squadron Leader Gibson stepped out of his bungalow onto the path closing the door behind him,   "Mr Robinson and I can manage perfectly well without you Mr Adams. We don't need you in your expensive suits. Mr Robinson will call on his own to see me so good bye"

I did make another appointment to see Squadron Leader Gibson, he was delighted with the performance of his maturing policy and I was able to arrange a new policy for him. He was pleased with the outcome, but was also pleased that any commission I had earned that evening was mine and mine alone and none of it helped to keep Mr Adams in expensive suits! The truth is though that had Jim Adams made the sale I would still have received exactly the same commission, when he accompanied me he was working for me and on my behalf. Clients always suspected that his involvement disadvantaged me. In an ideal situation, the Superintendents attendance should be an advantage to me. They had far more experience and expertise and very often sold a larger policy than the agent would have done had he been working alone.

I had another appointment to take Jim to see Larry who lived in the same village. Larry was expecting us but we were a minute or two early, as we walked down the path to his council house we saw Larry in the garden. He had prodded a straight line of holes in the soil and was popping seeds into the holes. He smiled as he welcomed us, "Hello, I will just finish this row of seeds and be with you in a minute."

Jim exploded, "You might have the common courtesy to stop what you are doing when the Superintendent  from The Prudential comes to see you!"

Larry exploded too, "Clear off, Mr Robinson does not need you living off his back. He will come back on his own and do business with me."

I learned a lot in those days! There are lessons even in the most negative experiences. When I became a Section Superintendent a few years later, I walked into some situations which made me think "What would Jim Adams have done?" then I would do the opposite.

One of the positives Jim had to offer was his historic knowledge of many of the clients and from time to time I was able to draw on this to my advantage.

When I took over my agency it did not include the RAF camp. I used to drive past the camp on my way to one of the villages I served and I looked at the row upon row of concrete type houses and felt sorry for the Prudential agent who looked after the camp, it looked so cold and sterile. However a couple of years after I started duties in Lincolnshire I was asked to take over the camp in exchange for a small village on the outer edge of my territory. It appeared that the agent who looked after the camp did not seem to be able to obtain much new business there and it had become a pressure to him. I agreed to the exchange and never had any regrets.

I had taken over a whole new list of customers and it would take me time to get to know them. Only a few weeks after taking over the camp, Mrs Lines, a client I had only met briefly rang me. She wanted to cash surrender a policy as she needed some money, but she would take out another one. I was working with Jim that evening so arranged to take him with me. Jim conducted the discussions with Mrs Lines, I was not really aware what was going on as I was in conversation with her two very talkative children. Jim took all the paperwork for the new policy home with him, and gave me the paperwork for claiming the surrender value to deal with. Less than a week later I was able to call and pay Mrs Lines quite a nice sum of money, and a couple of weeks later delivered the new policy which was on her husband's life. Mr Lines was serving in the RAF.

A few months later I had a phone call from my District Manager, Reg Hill had retired and Lou Winterton was now in charge of the District. Mr Winterton said that he needed to speak to me concerning a very delicate issue. He informed me that Mr Lines had died suddenly and that the RAF Welfare Officer was acting on the widow's behalf. The Prudential had refused to pay the death claim on the basis that information had been withheld from the proposal form which Mrs Lines had signed. Mr Winterton told me that when Jim had completed the proposal form for the new policy, Mr Lines was serving with the RAF in Cyprus but Jim had signed that he had seen Mr Lines that day and he appeared to be in good health. In truth, Mr Lines had developed heart problems quite a while before and had been on sick leave for quite a while. He was on medication which had not been declared on the proposal form and had been moved to a less demanding job in Cyprus. Due to the school needs of the children Mrs Lane had chosen to remain in their RAF house here in Lincolnshire.

Here were the issues, Mrs Lines had told the RAF Welfare Officer that she had told Mr Adams about the medication and that her husband was working in Cyprus. She had told him about the sick leave and had added that Mr Adams had written all this down on notepaper, and that more importantly, she had signed a blank proposal form having been assured that the form would be completed later with the information she had given. The Welfare Officer was challenging Prudential's decision.

Mr Winterton's question to me was "Is what Mrs Lines has said true. Think very carefully before you answer."

"I am sorry Mr Winterton, I remember the visit but I was in constant conversation with the two children and did not hear the discussions Mrs Lines and Jim had."

It appeared that the Welfare Officer had obtained a photocopy of the proposal form from Prudential's Chief Office and was threatening to inform one of the national Sunday papers about the situation. An appointment had been made for Jim to be interviewed by the RAF Welfare Officer, and Mr Winterton wanted me to go along as a witness before reporting back to him.

"Can't you go Sir?" Would that not be more appropriate?"

"David, I need to keep on the side-lines at the moment, my job is to gather the facts and report back to Chief Office, will you go along with Jim?"

So a few days later Jim and I were waiting outside the Welfare Office on the RAF camp. The officer had served in the RAF but was now a civilian. He was a slim, athletic looking man and his opening comments were pleasant enough.

There was an immediate heated confrontation, Jim announced that he thought that the Welfare Officer deserved a good pasting and that if he was a few years younger he would knock him out.

The Welfare Officer asked Jim to be careful what he said adding that he was an RAF boxing champion. Jim not wanting to clamber down from his attacking position threatened that he had sorted out better men than him. There was very little productive discussion during the meeting and we were shown the door. I reported back to my District Manager and a few days later I was informed that we were paying the death claim in full. Soon after one of the other Section Superintendents retired and the vacant area was more suited geographically to Jim so he transferred across to it. I had little or nothing to do with him after that. He had been with the company for very many years and to remain in his position for so long he must have given excellent service. I wish that I had known him when he was younger, he may have shown a different attitude then. How little we know though what is really going on in someone's life. Jim may have been facing and coping with issues which made him act out of character and I would rather give him the benefit of the doubt. I am grateful though for a succinct saying from the Old Book, which advises "A soft answer turns away wrath."

During the honeymoon period when I was new to the RAF camp I had a couple of unforgettable experiences. Ron, who had previously been the agent for the camp rang me to pass on a prospect for some new life assurance. Mrs Broadley, the wife of a squadron leader had contacted him asking for him to call and see her husband. Ron passed the enquiry to me but warned me, "David, I don't know how long you would usually expect the appointment to last, but you need to be prepared to be there at least twice as long. Squadron Leader Broadley , who is a lovely man has the worst stutter I have ever heard and it will take you a long time."

I made a suitable appointment by phoning Mrs Broadley and rang the doorbell at the allotted time and Squadron Leader Bill Broadley opened to door. I broke every rule in the book by prompting him as he tried to speak.

" K K K K K K K " he began.

"Come in?" I prompted. Soon we had shaken hands and I was sitting in the kitchen.

" K K K K K K K K K K "continued my host.

"Cup of coffee" I prompted, "Yes please"

The next half hour was difficult, Mr Broadley was alone and I tried not to look him in the face as he was trying to explain to me what he wanted. After what seemed a very long time he had made himself understood, then Mrs Broadley came in from work. He poured her a hot drink before sitting down beside her at the kitchen table. I introduced myself to her and she slid her arm across his shoulder and smiled at him. His stuttering was greatly reduced and conversation became more normal. Ron had been correct. I too had never heard such a bad stutter. I was completely ignorant concerning RAF job roles. In my naivety I thought that a squadron leader was the person who shouted SCRAMBLE as he ordered the planes to take off to deal with some dire emergency. I later found out that not all squadron leaders flew planes! As I drove away I smiled at the thought that by the time Squadron Leader Broadley had managed to shout "Scramble" the emergency would be over.

I was back at the home a few weeks later delivering the new policy and Mrs Broadley was alone, "Please come in David, Bill is delayed at a meeting. By the way please call us Sue and Bill, you don't mind if we call you David do you?" I was enjoying a hot drink with Sue when I asked her "What exactly is Bill's trade in the RAF?"

I was not expecting her response, "Oh Bill lectures in aerial warfare at the college. By report he is the best lecturer they have ever had."

"Good for him Sue, how does he manage?"

"Well, you know that Bill is Welsh, when he is lecturing he uses his sing song voice and he almost sings his words. People don't stutter when they are singing. He has problems though if someone asks a question. If his flow is interrupted he has difficulty starting again. So he comes out with a swear word and thumps the lectern. People don't stutter over swear words you know."

I felt a rush of admiration for Bill. What struggles he must have faced as he pursued his career, how many knock backs had he dealt with. How many times had he been laughed at, how many times had he thought of giving up the pursuit of his dream?

A few months later Bill's welsh origins were manifestly apparent. I had called at their home to be told that Bill was in the lounge and I should go through to him. He was standing there with stereo headphones on his head, in front of him on the mantelpiece was the sleeve of a long playing record. It was a record of five thousand male welsh voices singing hymns in the Royal Albert Hall. Bill was conducting the huge choir passionately, there were tears in his eyes, and he was singing at the top of his voice, flawlessly!

# Derek Murphy

Just a few hundred yards from the centre of the stately old Lincolnshire town, nestling behind the filling station and a farm implement showroom was the caravan park. It was so near the bustling hub of the busy market place yet so secluded and quiet that it would have been the ideal place to live, except for one thing- it was as the locals said "a bit on the rough side".

The site, holding twenty or thirty aged touring caravans was on a former paddock. The walk into the town centre took only two or three minutes and crossed two bridges which straddled the clear waters of the river from which the town derived its name in Roman times. The river divided into two just outside the town and flowed beneath the two old bridges, long strands of green streamer weed flowing in the strong current.

Whatever time you crossed the bridge, trout and grayling could be seen sporting in the crystal clear water. Sometimes they would just lie motionless, mouths facing upstream waiting to receive any particles of food brought down to them. Some of the trout were quite large, three to four pounds in weight and visitors to the town found them a fascinating and unexpected sight so near the busy shops.

Of course fishing was not permitted in the town centre but a local angling club held the fishing rights just outside the town boundary. I would walk Suzie our little terrier dog along the banks at night watching the trout rising and the occasional grayling, the "lady of the stream" sporting in the cool water. One lovely mellow autumn evening I watched a huge grayling just a few feet away from the supporting timbers of the old wooden foot bridge. The beautiful fish was motionless except for the fronds of the huge dorsal fin on the centre of her back which rippled gently in the current. I watched her for a few minutes and then pointed her out to an elderly angler, obviously a gentleman farmer. He looked every inch a seasoned angler in his Harris tweed plus fours and fly fisherman's hat which was decorated with flies of all colours and sizes.

I excitedly showed him where the fish was lying and as he thanked me with a tremor of excitement in his voice I was regretting that I had disclosed the resting place of the magnificent fish.

"She's a beauty " he whispered, "must be four or five pounds. I'll have her!"

His old fingers trembled as he cast his fly several feet upstream of the motionless fish. We both held our breath watching anxiously as the tempting morsel floated down towards the waiting fish She ignored it completely, so he tried again, and again. Each time the fly floated over her back on its journey downstream. . For at least ten minutes I crouched in the willows watching my angler friend pitting his skill against the cautious fish. He was not having much luck.

Suzie began to get restless and just as I was thinking of moving on the grand old fish seized the fly, and feeling the hook, leapt out of the water shaking its head angrily but it knew just what to do. Knowing from past experience that there was safety beneath the old bridge, she plunged amongst the old timbers snagging the line tightly against one of the wooden posts. She was safe and our angler friend was beaten. The fine line attached to the fly snapped, the heavy fly line wafted back to the angler in the breeze. He swore gently as he retrieved his line.

I strolled away, secretly glad that the lovely fish was still free and feeling guilty that I had betrayed her resting place to the tweed clad angler who called after me,

"I'll be back tomorrow night, I'll take her then..

Yes, all this went on within a few minutes of the local caravan site, it was as I have said, an ideal place to live if it were not quite so rough and run down. In fact the locals regarded it as the nearest thing they had to a slum and were suspicious of anyone who happens to live in one of its decaying old caravans.

The caravan park did provide the opportunity for some unfortunate people to find a roof over the head, even though it was a tin roof. The site became a resting place for homeless people and provided a low cost place to live if you did not mind the stigma bearing such an address brought. They all had one thing in common, they had fallen on hard times and needed somewhere to live, or perhaps they had chosen to live apart from husband, wife or parents preferring independence in a caravan.

Some of the old vans had been repainted in gaudy colours, some were streaked with decades of green algae, most of them boasted a broken window temporarily repaired with a piece of cardboard or plywood. Outside some of the vans, old cars were parked, not many of them were complete. Most had wheels missing and were propped up on bricks. The piles of rotting tyres and rusting metal grew week by week until there was sufficient to make a visit to the scrap yard worth while.

Some of the local "characters" lived here and the police were frequent visitors to the community. In the main the folk lived peaceably and I was quite happy to walk across the site in the darkness of night. I never felt threatened or afraid. In fact I enjoyed visiting here.

I am not sure why I enjoyed this, maybe it was because the people were so different. They were all open hearted and warm when a visitor came, and I don't expect that they got that many! They did not stand on ceremony. If they had no money they told you so, usually with a few mild expletives. If they had money in their pockets they paid me. On a hot summer evening there was always the offer of a long cool drink or a steaming hot mug of coffee and a seat near the gas fire on a cold winter night.. But they were all colourful characters and they made up a rather unique and interesting community.

I had to see two or three clients tonight and find Derek Murphy who had a couple of small policies with Prudential and who had moved to live here. The main problem was that his previous representative did not know the number of the caravan Derek had moved into. Ah well, I would just have to knock on a few doors until I tracked him down.

Business and coffee finished, I picked up my brief case as I prepared to leave the first client I had visited that night. As I was leaving I quizzed,

"By the way, I need to look someone up whilst I am on the site but I don't know the number of his caravan. I don't suppose you know where Derek Murphy lives, I think he has only just moved here?"

The young fellow gave a knowing grin as he replied,

"Oh Mucky Murphy ! You don't have to visit him do you? Still I suppose it takes all sorts. That's his van look over there and the best of luck mate"

Already beginning to wonder just what kind of challenge faced me in Mucky Murphy's caravan, I hastened across the grass towards his door. I rapped on the door and then took a step backwards as I waited for a reply.

The door swung open widely and a young man of about twenty three years of age stood there. He was splendidly attired in a pair of dirty well worn socks and a long white vest which fortunately reached almost to his knees. There is a fair amount of poetic licence in using the word "white" to describe the young man's vest. In the misty days of yore it had perhaps been white. Now it was dirty grey, several shades of very dirty grey with multitudinous stains marking the spot where unidentified dollops of food had dropped like multicoloured bird droppings released from a great height.

The grey vest matched the equally grey stiff stained table cloth and matching curtains I could see through the open door. I smiled at him as I asked,

"Mr Murphy?"

Through the grey green teeth came the friendly reply,

"Yes mate, I'm Derek Murphy. Who wants him?"

"I'm Dave Robinson your local agent for the Prudential Assurance Company. Welcome to my patch Mr Murphy"

I held out my hand to grasp his hand, and then began to think that perhaps this was not such a good idea but it was too late to change my mind. He grasped my hand in his greasy palm as I greeted him.

"Come in mate" Derek grinned, "Welcome just call me Derek, everyone else does."

As I followed Derek into the dismal little caravan my nostrils were assaulted by a sickening cocktail of the foulest of smells. I was so unprepared for the severity of this attack that I almost retched. What on earth was it? There was the familiar cocktail of stale food beer and cigarettes packaged together with stale sweat and urine. But there was a stronger smell than all these clamouring to be noticed and assaulting my nostrils with a vengeance, what on earth was it?

"What's the smell Derek?"

Derek grinned cheerfully back at me "It's my supper cooking in the pan"

On the greasy gas cooker stood a foul looking pan encrusted with grime and questionable looking residues from past suppers. The gas was burning fiercely and whatever was in the pan was bubbling and gurgling. The loose fitting lid rose and fell like evil bellows breathing forth a pungent smelling steam and allowing an evil looking liquid to spill over splashing into the gas flame.

I could not resist taking hold of the lid and lifting it to have a peep into the pan I whispered,

"What is it?"

The muddy water frothed and bubbled and whatever was soon to be eaten at supper kept appearing at the top of the witches brew. Pieces of flesh, bits of fur then a rabbit's ear rose up of the of depths . In disbelief I gazed transfixed as suddenly two eyes appeared in the foam and appeared to stare right at me. Derek took a spoon and began to stir the evil broth. Dark looking entrails coiled around the spoon like a snake and the smell belched out with a new lease of life.

"What is it?" I questioned huskily.

Derek grinned, obviously proud of his skill as a chef.

"Rabbit! I have been doing some casual work helping to get the harvest in. The rabbit got sucked up into the combined harvester and made chips of itself. Its too good to throw away though, it will make me a good meal."

"Really" I muttered incredulously.

Derek enthused, "It was a bit mushed up like and so I couldn't clean out its innards or skin it so I am boiling the whole lot to make a stew like. There will be lots of goodness in it. You are welcome to have some, will you stay and have some?"

I thanked him for his generous offer as I declined politely. My own meal would be waiting for me and I did not want to spoil it.

"Maybe some other time Derek" I said as we passed through the kitchen into the main part of Derek's little home. It was a lounge and a bedroom rolled into one with a black and white television in one corner . The bed took up the rest of the space and I wondered where Derek stood when he dressed and undressed. He had to lie on the bed so that I had room whilst I sat beside him to check his documents.

It was whilst Derek was reclining on the bed that I discovered he was not wearing anything under his grubby vest but he seemed quite unabashed whilst he paid me his premiums.. I promised to call every month at the same time before making my escape through the evil smelling steam bath in the kitchenette.

I called at Derek's little home for several months and during this time Derek's two brothers moved in to live with him. They were carbon copies of Derek, dirty but cheerful and warm hearted. They would do anything to help anyone in need and were very popular with the other residents on the caravan site.

Life's greatest mystery for me at that time was how they all managed in such a confined space. In my imagination I saw them having to dress and undress one at a time whilst the other two brothers stayed safely in bed out of harm's way.

I learnt that they slept three to a bed and that they all roamed round the caravan dressed in a pair of socks and a grubby vests. The amazing thing about their vests was that they changed colour becoming gradually darker and more stained as the weeks went by. I came to the conclusion that they wore vests most of the time because due to limited space it was almost impossible to get fully dressed before it was time to undress again!

Whenever I visited them I was greeted by a hearty shout "Come in mate"

I would discover all three brothers lying in bed laughing at some comedy show on the television. They were so easy going that I think that I would have been made welcome even if I knocked on their door at midnight.

I happened to be on the site one afternoon when I noticed that their window was open and so I knocked on their door.

Derek's two brothers were lying in bed a commentary on the horse-racing was blasting out from the television. Between the two brothers, underneath the sheets was a third shape. Obviously Derek.

Raising my voice I shouted:-

"Come on Derek let's have your money" My demand fell on deaf ears.

"Derek, let's see the colour of your money" Still no reply, but egged on by the giggling of the two brothers I continued. "Come on Derek don't be rude stop hiding under the blanket. Lets see your face and let's have your money".

I was obviously the cause of a great deal of merriment. Derek's two brothers seemed to be enjoying this futile exchange. I was anxious to get my money and get on. Not to be outdone I grasped the questionable looking blanket just where I thought Derek's big toe was and squeezed hard.

"Come on Derek, I don't have all afternoon. If you don't pay up quickly I will pull the blanket off you."

The two brothers lapsed into uncontrollable fits of laughter but my threat was unheeded. Spurred on by a sudden rush of mischievous confidence I took hold of the blanket and with a defiant thrust whipped it clear of the bed.

Oh no. It was not Derek lying there between the brothers. It was a young lady absolutely naked.. She giggled as she announced,

"I am not Derek I am Pauline"

I had no idea who Pauline was but I quickly dropped the bed sheet back onto her I mumbled with embarrassment,

"Yes, I can see that.". But the only person who seemed to be embarrassed was me! Before I could think what to say next, one of Derek's brothers giggled as he informed me

"Derek is out but he has left his money and book for you they are in the kitchen near the cooker". Red faced and embarrassed I fled into the kitchen and as soon as I had located the money, I beat a hasty retreat As I passed by the open window of the caravan I could hear the girl and the two brothers laughing. They had not enjoyed themselves so much at someone else's expense for years!

A few weeks later I was travelling back from one of the outlying villages, happy that another long day was over and warm with the glow of success as I had made one or two excellent sales. Only one more quick collection to make from the owner of the petrol station on the main road below the RAF camp.

Rex, the owner of the filling station was a recently retired squadron leader, and with his wife ran the successful petrol and tyre depot under franchise from Esso. I was secretly envious that Rex had been able retire at such a young age with a good pension. They were far too young to simply do nothing, so they had taken on the busy petrol station which was the nearest one to the RAF camp which had been their final posting. Many of their customers were air force personnel and they were able to keep in touch with former colleagues . They obviously enjoyed what they were doing..

As my tank was getting low, I decided to call at Rex's, fill up my car and relieve him of some of his money at the same time.

"Fill her up Rex"  I smiled as I unscrewed the petrol cap and took my wallet out of my pocket..

"I don't think there is enough petrol in to get me home so she should take about 12 gallons".

 Rex and his German wife Inge, lived in a detached bungalow  in a quiet village two or three miles away, but as they were always at work I had an arrangement to call at their filling station during the day time.  I was glad at this opportunity to avoid having to visit them late in the evening.  Rex shouted across to his wife who was manning their cash register in the static caravan a few yards away which doubled as their office and rest room whilst they were at work

"Inge, would you mind bringing out our premium books and cheque book so that we can pay David whilst he is here".

I glanced across and saw that Inge was speaking to someone on the telephone.  The door opened and a young lady I had not seen before came out holding Rex's cheque book and premium books.  She smiled as she handed my the books but suddenly her smile faded and a worried look creased her pretty young  face.

Turning her back on Rex, she motioned me to step away from the car before pleading in a low whisper,

"Please don't tell mum and dad where you saw me"

Not understanding her I questioned her huskily,

"But where have I seen you?"

Blushing almost to the roots of her hair , she turned her eyes away from mine and she croaked almost inaudibly,"I'm Pauline!"

# Mr Dyson's Teeth

The neat lawns and gardens looked like a picture of a model village. They were obviously the pride and joy of their owners. The owners invested hours of their leisure time in painstaking planning and cultivating their picturesque flower beds and billiard table lawns.

The crazy paving path led to a small tidy semi detached house which was just as immaculate as the gardens which led to it. No matter how closely I scrutinised the gardens, I could not find a single weed anywhere or any task which seemed to have been overlooked.

This was the home of Mr and Mrs Dyson, a local childless couple in their late forties. They married whilst still in their late teens and their greatest regret was that they had not been blessed with children. They were both out at work all day and made up for this separation by doing everything together in the house and garden.

The inside of the red brick semi was just as neat and tidy as the well tended gardens. Not a blemish anywhere on the sparkling white paintwork, not a stray book magazine or item out of its place. The home was a little palace and it was obvious on my very first visit one summer evening that there were no pets or children to put the home and garden into disarray.

Mr Dyson was a cheerful soul whose brick red face bore testimony to the fact that he was an outdoor man. His pipe always drooped from the corner of his mouth and would begin to glow red as he enthused about his vegetable plot, his strawberries, his lush green lawns or how he had achieved the mirror like finish to the white gloss paint in his kitchen. He took an inordinate amount of pleasure from the simple things in life which revolved around Mrs Dyson, the love of his life and his house and garden.

He knew what it was to work hard for living, belonging to that valiant band of council workmen who could turn their hand to anything. I had seen him during the harsh grip of mid-winter shovelling snow from the streets in the town centre. He only paused briefly to rub his hands together to try to revive his chilled fingers.

I had seen him sweating by the road side during the heat of summer, laying paving slabs or erecting new road signs. One afternoon I was walking through the large council estate just a few hundred yards from the busy town centre when I heard him loudly calling my name,

"Hello David! How are you this fine day?"

I looked round in vain; he was nowhere to be seen.

"Up here!" he laughed.

Shifting my gaze towards the roof tops I spotted him. He was sitting across the ridge of a house roof, bucket of cement and trowel at the ready, replacing broken or missing ridge tiles. It really did seem that there were very few tasks at which he did not excel.

Mrs Dyson was a perfect match for him. She had a responsible job in the accounts department of the local seed merchants and keeping the domestic finances under control was effortless to her. Her skill as a home maker complimented her husband's skills as a gardener and DIY enthusiast.

I was almost at the back door when I realised that Mrs Dyson had already seen me approaching, she greeted me with a cheery,

"Come straight in duck!"

As I stepped into the kitchen the mouth watering smell of roast lamb and mint sauce tempted my taste buds. She was busy washing the dishes and Mr Dyson had gone upstairs to get out of his working clothes, but he had asked me to wait as he wanted to see me as he had something important to tell me.

I sat on one of the high stools at the kitchen bench and Mrs Dyson poured me a cup of steaming hot coffee before coming to sit beside me bringing with her a plate of chocolate biscuits. We sipped our drinks whilst Mrs Dyson chatted about her job and the weather and began to ask me how my family were. There was something different about her tonight, she seemed more animated than usual and her eyes were filled with excitement. I began to wonder what Mr Dyson's news was all about.

Before long Mr Dyson, surrounded by a fragrant cloud of whisky flake, beamed as he came and sat beside his wife at the kitchen bench. His freshly scrubbed face glowed like a red bulb as he drew on his pipe. He gave his wife a knowing look and she nudged him on his arm smiling as she poured him a coffee. There was obviously something good on their minds, no doubt as soon as the stage is set, they will share their news with me.

A broad smile crease Mr Dyson's face as he made his announcement,

"We are going to have a baby and we want you to be the first to know!"

Mrs Dyson enthused,

"We had given up all hope. We have always wanted children but it has never happened for us. Now when we are old enough to be grandparents we are going to have our first baby!"

I was genuinely happy for them and offered my congratulations. The baby would make their happiness complete though I guessed that their little home would never be the same  I don't suppose they cared about their routine being shattered and I guessed that they would rather have adventurous fingers spreading food on the carpet and the paintwork  than remain childless. The best thing that could happen was going to happen for them and they were overjoyed. I was overjoyed and privileged that they had wanted to share their special news with me in this way.

In due time the baby William arrived safely. He looked strangely pale and fragile when cradled across his father's large chest. He beamed down at William with a pride and a love which promised that this baby would be the most loved, spoiled and cared for child for miles around. Nothing was to be too much trouble and there would be no end to the  number of toys proud dad would make for William as he grew up.

I visited the home regularly for a number of years after William's birth and at each visit there was a fresh account of little William's progress or news of some new words he had spoken. Weeks before William's birth I had been taken upstairs to see the nursery, brightly painted and wallpapered with the wooden cot made by Mr Dyson, safely in the corner where baby would not be in a draught when the door opened.

As the little one grew, there was always some new toy for me to see and they would hand William to me so that I could cuddle him until my coffee and biscuits were ready. I often thought how wonderful it would be if

William could have a baby brother or sister.

Over the years I had been privileged in seeing William develop into a very happy secure little boy and he had grown to know me and if he was still up, he too was pleased when I called at the home.

It was Monday evening again, and I was due to call at the Dyson's. I had become used to hearing their stories about William, and so always allowed plenty of time for their visit. What new things would they share with me tonight?

Mrs Dyson poured my coffee and looked at me with the same kind of expression she wore when they told me that she was pregnant. They sat me at the kitchen bench and sat beside me when Mrs Dyson, half laughing was the first to speak,

"We have something to tell you" glancing lovingly at her husband, she continued,

"Don't we dear?"

Mr Dyson's pipe glowed fiercely as he sucked eagerly nodding his head in vigorous agreement.

"We certainly have"

"My husband got out of bed this morning" grinned Mrs Dyson "and went to the bathroom to get his bottom teeth out of the soak, and they weren't there"

"Aye, that's right" the red happy face nodded in agreement. "I have a false set of lower teeth, and each night I put them in Steradent to soak. This morning they had gone!"

"Gone?" I questioned.

"Well, not so much gone, they had never been there. There was no water and Steradent in the mug either so it was obvious I had forgotten to put them in last night before I went to bed"

"Really, so where were they?"

"That's the point, couldn't find the blessed things anywhere. I only take them out at night so I must have gone to bed with them still in my mouth."

Mrs Dyson laughed,

"They may have been in when he went to bed but they certainly weren't in when he got up. They had completely vanished. Stripped the bed I did, but there was no sign of them anywhere."

"Aye, I worried sick" grinned Mr Dyson "if they weren't in my mouth where they belong then where the heck was they?"

"I even pulled the bed out and checked underneath" Mrs Dyson giggled," it was a waste of time though because they weren't there. They were nowhere to be found"

Mr Dyson grinned like a naughty schoolboy,

"I lit my pipe while I had a think about where they could be. Blow me; I could not hold the pipe properly without my bottom teeth in. The flipping thing slithered all over my mouth before dropping onto the floor."

"There only seemed to be one explanation" beamed Mrs Dyson, "I told him he must have swallowed them in his sleep."

"Aye and that thought got me really worried" said Mr Dyson, "I said to the wife, if I have swallowed them they will come out through the back end into the lavatory won't they? I'll be able to get them back then."

"You should have seen his face when I told him that he would need an operation to get them out "continued Mrs Dyson. "I mean how can an object shaped like a horse shoe pass unmolested through all those yards of pipes and tubes and come out at the other end. Stands to reason it is bound to get jammed somewhere. No! It would need an operation, and I told him so."

"Really"

"Yes, but to try and cheer him up I said that the operation wouldn't be as bad as having a baby, but he said that having a baby was natural, cutting open a man's stomach and letting all his insides spill out was not natural. Said he would rather have a baby any day"

"So what did you do?"

Mr Dyson chipped in,

"I had a bad day at work. You know I can't get through the day without my pipe, My mates asked me why I was not smoking, when I told them they jumped on the band wagon. They all painted gory pictures of me on the operating table and said I would be off work for months. I only came home for lunch to get out of their way!"

Mrs Dyson picked up the story,

"I think he only came home at lunch time to set his mind at rest. He was sure that I would have found them somewhere. I hadn't though, and he was really worried when I told him I had made him an appointment at the doctors for this evening"

Mr Dyson handed me another chocolate biscuit as he continued,

"Had a dreadful afternoon at work, was really worried about what the doctor would say tonight. I fully expected him ringing for an ambulance to take me straight into hospital."

"He looked awful when he came home from work at tea-time. I told him to have a good wash and to put his best trousers on with a clean shirt.. So he stripped down to his vest and underpants and started to have a shave at the kitchen sink."

I had listened with concern and amusement as I felt sure that there would be an amusing ending. I did not have to wait long for it as Mr Dyson continued,

"Aye, I was standing there at the sink, all lathered up with shaving cream when the missus said to me, 'by gum, your belly is a funny shape. Looks like you have a growth round your belly button'. So I put my hand there to have a feel and you'll never guess what I found"

Mr Dyson and his wife both lapsed into uncontrollable fits of laughter, with tears streaming down her cheeks Mrs Dyson continued,

"Right there, nestling in his belly button were the missing teeth. They must have dropped out of his mouth whilst he was asleep and dropped down his vest. They had gone down as far as the elastic in his underpants. They must have been there all the time"

"Aye," Mr Dyson laughed, " I was that pleased to find them, I nearly split my sides laughing. Can't understand how I had worked all day and not felt them. I have been digging holes and lying on my stomach on a roof. Wife always says I have a thick skin!"

Mrs Dyson interrupted,

"The only person who was not amused was the doctor's receptionist. Mr Dyson rang her up to cancel his appointment and she gave him a rough time."

"Rough time!" Exclaimed Mr Dyson, " when I told her where I had found the teeth she accused me of wasting their precious time. She gave me a good ticking off. Still I would rather have a good telling off from the dragon of a receptionist than have all my stomach cut open in hospital. That's not natural is it?"

As it was such a pleasant evening I had left my car a few blocks away, and it was quite a walk. I was still smiling at Mr Dyson's experience as I walked to the little parade of shops where I had left my car. It reminded me of the days in Holmfirth when we lived next door to the dentist's surgery.

Edith was still smiling one evening when I came home from work. As we were eating our meal she began to tell me that just a few minutes before I came home there had been a loud ringing of the door bell.

She opened the door to find a little old man there.

Edith informed him that I would not be long and that he was welcome to come in and wait.

The old gent continued,

"Nay there's no need for that. He will know why I have called. Bumped into the Master on the High Street yesterday and I told him what the trouble was. He said it would be in order for me to call here before seven o'clock and leave them with the cleaner".

"Cleaner!" Thought Edith " Is that who he thinks I am," but what the old man did next interrupted her chain of thought.

Reaching to his mouth, the old gent pulled his teeth out and placed them reverently into a blue sugar bag saying

"I told the Master where they are rubbing; he said if I popped them in he would have a look at them for me Cheerio Missus!"

Edith had called him back as he was disappearing down the path.

"I am sorry but the dentist's surgery is next door"..

Puzzled, the bewildered pensioner looked at Edith as she handed him back his sugar bag.

"Nay lass, there's the brass plate look beside the door".

"Yes" replied Edith," but it says Prudential Assurance Company. The surgery is next door!"

The old man did not believe her, out of his pocket came a twisted pair of spectacles which he placed on the end of his nose. When he had adjusted them properly, he scrutinised the brass plate, then with an embarrassed expression he walked backwards down the path, bowing every time he took a step saying

"Sorry Missus!"

# Church

Settling into a local church in Sleaford was so easy. We did not have to look round for a church family to become part of as we had attended the little Assemblies of God church in the town when we had been visiting there for three or four years and it was natural that we simply joined them as full time members

The church had been established quite a few years but had a small congregation and met in an upstairs room above a florists shop on the main street. Access to the room was gained by climbing some very steep stairs with a small landing at the top. Although adequate once we were inside, it was entirely unsuitable for weddings and funerals so a traditional church building was hired for such events. Wages were not high in this rural area so the income of the church was relatively small. Edith's mum and dad had moved to a village several miles away and her dad was invited to preach at the little Sleaford church who at that time did not have a pastor or leader. His preaching and pastoral heart must have endeared him to the congregation who asked him if he would consider becoming their pastor. He had a very demanding secular job as area manager for a large shoe retailing company and the manageress of the Sleaford shop and her husband were members of the little church. She ran the Sunday school and was known affectionately as Aunty Lucy. Not a few people referred to the Sunday school as the Lucy Show comparing it to a popular television programme of the day.

Edith's dad, David Jennings did not have much spare time as his area contained a large number of shoe shops and covered hundreds of square miles. He felt the call of God to care for the congregation there, and so in addition to his secular management role, he became Pastor Jennings. Blending the two responsibilities would not be easy, his job was very demanding and some days he did not get home for his evening meal until mid to late evening. However, with careful planning and much sacrifice of his own personal and family time, he successfully led and managed his shoe shop branches and loved and nurtured his congregation.

Local wages were not high, but over the years we had several serving RAF families join us, together with a self-employed company director who became a Christian through Pastor Jennings ministry. The editor of the local newspaper and his family joined us, and there was a mix of skills within the congregation. We had schoolteachers, a gardener, a civilian cleaner based at RAF Cranwell, and a high proportion of retired people. An elderly retired architect joined us and when we began considering building our own purpose built church, he drew up some quite fantastic plans. If unlimited funds had been available we would have loved to build according to Mr Mobbs design. When the day came we had to cut our coat according to our cloth! We still were able to build a lovely building though.

The Pastor who looked after the church prior to Edith's dad taking the responsibility, was Haydn Palmer. A lovely saintly gentleman, father of Hedley Palmer who was a well-known figure in Assemblies of God circles. Hedley was director of the Revival time Choir and the Radio producer for the Assemblies of God programmes. He was a gifted evangelist and a great preacher, he also sang like an opera singer.

Haydn's first wife had died and he had remarried to Myrtle, they had a happy life together and Myrtle was a great help to Haydn as he looked after the little church. Age and frailness meant that Haydn had to retire and as their rented cottage on West Banks Sleaford was demolished they moved into a council flat. However whilst the congregation were meeting in the upper room, Haydn had a longing to see the church have its own building, and he frequently went along to the empty plot of land where their little cottage had once stood, where he would kneel on his cap and pray that God would somehow provide for the new church to be built on that very spot.

His health declined and he was admitted into a care home. One night Myrtle woke up and could not get back to sleep. She made a hot drink and sat in the lounge intending to play some Christian music. She switched on her record player and the needle swung part way across the record before it began to play. She could not understand why the first few songs had been passed over, but she heard Alan McGill's tenor voice singing movingly,

"When I come to the river at ending of day,

When the last winds of sorrow have blown.

There'll be Somebody waiting to show me the way,

I won't have to cross Jordan alone.

When the darkness I see, He'll be waiting for me,

I won't have to cross Jordan alone"

Mrs Palmer told me later that she knew at that moment that Haydn had been called home and that God had been close to him in his final moments. A few hours later the local policeman came to break "some sad news" to her. She already knew the exact time Haydn had died.

Several years after becoming pastor of the Sleaford church, Pastor Jennings was able to lead the church into a building programme which resulted in them opening a brand new purpose designed building. It was built on the very spot where Pastor Haydn Palmer used to kneel on his cap and claim that piece of land for a church site.

The circumstances leading to acquiring that land were unusual to say the least. Danny McVicar a Scottish evangelist visited the upper room to conduct an evangelistic crusade.

He was a powerful preacher and lived a life in close touch with God. Whilst at Sleaford he told the church that God had told him that we must stop actively looking for a plot of land for a church. He told us that the land was already reserved for us and that at the right time it would be released to us. This brought a huge sense of release from the responsibility of finding a site, we also felt that here was confirmation that our desire for a new building was right and according to the will of God.

Pastor Jennings took his company car into a local garage for a service and the garage owner noticed a Bible with sermon notes popping out on the rear parcel shelf. When Edith's dad called to collect his car the garage owner quizzed him concerning his occupation. He thought Mr Jennings was a retail manager but the Bible and sermon notes had him guessing. Mr Jennings explained that he was indeed a full time shoe shop area manager, but he was also unpaid voluntary minister of a church. The conversation continued and our garage owner friend asked where the church was. It was then that Pastor Jennings shared that the church met in a rented room but hoped to have a church built.

"Where will you build it, have you a plot of land?"

"Not at the moment, suitable land is hard to find."

"I have a plot of land I have never used. I bought it several years ago but have not done anything with it. I am now wondering why I bought it in the first place. If it suits your purpose you can have it for the same price I paid for it all those years ago."

The land was the empty site where the cottages had been where Pastor and Mrs Palmer had lived. The plot of land Haydn had knelt on and claimed for a church had been offered to us out of the blue. The land which Danny McVicar had said was reserved for us to be released at the right time had been released. The site was ideal, but to be offered land at the same price it had cost several years before was a great blessing. It brought new meaning to the expression "inflation free".

The church congregation had gown under Edith's dad's care, and he had continued to build on the foundation laid by men like Haydn Palmer. Church income was now enough for us to take a mortgage from Assemblies of God Property Trust, one of my Prudential clients, Mr Cooling, was a self-employed builder with an excellent reputation and his tender for the work was accepted. He was aware that he was building "to the glory of God" and did us proud in every way. We had a grand opening and dedication ceremony, Myrtle Palmer turned the key to open the door and very movingly she shared the story of her late husband kneeling and claiming the site for a church.

There was a tinge of sadness overshadowing the joyful occasion, Edith's mum, who had been such a great support to her husband and had been very active in pastoral care for the ladies in the church was in reality too ill to attend. But she insisted and sat on the front row, propped up with a cushion anxious not to miss the occasion. Sadly we did not see her in church very much after that day. She was terminally ill and passed away at the age of fifty four leaving a huge gap. During her illness Pastor Jennings found it very difficult to maintain his work as pastor and his full time secular work. He reluctantly decided that he must relinquish his church duties. Michael Smith had just graduated from the Assemblies of God Bible College, and with his wife Christine they came to Sleaford as Pastor and wife. Michael worked alongside Edith's dad for a while, helping reduce his workload. Before long Pastor Jennings had retired from the church leadership and Michael had taken over. Edith's dad remarried a lovely widow, Molly Smithson and the wedding service took place in the church's new building. Edith's brother, Ian, conducted the service and I was honoured by being invited to be the best man.

Michael and Christine's time at Sleaford was a happy time of spearheading the work of the church from its new building. It was a time of more growth and maturity for the congregation.

There were very many happy memories from our time meeting in the upper room. One such occasion comes to mind. Edith's parents were away on holiday and I had taken the morning service. Pastor Jennings had arranged for Hedley Palmer to take and preach at the evening service. Hedley had tea with Edith and I, and I asked whether he would be singing to us in the service.

"Well that depends upon who will playing the piano or the organ."

"I am sorry Mr Palmer but Marjorie our regular pianist is away on holiday, but someone will be standing in for her."

"Oh dear, it's not the dear lady whose nose shines like a light bulb is it?"

"Yes, it is but she is alright you know"

"I can't possibly sing if she accompanies me. Thanks for the warning, I will choose some easy hymns."

It was a hot summer evening and the upstairs room was packed to capacity. The steward had to ask that we shared hymn books as we did not have enough for one each. Old Mr Wilson was heard to respond with a hearty, "We share the same bed so of course we can share the same hymn book"

Hedley Palmer began the meeting by announcing that the opening hymn was so well known that we would not need the hymn books.

"Number 619 in Redemption Hymnal, O Happy day that fixed my choice, on Thee my Saviour and my God." Let's all sing this together.

We began to sing, I looked at Edith and said "The pianist and the congregation are going to part company soon, the tune does not fit the words!"

One by one the congregation stopped singing and the hymn drew to a raggy untidy end.

Hedley Palmer beamed down at the pianist,

"Sister Brown, I am not sure what hymn number you are playing, but we are all singing number 619."

"That's the number I am playing Mr Palmer."

Hedley had his reply ready,

"Sister Brown, I know what has happened, your book is open at number 619 but number 620 is also on the same pages. Please don't play 620, play 619 O Happy day!"

"I am playing 619 Mr Palmer"

Hedley had another response ready, and he smiled at the congregation,

"I know what's happening. The music book Mrs Brown is using has a note at the bottom of the page it says Alternative tunes" and Sister Brown is trying to teach us a difficult alternative tune."

Looking at Sister Brown he continued," Please don't try to teach us a difficult alternative tune sister, just play the normal tune to number 619"

"I am playing the normal tune to 619 Mr Palmer"

Hedley looked at the congregation and in a serious voice continued,

"Shame on you all, I know what you are thinking. You are all thinking that sister Brown is playing the wrong notes. Sister Brown is playing all the right notes but because it is so hot in here they are coming out of the piano in the wrong order!"

Then addressing Sister Brown with a beaming smile said,

"Tell you what sister, I will sing it out and lead the singing and you just come in somewhere and follow".

So we were treated to hearing Hedley's fantastic voice after all.

Church is family and good families don't judge each other, they put up with each other's idiosyncrasies, they laugh at their own mistakes and support others when they put a foot wrong. No one thought any less of

Sister Brown and the experience did not put her off playing the instrument again.

Forty years after we had left Sleaford, Michael and Christine Smith were staying with us on one of their visits. We decided to visit the Sleaford Church, now known as Sleaford New Life Church and made the forty miles journey on the Sunday morning. We were overwhelmed at the welcome. Their pastor, Chris Bowater, had been made aware that we were going to visit as we had checked out the meeting time with one of the members. We did not expect to be honoured in the way we were. The four of us were invited onto the platform and we were presented with gifts. Michael and Christine were honoured as a previous pastor and wife whose labours had helped make the church what it is. Edith was honoured as the daughter of David and Linda Jennings who had also laboured there as pastor and wife. I was honoured as a past treasurer of the church. That was in the days when there was no money to treasure.

Seeing the church in its present form was very humbling. They had outgrown the building Mr Cooling had built. They were now in a complex with a conference venue which is in demand locally. They have a children's nursery, a coffee shop and effective initiatives to reach and bless the needy in the community. The church had been recognised by the local council for the part it plays in helping the underprivileged and the vulnerable. Gone is the congregation of seventy to eighty people, they are now well over two hundred strong. The four of us had been so favoured to have played a part in its story. Jesus said that He would build His church and that the gates of hell would not prevail against it. Here was just one vibrant example.

# The Hollies

As Edith's parents had invited us to live with them until we located a suitable house we had been able to move very quickly. I soon got to know the area and we were able to locate a modern semi-detached house on Meadowfield, which was only ten minutes' walk from the town. The house was on a very pleasant development with a mix of semi and detached properties. Just across the road from us was a detached house, home to a very friendly golden Labrador. When its owners were out at work the dog seemed free to roam around its garden and sit at the gate. Noticing what seemed like a placard hanging around its neck I approached it to have a close look. The notice bore the words, "PLEASE DO NOT FEED ME" I smiled as I thought that here was another Labrador which thought that the whole world was edible!

Sergeant Williamson, a local police sergeant lived a few doors away from us and I visited him and his wife on Prudential business. They always made me feel very welcome and although in sight of my own home they always offered me a coffee. Late one evening I was outside the post office opposite the cinema, I had just popped my mail into the letter box when I heard Sergeant Williamson's voice, "Hello David, are you OK. Would you like a laugh?"

"I certainly would, are you going to tell me a funny story sergeant?"

Sergeant Williamson raised his police radio to his lips and spoke into the microphone,

"PC Harper, report your position please."

"On Carre Street sergeant, all is quiet."

"Thank you PC Harper, over and out."

"PC Cooper, report your position please."

"Walking along Boston Road, all quiet sergeant"

"Thank you PC Cooper, over and out".

"PC Burton, report your position please"

"Hello sergeant, just walking past the builders merchants, all quiet"

"Thank you PC Burton, over and out"

Sergeant Williamson pointed across the road towards the cinema entrance,

"David, just keep your eyes on the cinema entrance."

Then he put out a call over his radio, "Calling all officers, incident outside the post office please attend"

For about a minute nothing happened, then the cinema doors burst open and PC's Harper, Cooper and Burton emerged like the keystone cops, as they ran out they were putting on their helmets and fastening up their tunics. Seeing their sergeant and I waiting for them, and realising that there was no incident and that they had been disturbed whilst watching a movie they began to show their embarrassment.

I realised that evening that the police officer's night shift in Sleaford was largely uneventful. In fact, even in the day time I discovered that if there were more than half a dozen motor cars waiting at the traffic lights in the town centre the constable would switch off the traffic lights and stand in the centre of the road directing the traffic.

I had Prudential business with several of the local police officers and they were all hospitable and friendly. The friendliest was Laurie, referred to by the local children as Uncle Laurie. The first time I called at his home I had no idea that he was a police constable. His wife Audrey welcomed me with a beaming smile and offered me a chair at the kitchen table.

"Laurie will be on his way home from his shift and his tea is ready, I have cooked plenty so you must join us" It was half past six and I had just enjoyed my own evening meal before starting my evenings collections, but Audrey would not take no for an answer. Within a few minutes Laurie walked in wearing his police uniform, he was a very large imposing man and seemed to fill the whole kitchen.

Audrey introduced me to him, and he too insisted that I have a hot meal with them. Laurie joked about his size and confided that he liked nothing better than immobilising a criminal by getting him onto the ground and sitting on him.

"Once I sit on them they can't get up" smiled Laurie, then adding ruefully,

"Come to think of it, I can't get up either unless two men pull me up"

As he was eating his tea he kept passing morsels to their black Labrador dog much to Audrey's disapproval. Laurie told me that one of his hobbies was shooting and their dog had been trained as a gun dog.

The Sleaford folk were so friendly yet they lacked the inquisitive attitude which had been prevalent in Holmfirth. I can't remember being quizzed about my own private business, the friendships shown were transparent and genuine.

We enjoyed living in our Meadowfield House, it was in a sunny aspect, had an integral garage and pleasant gardens at the front and rear. However we did not stay there very long.

Ron Hicklin who had been the evangelist in the Holmfirth Crusade came to Sleaford to visit and he and his wife fell in love with the place. He now had no commitment to the church he had pastored in Staffordshire and spent most of his time conducting crusades for Assemblies of God Home Missions Department. Ron and Connie his wife, decided that they would like to make Sleaford their base and we went with them to look at some houses. They fell in love with "The Hollies" a three storey Victorian house on Boston Road and decided to buy it. Edith and I fell in love with it too, and when for various reasons Ron and Connie had to pull out of the sale, Edith and I decided to buy it.

I needed to inform The Prudential colleague in whose area the Hollies was situated that we were thinking of moving to live on his territory as his permission was needed. He had no problem with our planned move and immediately indicated his interest in buying our Meadowfield house. He had been to see me there several times and had always liked the house. So our second property was bought by a Prudential colleague without the need for estate agents fees. A Prudential agent had bought our bungalow in Holmfirth, which had saved a lot of money in agent's fees.

The Hollies was a three storey Victorian semi house, very spacious with four bedrooms and large rooms with very high ceilings and skirting boards over a foot deep. The hall and passageway had the original mosaic floor. The house had not been modernised and it had no double glazing or central heating. Growing in the front garden around the front window was a beautiful mature wisteria which in the season was heavy with hanging blossom. The small front garden was screened from the pavement by a mature privet hedge which needed to kept well-trimmed in order not to block too much light from the front room.

The rear and side garden was very private with a cottagey feel and the rear garden seemed to be as long as a football pitch!

The downside was that there was no access for a motor car and no garage. The Hollies was situated on a trunk road, the main road out of town to Boston and Skegness and was an extremely busy thoroughfare. Consequently the road was well marked with yellow lines, and the closest place to park a car was New Street which was fifty or sixty yards away. There was only a four feet wide path leading from the pavement to the front door.

We were paying just over three thousand pounds for the property, but I could see that its value would be greatly enhanced if we could create access for a car and build a garage. We applied to the Council for planning permission and were successful. There were some stringent conditions however. The Council required the privet hedge to be removed so that visibility down Boston Road was not obscured when we drove out of the drive. Also it was a requirement that there was sufficient space to turn the car round in the rear garden to avoid reversing in or out from or into the main road.

We had waited to hear the outcome of our planning application before actually signing up to buy the house, the estate agent handling the sale rang me urging me to sign quickly. They were now aware that planning approval had been obtained for a drive and a garage and warned me that if we did not sign and proceed immediately they would withdraw the property from us and place it back on the market at double the price. Needless to say we recognised the good deal we had and proceeded with the purchase immediately.

We moved into The Hollies and for a while had to leave our car on an adjacent street, but it was quite safe. My parents came to visit us and we told them about the planning permission and about its conditions. Dad was incredulous as far as the removal of the privet hedge was concerned.

"David, you will never be able to remove that, it has been there donkey's years and will be impossible to move."

He also enquired how I would shift all the plants, shrubs and soil; and clear sufficient space for a drive, a garage and space to turn the car round...

When I told him that I planned to dig it all out with a garden spade he was doubly incredulous.

When they had gone I set about trying to remove the privet hedge. Once that had been cleared the four foot aperture in the front garden wall could be widened to create vehicular access. I found to my surprise that if I gripped each separate piece of the privet close to the ground and heaved with all my might, I could pull it out of the ground. It was hard graft, but within two or three hours the hedge was completely uprooted. Dad could not believe that I had simply torn it up by the roots, but I was strong in those days!

Mum and dad were back for a weekend, it was a bank holiday Saturday and the traffic along Boston Road was at a bumper to bumper standstill when I began digging out for the driveway.

A car was stationary outside our house and the driver was smiling at me as I started digging... Dad shouted to him,

"When you come past again on your holidays this time next year he will still be digging!"

But I wasn't! For weeks, every spare hour was spent digging out the topsoil. It was all moved further down the garden to create flower beds etc. Into the space created I shovelled between thirty and forty tons of hard-core which was rolled tight before a layer of pebbles were laid on top. We had our drive, we had our space to turn the car round, we had the space for a garage and I swear we had a much leaner David Robinson. A delivery of ready mixed concrete completed the garage base and we erected a sectional concrete garage. The first time I was able to drive my car onto our own drive and turn it round in the rear garden was a cause for celebration. All the hard work had been worthwhile. However there was still much to do INSIDE!

We were able to increase our Prudential staff house purchase loan so that we could have the property re-wired and have central heating installed, but there was still much to do. Where would the much needed money come from to carry out all the necessary improvement? Laurie our smiling policeman friend was an unexpected help.

It was after eleven o clock at night, I was sitting at the kitchen table completing my week's accounts when I was startled to hear a tapping on the window. Aware of someone standing outside I looked up, there with his nose pressed to the glass was Laurie beckoning me to let him in. He came into the kitchen apologising for the lateness of his visit but hoping that Edith and I could do him a huge favour.

"It's like this David, a lady has just called at the police station asking whether she could be allowed to spend the night in the cells. Her car has broken down and can't be fixed until tomorrow. She is alone and the local hotels are all full up. She is too frightened to sleep in the car hence she asked whether she could sleep in the cells. I had an inspired thought, David and his wife have a great big house and they must have a spare room. The lady will be safe there if they will let her stay. So here I am! Would you put the lady up for the night and give her some breakfast?"

Edith and I had no real thought of financial reward but we were anxious to help the stranded lady out. Within a few minutes Laurie was back with her, he assured her that we would take good care of her before leaving her in our care. We obviously had a spare room as my parents stayed with us from time to time. It did not take long to get the room ready, and the lady had some refreshments before retiring to bed. She had a good breakfast before she left, very grateful that we had looked after her so well.

I heard later from Laurie that she had gone straight to the police station to place on record her thanks and to assure them that they could send anyone to The Hollies for accommodation as they would be well looked after.

So began an unplanned and unimagined chapter which brought us much hard work, some amusing and touching stories, a series of interesting characters and of course, some financial help to improve The Hollies.

# Cloth Cap

Suitable head dress is a valuable part of the insurance agent's armoury. For many years, the logo on the Prudential Assurance Co business card showed a man proudly wearing a bowler hat. For a considerable time bowler hats were mandatory, and even when the bowler was no longer compulsory, agents were expected to wear a trilby. When I began my career with the company in 1965 there was no requirement to wear a hat. The reason for the army of Prudential men attired in a hat was down to politeness. How can the agent greet a lady on the street correctly unless he raises his hat? George Stocks who had held my Sleaford agency for very many years hated wearing a trilby but it was still mandatory. One morning as he was leaving home to commence his collections his mail from the office arrived. He took it with him and opened it, reading it as he was walking along the street passed a builders merchants. He read with difficulty as there was a gusty wind, but he saw to his great delight that the wearing of headgear was no longer a requirement. Whooping with glee he seized his despised trilby hat and threw it over the wall into the builder's merchant's yard. When he reached the entrance to the yard he discovered a young apprentice waiting for him, in his hand was the newly departed hat and on his face a huge proud smile"I believe that this is your hat sir, the wind blew it over the wall".

George made a solemn presentation of the hat to the young apprentice as a "reward for his honesty."

Before joining the Prudential, I worked for a while for another door to door insurance provider. My agency was in Huddersfield and was known locally as little Africa. A high proportion of my clients lived in overcrowded "Rooming Houses" in other words a four or five bedroomed house with a family in each room sharing one kitchen and usually one bathroom and toilet. Many of my clients were Indians, Africans, or Pakistanis with a smattering of Irish and Polish people. Many of them worked shifts so the kitchens never seemed to be idle. My clothes smelled of curry and other exotic foods, the money I took from the clients smelled of curry, and the handles on the doors of the people's rooms were usually sticky and fragrant with repeated applications of food residue from greasy fingers.

My solution! To acquire suitable headgear! I bought a cloth cap. I hardly ever wore it unless there was heavy rain, it was usually rolled up in my pocket, but here was my secret weapon to defeat dirty smelly door knobs. I simply put my hand inside the cap and used it as a sort of fingerless glove so that I did not touch the offending knobs and handles. I felt secure in the knowledge that if I needed to wear the cap I would not be contaminated by the odorous stickiness as this was on the outside. I completely lost sight of the fact that the cap spent many an hour rolled up in my pocket. We did not have meticulous health and safety risk assessments in those days. I carried over the practice of being armed with a cap for many years. By the time I was Section Superintendent in Grimsby I had been completely delivered from the habit. I sorely missed my cap though on one occasion. I was in the home of a local councillor who asked whether I would like a drink. He must have misunderstood my reply requesting a coffee as he brought me a tumbler full of neat whisky. I politely had a sip before discovering that I hated neat whisky. The damage was done though, I could not now offer it back to him. I waited until he had gone into the kitchen for his cheque book before quickly pouring the whisky onto the potted aspidistra plant. When I returned several weeks later the plant was dying. A cloth cap would have been a much more suitable receptacle for the unwanted whisky.

In my Sleaford days though I still used a cloth cap. True there were not many houses where it was needed, but Derek (Mucky) Murphy's home was one of them. My first meeting with Derek had been in his caravan when he was boiling some foul entrails on the gas hob. By now he had been housed in a council house had a wife and a young child. An elderly male relative lived with them and he was not able to get upstairs to the loo. Their simple solution was that he must do everything in a bucket in the centre of the lounge and at undetermined intervals they would transport the contents of the bucket upstairs to the loo. They did not seem to be aware of the existence of air fresheners, neither did they show the slightest degree of skill when it came to keeping a home clean. Here were stickier door knobs, here was a cloth cap home. This was in the 1970's and it seemed that no-one tried to intervene. There must have been a health visitor involved when the baby was born, and a council rent collector would probably visit them. I like to think that today they would have received an education to bring their home up to a satisfactory standard of hygiene. I had just left their home one morning when an electrician from the council greeted me.

"You are a brave man David going in there. I suppose you know that no council tradesman will go in their home. We simply refuse to go in as it is a health hazard."

Pleased to be outside and breathing some pure air I responded,

"Really, who does their repair jobs then?"

"Oh the Council employs a private tradesman who is not so particular and who needs the work"

I was aware that after spending a short amount of time in the Murphy household my clothes which had absorbed the smell, generously released it as I continued my visits. I remember one occasion when I had left my cap at home and had actually made contact with the Murphy's door handles. My next visit was a few doors down the road, and the lady asked whether I would like a drink. Thanking her, I declined saying that I would rather wash my hands if she did not mind. Pointing towards the kitchen she smiled "I think I know where you have just been."

I was walking along the main street one morning when Derek Murphy's cheery voice greeted me,

"Morning David hope you are OK"

Derek was standing at the bus stop looking as unkempt as ever.

"I'm OK thanks Derek, are you on holiday from work?"

"No, not on holiday David, I have visitors so can't go to work."

"Visitors Derek, why should they prevent you going to work and how long are they staying with you?"

"Not really sure David, the chemist has given me some stuff to get rid of them, it depends how quickly it works"

Sensing my puzzled expression, Derek enlightened me.

"We don't have people staying with us David, the visitors I have are the nits in my hair. They keep dropping off into the lemonade mix at work so they sent me home."

I suddenly remembered that Derek worked at the local soft drinks factory.

I thought, why don't food factories carry out a home visit before employing staff. Had they done so, Derek would not have been working there.

One hot summer evening, Derek appeared at our front door. I had just finished my tea and welcomed him in.

"It's good to see you Derek, how can I help you?"

"I am buying a car David and would like to get it tomorrow. I have never had car insurance before and will need a cover note. It will be a lost easier getting around with a car. We have our relative living with us you know and he does not get out much"

Explaining all the conditions and exclusions took a while and I was aware that our front lounge was beginning to smell unpleasant. After what seemed a very long time, I had the deposit premium and Derek had his cover note and he was ready to go.

"How did you get here Derek?" I quizzed,

"Oh a neighbour and his wife brought me along in the car I am buying from them tomorrow. They have parked on street just round the corner and are waiting for me there. Good night David.

Hearing the front door close, Edith came through with an air freshener and I paced up and down the room spraying copious amounts into the air. The odour was overpowering and it needed attacking. I was not aware that at that moment the car in which Derek was a rear seat passenger was slowly passing our window. Derek pointed at the house and said,

"That's where the Prudential agent lives, there look" Seeing me in the window spraying he went on,

"What is David doing, looks like he is spraying something."

His driver and his wife nudged each other before one of them answered,

"He is getting rid of the smell."

"It didn't smell "responded Derek.

"No it didn't when you went in Derek but it does now."

The young couple told me a few days later that the odour was so strong in their car that they sat outside it waiting for Derek and left all the windows wide open.

Ten years later, we had left the area and I was Section Superintendent in Grimsby when we had an unexpected meeting with Derek and his family. We were visiting the Christian festival known then as Grapevine which was held on the Lincolnshire showground. A young man from Grimsby was sitting next to me who had spent most of his life in Sleaford and had been part of the Assembly of God church there.

He pointed out a young family sitting on the row in front us I had noticed them and been impressed by them. They looked to be such a lovely family, well behaved children, well groomed, well presented. They were enjoying the service and entering in quite freely.

As my colleague nudged me and pointed at them he whispered,

"Do you know who that is?"

"No idea "I acknowledged.

"It's mucky Murphy and family they are part of Sleaford church."

I quietly thanked God for the part that local church had played in the life of a lovely but vulnerable young family.

# Guests

I was getting used to being stopped by a police officer as I drove along the main street of Sleaford. The first time my homeward journey was interrupted I was a little anxious though. "Are you on your way home?" was the beginning of what I hoped would not be an interrogation.

"Yes, just finished my duties and on my way home to relax!"

"Don't think you will get much relaxation. Your wife needs you quickly, we have given your address to two car loads of people asking for a good bed and breakfast address, so best get home quickly"

The Hollies was situated next to the local laundry and dry cleaners, and as I drove past their car park I had a clear view of my own driveway. Often the presence of one or more cars on our drive was the first indication I had that we had guests, unless I had received a smiling warning from a friendly constable.

The Hollies became a very happy home, it was always busy, there was always work to do as we improved and decorated the property. Being just a few minutes' walk from the town centre it was so convenient for church friends to drop in to see us, and on most market days at least one Prudential client would call in to bring their premiums or request a claim form or solicit some advice. We had a house full most Sunday evenings when the church service finished and we loved the warmth and friendship of our extended church family. Edith's parents sold their chalet type house just on the other side of town, and it was our privilege to provide them with a temporary home until they could move into their new bungalow just along the road from us.

The Hollies was more than just a happy home, it was ideal place for our two daughters to grow up. The beautiful River Slea was only two or three minutes' walk away and it was a popular place for children with their fishing nets. There were swans to watch, ducks to feed, fish to spot as they faced upstream in the long streamer weed, and such a peaceful safe environment to enjoy. A few hundred yards along the river was the open air swimming pool, a very popular recreation, which would have seen very few intrepid users had it been on the river bank in Holmfirth!

Just along from the open air swimming pool was Cogglesford Mill, a Grade 2 listed working water mill.  It is probably the last known working Sherriff's water mill in England. There is archaeological evidence of a Saxon mill on the site and records in the Domesday Book of later mills there. The red brick structure dates from the 18th century with alterations from the 19th century.   The ford from which the mill takes its name is where the Roman road, now called Mareham Lane crossed the River Slea.    Every time I passed the mill I was reminded of Flatford Mill on the River Stour in Suffolk.  This is a grade 1 listed property which was built in 1733 and was owned by John Constable's father The mill was immortalised in John Constable's water colour painting, The Haywain.

Those were halcyon days.  Our two girls could play out safely, there was very little fear of anything untoward happening to them and children's pleasures were not overshadowed by the dark clouds of health and safety.

Although the Hollies was such a happy home, in some ways it was a bottomless pit as there were always jobs to do and money to find to gradually bring it up to date without destroying its charming old character.

The last owner of the Hollies was a widow who had continued to live there after the death of her husband.  Her son who was a farmer lived further along the road from us and it was he who had signed the contract for the sale to us.

One evening he rang our door bell and greeted me pleasantly when I opened the door.

"Mr Robinson, I walked past the other evening and could see that you were painting the built in mahogany shelves in the alcoves beside the fireplace."

Wondering where his enquiry was leading I replied guardedly," Yes I have been doing some decorating. Mr Moore."

"It would be quite a big job Mr Robinson that is if you cleaned the shelves first and prepared them before painting."

"Oh yes, it was a big job Mr Moore but well worth it.  The room looks so much lighter."

"Did you find much dust etc. up there?"

Not quite sure when all this was leading I gave him a puzzled look before he continued,

"I am just interested whether you cleaned the shelves properly or just the front which is visible. Did you use steps so that you could see on the top?"

"Yes, I did a thorough job Mr Moore and there was quite a lot of dust."

"Ah, but did you find anything else on top of the selves. If you have found anything you will give it me won't you?"

"I'm not sure what you mean Mr Moore!"

"Well, my mother used to keep money hidden on the top shelf, and after she died I only found £65000 in the house, we were certain there was more than that, but we forgot to look on top of the bookshelf"

Needless to say, we had not found any money anywhere in the property. Had we done so I like to think that we would have done the honourable thing? I do remember though that when we were having the re-wiring done and the central heating installed, the tradesmen called me a few times to show me what they thought had been hiding places under the upstairs floorboards. I wonder how honest they were!

When discovering cost cutting repairs done by the previous owner, in spite of the fact that the son found £65,000 in the house after her death, I had to smile at some of her economies. A frosted glass panel in an interior door, only about 2 feet by 9 inches had obviously been broken. Instead of replacing the whole pane of glass it had been removed, a straight edge cut along the bottom before it had been refitted with a new piece of glass joined up to the old piece..

I could imagine the conversation with the glazier, "How much will it cost to replace the glass pane?"

"How much!" "How much will it save me if you just fit a new bit at the bottom?"

She could certainly have made her life at the Hollies a lot more comfortable had she spent some of the money hidden on top of the bookshelf.

I had never been a really proficient DIY man, but I excelled myself during our early time at the Hollies. Joy wanted some book shelves fixing onto the wall above the head of her bed. I visited the DIY shop and bought the wooden shelves and the metal brackets. I already had an electric drill and knew that even I could sort out this small job.

Joy went to bed the proud owner of new bookshelves. There was a cry in the night and we rushed into her bedroom. The shelves and the books had fallen on top of her whilst she slept. Edith insisted that we employed a "proper" man to refit the shelves.

Edith's dad was looking after Linda, his dying wife, and had handed over the leadership of the church to Michael Smith who had just graduated from Bible College. Until they were able to obtain their own house in Sleaford they stayed with us at the Hollies frequently, we enjoyed having them, they were our age and we got on really well together

One Saturday evening when they were staying with us a police constable paid us a visit. He hoped that we would be able to provide accommodation for one night to a lady who was presently at the police station. She lived in Boston but could not possibly get home that night. She was alone and we agreed to look after her. He returned to the police station and came back with her a few minutes later. She was in her forties and although pleasant enough, seemed very withdrawn and not very talkative. She asked if she could go straight to her bedroom and asked what time we needed her for breakfast. Christine took some refreshments up to her room and she seemed settled.

She was at the breakfast table promptly on Sunday morning and I took her breakfast in for her. She was still very preoccupied but was a little more talkative than she had been the previous night. She needed to get back to her home, 19 miles away in Boston but there were no buses or trains. Feeling sorry for her, I offered to take her home feeling that her need justified my absence from church. The journey to Boston was not easy, she did not want to say much but she directed me to quite a large modern house on a pleasant private development and we said goodbye.

I felt anxious about her as I made the return journey to Sleaford not really knowing how she came to be in Sleaford so far from home. The little mystery was soon solved though. A few days later the police officer who had brought her to us was on duty in the town and he enquired how we had managed with her. He thanked me for taking her back to Boston before adding that he had not been sure that we would find her alive on the Sunday morning. It seemed that she had decided to end her life and was going to jump into the River Slea when he came along and disturbed her. She went back to the police station with him and they talked about some of the issues which were troubling her. He told her that he knew of a good bed and breakfast address where she would be safe. She promised him that she would not harm herself but would not let him tell us about her mental state. Her husband was a Custom's Officer at Boston Docks and the constable had spoken with him on the Saturday night to assure him that his wife was safe and that she would be home next day. We often wondered how the lady was and hope that she had enjoyed the warmth and peace at the Hollies.

Michael and Christine were able to buy a house in Sleaford and the church were able to pay him a part time wage. Michael took a secular job for two or three days each week at Charles Sharpe's the large seed merchants just along the road. Their seed trials grounds were just opposite The Hollies giving us a beautiful view from our bedroom window like a well manicured park.

Michael had a morning break for his elevenses and if my car was in the drive he knew that I was in and would drop in for his coffee. It was always lovely to see him especially that day when I was trapped on the roof!

The laundry owner's son had been shooting birds from the window of their flat above the dry cleaners, and there were dozens of carcasses lying on the roof and in the lead drainage channels of our bay window. So one morning I used a ladder and went up onto the roof of the bay. I had to climb over the retaining wall and was able to clear away all the unfortunate birds. When I tried to climb backwards from the roof of the bay back onto the ladder I panicked and dare not do it. I could not make Edith hear and just hoped that it would not seem long before Michael came to rescue me. One of Michael's pastoral interventions on my behalf was to guide my rear over the parapet and safely engage my trembling feet with the rungs of the ladder.

My daily work with The Prudential was enjoyable and fulfilling, and Edith was skilled at looking after our bed and breakfast guests so well. Our sky always seemed to be cloudless and in many ways they were the happiest days of our life when such a store of precious memories were laid up.

We remember with a smile the gentleman who stayed with us frequently just "to break my journey" We were never sure where he was travelling to but he never failed to inform me as I was serving his breakfast that "the bottom has fallen out of all my pigs" His picturesque turn of phrase inspired our young daughters' imaginations as they considered bottomless pigs.

Then there were the two men who booked in together. One forgot to lock the bathroom door and Joy walked in on it whilst he was sitting on the loo. "Mum, dad, there is a man on our toilet wearing flowered underpants, flowered underpants!" I could not resist asking as I carried in their breakfast, "Which of you wears the flowered underpants then!"

We had sales reps staying with us, police dog handlers attending dog handling contests in the area, sightseers, a surgeon and his wife who were house hunting in the area, a man and wife came two or three times to take part in a cycling event in the area. He rode a traditional cycle, she rode a penny farthing which they brought here from Cambridge on the train in the guards van.

We had three young Frenchmen who we could not make understand that our Victorian bath did not have an overflow. They discovered when it was too late, they ran downstairs into the kitchen where water was dripping through the ceiling shouted "It has overflowded, it has overflowded!"

There was the gentleman who got up to use the loo in the night and mistook our bedroom for his. I heard our bedroom door open and he was just about to climb into our bed when I whispered, "You are in the wrong bedroom" He beat a hasty retreat.

There was the young lady who stayed with us during the hottest night of the year who knocked on our bedroom door in the early hours of the morning to tell us that burglars were trying to break in. "They are making an awful noise outside" she said. I gently told her that she need not worry. The noise was made by the guard dog at the laundry who could not sleep, he was dragging his kennel round the concrete yard.

There was the middle aged bank manager with the overbearing boring wife. He went to bed at 11 pm leaving Edith and I to put up with her monologue until the early hours of the morning. I was tired of hearing her say "My husband is a bank manager" I had heard enough when she told me that they had a son in law, just like me, so very old fashioned. We understood why her husband had escaped to bed so early. Unfortunately he was unwell next morning which was Saturday. His wife insisted that I phone our doctor to inform him that he husband has had a heart attack and needs a visit. She added arrogantly "Don't forget to tell doctor that my husband is a bank manager. Have you got that, a bank manager?"

I was amazed that our doctor came out so quickly. The lady and her husband took the doctor into our own private room, she was certainly overplaying the bank manager card! When the consultation was over she could not open the door as the door knob on the inside fell off and the spindle fell into the hall outside the room. I could hear her fumbling with the knob and trying her best to open the door. I had to use a great deal of self-restraint not to shout to her, "Tell it your husband is a bank manager!"

# Promotion

There had been several changes in the Prudential staff attached to the Grantham office since I transferred there from Holmfirth.  Reg Hill, the District Manager who had assisted with me moving to his district had taken his pension at the age of 60.  The new District Manager was Lou Winterton who would be in his 50's when he took control of the District. Some of the Lincolnshire Prudential Districts were known by the staff as Prudential Gold Coast areas.  They were the better areas often given to a successful District Manager as a reward for serving elsewhere.  The Gold Coast Districts were likely to increase the District Manager's earnings for the last 10 years of his career, thus making a welcome increase to the value of his final pensionable earnings.   These districts were also generally viewed as being likely to give the manager a fairly easy ride as he approached retirement.  Districts like Sheffield and Rotherham, which were within the same Divisional boundaries as Grantham were not as attractive and sometimes were dismissed as the Prudential man's graveyard.

So I knew when Lou Winterton came to Grantham that he was obviously held in high esteem by the Company.

So I had a change of District Manager and with the transfer of Jim Adams, had a change of section superintendent too.  I never addressed the District Manager by his Christian name, we referred to them among ourselves as Reg Hill and Lou Winterton, but when we spoke with them we addressed them as Mr Hill or Mr Winterton.  I never used Walter Slater's Christian name when addressing him, he and Jim Adams were always given the respect of Mr Slater or Mr Adams.  When David Hodge took over from Walter Slater there was a change in relationship.  After a few weeks I began to address Mr Hodge as David.  This did not mean that I had any less respect for him and his authority.

Lou Winterton had settled well into the Grantham District and was well liked and respected by the staff.  He too was a very fair man, generous in the praise he gave and excellent at creating team spirit.

I had just left the Grantham District Office building after my weekly visit there when I had a chance meeting with Reg Hill on the High Street.

Seeing me he registered nothing but pleasure, and even though he was no longer my manager I greeted him,

"Good afternoon Mr Hill, lovely to see you. How are you?"

"I am fine thanks David."

"How are you enjoying retirement Mr Hill?"

"Well David, retirement is fine, I have just recovered from a bout of dementia."

"Dementia Mr Hill, not you surely!"

"Yes, you see it's like this David, I retired at 60 but don't receive my state pension until 65. So I have signed on at the employment exchange and they have put me under huge pressure to find a job. I told them that I had been a very highly paid insurance company District Manager, and that if they could find me a job with earnings commensurate with what I had been earning, I would take it."

"Really"

"Yes I did not want another job but it would have been better than signing on all the time for unemployment benefit. They told me that there was an office job available and showed me the details. The salary was £15000 a year. I thought £288 a week on top of my pension was fantastic. I would not mind taking that job. So I had an interview and they seemed impressed with me and I was offered the job" Mr Hill continued, "I did ask whether it was a very demanding job as the salary seemed quite generous. I was informed that with my experience I would find the job very easy. All that I had to do was routine filing, checking office petty cash, checking invoices against goods received etc etc. So I accepted the job."

"Did you enjoy it Mr Hill?"

"Well yes I did. The only thing I did not enjoy was working 5 days a week, the loss of my retirement leisure. I obviously performed well because at the end of the first week the manager told me they were delighted with my work. He handed me my wage packet which I did not open until I got home. Imagine my surprise when the envelope contained only about a tenth of what I was expecting."

"Really, they must have made a mistake Mr Hill."

"No David, it was I who had made the mistake. I spoke to the wages office and they explained that I had misunderstood the advert for the job. I had read the salary incorrectly. It was not fifteen thousand pounds per year but fifteen hundred pounds a year. I had tied myself up five days a week for less than £30"

"Oh no, what did you do about it?"

"Well I thought it over carefully. They were obviously very happy with my work so there was no chance that they would not keep me on, so that night I became senile. The next day I knocked a bottle of ink over and it ruined a pile of invoices. I filed papers in the wrong cabinet. I spilt coffee all over the desk. When I answered the phone I could not remember the name of the company I was working for. They took me into the office and dismissed me. You know David, it's amazing but the very next day I had completely recovered from my dementia."

I had to award full marks to Reg Hill for ingenuity!

Lou Winterton rang me to let me know that Jim Adams was no longer my Superintendent. He was pleased that a newcomer was appointed in his place. He laughed as he said "David, it looks as though we are a right Christmassy area. I manage Grantham District and I'm called Winterton. The District Manager of Gainsborough is David Stuffing, and your new section superintendent is Dennis CAROLING. Mr Caroling will be calling to introduce himself to you David. I am sure that you will get on well"

Mr Caroling did call to see me, I found that his name was not Caroling but Carolan and he smiled when I told him the name Lou Winterton had blessed him with. It was not a material fact though because I never called him Mr Carolan, from the first day it was Dennis and David. I even introduced him to my clients as Dennis. We worked so well together he was a scrupulously honest salesman and was well received wherever I took him.

Dennis called for me one evening proudly showing me his new car. It was a lovely Volvo saloon, the same model used by the police motorway patrols. It was not new but was a super example. One of my appointments that evening was with a police officer who drove a police Volvo. I told them that Dennis had just bought a Volvo.

"Really" he enquired, "what do you think to it so far?"

"It's fantastic" replied Dennis, "At 40 miles per hour you can't tell that you are moving"

Our policeman friend laughed, "You don't buy a Volvo to cruise at 40 miles per hour, I drive one all day and you can't tell you are moving at 100 miles per hour"

The Volvo chapter in Dennis's life did not last long. Not many months later he called for me in a 3 litre bilious green Ford Capri. He had discovered to his horror that should his Volvo ever need a new clutch he would need to kiss goodbye to four hundred pounds. So chose to buy a British car with lower running costs. Later on in my career I was able to own a succession of Volvos beginning with pre owned ones before building up to new ones. I completed over 100,000 miles in some of them and none of them ever needed clutch repairs. Dennis was not prepared to take the risk however. But I certainly missed the comfort of his Volvo.

Dennis had a young family which was a reason we had so much in common. He trusted me to get on with my job without interference but we worked together twice a month when I set up potential sales calls for him. Sometimes we decided to take half the appointments each, working separately in order to have more time to do them justice. Dennis rang me occasionally seeking my advice on how best to deal with a Prudential issue he was facing, and it was Dennis who first said to me, "David, have you never thought of going for promotion?" So now two voices kept coming to mind. Walter Slater's voice "You will never mek owt in this job" and what was becoming a louder voice that of Dennis Carolan asking "Have you ever thought of going for promotion?"

The Divisional Sales Manager made a huge impression on me, but for all the wrong reasons. I am sure though that I was partly influenced by him when I began to consider applying for promotion.

The Sales Manager, Mr S R Edrich had requested that he conduct a sales meeting for all the staff attached to the Grantham office. Lou Winterton had booked the conference room in a Grantham hotel and about thirty of us were sitting in a semi-circle facing the table where Mr Winterton and Mr Edrich were conducting the session. This type of meeting was held periodically and was intended to have an encouraging and motivating effect.

After being introduced by the District Manager, Mr Edrich decided to conduct his input whilst standing and walking to and fro around the room. He seemed to have a haughty superior manner which I had difficulty engaging with. He looked at one staff member who was sitting cross legged as he asked loudly,

"Are you a queer?"

Our embarrassed colleague mumbled "No sir."

"Then why are you sitting like that with your legs crossed! If you don't uncross them I will kick them into a normal position"

There was no way he would find it easy to motivate a group of people to achieve better things. People were seething at his attitude. Then when he wanted to ask a chosen person one of his questions he simply pointed at the individual as he barked to Lou Winterton, "What's this man's name"

"That's Samuel Brown Sir"

Then Edrich posed his question "Brown, what is your opinion of?"

It was not long before it was my turn. Pointing at me he asked the District Manager for my name.

"That's David Robinson Sir."

"Robinson, why is the opening sentence of a Prudential salesman's presentation so important?"

I knew the answer and I knew it off by heart. I had completed hundreds of the official Prudential prospect forms which were handed to the specialist salesman before he visited the prospect. There was a section which asked for details of any known activities which the prospect was engaged in, adding the words ESPECIALLY IF A TV VIEWER.

I looked Mr Edrich in the eye, "Well sir, if the salesman's opening remarks are less interesting than what's on the TV he has no chance!"

"What sort of rubbish is that Robinson, where did you get that stupid idea from? Do you seriously think that TV is a serious threat to one of our salesmen?

I happened to have a completed prospect form in my pocket which I pulled out and unfolded before answering,

"Yes sir, I think that TV is a threat and the Prudential consider it a threat also. I quote from our official prospect form "Please give details of any known activity" before saying the last few words loudly and with great relish "especially if a TV viewer"

Edrich grunted at me and my remarks received much enthusiastic approval from some of my colleagues in the room. Our paths were to cross again when I was Section Superintendent, he tried to pay me back.

If Edrich had not already slumped in my estimation, he was yet to excel himself. Present at that meeting was the senior superintendent of the Grantham office who had worked for the company for 28 years. He had been absent from work for months due to a serious heart problem and he had decided to call it a day and take ill health retirement.

Lou Winterton paid a short tribute to the retiring colleague simply saying that he admired him for attending the meeting as he was still on sick leave, and briefly paid tribute to his 28 years' service. Then he invited Mr Edrich to say something,

"In view of the special occasion would you like to pass on Senior Management best wishes to our retiring colleague Mr Edrich?"

Dismissively Mr Edrich replied, "No, not necessary Mr Winterton, not necessary."

I felt incredibly sorry for Frank Padget the retiring staff member, he was a good man and worth more than that. I felt like standing up and saying "If you won't wish Frank a long and happy retirement sir, then I will" but I had the sense to do it privately in a letter to Frank a few days later.

I drove back to Sleaford with a deep sense of unease that such a man as Edrich had progressed up the ladder and was now probably only one grade below that of Divisional Manager. "The company don't need men like him at the helm. What were they thinking of when they promoted him? If he can do it I can!"

A few months later, Mr AW Robberts our Divisional Manager visited Grantham office to interview selected members of the staff. I understood that he would interview the District Manager and all the Section Superintendents before speaking with six selected agents. Three who needed a kick up the backside and three who he wanted to congratulate for a successful performance. I was sent an appointment not really certain which category I had been placed in. However by the end of the interview I was in no doubt which category I was in.

The session was informal, Mr Robberts was very expansive, and concluded by saying "Mr Robinson, have you anything you would like to ask me?" Knowing that this was the most important part of the session I took a deep breath before answering, "Yes Mr Robberts, How do I go about a promotion to Section Superintendent?"

With no hesitation Mr Robberts gave my answer "You do know that if promoted you would have to move."

"Yes Sir I do."

"Then, Mr Robinson, we will get you included in the next promotion selection course."

# Moving Again

The day after my interview with Mr Robberts I had a phone call from Lou Winterton. After discussing the purpose of his call and exchanging a few pleasantries about the interview, he warned,

"Don't get too excited David. Things don't happen quickly and it could be 18 months before you hear anything about a promotion selection course. So I guess that it's just business as usual until then."

This did not concern me too much as we were very happy in Sleaford and I was very fulfilled in my work there. I was still in my early thirties and the physical effort of walking many hours a day from client to client was no problem. I was just unsure how I would feel if I was still pounding the beat when I reached my sixties.

So I settled down to what Lou had called "business as usual" It was a lovely time of the year, autumn was painting its gorgeous colours, it was still mild and very pleasant and we never had hard winters in Sleaford so there was a lot to look forward to.

Then out of the blue the phone call came from Lou Winterton,

"David, things are happening sooner than I thought. The Divisional Manager wants you to attend a promotion selection course in two weeks' time. It will be held at the Golf Hotel at Woodhall Spa and you will be there for a couple of nights. I will send you the official paperwork but you need to provide a passport photograph in advance of the course."

"Really, that's no problem but why do they need a photograph?"

"Nothing to worry about David. Each member of the selection panel has a score card for each candidate. The card has the attendee's photograph and name on it, and the panel member makes his observations on the card. The photograph ensures correct identification until each face has become familiar. It's just routine David"

So the required photographs were posted off to Nottingham Office with the completed enrolment form acknowledging that I would be at the Golf Hotel in time for lunch on the Wednesday. So here I was, attending a selection course within only 4 weeks of my interview with the Divisional Manager.

I was surprised but pleased at the choice of venue. I had expected that the course would be held in Nottingham, but preferred the Woodhall Spa venue.

The small town was about an hour's drive from Sleaford. It was a former spa town and was beautifully situated on the southern edge of the Lincolnshire Wolds just 6 miles from Horncastle and about 17 miles from Lincoln. We had visited Woodhall spa a few times and it had a charm of its own. It seemed to have its own gentle pace of life as though the residents regarded every day as a Sunday.

The little town was famous for the Kinema in the Woods, a cinema dating back to 1922 which was still the only functioning cinema in the United Kingdom to use back projection. The building which is the home for the Kinema was originally a farm building, then a concert pavilion. In 1906 it became the cricket pavilion for Petwood House, which later became The Petwood Hotel. It was in 1922 that the cricket pavilion was converted into a cinema, and was only the 68th cinema to be opened in the whole of Britain.

Later a magnificent Compton theatre organ was installed in the Kinema. The organ began its life when it was originally installed in the Super Cinema, Charing Cross Road London in 1928. The wonderful organ can be appreciated by all as it is still played regularly during film performances, being raised up onto the stage via a central lift. One of the pieces of music played on the organ at its inaugural concert in the Kinema was The Dam Busters March. A fitting choice as Lincolnshire is widely known as The Bomber County. The Dam Buster's flight actually flew from RAF Scampton just a few miles from Woodhall Spa in May 1943.

I knew though, when setting off for The Golf Hotel that Wednesday morning that there would be no time to savour the delights of Woodhall Spa or the Kinema in the Woods. I expected that the few days would be challenging and intense but I was determined to enjoy the experience. During the drive to Woodhall Spa I played a track from the Sound of Music over and over again. I felt that I needed confidence, so I allowed the encouragement from Julie Andrews to wash over me,

"Let them bring on all their problems,

I'll be better than my best,

I have confidence in confidence alone,

Besides which you see, I have confidence in me"


As I entered the hotel, Julie's words were ringing in my ears,

"Let them bring on all their problems,

I'll be better than my best,

I have confidence in confidence alone,

Besides which you see,

I have confidence in me"

I felt completely relaxed as I mingled with the Selection Panel and the other candidates. There were about ten of us and I guessed that I was probably the youngest. We all had a drink at the bar before going through to the dining room. I could not help but notice that some of the candidates did not seem to be enjoying the excellent lunch.

Then at half past two we began in earnest. A small conference room had been prepared for us, we all had own own table with course materials etc laid out and we faced the long table where the three man selection panel presided.

Mr Robberts, our Divisional Manager was in the centre seat flanked by Stan Keene the Prudential District Manager from Chesterfield and Mr Futter who was the Divisional Fire and Accident Manager based at Nottingham office. Mr Robberts quickly dealt with the health and safety formalities before passing a bag around which contained pieces of paper each numbered 1 to 10. We took a piece each wondering what this was a prelude to.

"Right" said Mr Robberts, who has chosen number 1?"

"I have Sir" was the nervous response.

"Then welcome as opening batsman! You have exactly five minutes to give a talk on any subject you wish. At the end of five minutes I will tap my cup with my spoon and we expect that you will be concluding as the signal is given..."

I felt sorry for number 1, he had no time to prepare. I was pleased that I was number 5 until I realised that I had more time to become nervous and anxious.

Not many candidates finished exactly on cue. When we had all made our contribution we had to give feedback and express our opinion of each colleague's performance. Then the selection panel gave their feedback, not just concerning each man's performance but also our criticisms and appraisals of our colleagues were put under the spotlight. The man who had been savagely critical of a colleague put under pressure to justify his attitude.

One of the candidates was out of his depth and told mother in law jokes for three minutes. He was told very firmly that his presentation was not what the panel were looking for,

A coffee break mid-afternoon broke up the afternoon nicely. Then the session concluded. We were able to go to our rooms, unpack, unwind, as we prepared to meet later for dinner.

The cards bearing our passport photographs had been very much in evidence all afternoon. The panel were watching us all and listening to all we said, even conversations at lunch and off the cuff remarks were noted on the correct card. It was no different at dinner. They were listening and watching. I began to understand the expression "your card is marked." After dinner we were entertained to drinks etc. in the bar until bed time. The time spent together was punctuated by the regular appearance of the cards followed by a hasty scribbling.

We all assembled for breakfast and Mr Robberts noticed that there were only 9 of us. Discovering who was missing he enquired whether anyone knew where he was.

"Yes sir, I have just knocked on his bedroom door and he is laying on the floor crying. He says that he is too scared to come down for breakfast."

Possibly speaking out of turn I said "Oh that's not necessary. Tell him there is no need to feel like that. The Panel know we are nervous and make allowances."

"Mr Robinson" retorted one of the Panel, "We make no allowances at all. If you can't hack it you should not be here."

The course resumed after breakfast and the various sessions were designed to test us on product knowledge, Company procedures, management issues, personal opinions on a wide area of related subjects. The attitude of the panel was in the main non-threatening and warm, however if they perceived a possible weakness in a candidate they probed to get as close to reality as possible. It was interesting how many opportunities there were to score points over a colleague by making oneself look big at their expense. I soon sensed that this kind of attitude did not please the panel. There was pressure though to get a candidate to change his mind by playing a colleague against him. The Panel asked me how I would deal with a certain situation. I knew that there was a correct company procedure recommended and so recited that as my answer. I was confident that my answer was faultless, until one of the panel threw a spanner into the works,

"Really Mr Robinson, are you sure that is the right thing to do? Let's see what your colleagues think" then he invited contributions from the others. Sensing that he had hinted that my answer was not right, one by one they followed his lead.

"I am not sure that's the right thing to do Sir. I think that I would handle it this way."

"Really, do any of you others think the same way?"

"Yes sir, most certainly. I think that David Robinson is quite wrong."

Then I was put under pressure,

"Mr Robinson, you have heard what your colleagues think, they all think that you are wrong. Would you like to reconsider your answer?"

"Thank you sir, but no, I will not reconsider. I believe my first answer to be the right one."

"Excellent, because you were exactly right and all the rest of your colleagues are totally wrong.   Next question is….."

So it went on. There was no privacy apart from the time spent in our room.  A brief conversation with a team member at the bar was overheard and out came the cards and out came the pencil.

My admiration for the panel members increased as the course proceeded. Mr Robberts, every inch a successful divisional manager with excellent personal qualities.   Stan Keene became the manager I would love to work for if I was not working for Lou Winterton.  And Mr Futter, such a gracious self-effacing but successful divisional fire and accident manager. How privileged we were to rub shoulders with these guys for two or three days.

The weather was really kind to us and we took our coffee outside for one of our breaks.  I noticed this superb Saab motor car on the car park and edged over to have a close look at it.  I was looking through the windows drooling and dreaming when Mr Robbert's voice broke into my reverie,

"Here are the keys Mr Robinson, have a sit inside"

As I was sitting inside Mr Robberts confided in me that he had always had Rover cars, until his last one! Driving at speed on the motorway one day he needed to brake but when he applied the brake pedal nothing happened. He informed the Rover dealer who told him that they were aware of the problem because it keeps happening but no-one knows why.  It happened again, and again the dealer had no answers.  So Mr Robberts asked Mr Futter to help him.  He asked him to obtain the official Prudential list of the three safest cars on the road.  Saab were clearly number 1, so I changed loyalties and am now a Saab man, and have no regrets.  I handed him his keys back hoping that he had not seen my modest Ford Cortina parked near to his Saab.

It was the last session of the course and we had broken mid morning for coffee.  I chose to go back to my room and bring all my luggage down and pack it into my car.  When I returned to the conference room all my colleagues were already seated and I noticed a note on my table.  It said,

"In your absence we have decided unanimously that you are the right person to give a vote of thanks when the course ends."

Mr Robberts and his team thanked us all for attending, wished us all a safe journey home before adding, "Please don't rush away. I will go to the door and I would like to shake you all by the hand as you leave."

I seized my chance and standing tapped on my table with my pen. I gave a brief sincere vote of thanks, then it was all over. The only people in that room I ever saw again were Mr Robberts and Mr Futter.

Mr Robberts true to his word was waiting at the door, we all received a hearty handshake. As he pumped my hand he said quietly, "David, view this as the next step from your promotion course. Go back to your agency and find someone to replace you."

Surprised at his parting greeting I could only manage to say "Just like that Mr Robberts?"

"Yes David, just like that!"

It was early Friday afternoon when I arrived back home. Edith was interested to hear how the selection course had gone. When I explained to her that I had been asked to find someone to take over from me she smiled. "A young man called to see you whilst you were away. He is coming back tomorrow for a cover note. When I told him that you were away on a promotion selection course he said that he would love to apply for your job if you move on. He is called Trevor Newton."

"Oh I know Trevor, he has an office job, and I think that he works for the council. He is a capable likeable young man and I think that he would make a good Prudential agent. I will have a chat with him when he comes for his cover note"

Sure enough, Trevor called next day and enquired whether I had enjoyed the course. When I told him of the Divisional Manager's parting comments he displayed great interest in applying for my job. I promised him that I would let Mr Winterton know about him on Monday.

I did not need to ring Lou Winterton as on Monday morning, bright and early he rang me to ask how I thought the course had gone. He obviously had not received feedback from Divisional Office because when I told him of Mr Robberts request followed by my recommendation of Trevor Newton, he stopped me in my tracks.

"Oh David, nothing will happen so quickly. It will be at least 18 months before you hear anything" then came the phrase I had heard before, "until then it is business as usual."

A couple of weeks later I had another phone call from Mr Winteron. "David, please don't read too much into this but you are requested to attend Nottingham office for an interview with the Divisional manager. He wants to see you next week at 10 o'clock. It will only be to give you feedback from the course so don't get excited."

Then he added as an afterthought,

"By the way David, be sure to be there on time. I have known of occasions when due to late arrival Mr Robberts has changed his mind about offering promotion. If you are even ten minutes late he is quite likely to say " if you can't be bothered to get here on time for something as important as a promotion interview I will offer your promotion to someone else. Good bye"

So when, a few days later, I was driving to Nottingham I was agitated. I had left home in good time but I encountered fog and black ice I tried to ease away my anxiety by thinking that in all probability I was not going to offered promotion, just given some course feedback. Lou Winterton's remarks came back to me, "If he is going to offer you promotion David, there will be seven buff folders on his desk with a map folded up on top of them."

Miraculously I arrived at the office with minutes to spare, the lift was in use so I ran upstairs to the top floor, known as the corridor of power, where Mr Robberts was at his office door, beaming and with outstretched hand...

As he welcomed me inside he said "Please accept my apologies David, I should not have expected you to be here by ten o clock, it was thoughtless of me, sit down and get your breath back. I sat just in front of his desk as he made his way behind it. There on the highly polished desk were several buff folders and a folded map.

"I want to offer you promotion to Superintendent David, but it will need you to move. Will you go anywhere for me?"

"Yes, I will go anywhere for you Mr Robberts except Sheffield or Rotherham, they are industrial areas which would be bad for my health"

"I am not going to ask you to go to Sheffield or Rotherham, I am going to ask you to go to Cleethorpes attached to our Grimsby office. Will you go there and do a job for me?"

Within 20 minutes I had been given a rundown of what would be my area. I had thumb nail sketches of my staff and had agreed a start date of 5th January. Wishing me every success, I was then handed over to the personnel manager with whom I spent a very profitable hour. He offered me interest free bridging loan facilities to help us move house quickly, agreed an expense allowance to cover the full cost of accommodation until we moved and extra costs of travelling to and from Grimsby. I signed all the papers including the new contract as Superintendent before being handed over to none other but Mr Edrich, who I remembered well from the meeting he conducted in Grantham.

I had just been sitting with my elbows on the Divisional Manager's desk and with my feet under the Personnel Manager's desk, but no such closeness here. Mr Edrich's desk was across the corner of his square office and ten feet in front of it was a solitary chair. He barked, "Morning Robinson, sit there."

Assuming a position of arrogant authority behind his desk, he continued,

"Well boy, you are here because you are hoping to be offered promotion, is that right?"

"No Mr Edrich, it is not quite right, I have been offered promotion and begin on 5th January as superintendent in Grimsby."

"I don't think so Robinson, I don't think you have been offered anything. You have misunderstood."

"I don't think I have misunderstood Mr Edrich, all my expenses are agreed and I have signed a contract."

"I don't think you have signed anything Robinson but I will soon find out" as he stormed out of his office.

Very soon he was back, "It seems that you have been promoted Robinson but I had no knowledge. So what are you going to do with these guys on your first day in Grimsby on January 5th? I will tell you what you are going to do. You will go in there waving the big stick. Do I make it clear, do I make it clear?"

"Yes you make it very clear Mr Edrich but I will treat each man as an individual after deciding the best way to motivate him"

"You will go in there waving the big stick, do I make it clear?"

I was rescued by a secretary informing him that Mr Futter was ready to see me and she conducted me to his office. "Hello David, lovely to see you and congratulations. Come and pull your chair up to my desk, coffee?"

"Thanks so much Mr Futter, coffee please."

"David," he smiled, "I observed you on the promotion course. No doubt someone has just told you to take a big stick to Grimsby, you and big sticks don't go together. My advice is just do it your way David, just do it your way"

I spent a very pleasant and profitable time with Mr Futter. He headed up the section of the Prudential which conducted house and contents insurance, motor car and commercial insurances etc etc and pledged the support of him and his team The time engaging with him seemed to wash Mr Edrich right out of my hair.

I left Nottingham office on cloud 9. The fog and the black ice had gone, my promotion was secure and I could not wait to get home to tell Edith. Mr Robberts had warned me that the Grimsby Manager, John Stoner would no doubt ring me and I found myself looking forward to his call.

The phone call came soon afterwards. Mr Stoner wanted to meet Edith and I and he invited us both to visit him and his wife at their home just outside Grimsby. On the Saturday morning we set off into the unknown, to make our first acquaintance with John Stoner District Manager of the Grimsby District. His directions were just right and soon we were 50 miles away enjoying a hot drink with Mr and Mrs Stoner. He was forbidding, he was business like, he seemed to be the type of man who would not suffer fools gladly, and he had the look of inscrutability which made it difficult to know what he was thinking. At times he wore his heart on his sleeve when it was obvious what he was thinking. After recommending suitable areas for us to consider moving into to, he began to hit from the shoulder. He told me that he thought that I was far too young to be a superintendent. He told me that all my stars must have been shining during my promotion course. He told me that I had no idea what hard work is, he told me that I would be so busy in his District that I would hardly have time to see the sea. He told me that I should not have been promoted direct to Superintendent but should have been placed in the equivalent of a locum superindent role first to gain experience first.

As we drove back to Sleaford I was feeling decidedly unsettled. I am a great sleeper and never know what it is to have a sleepless night. That night was different. I could see John Stoner's face, I could hear John Stoner's voice, I could sense John Stoner's attitude and I lost all sense of confidence. The "I've got confidence in me, I'll be better than my best" attitude had melted like a snow flake in the river. I battled all night and decided that promotion was too big a challenge, the job was too big for me, I was not suitable for it. I decided that on Monday morning I was going to phone Nottingham office and tell that that I had decided not to accept the promotion. I told Edith and I think that she understood how I felt and she was encouraging but did not try and convince me against my will.

I still felt the same in church on Sunday morning. I could not wait for Monday morning to put an end to the agonies. We had a visiting preacher, Barry Benney who was now the editor of the Assemblies of God magazine I had written a weekly article for several years previously. Michael Smith was conducting the meeting and quite suddenly he announced that Brother Benney was going to read the Scriptures to us. I could tell by the expression on Mr Benney's face that this had come out of the blue, he did not seem to be expecting this or prepared for it. Walking to the lectern he said "Let us read a Psalm, its Psalm number 75" and he began to read.

I was sitting there thinking that this was a fairly uninteresting reading when the words from verses 6 and 7 hit me right between the eyes, *"For promotion cometh neither from the east neither from the west, nor from the south. But God is the judge. He puts down one and sets up another."*

Edith elbowed me and smiled. Some powerful transforming dynamic was active. I had the same experience as John Greenleaf Whittier, who many years before had written,

Drop Thy still dews of quietness till all our striving cease take from our souls the strain and stress and let our ordered lives confess the beauty of Thy peace.

Breathe through the heat of our desire Thy coolness and Thy balm.

Let sense be dumb let flesh retire, speak through the earth quake, wind and fire, O still small voice of calm"

God had spoken. I shared what had happened with Barry Benney who admitted that as he walked towards the lectern he opened his Bible at random and read the page it had opened at. Smiling he quizzed, "What do you think the chances are that this is a coincidence"

I enjoyed my Sunday lunch. I never made the phone call to Nottingham. I enjoyed every minute of our new chapter in Grimsby and Cleethorpes.

# Grimsby

On Sunday 4th January 1976 our phone began to ring. I assumed it to be a Prudential client facing some emergency and that would have been fine. Even though I had relinquished my Sleaford agency, I could have still come to the rescue of a client in a time of need. I would of course also have involved Trevor Newton whose application to take over my job had been successful. However Trevor had literally just started his career with Prudential and I was sure that he would welcome anything I could do to help him. The phone call however was not from a local client. The issues needing attention were massive and would present me with a huge challenge and take up weeks of my time.

When I answered the phone I was greeted by John Stoner, soon to be my boss at Grimsby.

"Sorry to disturb your Sunday afternoon sleep David. What time are you expecting to arrive at Grimsby office tomorrow?"

"Hello Mr Stoner, I was intending having an early lunch so that I can be in your office about 2.00pm if that's ok"

"It will be better if you can get here first thing in the morning David, the sea defences have been breached and hundreds of homes are flooded. All of the affected houses are situated in your territory." He went on to explain that the railway line between Grimsby and Cleethorpes had been washed away and the open air bathing pool in Cleethorpes had been wrecked by the water and the gales.

Needless to say, I promised to be on hand soon after 9 am next day, apprehensive of what appeared to be a huge challenge waiting for me. Michael Brotherton, the M P for the area raised the issues in the House of Commons and he addressed The House with these words

"I should like to bring to the attention of the House the necessity to build up more strongly the sea defences of this country, particularly following what happened in January this year with the gales and floods, especially on the East Coast, and what has happened in Cleethorpes in my constituency. In Cleethorpes 402 houses were flooded and damaged by flood water. I do not know how many honourable members have seen what has happened in a house when water has come over the nearby sea wall. It is a grotesque, nasty, horrid and revolting sight. On the Monday following the weekend of the floods, I went to look at Oliver Street in Cleethorpes and I saw the most horrifying sights. The damage suffered by people who had, perhaps, just bought their houses, and damage to freezers, new carpets and so on, was immense. The whole thing was mayhem and destruction. I believe that the Louth constituency is entitled to ask that compensation be given to the people in the constituency whose houses were damaged. What sort of help can be given, for example, to my constituent whose motor car was hit by flood water? The vehicle was insured for third party risks only, and its owner was told by the Council that the flood was an act of God and so the Council could not help him. We ask the Minister to help the Council look after such cases. We in Cleethorpes know that before the winds come again and the tide gets high, it is the duty of ratepayers and taxpayers to help us. Helping the people of Cleethorpes by the provision of a sea wall is just as important as helping those in Wallasey, Norfolk, on the Thames or in any other part of the country. Defending our people from floods is just as important as defending them from the Russians, the Chinese or anybody else" Hansard 21st January 1976

I was in the Grimsby office just after 9 o'clock next morning and warmly welcomed by John Stoner. When Edith and I had visited him at his home a few weeks ago, I noticed a polished wood name plate on their mantel piece. It obviously belonged to a previous life and proudly displayed the name in gold leaf CAPTAIN N. A. J. STONER. There was an atmosphere of calm in the office, I felt as though the captain was on board and therefore everything was under control. I soon learned that whenever John Stoner returned to the office following a short break or holiday it seemed as though the captain was back in control. John was already getting to grips with the handling of all the flood claims. He had brought his caravan onto the car park of Darley's Hotel on the main Grimsby Road, it was positioned there with a large sign informing the public that PRUDENTIAL FLOOD CLAIMS ARE SETTLED HERE. The caravan was just a few hundred yards from the streets of the most devastation, and made it so much easier for a client to obtain help. John had also been in touch with Lincoln sub divisional office and they sent a staff member with a portable safe in the boot of his car. The safe contained enough money to ensure that policyholders could receive cash immediately to obtain essentials such as food, clothes, toiletries and cleaning materials.

He had also arranged that I had authority to handle and settle claims up to £5000, which was a great help. People often speak of a baptism of fire, this was a real baptism of water initiating me into the responsibilities of a Prudential Superintendent.

Grimsby District employed four section superintendents. I was the only one to be affected by the horrid disaster, but in the early days all four of us became involved in the soul destroying job of inspecting so much damaged property and trying to ensure that our clients were not left out of pocket. Air force personnel were brought in from Binbrook, they helped remove smelly saturated carpets, floor coverings and furniture before stacking everything up in the garden for our attention. The RAF brought with them huge powerful electric hot air blowers and left those running in people's homes to try and dry them out, the huge electricity cost became an allowable claim under the Prudential home insurance.

In those early weeks I tried to keep each evening free to accompany my staff on their sales programmes, but we could not avoid having to deal with some flood claims during an evening. The impact made upon normal routine was significant.

The timing of the flood was vicious. The homes in the flooded area were among the lowest cost in the area, many just bought by first time buyers, very many owned by young couples with children. Many people had stretched themselves financially to give the children a good Christmas at the risk of emptying the bank account and now had this unexpected tragedy to contend with. Yet I cannot recall hearing any affected people grumbling or complaining. There was a cheerful resilience which made my job of claims settling much easier. I had to keep my wits about me though. I was completing a claim form for one client and most of the items claimed for could still be seen piled up in the back garden. Just as I thought we had included everything he added,

"Oh Mr Robinson, there is one other thing I almost forgot. I lost my excellent Canon camera in the aftermath of the flood. "

"Really, sorry about that, can you tell me more?"

"Yes, I took loads of pictures showing the water level in the house and showing the piles of damaged goods in the garden. Then I put the camera on the mantel piece but when the fire service left after pumping us out

I discovered that the camera had gone. I don't think for a moment that they stole it. I think it got knocked onto the floor and swept up with all the debris."

I took details of the camera and added it to the claim form. Our paperwork all done I was offered a hot drink, whilst relaxing with my hands round the hot mug, my client continued,

"Would you like to see pictures I took of the water lapping up the stairs and the piles of damaged goods?"

"Yes I sure would"  letting go of my coffee mug I held my hand out as he shared his photographs with me.

"Wow these are amazing pictures, they must have been taken with an excellent camera."

"Yes, they were taken with my Canon camera!"

"Then, my good friend, I need to delete your Canon camera from the claim form"

Giving me an embarrassed grin, he replied,

"Sorry, I slipped up there didn't I?"

We earned a great deal of goodwill during our response to the flood. Some of the other insurance companies were not as quick to pay out or as generous as we had been and word spread. Some dissatisfied people changed their insurer and came to us at renewal, and there were many recommendations for us to call and see relatives and friends to insure their homes and contents. One of the most fulfilling outcomes though was that years later, I would visit a home to try and sell some new business, and there was a real welcome, "Come in, we remember you, you were brilliant when we were flooded"

Even though I had been busy all day assessing flood claims I was still expected to accompany one of my staff that evening to sell on his behalf. John Stoner had planned my diary for the first week, from then on I was master of my own diary. John said,

"If you had arranged your own diary for this week, who would you have worked with?"

"That's easy, I would have worked on the first night with the least experienced agent working my way through them all leaving the senior ones until last"

"I thought you would do that David, but I have thrown you in at the deep end. Tonight you are working with the oldest most experienced agent. Let's see whether you can teach him anything."

So following a quick sandwich back at my bed and breakfast address I waited for my colleague to call and introduce himself. The lady who owned the B&B was Lil Parker and the colleague I was to work with that evening was her Prudential agent.

"Oh you will get on well with Bill Bartlet. He is lovely. He has been with the Prudential for donkey's years and there is nothing he does not know about insurance."

"Thank you Mrs Parker" I thought. "You have made me more nervous now"

Soon Bill rang the doorbell and we were off in my car, following his directions to visit his first appointment. We were going to see a school teacher to discuss his maturing endowment policy and to try to arrange a replacement policy for him. Bill introduced me as "Young Dave" and having set the stage left it all to me.

An hour later we were back in my car and I heaved a sigh of relief that my first appointment seemed to have gone well. Imagine my surprise when Bill, as he fastened his seat belt said gently,

"Young Dave, that's it. I don't want to work with you again"

"Sorry Bill, I don't think that I understand."

"Oh there is nothing wrong young Dave, in fact just the opposite. Now that I have seen you work I know that I can send you anywhere. When you and I are programmed to work together in future we will do half the appointments each and then meet up in the pub to see how we have both succeeded" As there was nothing Bill did not know about insurance, this seemed a good idea, but I did insist from time to time that we work together.

First day over, I was glad to get back to Lil Parker's guest house and glad to go to bed thinking "I am really going to enjoy this job"

# Team Building

Until we moved house to live in Cleethorpes in March 1976, I was made very comfortable at Mrs Parker's guest house just off the sea front. I could not fault the accommodation and the friendship shown by the Parker's however when I think back to my time there, one word comes quickly to mind, FREEZING. I was so cold that I slept in a woolly jumper and my dressing gown and pyjamas and still woke every morning with my teeth chattering. Lil Parker plugged in an oil filled radiator in my bedroom, it was certainly hot to the touch, but I still woke shivering uncontrollably. My teeth chattered so much that I found normal conversation impossible at breakfast. Yet when I went back home to Sleaford mid week for a night I discarded the woolly jumper and dressing gown and was perfectly comfortable.. It made me realise just how much colder it was 40 or 50 miles away at the coast. I was beginning to hope that Cleethorpes was not always as cold when Spring dawned followed by a long baking hot summer which seemed to go on and on and on. I was still enjoying hot sun right into October.

June 25th was the hottest day on record in many places in the United Kingdom. In some areas the temperature was pushing 100°F and the UK had the worst drought in 300 years. The unbearable heat was not confined to Cleethorpes alone. In Yorkshire the surface of the M1 began to crumble in the heat. The Wimbledon umpires were allowed to remove their jackets for the first time in living memory. Newcastle Hospital laundry staff walked out due to the intolerable heat. The AA reported that almost every major road in the UK was littered with overheated motor cars. Debenhams in Southampton city centre had air conditioning fitted 8 months before the heatwave. However they could not afford to switch it on. Dealing with the intense heat was costing £2500 per hour, which was the usual amount spent on electricity in an average month.

In the London Underground the suffocating heat was only alleviated slightly when passengers began stripping to the waist and smashing the carriage windows. The intense heat caused some people to behave strangely. An Egyptian spectator at Wimbledon began pinching women's bottoms and when arrested immediately claimed Diplomatic Immunity.

A few months ago I had struggled with the cold. Now I was struggling with the oppressive heat. A traditional suit was so uncomfortable that I bought a beige safari suit and did feel a little cooler in it. One afternoon I went into Grimsby office wearing it to be greeted with a question from John Stoner,

"Have you forgotten part of your uniform David?"

" Sorry Mr Stoner, I am not sure what you mean."

"I am referring to your peaked cap which you seem to have forgotten, you are a park keeper are you not?"

He then made it clear that he expected that a normal suit and tie be worn at all times. I heard a few days later that he had visited a Prudential client and his wife to deal with a death claim.

They said to me, "We wondered who was walking down our path looking so casual. No jacket, sleeves rolled up and no tie, shirt collar wide open. When he told us he was the Prudential District Manager we would not believe it"

I remembered Mr Stoner's criticism of my safari suit but continued to wear it. After all, had he not now given me diplomatic immunity!

During my first week in Grimsby I worked with my two most senior staff on the Monday and Tuesday. On Wednesday afternoon Mr Stoner had arranged for all my team to meet formally in his office so that official introductions could be made and giving me the opportunity to address the team and begin building team spirit right from those first few days. That evening I was scheduled to work with another of my senior staff, Bert, who also happened to be the chairman of the local branch of the staff union. I found him to be inscrutable at first, and considered him to have no sense of humour. As we got to know each other I discovered a dry sense of humour and a warm personality. He played the organ at the local Catholic Church and did a lot of voluntary work for the local Polish Association. His wife had inherited her fathers well established printing business and ran it successfully with a very small staff. They produced the invitations and order of service for our two daughters when they were married. One of my memories of Bert still brings a smile to my face. He had a late afternoon appointment for us both, and as the weather was warm and pleasant, I left the sun roof of my Volvo wide open whilst we were doing our visit. We were completely unaware that whilst indoors there had been a tropical downpour but as we made our way back to my car we saw no evidence of the rain. The heat had ensured that the pavements, road and my car were dry. The car seats however were soaking wet, a fact we did not discover until we sat on them. We both exclaimed together, "Oh no, my backside is soaking wet"

Bert took me to his next appointment and the lady invited us in and invited us to sit down on her pink settee. Bert, inscrutable as ever, moustache quivering, serious as a judge, said to our hostess,

"We would rather not sit down if you don't mind. We have both wet our trousers and don't want to leave half moon marks on your settee"

The lady trying not to look amused, responded,

"Oh you won't be wanting a drink then!"

Following introductions at the section meeting I expressed surprise to John Stoner that my team only comprised of six men whereas at my promotion interview in Nottingham there had been seven buff folders on the divisional managers desk, and he had given me to understand that I would be responsible for a seven man team.

John Stoner, looking very serious replied,

"Yes David, there were seven men on your team, but I made the decision to take one of them from you and have transferred him to another section. He is unmanageable and he would have broken you within a year. He has caused two superintendents to have nervous breakdowns, and I did not want you, as a rookie to have to try and manage him."

Three years later, John Stoner retired and the new district manager Roland, advised me after a few months that he was transferring the unmanageable staff member back to my team.

"David, we need to manage him out, and you are the man to back me as we get to grips with him. You will keep your cool and he will find it difficult to provoke you"

"Thanks for showing confidence in me, but at this stage I can't give you an assurance that I will work towards getting rid of him. He may work well with me"

Three years later, after a very interesting journey, our unmanageable man was dismissed after being placed under disciplinary measures from the very first week he was part of my team. It had been a hard three years but I learned lessons which would prove valuable in later life.

I was happy with my team, I felt certain that my six men with experience varying from just a few months to thirty years would be loyal, responsive and hardworking. When I addressed them all at that very first meeting, I completely ignored Mr Edrich's orders to wield the big stick. That would be used later when managing the unmanageable !

Bill, who I had worked with on my first day was a very gentle soft spoken Irish gentleman and was a practising Catholic. One of my memories of Bill concerns his caring attitude. One of his clients was a nurse who worked shifts. She did not want Bill to have to make a repeat visit if she was at work or in bed, so she hid a key for him so that he could let himself in and collect the money which would be ready for him. She had told him that he was welcome to make a hot drink if she was not in and that he could use her telephone if he needed to. She was in bed when Bill called but was still awake. She overheard Bill making a phone call to a local coal merchant. He had just left an old ladies house, and she was sitting shivering with no fire in the grate. As he left he lifted the lid of the coal bunker just beside her back door. It was empty.

"Please deliver 5 bags of coal to this dear old lady who is sitting with no fire. Please send me the bill and don't tell the old lady who has ordered the coal". Our nurse friend never let Bill know that she was aware of his kindness. But she told me, after Bill's death.

Willie, who was due to retire in six month's time was the joker. He was a sharp bright eyed Lancastrian, always ready with a joke, always clean but often corny. He played the cornet in a local band and his writing was like hieroglyphics. His previous superintendent said to me,

"If you can't read Willie's writing, just ask him what it says and trust him."

I did Willie's final audit in the scorching hot June. I called for him on the first day of the audit to find two pedal cycles waiting beside his door.

"It's too hot to use the car David so if you don't mind we will cycle, get the breeze up our trouser legs!"

I should have suspected that foul play was afoot as I cycled along behind Willie. He kept looking round to check that I was still close behind and kept giggling.

"Whats wrong Willie?"

"Nothing at all young Dave, nothing at all!"

I hit a pot hole in the road and the stem holding the cycle seat retracted at great speed into the tubular frame. I had a high pitched squeaky voice for a while. Willie had another fit of the giggles. I realised that he had slackened off the bolt holding the seat, and he was joyfully anticipating my discomfort when the inevitable happened.

Rob was a member of my team. Single, living with mum and dad but engaged and due to be married later that year. Rob was still quite new to the job. New agents were subjected to a confirmatory audit after 6 months service. This audit confirmed whether or not they were considered suitable to be confirmed as a permanent staff member. The previous superintendent had done Rob's confirmatory audit just a few months before and it was satisfactory. Rob's agency was due shortly for its routine three yearly audit, and I would be conducting that within a few months. Rob was a cheerful likeable young man in his early twenties. He had experience as a journalist with the local newspaper and was skilled at painting pictures with expressive words and phrases.

We have kept in touch over the years and Rob is a frequent welcome visitor to our bungalow. Last time he came he went home to fetch his wheel barrow, rolled his sleeves up and moved a huge pile of bark chippings from our front to the back garden and then spread them over the prepared bed.

Steve was a valued team member, he was older than Rob and was married with two young children. He had been with the Company for only four months, and I would be doing his confirmatory audit within a couple of months. I was beginning to think that there was some truth in John Stoner's warning that I would be too busy to enjoy the seaside! Steve and his wife were very supportive of the premature baby unit at the hospital and helped raise funds for it. They often took gifts to the unit to bless young mums who needed a little help and support.

Then there was Dave, a fellow Yorkie from Rotherham.    I was from a posher part of Yorkshire, Wakefield,  Dave was a godsend in helping me settle in Grimsby. He sensed when I was busy and would always volunteer to help.  If an agent was on holiday Dave would gather up all the money collected by Inge McDonald our highly efficient Deputy Collector.  Inge retired shortly after my move to the area, and her very worthy successor was Rose Molson who gave many years of loyal service.  Having relieved Mrs McDonald of all the cash she had collected, Dave would complete the weekly account for the colleague on holiday, and often would deal personally with any urgent messages. I was grateful for this very practical and thoughtful help. Dave even came to our home just after we moved in and helped to get the place ship shape. He worked for the Prudential in Rotherham before transferring to Grimsby.    One day he received notification that a Rotherham policyholder had moved to live in his area in Cleethorpes. He called to introduce himself and discovered that he knew the clients Rotherham agent.

Making conversation, Dave commented,

" It's a small world,  I used to work for Prudential in Rotherham and I know your previous agent."

"Really, I don't like him, in fact I could not stand him,"

"Why is that then?"

"He wears a wig!"

"That's not a good reason for disliking someone, I wear a wig"

The lady reached out her hand, as she was saying,

"Rubbish, that's not a wig it normal hair". She grabbed Dave's wig and pulled.  To her horror she exposed Dave's bald head as she waved  his wig in the air.  They both laughed and got along just fine from then on.

Dave still lives quite close to me, and often walks past our front garden, now that we are both well and truly retired we have time to catch up on old times. Our reminiscences are pleasant and refreshing.

Yes, I was pleased with the team I had inherited. I hoped that they saw in me a leader and colleague they could trust as I sought to encourage them when they were down and bring them down when they thought too highly of themselves. My success was in their success, we all needed each other. I was sure that I had excellent material to work with and felt privileged to be able to lead them.

# The Chuffings

It was my evening to work with Steve and he arrived at my home just before six pm he seemed unusually excited.

"You are in for a treat tonight David, we have an appointment with the Chuffings".

This was music to my ears because the family were much younger than Steve usually took me to. Steve seemed to have such a high number of older people on his patch and getting into the home of a young family was a refreshing change.

I had met this family before. They were from Barnsley but had made Cleethorpes their home, and who could blame them! They lived less than five minutes walk from the town centre and could be on the promenade in ten minutes. The short distance to the town centre did not prevent Frank from driving his large car there. I had seen him several times park his car on the high street before climbing out bare footed to disappear into one of the shops. He was a thin wiry man with sharp pointed features and a broad Yorkshire accent. He reminded me of Seth who years ago was a character in Emmerdale.

His wife, Cathy, although a Barnsley lass, had black hair and a pale complexion. She reminded me of an Irish Colleen, until she opened her mouth.

Before long we were sitting in their comfortable terraced house enjoying a coffee. I always liked to explore for myself the reason for the appointment, so between sips of coffee, I asked,

"I know that Steve has made an appointment to see you tonight, but what would you like us to do for you?"

This was a very open question and often revealed that our client had bigger expectations for our visit than we had anticipated. It helped us to avoid small thinking when they had more substantial plans for saving.

Cathy smiled at me, "I want to cash a small chuffing policy in, but I would like to take a chuffing bigger one out."

To avoid pre-judging how much Cathy wanted to save, I worked out three examples and outlined them for her consideration. As often happened, Cathy chose the middle example and I asked if it was ok to go ahead with the paperwork.

I tried not to smile each time Cathy used the word "chuffing" but I was trying to keep a tally in my mind of how many times she used the word. So Cathy chose the middle chuffing example, at twenty chuffing pounds per chuffing month. She asked whether she could pay the chuffing premium by chuffing direct debit, and I nodded in agreement.

We were offered another chuffing cup of coffee and were invited to help ourselves to the chuffing chocolate biscuits as I proceeded with the completion of the proposal form. Cathy told me her chuffing date of birth, the chuffing place of her birth, what her chuffing job was adding her chuffing height and weight.

I needed to gently explore her medical history, and asked whether she had ever had a surgical operation.

"I had a chuffing hysterectomy."

"Thanks Cathy, where did you have the operation?" I expected her to say, "I had the operation in Grimsby hospital" but this was too simple for her.

"Where do you think I had the chuffing operation, don't you chuffing know anything about a woman's chuffing anatomy?"

Eventually, having lost count of the number of chuffings's I had heard, the paperwork was finished.

"Where do you want me to chuffing sign, can I borrow your chuffing pen?"

As she handed the signed form back to me, Cathy said,

"I suppose you will want a chuffing cheque for the first chuffing month's premium. I will just go into the chuffing kitchen for my chuffing cheque book."

Steve had not said much during the interview, and although he was usually very serious, he smiled at me as he asked,

"Excuse me sir but would you like me to make out a chuffing receipt for the first chuffing premium?"

Not wishing to leave Frank out of the interview I gently enquired whether I could speak with him about savings or life assurance. Frank obviously had the same affliction as his wife,

"Not chuffing tonight if you don't chuffing mind!"

We saw two or three other appointments that evening but none as colourful as Cathy and Frank. As Steve and I concluded our evening's work at about nine pm Steve with uncharacteristic humour was still trying to fit the word "chuffing" into his conversation as often as he could.

A few weeks later I was shopping in Cleethorpes and as I walked out of Boots Chemists onto St Peter's Avenue I almost collided with Cathy. I smiled at her as I greeted her,

"Lovely to see you Mrs Chuffings."

With a puzzled expression clouding her pleasant face, Cathy responded ,

"Mrs Chuffings, I don't know where you chuffing well get Chuffings from. I'm chuffing Cathy chuffing Smith."

# Team Changes

The dynamics of my team were soon to change as I lost two of my three senior men. The first audit I did was Willie's final audit which was conducted in the searing heat of June. I did not find the audit challenging as everything was shipshape. The main problem was understanding Willie's writing. I followed the advice from the previous superintendent who had moved to the Louth District, " Just ask Willie what it says and trust him".

When I left Sleaford, Lou Winterton the District Manager asked me to do my own final audit.

He felt that it would be good experience for me which would stand me in good stead when I began doing audits in Grimsby. After all, I was not leaving the Company so I could soon be contacted should there be any irregularities with my own audit. Happily there were no issues.

I always found that I got to know my staff a little better whilst auditing them. We practically lived together for at least three weeks with a very late night finalising all the calculations. It was also interesting to see first hand how the agent and his clients related to each other. I regarded an audit as  successful not simply because it showed accuracy and competency, but because it produced a lot of leads to follow up in pursuit of new business. It was surprising sometimes how blinkered an agent could be, he was visiting a home every month and chatting to the lady of the house, but had never realised that the eldest son had begun his first job, or the daughter had just got engaged. Having gleaned this information myself whilst doing the audit I would ensure that suitable follow up sales appointments were made. John Stoner, my first District Manager in the Grimsby District always referred to an audit as " the Lord Mayor's Show". He viewed them not just as irksome routine administration but as an opportunity. An opportunity for the superintendent to role model good practice and to demonstrate to staff how to prospect for new business.

So even though Willie was retiring, I found myself compiling a list of prospects which I would follow up with his successor.

Early on during Willie's audit I saw something which caused me deep concern. Bill was out collecting on his own agency, but he was not walking in a straight line and needed to lean on a fence to support himself. I stopped my car and spoke with him, but he insisted that he was fine but was struggling in the heat. I was not convinced, so I phoned Mrs Bartlett to tell her that I had arranged for the deputy collector to do that afternoon's collections for Bill which left him without excuse when she insisted that he saw the doctor. Bill did see his GP that evening who insisted that he be admitted to hospital immediately for tests.

Three weeks later was Willie's final day with the Prudential. All the staff attended his lunch time retirement presentation at The County Hotel. A suitable gift was presented to Willie, and John Stoner and I paid tribute to his long devoted service. We all said our goodbyes, and quite soon only John Stoner and I were left in the room.

"David, I did not want to spoil Willie's send off by breaking some bad news to the staff. I am afraid that you have lost not just one team member today, but two. Bill passed away in hospital late this morning. I have told Mary his wife that you will contact her to arrange to collect everything connected with Bill's Prudential work."

I was still trying to take this in when Mr Stoner continued,

"You will need to do another final audit of Bill's agency David. It won't be easy because you will be doing it without him. But I don't expect there to be any problems, do you?"

Later that day I was sitting once again at the bureau which Bill had used for many years as his office base. Soon after Bill had been admitted to hospital I had called and picked up all cash and cheques he had not banked together with his account books etc and had taken over the running of his agency whilst he was ill. I never imagined then that Bill would never return home alive and that within a few weeks I would be removing everything connected with the job from his home. Mary was so helpful, making me coffee and supplying biscuits. She was trying to keep busy as a well proved coping mechanism at such times. There was a touch of humour even in that sad scene. I had cleared Bill's desk when Mary handed me a small clear cellophane bag containing a set of false teeth.

"Would you mind taking these as well please David, they are Bill's spare teeth. Please dispose of them"

As I was driving away I began to realise just how much work was ahead of me, but for Bill, nothing was too much trouble.

I was surprised how many of Bill's clients were not aware that he had died. Several greeted me brashly exclaiming,

"Where's Bill then, is he sunbathing on the beach?" Breaking the news of Bill's death became part and parcel of carrying out his final audit.

The audit went well with no issues. Joyce Schofield who was John Stoner's clerk decided to leave her responsible clerical job and take over Willie's agency. Dave Winslow who had been a successful agent in Grimsby for several years applied to take over Bill's agency. So I was blessed in that I did not have to carry the weight of two vacant agencies for long.

My first two audits had been carried out in glorious summer weather. There was to be yet another one, another three weeks pounding the beat being smiled upon by the hot Cleethorpes sun.

Rob's agency was due for its routine three yearly audit, however a full audit had been completed a few months prior to me taking over the section. This had been Rob's confirmatory audit when he had concluded six months service, and it had been concluded that as there were no issues Rob should be given a permanent contract.

I liked Rob, he was young, transparent, pleasant and full of enthusiasm. He reminded me of a young puppy, eager to please it's master but not quite sure what was expected of it! One thing Rob did expect, was that I would be a passenger in his car for the duration of the audit. This was his first car and he was so proud of it. He frowned when colleagues described it as a plastic pig, but it was a huge step up from his bike. He had to brake harshly which is when I discovered that my seat was not secured to the floor. I rolled over backwards, knees and legs in the air, my papers scattered all over the car floor.

We called at a small convenience store to check the owner's premium books etc. We were greeted with a tale of woe,

"Would you believe it, someone has stolen my half ounce and ounce weights" the proprietor grumbled as he nodded towards his old fashioned scales.

"What good are a couple of weights to anyone? I don't think I will be able to replace them, they are a hundred years old"

Rob trying to show sympathy replied,

"That's bad, I do hope that you get them back. Did you inherit the scales when you took over the shop or did you buy them new?"

Our shopkeeper friend was not amused but we both bought some sweets to try and make amends. As we walked along the road, Rob warned me about his next client,

"Our next client is not a pretty sight, on a hot morning like this she will be sitting on a high kitchen stool having a smoke. The only clothing she will be wearing is a grubby underskirt and it is hard to see where the underskirt ends and where the dirty flesh starts! She does not look human, she has places where normal women don't have places."

True to Rob's description, there she was, resplendent in her unwashed sweaty state as she held court from her kitchen stool, she blew clouds of cigarette smoke from her toothless mouth.

Rob introduced me as his boss as he picked up her money from the kitchen bench. Keeping a sensible distance from her I said,

"Good morning Mrs Francis, I am doing an audit and need to see your premium receipt books."

"Oh I don't know where they are Mr Robinson, I have not seen them for months."

"Please call me David, and I am sorry to inconvenience you but it is absolutely essential that I inspect your books"

After a frantic search punctuated with heavy sighs, unrepeatable swear words and voluminous clouds of smoke, her books were safely on the kitchen table. The only problem was that they were not up to date and the last entries in them were several months old. Rob volunteered,

"Oh it's alright boss, there is nothing wrong, just assume that they are all marked up to date"

"But they aren't marked up to date Rob. Please refer to your collecting book and ensure that all monies you have collected are clearly shown in Mrs Francis's books". It did not take Rob long to do this, but his collecting book was quite new and the records in it did not go back far enough.

"Your old collecting book is in your car Rob, please pop out and get it so that we can ensure these books are brought fully up to date before I check them"

"There's no need to do that, it will take too much time, I am sure that everything is fine"

Quite suddenly Mrs Francis exploded into action as she leapt up from her stool,

"Rob, who is the boss, you or him"

"Him"

"Well do as he bleep bleep tells you then, go and get your old collecting book from your bleep bleep car"

Rob left the kitchen like a scalded cat returning a few minutes later with exactly what I needed to complete the records and make it possible to satisfy myself and Mrs Francis that everything was satisfactory.

In the privacy of Rob's car I told him that he had deserved Mrs Francis's wrath, and that I expect him to follow my instructions at all times.

The audit was beginning to go badly. I was making a list of errors, omissions and any breaches of company regulations. Rob pleaded with me not to add any further issues to my list. I gently took the stance that everything needed to come to light. There was no suggestion of dishonesty, no money which was not accounted for, the issues were that record keeping and compliance were slipshod. The regulations of the relevant Industrial Assurance Acts were in some cases not being observed.

One example was incorrect use of premium receipt books. The books were colour coded depending upon the date and types of policy they referred to. The brown book was used only for policies with premiums due on a four weekly basis. The green and the pink books were for weekly premiums and their use depended when the policy was dated. The correct use of books was strictly regulated as their preamble legally defined the regulations affecting the policies listed in that book.

Rob had a unique system. Whilst checking one clients books, I handed Rob one of the ladies brown books which had PINK BOOK written on the front.

"What colour is this book Rob"

"It's a pink book"

"No Rob it's a brown book"

"No, I have changed it from a brown book to a pink book. Look, I have written pink book on it"

So here were more issues to be mentioned in the audit which was duly presented to John Stoner.

Our district manager carefully studied the audit for a while before speaking.

"Rob, it's obvious from all this that you can't do the job properly, I am asking you to resign."

Shaken to the core, Rob responded,

" I have diarrhoea and I get married in three months, I need this job "

Mr Stoner looked at me expecting my support. Instead I challenged him,

"Please let me have six months to sort Rob out, I am confident we can do it"

Then looking at Rob I said,

"Rob, Bert the union chairman is outside, please ask him to come in"

After some probing from Bert, Mr Stoner conceded that most of the things I had discovered to be wrong were apparent a few months previously but had not been discovered by the previous superintendent when he conducted the audit.

Bert addressed the district manager,

"Can I ask who did Rob's confirmatory audit several months ago."

"You know who did the audit Bert, the previous superintendent did it."

"Then can I ask Rob how long his previous superintendent spent doing the audit?"

"You can ask him but he does not have to answer. Do you want to answer that question Rob?"

"Yes sir, my previous superintendent spent two hours with me."

There was no room for further argument, Rob was reprieved, the diarrhoea cleared miraculously and Rob was married three months later.

I was given six months to turn Rob round. Two years later, he was selected to attend the Prudential Star Dinner held at the Savoy Hotel in London. This was an honour very few attained to. It was a reward for giving a star performance in the job in the previous year.

A worthy investment of my time and a well earned reward for Rob who had worked his socks off to do well.

# The Family Grows

We were settling in well in the Grimsby area and had bought a large semi detached house with sea views from the rear bedroom window. It was a happy home, my staff were dropping in regularly to see me and being so close to the beach it was an excellent place for our daughters to grow up.

However, the weather was not welcoming on the day in March when we moved from Sleaford. It had been very wet and there was a biting cold wind. We arrived at our new home on Seacroft Road at around lunch time and the removal contractors brought three tea chests containing some of our possessions into the kitchen and then decided that they would like some Cleethorpes fish and chips, it seemed a good idea and we all sat on packing chests eating them out of the paper wrappings. One of the removal men switched his radio on, a comedy programme was just starting. Arthur Askey's voice filled our kitchen, "Hello playmates, when the red light is on all the world and parts of Cleethorpes can hear us."

Many people referred to Cleethorpes as "the last resort" it did seem to have been left behind in the popularity stakes. There had been a lack of investment into the area and a certain parts of the resort were looking down at the heel. The Butlins Holiday company had tried to get planning permission to build a hotel in Cleethorpes but those resistant to change thought that such a development would spoil the area. Many of the guest houses were looking rather run down, but their fortunes began to change when the construction of the Humber Bridge began in 1972. Hundreds of contractors were brought in and suddenly Cleethorpes guest houses were in demand. The renaissance of the area had begun.

But on the day we moved in, with a biting cold wind and puddles of water everywhere Arthur Askey's comment about parts of Cleethorpes added a touch of humour. We hoped that we had chosen a good part of Cleethorpes but in truth we soon had regrets.

Directly over our rear garden fence was the car park for the Winter Gardens. In the summer the car park was full and all the coaches backed up to our fence and sat there for long periods with their engines running filling our back garden with acrid diesel fumes.

The Winter Gardens was the venue for Northern Soul concerts which went on virtually most of the night. The volume levels were unhealthily loud and we could feel the beat making our bedroom vibrate and the noise disturbed our sleep. I rang the Winter Gardens one night to complain about the loud music, the lady who answered the phone apologised that she could not hear what I was saying because of the music.

Then at two and three o'clock in the morning we were awakened by the crashing noise of large quantities of empty bottles being dropped from the Winter Gardens fire escape into the refuse skips below.

At three o'clock one morning I rang the police to ask them if they could do anything about the miserable wailing noise caused by someone playing bagpipes quite close to our rear garden.

The police reminded me that it was Burns Night and there was no doubt a celebration going on in the Winter Gardens.

So although our Seacroft Road house was a happy home, we knew that we would not make it our permanent base.

It was whilst living there that we applied to local Social Services to become foster parents. Quite soon our family was enlarged temporarily as Nina a gorgeous baby girl was placed in our care. Our two daughters thought the world of her and as we had Nina for several months they became very attached to her. It was a sad day for us when our social worker took her away from us to re-unite her with her mum. There had been a process of gradually returning her to her mother, but we knew that she would be back with us within a few days. This time though, the goodbye had to be a final one. We heard years later that Nina was working as a hairdresser, so Edith made an appointment to have her hair done where she was working. Edith recognised Nina but did not communicate with her. She had grown up into a beautiful young lady.

When Nina had left our care, we had Danny placed with us. He was about three years old and needed care whilst his mom recuperated from hospital treatment. Danny was a bundle of energy, he followed me everywhere and if I was working in the garden with tools, he was like my shadow, copying my movements. If he could pick up a hand tool I had discarded and pretend to use it as I had done, he was in heaven. He was always on the move, and we had difficulty getting him to sit on the toilet until the task was done. He would look at me intently and say, "I have finished, I have finished."

He was sitting on my knee in church one Sunday morning and he obviously thought that the sermon had gone on long enough. He began to shout " I have finished, I have finished." Danny had heard enough, but the preacher was far from finished!

After six weeks there were sad goodbyes again when Danny had to leave us. He clung to us as he did not want to go. Our two daughters found this difficult to cope with.

Then Cathy was brought to us complete with plenty of nits but with a shortage of clothes. Edith had to deal with the head lice and provide clothes quickly. Cathy was about ten years old and we looked after her for several weeks during her mum's illness. Although she only lived ten miles away she had never been on a beach before. I took her for a walk along the sands and she picked up a handful of sand exclaiming "What is this?" She had never seen sand before. Her home address was on a street called Spring Street, and Edith was enthusing with her one day about how nice her address sounded. Edith asked, "Have you really got springs of water in your street?"

"No " protested Cathy "the street where I live is grotty. Do you know aunty that there is a brothel on my street!"

When Edith reported the conversation to our social worker she confided, "Yes there is a brothel on her street, she does not know it but she lives in it." When Cathy left us to go back to her mum she was proudly carrying a bag full of new clothes and as many tomatoes as she could take from our greenhouse as a gift for her mum.

Edith and I decided not to foster again, but to apply again to The Mission of Hope in London in the hope that we could adopt another child through them. Our application was approved but we needed to immediately resign as foster parents. They would not place a child with us if we were actively fostering. Our social worker was sad to lose us, but she understood and wished us well.

Several months later she popped in to enquire whether The Mission of Hope had placed a child with us yet. Upon hearing that we were still waiting, she asked that we consider fostering a baby boy, but with the intention of adopting him.

The baby was ten months old and was called Trevor. We went to see him in the lovely home of his temporary foster mum who was getting too attached to him, and wanted to see him settled in his permanent home as soon as possible. He was as fat as butter, so placid and sitting happily playing with saucepans on the lounge carpet. We were smitten and were keen to take Trevor as soon as possible. The day after he came into our care, he was asleep in his pram in our back garden (we had moved away from the diesel-flavoured garden!)

Without warning , Mrs Edwards his previous foster mum knocked on our door and asked to see Trevor. She saw him sleeping contentedly and after chatting with Edith left us quite happily. She rang later to let us know that she sensed that Trevor was in a lovely home and that she was happy for him

There was no chance that a social worker would come and take Trevor away, so our two daughters felt secure. They needed to know that they would not have to say a tearful goodbye at the end of a few weeks, so they felt relaxed.

The whole adoption process took about 6 years but the day finally came when we left Grimsby Magistrates Court with the piece of paper which said that Trevor was ours for ever.

Our little family was now complete.

# Mr Stoner

I got on extremely well with John Stoner the Grimsby District Manager. There was always a sense of security when he was in the office. It was not easy to read what he was thinking and it was easy to make a wrong assumption. I remember distinctly feeling that he did not think that I was doing a good job and this made me feel insecure with him. This feeling was kicked into touch by a comment he made about me to the Divisional Manager at one of his visits to Grimsby. It was my turn to be interviewed and as the Divisional Manager and I shook hands, Mr Stoner said to him,

"If Mr Robinson's section does not do well, it won't be his fault."

Just knowing that he had confidence in me was like a shot in the arm. If I was pleased with my staff I let them know. It was always my priority to praise my team for what they had done well before drawing their attention to areas needing improvement. I had the right to challenge them if they were under performing, but I too was in some way accountable to them. They provided a programme of sales calls for me to see when I worked with them, I needed to perform well when I worked with them. If I failed to make sales or made inappropriate sales they had the right to let me know that they were disappointed with the results. If it had been my fault I had to be man enough to admit it and not take their criticism personally. I tried to cultivate this kind of relationship with my team. They all knew that I would be quick to support and encourage them if they were going through a bad time. In a sales job it is important to feel confident, buoyant and enthusiastic and one of the secrets of a team's success is their mental and emotional health.

That is why I had very little time for Mr Edrich, the Division Sales Manager who I suspect did not know the meaning of the word "encouragement". John Stoner was within a year of retiring when Mr Edrich visited the District to hold a meeting with the manager and four superintendents. Mr Stoner spent some time with Mr Edrich first before calling the four of us into his office. He introduced us using our full names,

"This is Malcolm Catley, this is David Howard, this is Peter Bradshaw, this is David Robinson"

Very brusquely Mr Edrich declined to shake hands, he nodded towards the four empty chairs saying,

"Sit down Catley, sit down Howard, sit down Bradshaw, sit down Robinson."

We all felt unwelcome and patronised, as he continued,

"Before I begin this meeting I want to say a few words. You guys will come up with the goods or I will have your jobs. Do I make it clear?"

Oh yes, he made it clear. He made it very clear that although he was Sales Manager for the whole Division the only man management skills he had involved using the big stick. A few minutes into our meeting he singled me out,

"Robinson, do you have any opinion about what I am saying. I can't read you, I don't know whether you are taking it all in or whether it is just going over your head. Do you have any opinion about what I have just said?"

"Oh yes Mr Edrich, I have a very strong opinion about what you are saying and about you as a person!"

"What's that supposed to mean Robinson?"

" You can make it mean whatever you wish Mr Edrich."

He ignored me for the rest of the meeting. That afternoon I rang John Stoner to remonstrate with him.

"Mr Stoner, may I respectfully say something to you. I would not have allowed Mr Edrich to speak to my staff in the abusive way he did. You have less than a year to retirement, what can he do to you at this stage, you had nothing to lose?"

Mr Stoner replied in a tired voice,

"David, you will still be giving excellent service for the company long after they have weeded out Mr Edrich".

Within a few years there was a news item in the Prudential Staff newsletter, 'On the 30th September Mr Edrich , Divisional Sales Manager, relinquished his position and has left the Company's service'. I knew how the Company complies strictly with employment laws, I also was aware that employees were given generous time and space to rectify their deficiencies or change their behaviour. I therefore imagined that the road leading to Mr Edrich's departure had been a long one, and that leaving the Company had been the last resort

Seeing that announcement gave me a pleasurable feeling. I felt reassured that bullying and abusive attitudes would eventually be rooted out. I also felt that my own style of management had received a "thumbs up." At one of my annual appraisals, the District Manager commented,

"David, I sometimes wish that you would lose your temper with some of your staff and give them a good kick up the backside. But at the end of each year you have come up with goods, and done it pleasantly generating a good team spirit. So what have I got to complain about! "

I spent three very happy years working for John Stoner and I was fortunate in having a superior who modelled so much that was good and wholesome. John retired and my new District Manager was Roland Huitson who I was privileged to work for fifteen years.

I think that John Stoner would have retired a year sooner than he did, were it not for sad and unfortunate circumstances. He had an open door policy in his office, and when the door was open we knew that we could step into his private domain if we needed to speak to him. If he wished to raise a sensitive matter, he would ask that we close his office door, and we knew that we were either in trouble or there was a sensitive matter he needed to discuss. I had just sat down in front of his desk one day when he asked me to close the door. Then, finding it hard to control his emotions he told me that his wife, who he always referred to as "Mummy" and to whom he was devoted, was in hospital recovering from a hysterectomy. He explained that the consultant had discovered terminal cancer during what should have been a routine operation. The cancer had spread into vital organs and the prognosis was that "Mummy" only had several months to live. After expressing my sympathy I enquired whether John would bring his retirement forward.

"Oh no David, that's the last thing I would consider doing. I am going to need this job more than ever in the months ahead."

John took some encouragement from the way "Mummy" seemed to improve after being discharged from hospital. She put on some weight and was soon able to potter about in the garden. John spoke with the consultant about this, in the hope that the prognosis could have been wrong. The consultant's response did nothing to alleviate John's fears.

"I am sorry but I have seen how much cancer there is there. I did expect that she would show signs of getting stronger after the operation, but that is only short term. She will deteriorate I am afraid and we must expect that."

This was an awful burden for John to carry and his team did all we could to make his work duties as light as possible. John had seen a similar situation in the life of a long standing friend who lived close to him. He had recently died from cancer and John had visited him most evenings and had sat with him to give his wife a break. Having seen his friend slowly sinking he knew what to expect for his own dear wife.

One lunchtime I received a phone call from Mr Stoner's clerk at the office.

"David, Mr Stoner asked me to ring you. He has been called home unexpectedly and wants you to take over management of the office."

It did not take me long to get into the Grimsby office. It appeared that Mrs Stoner had suddenly become very ill and John had been called home immediately. I had not been in the office long before the sad news came that "Mummy " had died.

John told me later that "Mummy" was feeling stronger and that she was doing some gentle tidying up in the garden when a bee settled in her hair. It caused a panic attack which in turn caused a heart attack and so she died, no lingering week after week in pain, no prolonged suffering. When John arrived home the Anglican Vicar, Canon Hugh Oakes was with "Mummy" and was a great comfort at that time.

Although John was quite a private person who did not discuss his faith, he did see the providence of God in the way in which "Mummy" had been taken. I feel certain that he was right. The God who used ravens to feed one of his prophets during a national famine, and who could instruct plagues of frogs and flies to invade Egypt prior to the exodus can so easily divert a bee from its pollenating duties to settle in a ladies hair.

So the loss of "Mummy" was still a huge blow to John, but it had been made easier by what some people would claim to have been a coincidence.

After "Mummy's " death John continued to manage Grimsby District. Love blossomed again for him and he married the widow of the friend he had helped look after at his journey's end. The four superintendents and their wives were privileged to witness Canon Oakes join John and Betty together in marriage and share in the wedding reception at the Coach House in Humberston, Grimsby.

Roland Huitson who took over from John Stoner, also had an open door policy at his office. He too would ask me to shut the door if he wished to discuss something sensitive.

He rang me one morning to discuss a routine matter, and then asked me to hold on whilst he closed his office door. I was not prepared for what Roland shared with me. He told me that he had cancelled his holiday which was just a few weeks ago because his six years old grandchild was terminally ill. He had gone into hospital in Sheffield for an operation for appendicitis. The surgeon had discovered cancer which was so far advanced that they just closed the little lad up as there was nothing they could do. He had been given just a few short weeks to live.

Roland said,

"I know that you are a Christian David, so perhaps you could pray for my grandson, the Catholic Father has already given him the last rites."

I expressed sympathy and said that I would pray for the little boy. A few weeks later Roland rang me again with an amazing story. It appeared that the surgeon who discovered the cancer had asked the boy's parents for permission to operate again. This would not save the boy's life but would help ensure that he would not suffer as much pain in the final stages of the illness. Consent was given, but when the surgeon opened up the abdomen there was no trace of the cancer. He told the parents the good news adding that if he had not personally seen the cancer for himself he would not have believed it.

Roland added that the story had become a news item in the Sheffield press under the heading "Miracle boy"

When I checked out with Roland several months later, the boy had been back at school for a while and was doing well.

I am not claiming that my prayer was responsible for the outcome. No doubt others in the Catholic Church in Sheffield would have been praying too. What I am claiming is that God does have an intimate hand in the affairs of men. One day we will discover just how many coincidences were actually not coincidences but interventions by a loving and gracious God.

# Echoes of the Past

Three times during my eighteen years in Grimsby as  part of the management team of the Prudential Assurance Company I was unexpectedly confronted by voices from the past.  Two of these incidents were a direct link with my Holmfirth days. The other, a much earlier link to my teenage years in Wakefield, the place of my birth.

I turned the first of these links into an amusing way to impress one of my staff.  The second one I used as an opportunity to try to  revive a past relationship. The third link, and its later implications shows that seeds we have sown many years ago provide God with the opportunity of producing fruit at exactly the right time.

Rob, my youngest staff member asked me to go door knocking with him.  I remembered my early days in the insurance business with the United Friendly Insurance  Company, when I tried to generate business by knocking on doors.  At first I was so nervous that I hoped that no one would answer the door. It was at that time that I came under the guidance of Harold Crawshaw an insurance colleague who I was able to accompany and observe in action.  Harold had been a traditional insurance agent, but the collecting duties frustrated him. He paid his wife to do his collections for him using the time freed up to knock on doors trying to sell new business.  He was so successful at this that his local manager relieved him of his agency and promoted him to the rank of full time door knocker. He was attached to the local office who deployed him across all the agencies to knock on doors of houses where their representatives did not have any business. Harold rejoiced in the job title, " District office knocker man." The amount of new business he generated was incredible.  His fame spread and before long he was promoted to the rank of "Chief Office knocker man."  Chief office in London sent Harold all over the country to do nothing else but knock on doors.  He was incredibly successful, and watching him in action was an inspiration.  I could never claim anything like Harold's success rate, but I learned enough to ensure that I was not nervous anymore and even began to enjoy knocking on "cold" doors.

So when Rob said " Please take me door knocking."  I knew that I could not let him down.

I was knocking on doors on St Heliers Road Cleethorpes with Rob in attendance when a pleasant young lady answered the door. Suitable introductions were made and the lady obviously trusted us because she invited us in to arrange some home contents insurance for her. She accepted the quotation I worked out for her and I invited Rob to complete the proposal form.

As Rob was completing the paper work I had more opportunity to relax in the easy chair and study the contents of the room. There was a photograph of the young lady with a young man beside her. Indeed a voice from the past. A voice crying out loud and clear from my days in Holmfirth.

When Rob had completed his paperwork I drew the young lady's attention to the photograph, asking her,

"Is this your young man?"

"It certainly is Mr Robinson."

"He is not a local boy is he.?"

She shook her head in reply as I continued,

"That's right. The countryside is very flat in this area but where your young man comes from it is very hilly. Yes it's very hilly. In fact he used to live at the top of a very steep hill. Yes I can see it all, he lived in a tiny cluster of houses called "The Hill"

She and Rob were intrigued as I continued,

" Yes, I can see the house he used to live in, it's number twelve. He lived there with his mum Molly and Derek his dad. Derek has a very unusual job, in the winter he drives the snow blower and tries to keep the roads over the moors clear."

I was really impressing her and Rob now, so there was no stopping me

"Your young man got  job in a butchers shop when he left school. It was at the bottom of the hill on the corner with the main road. Yes I can clearly see the name above the shop window, it is called Mettricks Butchers."

A few minutes later we were leaving the young lady's house with her cheque for the insurance premium and the complete proposal form. I had thought that Rob held me in some admiration, if that was true, then the admiration level had just soared. Rob gave vent to his amazement,

"Wow, that was amazing, how did you know all that.?"

"I know everything young Rob!"

"Wow"

"It's simple Rob, his name is John Pickersgill and I sold him his first endowment policy when he left school."

John is the son of Molly, the lady with the loud voice and the heart of gold who befriended Edith when we lived in Holmfirth.

The second voice from the past occurred one morning when I was keeping an appointment for Steve, one of my staff. He had arranged for me to visit the widow of a skipper to discuss investment of a lump sum. I enjoyed coffee and biscuits whilst discussing investments and we had just concluded our business when we heard a car pull up outside her house. My client was sitting with her back to the window which I was facing, so she asked

"Is that a white car which has just pulled up outside?"

"It certainly is Mrs Nielsen."

"Then it's my brother, he is coming to see me today from Huddersfield."

I offered to leave immediately but she chose to ask me to stay and outline the business we had discussed with her brother. He was friendly and I mentioned to him that I had worked for the Prudential near Huddersfield.

"Really, that's where I live, in a village just outside Holmfirth."

I discovered that he actually lived next door to Walter Slater who had been my superintendent during my first two years in Holmfirth. At least ten years had passed since I attended Mr Slater's pie and pea retirement supper, so I was interested to hear how he was going on.

"Oh, he is very sprightly, plays golf two or three times a week, changes his car every year and looks very dapper when he is dressed up."

"Would you please do me a favour and pass my business card on to Mr Slater and give him my best wishes."

I wrote on the back of my card,

"Hello Mr Slater, hope you are well.

You did not think that I would ever mek owt in this job, but I have not done so bad.

Thanks, sincerely

David.

The third voice from the past spoke loudly and clearly when I was standing in for young Rob who was on holiday. My staff always tried their best not to leave me any outstanding matters when going on holiday.Rob was no exception. He had cleared up all matters needing his attention, but expected a cheque whilst he was away, which needed delivering to a retired lady. The lady, Miss Lucy Frederic lived alone and was not keen to answer the door to unannounced strangers. Rob asked me to check his pigeon hole in the office to keep any eye open for the cheque. He left me Miss Frederic's phone number so that I could ring her and arrange to deliver her cheque.

The cheque was in settlement of a maturing policy. I made the phone call, simply introducing myself as Rob's boss without mentioning my name. I arranged to call with the cheque and soon found the house. It was situated on one of the streets which had recently been badly affected by the floods.However I had not been to the house before and to the best of my knowledge had not met Miss Frederic.

As I walked down the garden path I could see that a lady was watching out for me, and she answered the door with a courteous smile.

"You must be Rob's boss, thank you for coming"

"My pleasure Miss Frederic, Rob wanted you to receive your cheque quickly. It only arrived at the office today."

"Well now" she quizzed, " you are not from this area are you?"

"I live in Cleethorpes but was not born here"

"That's right, you were born in Wakefield. Tell me, do you remember Flanshaw Lane?"

"I do, I used to deliver newspapers on Flanshaw Lane but that's a long time ago"

"Yes, it is Mr Robinson, but I never forget a face. Do you remember Flanshaw Lodge?"

"Oh yes, it was a children's home, I delivered newspapers there and once a month used to collect the money."

"You certainly did Mr Robinson, and I was the matron there who used to pay you very month. I watched you park your car just now and as soon as you began walking down my path I remembered your face. At first I thought you were one of the boys who had been through my care, then I realised that you had been our paper boy. You see I never forget a face.'

Miss Frederic went on to tell me that although she had never married, she had been able to adopt a little girl who was now married and living in Cleethorpes. Now retired she had come to Cleethorpes to live near her daughter.

Then, as we enjoyed a coffee together, she reminded me of things I had long forgotten. But as she reminisced the memories came flooding back. She reminded me that I had spoken with my boss at the newspaper shop, and he had donated a large quantity of children's books to the orphanage, I had recently passed my driving test and had borrowed dad's Volkswagen Beetle to deliver all these books to the home. She smiled as she remarked that she was surprised that the books were in the boot which was at the front of the car, the engine being at the rear. This was a novel thing to her.

She recalled how she had told me how disappointed she was with the local vicar who had asked her not to bring any of the children to church, which he said was for adults not children. She reminded me that i had offered to visit the home once a month with a colleague from church to hold a Sunday School for the children.

She reminded me that one Sunday afternoon when we had visited to take the Sunday School, she had not welcomed us and I had asked whether Matron was on holiday. Upon being told that Matron was upset and was in her office, I had tapped on her office door and found her in a tearful condition. She had told me that one of the young boys in her care had been hit by a motor car and was seriously ill in Pinderfields Hospital. The prognosis was bad. The little boy was in a coma and he had suffered brain damage. If he came out of the coma he would have no quality of life whatever. Miss Frederic reminded me that I had asked whether she would like me to pray for the little boy. I prayed that the Lord would either heal him completely or graciously take him whilst he was in the coma. During that afternoon's Sunday School, the hospital informed Miss Frederic that the little lad had slipped away in his sleep.

She reminded me of other things, which I had long forgotten but which had obviously made a big impression upon her which had lasted for eighteen to twenty years.

I left Miss Frederic after thanking her for sharing these memories, and although our conversation had made a big impression on me at that time, I was so busy that it soon slipped to the back of my mind. It was at least 15 years before I met Miss Frederic again.

I had taken early retirement at fifty years of age to launch a Christian charity in Cleethorpes. The local Churches Together group had invited me to share my vision for the Charity, Christian Action and Resource Enterprise (CARE) at one of their meetings, I had done this quite often in Christian and secular circles and always enjoyed it and felt free to express myself. This occasion was different. We were assembled in the church hall. The lady who was acting as Chair told me to sit anywhere in the hall, she would invite me to speak at the appropriate time. I found a seat several rows from the back of the hall, and sat through the preliminaries.

The Chair invited me to stand and deliver my talk. It was clear that I was not expected to stand at the front facing the audience. There I was, three quarters of the audience sitting in front of me with me speaking to the backs of their heads. A quarter of the audience were behind me, and they were looking at the back of my head. The only faces I could see were those of the Chair and the Secretary who were sitting at the table facing the audience.

I could not engage with the audience, in fact I could not engage with the Chair at her table. She was expressionless with no encouraging smiles or nods. I spoke for 15 to 20 minutes and it was the most difficult address

I had ever given. Not a sign that the audience were engaging with me, I tried every angle but it was like trying to stir thick pudding. At last, it was over, I heaved a sigh of relief and sat down.

The Chair in a rich fruity voice simply said, "Thank you for that, the next item on the agenda is item number seven, which is...."

But she never finished her sentence. She was interrupted by an equally loud voice coming from somewhere behind me.

"Madam Chair, how dare you move on to the next item on the agenda. We have just heard a voice from God tonight, and we need to pause to consider what we can all do to get behind this enterprise. I knew our speaker when he was a very young man, and he was a person of integrity then. He is a gentleman of integrity now, and we need to listen and get behind this project'"

I turned to see who was so bravely interrupting the meeting. It was Miss Lucy Frederic.

In 2002 when we celebrated the tenth anniversary of the Charity at the Ice House in Grimsby, Miss Frederic was there as were Lord Yarborough, the Mayor and other VIPs. Miss Frederic sought out the newspaper reporter to let her know that the founder of the charity had been known to her since he was a young lad, "He was a young man of integrity then, and he is a man of integrity now. We need to get behind this Charity.

# All in a day's work

I was fortunate in meeting so many members of the public who were policyholders of the Prudential Assurance Company. They formed a rich tapestry upon which could be seen people of all temperaments, viewpoints, political and religious persuasions and of course different occupations. Some people were exhausting to be with, dealing with them seemed to suck the vitality from you, and others left you walking on air. I regularly called upon a retired couple in Sleaford. She had been a teacher and he had been a self-employed builder. They were pleasant, friendly, welcoming and never said an offensive or unpleasant thing. The subject matter of their conversation was always interesting and topical, but I hated calling on them - when I left their home I usually felt that all vitality had been sucked out of me. This was when I was pounding the beat collecting premiums and this couple were a regular monthly call. If I was short of time because unexpected duties had needed attention, I would look through my collecting book at the rest of that session's calls and decide who I could miss out and leave until the following month. This couple were hot favorites for omitting from my visits. There was nothing not to like about them except the way they sucked. I did not like visiting them.

I did not know that an elderly gentleman I loved visiting, was related to them. At one of my visits he produced their premium book and money, commenting that he understood that I had not caught them in a few days ago, and so they had brought their money to his home as they knew that I called there too.

"I did not know that you were related to Mr. and Mrs. Robertson Mr. Wollerton!"

"Oh yes, she is my sister. You should get along fine with them because they are Christians like you."

"Really Mr. Wollerton, I never knew that. We have not spoken about faith and religion. Which church are they members of?"

"Oh they are leading lights at the Christian Spiritualist Church

I left Mr. Wollerton's home thanking him for the information and realising for the first time why I felt uncomfortable in visiting his sister and her husband. I could not accept that there were such people as Christian Spiritualists. Christianity and Spiritualism are poles apart and however hard you try to reconcile them it is impossible. They are as opposite as light and darkness which actually is an accurate analogy. What I had sensed in their home was a different spirit which, had I let it, would have oppressed me and taken me into bondage.

As soon as I realized that, I was fully prepared for future visits, I asked the Holy Spirit to accompany me and protect me from subtle attacks from unknown spirits which motivated them and directed their lives. I could not refuse to deal with them, visiting them was part of a day's work, but I could deal with it forewarned and forearmed!

The opposite of this is true, I have felt drawn to certain people, as though warmed by their presence only to discover later that they are practicing Christians. We need to be careful that we carry the right Presence with us as we go about our duties.

I was with Rob for an afternoon and evenings sales session, always an enjoyable experience. Rob and I got on so well together and he had a great rapport with his clients. He had an appointment with a middle aged couple who ran a guest house. The general idea was that I would try and replace an endowment policy which had just matured. I turned the subject round to investment of a lump sum, they liked the idea and we completed the paperwork but left the amount of the investment blank until they had left the room and chatted together about how much they had available to invest. Rob and I were sitting in their own private lounge and we realized that they were going upstairs.

"Listen" said Rob, "You will hear them moving furniture about as they get the money from under the floor boards"

"Really Rob"

"Oh yes, they often do that when I am here."

I was gratified to know that Rob was held in such high esteem by this couple that he was party to knowing where they stashed their money. But that was the kind of relationship most of our staff had with their clients. A few minutes they came back into the room, smiled at me and said,

"Here is seven thousand pounds, it will do for a start, we can add to it later on."

The seven thousand pounds was in ten and twenty pounds notes, Rob, with a glint in his eye, checked it before handing it back to me. I thought quickly about where I should put the money. Suppose I put it in my brief case and someone snatched my case from me. If I place the money in my brief case it will be on show in each home we visit when I open my case. So I decided to split the money into two piles before stuffing it all into my two inside pockets of my suit jacket. It felt safe there.

Rob took me to his next appointment and introduced me, with a grin the man of the house said to me,

"By heck Sir, you look as though you could do with wearing a bra."

That settled it, as soon as we left there, we went straight to my home and much to the delight of our two daughters put the money in a pile on the coffee table with the request that they count it and let me know how much there is when I return from work.

This reminded me of an incident which happened to me just after Bill had died. I called on one of his clients to collect four hundred pounds in annual premiums. He had never seen me before, but he checked my business card before saying,

"Come with me and I will get the money."

I followed him out of the back door and onto his drive. He started up his car and reversed it a few yards to reveal the large manhole cover. He levered up the cover with a screwdriver, and there, a foot down, hanging on a brass hook was a leather night safe bag. He removed four hundred pounds for me before replacing the bag and the manhole lid.

"No burglar would ever think of looking there." He smiled.

"Have you thought what would happen if the sewers became blocked and the water backed up? You would need to do some serious money laundering!" I laughed, assuring him that his secret was safe with me.

One of my fellow superintendents in Grimsby actually witnessed a very strange sight. His client got his spade from the garden shed and dug up a coffee jar from the back garden before taking from it one thousand pounds to be invested into unit trusts.

"Hang on a minute! I will make it two thousand pounds." As he dug up a second jar with another thousand pounds in it.

"He grinned at my superintendent friend as he warned him,

"If I ever see you at midnight outside my house with a spade, I will call the police."

"I don't think you will" replied my colleague, "because I don't think that you will want the tax man to know about that secret stash."

Two or three minutes' walk from our home lived a retired fishing trawler owner and his wife. They too had been clients of Bill, and I had called on them to complete paperwork for a maturing endowment policy. There was two hundred and fifty pounds less than ten thousand pounds due to them. I outlined a lump sum investment plan which was performing really well, adding,

"If you transfer your nine thousand seven hundred and fifty pounds into the investment, the Company will add one percent to it as a loyalty bonus. Also, you can add other money to it and get the one per cent bonus on that too if it is all done at the same time."

"That's a great idea, I will leave the money invested and add two hundred and fifty to it."

After I had completed the paperwork I looked at my client expectantly,

"I just need your cheque for two hundred and fifty pounds please Mr. Jensen."

"I never said anything about two hundred and fifty pounds, I meant two hundred and fifty thousand pounds, is that alright?"

It was alright! But I gave them time to think about it and returned a few days later with a colleague with more experience in our investment plans. True to his word, Mr. Jensen gave us a cheque for two hundred and fifty thousand pounds.

Then his wife spoke up,

"Can I have one of those investment plans?"

"You certainly can Mrs. Jensen."

"I can't give you two hundred and fifty thousand but I will give you fifty thousand pounds."

Mr. Jensen spoke up,

"Where have you got fifty thousand pounds from?"

"Keep your nose out of my affairs, I did not ask you where you had got your two hundred and fifty thousand pounds from."

So we left their home with three hundred thousand pounds fortunately the money changed hands in the form of two cheques, otherwise I would have needed a very large bra.

Some responsibilities are far from pleasant. Death Claim Unit based in Reading wrote to me asking me to visit Mrs. Lamb, a Cleethorpes lady who had just been widowed. They asked me to formally inform her that we were not paying out on a life assurance policy she had recently taken out on her husband. They alleged that she had withheld information from the proposal form and had failed to inform the Company that her husband was taking medication for heart trouble. The policy had been arranged by my "unmanageable man" and before visiting Mrs. Lamb I checked out the details with him.

"I did not put a foot wrong David. I did everything by the book. I called at tea time to collect some premiums. Mr. and Mrs. Lamb and the two children were all having their tea before Mr. Lamb went off to work his night shift. Mrs. Lamb asked me if I could call back to discuss a new policy with her so I went back later that evening. Mr. Lamb had already gone to work"

"Did Mrs. Lamb give you any medical information about her husband which you did not enter onto the paperwork?"

"Definitely not David, that's more than my job is worth."

"Can you tell me anything about the family?"

"Yes they are a lovely family, two smashing young kids. Mr. Lamb is quite a bit older that Mrs. Lamb, and she worries about the age difference. But they are as honest as the day is long"

"Ok, I will call and see her, but please don't say anything to her about the claim being rejected."

I called upon Mrs. Lamb, a slim whisp of a lady who looked as though a puff of wind would blow her over. She looked weak and vulnerable, but she had just lost her husband suddenly, had had to tell her two children that their father would not be coming home from work and faced the harsh reality of being a single mum.

I had decided that I would disregard Reading's instruction to inform her that we were not going to pay the death claim. I chose rather to tell her that I needed just to ask her a few questions before reporting back to Chief Office. The policy would provide a lump sum on death worth a few thousand pounds followed by a weekly income for the next fifteen years. So there was a lot at stake here.

Mrs. Lamb told me that until she saw her husband's death certificate she had no idea that he had recently been diagnosed as having a heart problem. She did not know that he was taking tablets to treat the condition. There were no heart tablets in the house, he left them at work and took them each evening when he arrived at work. Following his death she had seen the GP who told her that he had been informed by Mr. Lamb that he did not wish to worry his wife, so he did not intend to inform her at this stage, and that he would take his tablets at work.

I was able to confirm these details with the doctor, and so in my mind there was no doubt. Mrs. Lamb had not withheld the information about her husband's heart problem and his prescribed medication. She just did not know about it.

I left Mrs. Lamb with the promise that she would be hearing from us shortly, went to my desk and wrote to Reading office reporting my findings and recommending that the claim should be paid in full. It ended with an impassioned appeal,

"If this great Company has an ounce of compassion, it will give Mrs. Lamb the benefit of the considerable amount of doubt, and hasten to pay this claim in full."

I popped the letter into Grimsby office along with my other mail. The District Manager saw it and rang me to say that he did not think it was up to me to challenge a decision made by Chief Office. My response was that if I could prevent an injustice being committed then it was entirely up to me to do something about it.

Two or three days later I was at home gardening when Edith called me in to take a phone call. It was from Mr. White, head of the death claim unit in Reading office.

"David, I have just read your report and recommendations about Mr. and Mrs. Lamb. Thank you for the trouble you have taken. I have just finished crying into my coffee, please apologize to Mrs. Lamb for any anxiety caused and tell her that we will be paying the death claim in full, and thank you again."

We did not need to apologize to Mrs. Lamb for the anxiety caused because she had no idea that initially the death claim had been rejected. I rang my "unmanageable man" and told him that within a few days he would receive the cheque for Mrs. Lamb and asked him to pay her as soon as possible, adding that there was no need to let her know that there had been a problem.

But he was a bigger man than that! He realized how I had saved the situation, and without my knowledge he told Mrs. Lamb that she had me to thank for challenging the decision of the Company.

A few days later, Edith and I were shopping in Grimsby when a person completely covered in motor cycle leathers, crash helmet and visor rushed up to me, threw the leather clad arms round me, pushed up the visor and gave me a kiss. It was Mrs. Lamb. I knew then that our "unmanageable man" had told her all and that she was just showing her gratitude.

The decision to decline a claim was a rare one. When I was still in my first few months with the Prudential, and attending Les Jackson's training sessions in Leeds, I heard a remark which increased my admiration for the Company. Les told the assembled group of eager students that his niece had started a job in the claims office of a rival insurance company. On the first day of her training she was instructed to look for reasons for declining to pay a claim. This was in direct contrast with the Prudential who trained their claims staff to look for reasons why a claim should be paid. Of course any attempt at making a fraudulent claim was thrown out by the Prudential, but they had to be sure of their facts. Declining a claim was something I dreaded doing, fortunately I was not often called upon to do it.

I saw an attempt to make a fraudulent claim first hand, and responded to it with no mercy.

I was auditing Steve's agency when a lady invited us through to her kitchen to have a coffee. Her kitchen window gave a clear view of her neighbour's back garden where we saw a mattress leaning against her neighbour's kitchen wall. It was obviously fire damaged, and she volunteered the information that her neighbours had suffered a small fire. They had left the electric blanket on in their son's bed, and when they returned from the pub could smell fire. They rushed upstairs to find that the bed was on fire.

They unplugged the electric blanket, doused the mattress and bedding with water, and managed to man handle the mattress downstairs. As they were trying to get it through the back door they smashed the pane of glass in the door which had needed to be replaced.

"A charred mattress is not a pleasant thing to see each time you look out of your window," I remarked, "how long has it been there?"

"Oh, five or six weeks, I am getting used to it now."

Steve and I thanked her for our coffee as we left. I was surprised that we called next door and asked Steve whether they had fire insurance with the Prudential.

"No David, we don't need to take a claim form with us, they are not insured with us for fire."

We were invited in and the premiums were waiting on the telephone table in the hall. As I was checking the premium receipt books we were asked,

"Do you do fire insurance?"

Before I could give a suitable reply, Steve jumped in with both feet,

"Oh yes we have excellent house insurance policies which include fire."

Our client, Mr. Hindle , could not reply quickly enough,

"Can I have a fire insurance policy please?"

Steve assured him that he could have one, and that he would call back that evening to arrange it. I assured Steve that I intended to accompany him, and that he must leave the sale to me.

When all our collecting duties were finished we called at Mr Hindle's and I began completing the Home Insurance proposal form. There is a question on the form, "have you ever sustained any losses caused by an insured peril" I put this question in several different ways to our client.

"Mr Hindle, we need to be sure that you understand this question. It is not asking whether you have made any claims for fire etc. It is more specific than that. What we need to know is whether or not you have suffered any loss which you could have claimed for had you been insured. Whatever angle I came from, the answer was just the same, an emphatic denial that there had ever been any loss for which they could have claimed had they been insured.

We left the house and sat in my car reviewing the matter.

"What are you going to do with this proposal form now Steve?"

"Send it to Lincoln Office in the normal way."

"No Steve, not in the normal way. You must attach a letter notifying Lincoln Office that this morning we both saw a fire damaged mattress in Mr Hindle's garden, which the neighbor confirmed has been there five or six weeks."

"OK boss"

"Well it covers us both Steve and puts Lincoln on the alert in case Mr Hindle tries to claim for something which happened before he took out the insurance."

It all seemed perfectly obvious to me. I assumed that he had complied with my instruction and had forgotten about the matter, until I received a phone call from Steve.

"Morning David, I have just had a phone call from Mr Hindle who wants to make a fire claim

"Let me tell you what he wants to claim for Steve! The son's bed has been on fire."

"That's right boss."

"Did you attach the report I requested when you sent the paperwork in to Lincoln.?"

"No, sorry Sir, I forgot. But I have delivered the policy and collected the first year's premium."

"I bet you have Steve, and now Mr Hindle hopes to get all his money back and more? Don't go near him. Leave it to me. I will call and sort it out.

I rang Mr Hindle and arranged to call that evening, and then I called at the local glazier, the only one in Cleethorpes, and introduced myself. I explained that I was handling a fire claim for Mr Hindle and I understood that they had possibly attended to replace the large pane of glass in the back door,

I had hit the jackpot, they asked whether I would like a copy of the invoice, which I took away with me. They had attended eight weeks ago. Bingo!

That evening I was working with Rob who I asked to attend as a witness. Mr Hindle expressed surprise that we had responded so quickly to him notifying his claim.

"Oh that's how good we are Mr Hindle. We respond very quickly when there is a genuine claim."

"Oh this is a genuine claim Mr Robinson, it only happened last night."

"Well, we shall see Mr Hindle, we shall see. Please tell me what happened."

I heard a well-rehearsed story. They had been at the pub. They had left their son's electric blanket on. They came in from the pub just after ten o'clock and could smell burning coming from upstairs. They discovered the burning bed, managed to douse the mattress with water before getting it out into the back garden. They were in such a hurry that they smashed the pane of glass in the door, which had to be replaced.

The three of us stood surveying the mattress in the rear garden.

"It looks to me as though this has been here several weeks Mr Hindle,  it is going mouldy look.  This mould has not been caused by the water you say you poured on it last night.  It has rained quite a lot recently, and this mattress looks as though it has been soaked repeatedly."

"Yes that's right Mr Robinson.  It has been wet through several times but not by the rain.  You see my son wets the bed."

"And you let him use an electric blanket!  How old is your son?"

"He is fourteen sir"

"I am just looking at the pane of glass in your door Mr Hindle.  When did you have it repaired?"

"This morning Sir, the glazier came out straight away."

"That's remarkable Mr Hindle, look how hard the putty is.  This was not repaired today, the putty has had plenty of time to harden!"

"Yes Mr. Robinson, but modern putty is remarkable.  It goes hard straight away."

"Really!  Please can we see the bedroom where the incident happened?"

Within a few minutes we were in the back bedroom, Mr Hindle was strutting back and forth with his nose in the air,

"You can smell it can't you.  You can still smell the smoke.  It's very strong. Can't you smell it?"

I too began to strut around the room with my nose in the air, between sniffs , much to Rob's surprise said,

"Yes I can certainly smell something Mr Hindle, I can't smell smoke though, all I can smell is fraud!"

For a few moments I thought that Mr Hindle was going to punch me.  I dealt with his protests by producing the glazier's account.

"You smashed the door glass eight weeks ago Mr Hindle, the bed caught fire long before you even took out the insurance.  You don't have a claim. Furthermore I intend to cancel your policy and get you a full refund.  We don't really want your kind of business.

I did not like declining claims, but I enjoyed declining this one!

# Just Another Day at the Office.

I answered my home phone to hear my District Manager's voice.

"David, there is an interesting little job for you. It might lead to some new business, are you up for it?"

"Tell me more Roland"

"Well, a gentleman who works on the oil rigs has just phoned the office. He and his wife have recently moved to Cleethorpes and don't have a local agent. He has two or three life assurance policies with us which are paid by direct debit. He has been approached by a broker up in Aberdeen who has really soured him up against the Prudential"

"Really, in what way."

"This unscrupulous broker has convinced him that as he works on the rigs, none of his Prudential policies are any good as they don't pay out should death occur due to an accident whilst working on the rigs."

"This broker sounds like a really friendly guy Roland. But if our policyholder reads his policies he will know that the broker is lying to him just to line his own pockets."

"Yes David, I know that, but I have promised that you will phone him and arrange to visit him and set his mind at rest, here is his phone number."

Bill, the oil rig worker was home for a few days so I had no difficulty catching up with him. He lived in a smart, tidy semidetached house in the resort. One side of the road was made up of houses whilst on the opposite side were bungalows.

He welcomed me in, and I soon discovered that he was renting the house on a six months Assured Shorthold Tenancy Agreement. He had only been there a few weeks. He handed me his life assurance policies which were all in his name. Our broker friend had certainly cast doubt over the validity of his Prudential policies. Luckily for us, Bill was not an impulsive man otherwise he may have immediately cash surrendered them without being open to other advice.

It did not take me long to prove to Bill that his policies were completely valid, he was surprised when I explained to him that should he die due to an accident, whether at work or not, the death benefit was actually doubled.

"Bill, did you actually show these policies to your broker in Aberdeen."

"Yes, he had a good look at them, I just thought that I could trust him. I am completely happy with my policies now"

It had not taken me long to prove to Bill how valuable his policies were, it did not take me half as long to completely rubbish the Aberdeen broker, and Bill agreed that he wanted nothing more to do with him.

Seizing the opportunity I began to speak with Bill about increasing his business with Prudential and he was prepared to listen to my suggestions.

"Before you go any further, let me ask my wife to come through and make us both a drink, she is in the other room."

He introduced me to his wife, Ellie, who had a feisty and fiery disposition. I discovered that she was eighteen years younger than Bill. He explained to me that English was not her first language and that she was not used to British customs and regulations.

Over a welcome coffee it did not take me long to recommend some additional business and when I left the home a short while later I was able to report back to Roland that I had conserved our existing business and sold new business worth a hundred pounds a month in premiums.

I thought it only courteous that I deliver the new policy myself when it was issued a few weeks later, and I was fortunate in discovering that Bill was at home again. The business concluded, I was about to leave when Bill said,

"I have a favour to ask you David. We don't know anyone around here, and Ellie is vulnerable when I am away. If anything crops up that she does not understand or can't handle, could she ring you. We know that we can trust you!"

I agreed to this unusual request never dreaming that I would soon receive a cry for help.

Ellie rang me one morning in distress. Bill was working on the rig, she had just got up and come downstairs to make a drink. To her horror two men were asleep in the lounge. She disturbed them and demanded to know what they were doing there. One of them told her that actually he was the owner of the house and had more right to be there than she had. It appeared that he had lost his job and needed to return to his house to live. The fact that Bill and Ellie had the security of a six month's tenancy agreement did not matter. He was back living there and she would just have to make the best of it.

Within a short while I was ringing Bill and Ellie's door bell and was soon invited in by a tearful Ellie. I did not like what I saw. The two men looked rough and questionable.

I quickly assessed the situation. Ellie and Bill had a legal right to be there and the owner of the house had no legal right to move back in. I also knew that this was a civil matter which the police would not be interested in. Enforcing Bill and Ellie's position would not be a speedy matter. I felt, rightly or wrongly that in order to guarantee Ellie's safety I needed to get her out of there.

Ellie gave me a phone number on which I could contact Bill on the rig and I rang him and explained the situation. He agreed with me and asked if I would mind getting Ellie out of the house immediately and into a hotel. Within a few hours I had arranged for her to have a room at the Kingsway Hotel in Cleethorpes and she packed a bag with enough emergency items to last until Bill, who obtained compassionate leave, could join her at the Kingsway Hotel.

They were able to move back into their rented home, without the threat of a live in landlord. Whilst there I they were able to source a mortgage and they bought their own home in a nearby village. Their new address was still in my area so I was able to maintain contact with them for several years until due to changes I had to take on a much larger area which did not include their village.

Years later, I was walking across the car park on St Peter's Avenue in Cleethorpes when a loud voice called my name.

"David Robinson!"

I turned, it was Ellie, as feisty and fiery as ever.

"You know that hundred pounds a month policy you arranged for me and my Bill. Well you promised us that when it matured we would get seventeen thousand pounds back. You were wrong"

"Really Ellie."

"Yes your calculations were rubbish. You promised us seventeen thousand pounds back, but we only got twenty four thousand pounds back. What have you got to say for yourself?"

I was tempted to say "It's a good job you trusted me and not that broker in Aberdeen." But I just smiled and said "Happy to have been of service."

Not long after Bill and Ellie moved out of their rented house into their own home, I received a phone call requesting me to visit them. I think that every superintendent in the District had a small number of policyholders who preferred to deal with them rather than with the local agent. This was the case with Bill and Ellie, and I could well understand that having built up a relationship of trust, they would rather deal with me.

So I popped in early one evening and walked straight into an atmosphere which was almost tangible. Bill seemed quite relaxed in front of the television, but Ellie was like a volcano waiting to erupt.

"If I have picked a bad time I can come at a more convenient time" I volunteered.

Ellie , feisty and fiery as ever, glared at Bill and said to me,

"It's him not you! I will make you a coffee"

When she had gone into the kitchen I said to Bill,

"What's up?"

"Oh it's Ellie making a mountain out of a mole hill. She will get over it."

"Get over what" shouted Ellie from the kitchen, "I'll tell you what he has done. You won't believe it."

She brought my coffee in, and began her account of the latest thing that Bill had done.

"I walked up the road on my way home from work, and one or two of the neighbours were in their front gardens working. As I passed they gave me a funny look and started giggling and then looked away"

"Really Ellie, what were they laughing at?"

"I thought that they were laughing at me, so I said "don't laugh at me like that" what's wrong?"

"Nothing at all Ellie"

"But they gave me that kind of look which suggests that they know something which I don't"

"Oh dear Ellie"

"Don't 'Oh Dear' me David, it's Bill you should be saying Oh dear to. It's him that did the stupid thing, it's him you should feel sorry for."

"Why what has he done Ellie?"

"I told him this morning before I went to work that I expected him to paint the kitchen walls and ceiling today whilst I was at work, I did not think he would make a mess of it."

Then looking at Bill, she continued,

"Shall I tell David what a stupid thing you did or will you tell him?"

Before Bill could get a word in, Ellie continued,

"He went to the supermarket and bought a huge tin of paint, then he read on the side of the tin that he needed to stir it well. He could not find anything to stir it with, so he put it in the spin drier and switched it on. It got faster and faster before it started to wobble about all over the floor, so Bill lifted the lid to stop it spinning. As he lifted the spin drier lid, the lid came off the paint tin and paint came out like a fountain, all over the walls, ceiling, window, blind and the kitchen units and the floor."

I was having difficulty keeping a straight face but seeing the deep trouble Bill was in I managed to remain serious.

"Oh no Ellie, poor Bill, what did he do about it?"

"I'll tell you what he did, he went and asked the neighbours for help. Those men who were giggling and laughing at me when I came home from work had been here most of the day cleaning up the mess."

Ellie was not prepared to give any credit to Bill for the fact that he was eager to please her and decorate the kitchen whilst she was at work. I am sure that he would rather have cleaned his vintage MG sports car, and had a drive in it. But no, he wanted to do something which would please Ellie. It was not his fault that it had all gone wrong!

Ellie disappeared for a while and when she came back into the room she had a hand full of important looking documents. Waving them under Bill's nose she recited to him what they all were. Higher National Certificate in this, Award of merit in this, Diploma in something else, she threw all Bill's qualifications into a sizeable pile on the carpet and began dancing on them shouting,

"What good are certificates if you are an idiot?"

There was a resigned look on Bill's face. I thought that this was not the first storm he had weathered, and no doubt it would not be the last. I stayed long enough to ensure that Ellie did not murder him before I got into my car and drove off- laughing.

I wish that all my interactions with clients were as amusing, many were. Sadly tragedy was never far away. In an expanding village just outside Grimsby lived a lovely family. Mr. and Mrs. Boyle had four or five children who were all an absolute pleasure to be with. Mr. Boyle was a quietly spoken Irish gentleman and it seemed to me that every member of his family had a warm personality and an infectious sense of humour.

I had taken over some additional territory in a reshuffle, and was privileged to have Adrian, the agent for this area, transfer to me from his original office in Louth. Adrian had taken me to see the Boyles two or three times, there always seemed to be some new business to secure and we left the home feeling as though we had drunk a strong tonic!

When we rang the doorbell, all the children rushed to the door, each wanting to be the first to welcome us. Most of them were working but they all seemed perfectly happy to remain living at home with mum and dad.

It was my day when I was programmed to work with Adrian, but he could not accompany me as it was a collecting day and the deputy collector was working elsewhere. I arranged to meet him on the car park behind the village hall in Tetney at half past two. It would be a quick rendezvous just to give him long enough to give me his list of appointments and the reason for my visit. Adrian beamed as he began to go through his list,

"You are in for a treat David, your first appointment at three o'clock is with your favourite family, the Boyles. That will set you up for the rest of the programme. He explained that the eldest child, Sam, had got engaged and wanted to discuss some life assurance and needed some mortgage advice. I promised to give Adrian a ring when I had finished his appointments and let him know how successful I had been.

I parked outside the Boyles and walked up the front path. There were no twitching curtains, they did not seem to be looking expectantly out of the window for me. The bungalow seemed strangely quiet and there was no stampede to be the first to open the door. After a while Mrs Boyle and the children all came to the door. There were no smiles, no cheeky welcomes, in fact there did not seem to be any indication that they had recognized me. They were all ghastly white and looked as though they did not really know what they were doing. Something was clearly wrong, and I did not immediately feel that I could ask what.

I noticed that Sam was absent, and thought that just asking whether he was in was a harmless question

"Sam is expecting me, are you all OK?"

We stood in a circle in the front room, the family were all holding hands and they included me so that I had both hands gripped tightly.

I was wondering where Mr Boyle was, but I was hesitant to ask.

Mrs Boyle broke the silence,

"We think that Sam might be dead."

There was no response from the children, just ghastly white faces with distant far off expressions.

Mrs Boyle continued,

"Sam worked all night last night repairing a level crossing near Lincoln. He went into the works van to have a break and make a drink on the gas stove. There must have been a problem with the gas. When he did not come out, his mate checked and found him lying on the bunk, dead. Mr Boyle has gone to Lincoln to identify the body. We are all hoping that it is not Sam." Then she broke down.

At times like this you feel so helpless. I did feel that I was intruding into this families most private moments but they clearly did not want me to leave. I can't remember what I said or even whether I said anything to them. What seemed important to them was me just being there. We held hands, we hugged, and we waited.

Perhaps it was half an hour before Mr Boyle returned. He walked in with silent dignity, the family did not need to address him with words and he did not need to vocalise a reply. The question was in their eyes, and the answer they did not want to hear, was in his eyes.

They all burst into tears and Mr. Boyle stood where I had been in the circle. As the circle closed, I quietly left them.

Sometimes we avoid a grieving person because we don't know what to say. I don't think that the grieving person knows what to say either. The important input comes from just being there, a visible sign that you are sharing their grief and trying to bear their hurt.

I did not say very much in the Boyles home that day. But on subsequent visits I always sensed a special bond between us. Had I known what I was walking into that day, I would have been tempted not to ring their door bell. I am glad that I did.

On another occasion I was scheduled to meet Adrian at half past two on the car behind Tetney Village Hall. I always looked forward to working with him, he tried to make enough appointments to keep me busy and even though we were meeting in the early afternoon it would most likely be nine o'clock in the evening when we finished. Days like that could be long ones, especially if I had been in the Propserity Office that morning, But when you are having a good time, time flies by. Adrian was always a pleasure to work with. His agency was a country one, and the pace was more gentle. His clients always seemed to have more time and they were very loyal to Adrian and the Company he represented so well.

I had just finished my lunch and was looking forward to my time with Adrian when our phone rang. It was Adrian,

"I am so sorry David but I won't be able to meet you and work with you this afternoon."

There was a seriousness in his voice, but he could appear to be serious when he was joking with me. I was just about to respond with some wise crack, such as "Why, have you had a better offer Adrian?" when something checked me. There was more than just a serious note in his voice, I sensed that he was finding it hard to speak to me.

"That's OK Adrian, obviously something urgent has come up, I have plenty to do and I can work on my own."

"David" there was a trembling in Adrian's voice, "it's my dad. I have just come in for my lunch and found him dead. He has hung himself on the stairs."

How Adrian found the composure to phone me I will never know. I had not met his dad but had met his mum several times. Quite often she had prepared a platter of delicious sandwiches so that Adrian and I could pop in there at tea time and refresh ourselves for the evening session.

There was a large family and they needed each other at a time like this. Some people think it is thoughtless to try and continue with the daily routine when something like this happens. I am sure that Adrian needed the diversion of his job, the sympathy and support of his many clients. He certainly did not neglect his family responsibilities, but neither did he neglect his job. There was very little that I needed to relieve him of, if he needed my help he knew that I was there for him.

I still remember Adrian's dad's funeral... The Methodist Minister from their village took the service at the crematorium. He had the advantage of knowing the family, so his eulogy was warm, personal and relevant. but he did not mince his words. Some of his remarks were directed at those who were sitting in judgement of someone who has taken their own life. He challenged any mourners who held to such an ethos,

"How dare you judge? Unless you have a strong love for your family, and an immense work ethic, unless you had been made redundant time and time again because of mechanization, unless you have picked yourself up only to be thrown on the scrap heap again, you have no right to judge. Unless you feel worthless because you can't get a job to support your family, then don't judge."

Adrian's dad had been a hard worker on the farms. He had become victim to job losses due to mechanization more than once. He had obtained a job which he thought would be a permanent one, but the same axe fell again, he just could not get up from the blow.

I had a window into the type of family Adrian had been born into. It was no surprise to me that he was a grafter, loyal, committed, eager to please, as honest as the day is long. Eager to be self-reliant and with his shoulder to the wheel, do more than a fair day's work for a day's pay.

It was our privilege to attend Adrian's wedding a few years afterwards. I looked at his bride and was so glad that she was marrying into a lovely family.

My role was more than just heading up a sales team. It was a privilege to share people's lives with them. To try and be there for them when they needed something extra. Although I had no ulterior motive for being there to serve them when necessary, I was not the loser. When due to illness or staff shortages I was snowed up with work, I did not need to put out a cry for help. They rang me, they turned up at my door to ask, "David, is there anything I can do?"

There is something very special in working with that kind of team.

# PHEW!

Although I began duties in Grimsby on the first working day of 1976, I remained in a local bed and breakfast until March. Each week I travelled back to Sleaford mid-week for one night, and then returned to Sleaford late on Friday evenings for the weekend. Dennis Carolan my superintendent in the Sleaford area had changed areas, and I was really sorry to lose him. Nigel Pengelly took over from him but we did not work together for long as quite soon after he came, I was promoted to Grimsby. However, when I was back in Sleaford at the weekends, Nigel often got in touch needing some advice if he was uncertain about anything. This in no way reflected upon his knowledge or ability, but as he had been in a Prudential sales role for several years, he had grown out of touch with routine agency matters, so he often rang or visited me at the Hollies, and it was always a pleasure to resume contact with him. He did not remain in the section superintendent role for long, as I had not been working in Grimsby area long before he was sent to work with us for a week as a sales inspector.

Rob had arranged an appointment for Nigel and me to discuss investments with Stephen Knox, the proprietor of Pattesons Pickles, a picked onion and chutney business which had been established since 1910. Their factory was adjacent to a large supermarket, and the smell of onions, vinegar and chutney always seemed to invade the car park. Fortunately for Mr. and Mrs. Knox, they lived in a very impressive old house quite near the sea front. They were safe from the pervading aroma of pickled onions.

Mr. Knox, was a very astute business man and asked all the right questions. Nigel had explained the benefits of one of our investment bonds by comparing it to money saved in a building society.

"Mr. Knox, if you put your money into the building society, you will only be making about 8% interest. Our Bond is making far more than that at present, you will be quids in with the Prudential."

"Yes Mr. Pengelly, but I know I am getting 8% in the building society, exactly what rate will I earn in your Bond?"

"Well Mr. Knox, your building society interest is down there." proclaimed Nigel, pointing emphatically down at the ground, "whereas our rate is right up there" he continued, stretching his arms heavenwards.

Mr. Knox was quite correctly trying to extract from Nigel some concrete evidence of how our bond was performing. Gesticulating earthwards and skywards, and veiled references to "down there" and "up there" would not cut it with a shrewd business man like Stephen Knox.

"Tell me Mr. Pengelly what is the exact rate of interest your bond has made over the last couple of years."

Holding both hands at face level, Nigel continued valiantly, "Well Mr. Knox, imagine that in my left hand I am holding all your building society investments. The label on it says 8%. Now imagine that in my right hand I am holding all your investments in the Prudential Bond, the label on that says "PHEW". Not 8% Mr. Knox, but PHEW" as he said that Nigel raised both hands towards the sky, adding "PHEW the skies the limit Mr. Knox."

Mr. Knox thanked us for our time and promised to consider Nigel's proposition if he submit an official quotation in writing. As we left I commented to Nigel, "Exactly how are you going to define PHEW rate of interest in writing Nigel."

Needless to say the official quotation was never forthcoming. We maintained excellent relationships with Mr. and Mrs. Knox but they never invested with us at the PHEW rate of interest.

So, in March we said a fond "Good bye "to the Hollies, to all our Sleaford friends and to our extended church family. On the occasion of our last church service, we were presented with a lovely carriage clock as a token of affection and esteem. The Hollies had been such a happy home, and as we saw all our possessions being loaded into the removal van, except for the pianola which we had sold, we felt a tinge of sadness. We knew that we were heading for a new chapter in our lives and that there would be more happy memories to create, friendships to forge, challenges to face plus the excitement of finding and settling into a new church family.

Becoming part of the Grimsby and Cleethorpes community made my job far easier. It cemented the idea amongst my staff that my appointment was permanent. They could visit me at any time they needed, our clients knew that I lived among them, and this made a positive difference. Human nature is such that a person would rather buy from someone who lives close by. I think that part of the reason lies in the feeling that a local man will not rip you off. After all if you know where he lives you can always go and sort him out. I think too that building up a local reputation for honesty and fair dealing is priceless. The Prudential has always been a home service insurance company, and making your own home amongst the clients is a positive thing.

Finding and settling into a local church upon moving to Cleethorpes was our priority. Saint Augustine famously said "Man's chief end is to know God and to enjoy Him forever." Embraced within thirteen words is the entire message of the Gospel. We are not temporal creatures with a seventy years span and then nothing. We are eternal creatures allocated a seventy years earthly span in which to come to know God in order that we may enjoy Him forever.

So our life consists of what A J Cronin called, "Adventures in two worlds." Cronin was a doctor by profession and became a hugely successful novelist. From his pen came classic works such as The Citadel, The Stars Look Down, The Judas Tree, Shanon's Way, Doctor Finlay of Tannochbrae, The Keys of The Kingdom, Beyond This Place, The Green Years, The Minstrel Boy and others. All well worth reading and re-reading. In my view, A J Cronin's most powerful book is the story of his life entitled "Adventures in Two Worlds."

Some reviewers have completely missed the main issue Cronin writes about in "Adventures in Two Worlds" their assessment is that the book chronicles Cronin's two worlds as the world of a doctor and the world of a novelist. In the early part of the book, A J Cronin is studying to be a doctor. Witnessing his first post mortem has a profound effect upon him. Seeing the amazing structure and intricacies of the human body, something inside him rebels at the idea that all this just happened by chance. In his mind he is accepting the concept that the amazing human body has been designed and that it owes its creation to a Great Designer. So there begins a new adventure in a new world, the world of the search for God, which, to use A J Cronin's own words, ends when he utters the life changing prayer, "God be merciful to me, a sinner."

During his search for spiritual reality, Cronin becomes unwell and a colleague invites him to share a holiday with him in Germany. This friend informs Cronin that the next day being Sunday, he will be going to the local church and invites him along to. He warns him though that the entire service will be in German, and as Cronin knew no German he would not be able to understand the service. Cronin wishes to go along completely unaware of the impact the German speaking preacher would have upon him. He writes about the service, saying that he was greatly impressed by the enthusiasm and passion of the preacher. There were only two words in the whole sermon which he understood. These two words were thrust at the congregation more than once, and were Christos Fuhrer, "Christ The Lord"   Not being able to understand what the preacher was talking about, Cronin let his imagination loose and in his mind he pictured all kinds of scenarios.  Walking home from church he explained to his friend the subject matter of the pictures he had seen in his mind as the pastor was preaching. "That is amazing" replied his friend, "what you were seeing as mental images is exactly what the preacher was describing in his sermon." Basically mountains of the world's ills and problems crumbling in the presence of Christos Fuhrer, Christ the Lord.

It is no surprise to me that after such adventures in two worlds, A J Cronin bows the knee to The Lord Jesus Christ as he prays the sinner's prayer "God be merciful to me a sinner" and in his way, he invites us in the book to breathe the same prayer.  God had spoken to Cronin through what he saw at an autopsy and through what he heard in a sermon he could not understand. There are many roads leading to God, I believe that God is not short of pathways along which to lead us. There may be many roads leading to God, but there is only one door! Jesus taught that he is the door, and that He knocks upon our door seeking an entrance.

Edith and I were both privileged in coming to know God at a relatively early age.  But that is not the end of the journey.  Christian faith needs to be fleshed out in the real world. Christians are called to be salt and light in their community, and God has chosen the church as the environment where we continue in our discipleship training.

So it was important that we settle into a church family in Cleethorpes where we could continue our adventures in two worlds! That search led us to Cleethorpes Assembly of God Church, which we first visited in March 1976.

# Sea View Street

So by March 1976 we had moved into our first Cleethorpes home on Seacroft Road and visited our new church family for the first time. Edith and I had been brought up in Assemblies of God churches and their heart and ethos were our native air. So we went along to the Cleethorpes Assembly of God on Sea View Street simply because it was the closest to us. We were quite prepared to try the Assembly of God Church in Grimsby if necessary, however we felt at home with the Cleethorpes congregation.

The building was not an inspiring looking one, it resembled a converted warehouse, which it probably had been. It was situated at the end of a row of terraced properties, and would have needed change of use planning permission before it could operate as a church. Being situated on a domestic street, parking was limited, but being a seaside resort there was a large public car park quite close by.

We only had our two daughters at this time, and the four of us were able to find four seats next to each other and we were warmly welcomed. The pastor, Allen Wooffindin, who had pioneered the church had a chat with us and we immediately liked him. He was around retiring age and had built up a church family by caring for them and encouraging them. He was a deeply spiritual man but also very practical in his pastoral care. He was supported by his wife Gladys, who though in failing health was a very competent preacher. Their son Philip and his wife Jean and two boys Andrew and Mark were part of the congregation. Jean was an extremely good musician and she played the electronic organ to lead the singing. Philip was a senior executive in a large company and shouldered heavy responsibilities at work. He preached from time to time at the Cleethorpes assembly. We never imagined then that our daughter Joy and Mark would one day fall in love and enjoy a very happy marriage.

In those days we tended to have two services on a Sunday. The morning service was the traditional communion service with a devotional type sermon. In the evening was the gospel service, usually better attended and livelier with a sermon presenting the simple gospel of salvation through faith in Jesus Christ. Today almost 45 years later, the thought of attending two Sunday services seems rather heavy. Yet in those days we also had the Sunday school in the afternoon as well. So some of the congregation spent almost the whole day in church on a Sunday. We were such gluttons for punishment that within a few years the Cleethorpes Assembly of God church were adding a fourth service to the Sunday menu. The gospel service which ended about eight o'clock was followed by an after church rally beginning at eight fifteen. I sometimes imagined that I could hear the Apostle Paul repeating some of his well-known words over us, "Do you not have homes to go to."

There was a lovely family atmosphere and we felt that here was the church family we could commit to and be a part of. Soon, we were accepted as members. We met people there who became lifelong friends. David and Gwenda Thomas were among the first to invite us to their home. We reciprocated and it soon became a tradition that David and Gwenda and their two children, Simon and Sarah spent every Sunday afternoon at our home. We, and David and Gwenda took our caravans to the Isle of Wight for a memorable holiday spent in the rain. I took a picture of them all standing in the rain looking miserable, and wrote the caption beneath it in the album "You will enjoy this holiday". Many years later we attended the marriages and Simon and Sarah and they supported us at our own children's weddings. When Simon Thomas was married in a very old picturesque Anglican church, Simon Cowell, his partner and his mum were guests. It was lovely to see the unaffected way that Simon Cowell mingled with the guests at the reception. As we were watching the photographs being taken, I noticed a brand new gleaming Rolls Royce parked beside the church. I nudged someone saying "The bride and groom have done themselves proud in the choice of taxi" my unknown conversation partner replied, "Oh that's not the bride and groom's taxi, that Simon Cowell's car with his personal chauffer!" It was revealed to us later that Simon Cowell was the bride's uncle.

Many years later Gwenda lost her fight with cancer, and although they were living in Exeter, Gwenda was buried in Cleethorpes. She had requested that I should give the address at her funeral service which was a great honour.

The congregation of the Cleethorpes church were by and large ordinary people, an encouraging sign was the number of young people coming to the church. There was soon a large group of young people congregating in Philip and Jean Wooffindin's home after the Sunday evening service. Possibly here were the seeds leading to the commencement of the After

Church Rallies!

Jo Humberston was one of our members. He was elderly and had moved into Beacon House Care Home. I frequently visited him there. He was a war veteran and told me that one day shortly after the war had ended, he was in St Peters Church Cleethorpes reading the list of names of the men who lost their lives in the war. He was surprised to find his own name there, "Private Joseph Humberston missing presumed dead." He made it known to the church authorities that he was very much alive and the unfortunate error was rectified! Jo had a last wish, he confided in me "I want the Lord to call me home during a communion service at church. That is where I want to die." He had made his strong desire known to others, and Jean Wooffindin was aware of his dearest wish. Unfortunately he sometimes fell asleep in church and Jean, sitting at the organ had a better view of him that I did, as I was sitting behind him. Jean mouthed to me one Sunday morning "I think Mr. Humberston has died." It fell to me to discreetly go and check that he was just asleep.

One Sunday evening Jo had a heart attack whilst in church and I went across the street to a neighbouring house to use their phone to call an ambulance. The prognosis was not good and he was rushed into hospital. I followed the ambulance in my car and waited anxiously in the corridor. The next few hours were critical and he was not expected to last the night.

Early next morning I rang the ward to enquire how he was. "Oh he is fine, he has enjoyed a good breakfast and is helping to collect up the breakfast utensils. He can go home later today" He lived a few more years but fell asleep in church many more times. I still have a book which I loaned to him whilst he was in Beacon House. He has written in pencil on the fly leaf "Loaned by D Robinson to Jo Humberston, Beacon House."

Philip Wooffindin's aunt Lillian and her husband Reg were members of the Cleethorpes church. Reg was elderly but kept himself very active. He played a mouth organ and sometimes played a comb and paper. I often heard distant strains of a mouth organ whilst in my front garden and knew that Reg was approaching, Jean was ill and absent from one mid-week service, and we had no musician and sang the hymns without accompaniment. I said to Philip later, "Could Reg have played his mouth organ, it would have been better than nothing." Philip smiled as he informed me "I am afraid that there are not many hymns which fit the

Scotland the Brave tune, David."

My first real memory of Reg is of one Sunday morning in 1976 when I was asked to help count and check the collection at the end of the service. We had a strict rule that the money had to be checked by two people before entering the amount into a book and signing it. It was a good five years since decimalization, and I was amazed to see how he was counting the money. "Four and five pence, four and six pence, four and seven pence, four and eight pence, four and nine pence four and ten pence, four and eleven pence, five bob, five and a penny"

"Reg, what are you doing, we don't count money like that now, we have changed to decimal currency!"

I shared my amusement with Philip later who said "I know, but he always gets the amount right in the end"

Reg never gave anything away which he thought "Might be useful later" He had a leaning garden shed ready to fall over, but stuffed with things which could at some future time find a use. Every time I visited him the shed seemed to leaning more, as though it were sinking into the ground at one side. When he became ill with lung cancer and was not able to attend church, Herbert Thomas and I called one Sunday morning after church to serve communion to him and Mrs Watson. We had the bread and wine in a portable communion set. Reg very graciously but firmly took the communion set from us, and as he set out the bread and the wine said to us,

"It will be my honour and privilege to serve communion to you" He read a portion of Scripture, sang a verse of a hymn in a weak shaky voice before praying over the bread and wine and serving us. He was only weeks away from death, no sign of fear, no wanting to be the centre as we served him, no special treatment, just gratitude for all the goodness of God and his desire to put others first. I have never forgotten that spirit of gratefulness humility and servanthood. The Lord called him home not many weeks later. When the doctor came out to their bungalow to certify death, Mrs Watson said, "Do you know doctor, today is Reg's birthday."

The doctor smiled as he responded, " I think that The Lord has given Reg a wonderful birthday present."

Mrs Watson's loss was our loss, we all felt it. Were we not all church family? Sadly, some churches have become preaching centres. There is nothing wrong with excellent Biblical preaching but excellence in the pulpit does not necessarily build the kind of church which is close to God's heart. God's heart is to set the solitary into families. He intends that church should be a living organism with every member finding his or her place there and functioning as He enables. All in a place of meaningful relationships where variety and diversity is a key. I remember reading that when R T Kendall went to Westminster Chapel as its leader, he was concerned that the church was not really a church, but a preaching centre. Anonymous visitors came week after week because they enjoyed the preaching, but there was no commitment from them to the church, no sense of belonging, no real opportunity for the church to provide pastoral care or to bring them under any form of discipleship training.

The Cleethorpes Assembly of God church was small enough to be intimate without being obtrusive. It was easy to notice when someone did not seem quite right. One member rang me after one Sunday evening service to express concern. "I feel really anxious about you David, you seemed to have a pained expression on your face tonight and I am just want to enquire whether you are alright." I soon assured him that I had eaten too much tea and that the cause of my discomfort had been physical! It was so good to know that people had a caring interest, and were prepared to offer help should there be anything wrong.

One Sunday morning I noticed that a lady member, although with us in body, seemed far away and pre-occupied. She looked to be on the verge of tears and concern for her gnawed at me. By this time, Alan Wooffindin had retired and his son Philip had become our pastor. I phoned Philip after lunch to express my concern about this lady and to enquire whether any steps had been taken to offer support. Philip had noticed too, and suggested that I pay her a visit that afternoon to conduct what he called a "reccy" a reconnaisance! I popped in to see the lady and her husband and asked a few gently probing questions. She had fallen behind with their mortgage payments and had kept the problem from her husband. They were now under threat of losing their home unless they were able to pay a minimum of three hundred pounds by the next day they did not have the money. In the late 1970s this was a lot of money. I prayed with them and obtained their permission to share the problem with Philip.

Philip agreed with me that we ought to try and help them and promised to ring me back immediately he had checked out with his father who was still a member of the church leadership team.

When Philip rang me back a few minutes later he was upbeat. "David, Mum and Dad had also noticed that the lady was far from her normal self. There were people around and so they did not get chance to ask her if anything was wrong. However over lunch their concern increased and they prayed about it and felt that they must offer help. They felt that they should scrape together all the money in the house and offer it to the lady as an interest free loan. They have put three hundred pounds into a Tate and Lyle sugar bag and intend taking it to church with them this evening.

The chances of this kind of response with its uncanny accuracy being the result of some kind of coincidence is not a credible conclusion. Clearly God was at work leading and guiding and the caring church members showed once again that when the Spirit of God is at work in a company of people, they really do "weep with those that weep and rejoice with those that rejoice."

I have alluded to the fact that Alan Wooffindin had retired and that Philip had taken over as our Pastor. By the time Mr. Wooffindin senior retired I had been appointed to the role of Deacon within the church, and it was a joint decision of the deacons that we invite Philip to consider accepting the role of Pastor. I had been designated to go to Philp's home and present our invitation to him  I could not imagine how he could ever find time to care for the church as he held down a very demanding job. I understood that should he become our Pastor he would be forfeiting a great deal of his relaxation and family time and that the cost would be great. He counted the cost, was prepared to pay it, and became our Pastor, leading the church into a new and exciting chapter.

# Grimsby Transitions

After more than twenty five happy and successful years with the "Prudential Assurance Company", dramatic changes began to shake our foundations. During the first few years of the 90s, some new training seminars were introduced including "Planning the plans", "Managing Change", "Change is here to stay" etc. etc. whose titles alone were the precursor of what was in store. One seminar "Effective Communication" was arranged to be held at a hotel in Nottingham and all the District Managers in the Division were expected to attend. Twenty or thirty extremely busy District Managers arrived at the hotel to discover that the booking for the event had been cancelled. One District Manager rang Prudential's Divisional office, which was also in Nottingham.

"What is going on" he asked, "We are all at the Royal Hotel for the 'Effective Communication' seminar but is seems to have been cancelled without our knowledge."

"Oh, the seminar has not been cancelled, it is just the venue which has been changed, it will be held here at Divisional Office and the trainers are expecting you all now."

"But this is supposed to be a training session on effective communication and no one has bothered to communicate to us that there has been a change of venue"

"Really, we thought that we had let everyone know."

"I have news for you, there are between twenty and thirty of us here at the Crown Hotel, and none of us have been informed of the change of venue. If this is an example of effective communication you can forget it, we are all going back to our Districts, and we have more important things to do."

So all the District Managers returned immediately to their offices. This fiasco was not the norm, in fact such an embarrassing gaffe on the part of senior management was previously unheard of. But now it was the start of a series of muddles and mix ups caused solely because "The times, they were a changing" and extra work, last minute changes, extreme pressure to have things done within an unreasonable time scale and continually changing deadlines were becoming the new normal.

In my twenty five years with the Company there had been little change to affect how we did our daily work. The Mighty Prudential had decided that major structural changes were needed in order to retain its position as the largest insurance company in the UK.

Various scenarios had been discussed with the trade union, and after much time consuming discussion and engagement with the staff, Scenario Three became the chosen option. It quickly became known as S3 and was the most massive item on the Companies agenda. During the preparation for the introduction of S3 many routine practices were put on hold. If a staff member happened to qualify for being awarded his or her clock for 25 years' service during this hectic time, the presentation was put on hold. I personally did not receive my clock until more than 6 months after I had retired from the Company in reality it was almost 4 years late!

In a nutshell it was all about a total restructure and redeployment of staff. The District I was privileged to serve as a section superintendent had 27 full time agents who collected all the premiums and looked after their own policyholders. The 27 staff would be reduced to about half that number, with the displaced staff members being lost to natural wastage, redundancy, or staying with the Company as sales representatives.

The four Section Superintendents managing the 27 staff would be reduced to two only. So there would be an enormous increase in workload only partly eased by the fact that unless you were a sales representative, there would be less pressure to make personal sales.

A major change for the District Manager was that he would now be able to choose his management team personally. Prior to S3 Divisional Office decided which office to allocate a newly promoted superintendent to, as happened in my own promotion. John Stoner was informed that I was being promoted to serve in his district and unless he had a valid reason for objecting, that was it.

What did I have to look forward to? Instead of being responsible for a quarter of the District's territory, I would have to look after half of it. A significant increase in workload in itself, but when we consider that the staff I would be managing were also struggling to cope with a hugely increased number of clients and with the changes in their own job role, the future was certainly challenging. Even more challenging was the uncertainty of whether I would still have a job when S3 rolled out.

It was during this hectic time, and I hesitate to use the word hectic because that word alone does not adequately describe the experiences we were going through. Two brothers worked for the Company and one of them, Dave, was sent to Grimsby to assist with all the changes and the almost unbearable workload. Whilst he was helping us in Grimsby, his brother had not been able to cope with the pressures and had taken his own life. Dave was in the process of taking the Company to court and was being supported by a barrister and the staff union. He was instructed by his lawyer not to take part in any official meetings with Prudential management in case he said something which could prejudice his case. We felt that in addition to carrying our own workload we were in some way also helping to carry Dave's pressures too. I had always completely enjoyed my work with the Company but things were getting to be intolerable. It was during this stressful time that Granville Cox, Steve Briggs and Jonathan Dixey, all members of the church I belonged to, and myself went to a large Christian event in the De Montfort Hall in Leicester. It was a national mens day event, and we really looked forward to attending. I drove the four of us in my car, and as we were approaching Leicester, one of my colleagues asked,

How are things at the Prudential at the moment David."

I was caught completely off guard and had no time to think through what my answer would be. I found myself responding,

"It's dreadful at present. No one seems to be able to cope with the workload, people are stressed out. I know of two people who have taken their own life. To be honest I feel like a piece of elastic being pulled at both ends. I am nearly at breaking point and don't know how much more I can stand before something breaks."

I parked on the De Montfort Hall car park and we went into the packed hall. Several hundred men were there and following a time of singing, the preacher was on his feet. He placed his Bible on the lectern, looked straight in my direction and said loudly and clearly,

"You have said "I feel like a piece of elastic being pulled at both ends and you wonder how much you can take before something breaks.

Understand this that God is in control, He will not let you be stretched beyond what you can stand. Also understand this, that when both ends of the elastic are released you will not shrink back to what you were before the stretching took place."

Experiences like this are very humbling and confirm that God has a plan for our lives.

Although the principles of S3 were known up front, the full impact of all the number crunching exercises seemed to creep up on us unawares. During 1990, the management team from each "Prudential" District attended a "course" at a conference centre, Eagles Nest on the shores of Windermere. It was presented to us under the guise of being a team building exercise, but looking back it was obviously an opportunity for the Company to begin marking the cards of the staff as they decided which managers and superintendents still had a future with the Company. We discovered that our own Grimsby District would not be alone on the course, another District would be attending too. We would be in competition with each other as we played "executive games."

I was a passenger in Roland Huitson's car for the journey up to Windermere and we stopped for a welcome relaxing coffee at a hotel on the shore of Lake Windermere. This was to be the last time we would have chance to relax for a few days. By the time we arrived at Eagles Nest the weather had turned nasty and heavy rain was falling. The organisers led us out to a barn where there was lots of waterproof clothing and boots, helmets etc. before leading us out like a herd of sheep into an extremely wet and muddy field. They assembled each team beside what resembled a set of football goal posts, however the cross bar was considerably higher than that in conventional goal posts. They provided each team with two oil drums before setting the task. "You have to get every member over the cross bar and the only equipment you have is the two oil drums." I looked at the size of the drums and thought "Even if one drum is placed on top of the other, there is still an insurmountable gap between the top drum and the cross bar."

There was no shortage of suggestions and no limit to the number of times one of us fell headlong into the mud. Whilst all this was going on the adjudicator was watching, stop watch in hand and clip board upon which he was making notes. Someone suggested that someone should stand on the top oil drum and that we should hoist another member up onto the drum from where he could somehow clamber onto this colleagues shoulders, if we were able to perform this acrobatic feat he would still not be able to reach the cross bar, let alone clamber over it.

We had just arrived after an early start and a long journey, it was March, it was cold, it was wet, it was muddy, and we all felt determined to achieve the target. I was hungry and frustrated and suddenly yelled out "Let's stop wasting our time. It's impossible to do this."

I was greeted with a chorus of disapproval, "Of course it's possible to do it, we just haven't discovered how."

After a few more minutes our time was up and the whistle blew and the stop watch stopped. The adjudicator said "Right lads, back to the barn and get your wet gear off"

"How did we do Sir?" someone dared to ask. The taskmaster barked back at him, "You didn't, it should have taken you less than a minute to decide that the task was impossible. You have just wasted your valuable time."

After lunch the two "Assessors" inducted us all. They explained the facilities at the hotel, they familiarised us with the layout of the gardens which would be the "stage" for some of the activities, they explained that there was a tool shed with a supply of available tools, that they had a twelve seater mini bus which was available should we need transport in pursuit of some of the "executive games" adding that the local swimming baths were available. Then we were pitched back into our two team rivalry.

When each task was described to us, both Prudential District teams were together, immediately we understood the task we were separated into two adjacent portacabins where we each planned our strategy. Each of us had in turn to be team leader instructing and driving the team on to success.

One task was to build a raft and launch it successfully in the lake before paddling it a hundred yards out and back. Each team had some of the materials necessary, but neither team had the same things. The items we did not have would be available in ten minute's time at an auction sale in the barn. We had ten minutes to do an inventory of what we wanted, and decide exactly what we needed in order to be able to build our raft. We appointed a member to attend the auction and bid on our behalf and gave him a list of what we needed.  Neither team knew just what the other team already had.  Success at the auction was crucial, failure to buy all that was needed to complete the kit meant that the raft could not be built unless what was lacking could be found somewhere in the grounds and outbuildings, but there was no time for that.

One of our team had frequently bought cars at auction sales and was experienced, so we sent him to bid.  He was successful and we obtained all that was necessary to build our raft and sail it.  We needed enough oil drums, rope, planks of wood, paddles to propel the raft plus of course necessary tools and life jackets to protect us once we were afloat.

During the ten minutes planning meeting, the auction, the construction of the raft, we were observed at all times, stop watch and clip board at the ready.  Fortunately we won that project and were congratulated. Both teams were assembled together and we were given feedback, the defeated team were left in no doubt why they had lost, and we were given constructive feedback highlighting the things we could have done better and quicker.

One task was for one man from each team to be completely submerged at least one foot underwater for two minutes.  We ought to have remembered that at our induction we were told that the mini bus was available as was the local swimming baths, but we didn't.  One of our team, bowled over with enthusiasm rushed out to the tool shed and found a coil of hose pipe.  He cut off an eighteen inch length before stripping down to his underpants and lying down under water at the margin of the lake, using the hose as his breathing tube. It was March and snow meltwater was running into the lake and our valiant colleague had asthma.  He managed only a few seconds before he was overcome with the cold and had an asthma attack.

The opposing team had instructed the mini bus driver to take their man to the swimming baths, and he with a similarly obtained piece of hose, completed the challenge.  We were heavily criticised for not listening at the induction and for not preventing such a fool hardy escapade.

One morning we all tumbled into the mini bus to be driven to our next task.  None of us expected that we must abseil down a sheer rock face. We had a few minutes of instruction at the top of the rock face before being kitted out with safety helmets and harness etc.  Roland our District

Manager took the lead offering to be the first over the edge. I could tell that he was nervous, he was a big man and all credit to him, he insisted on showing the way to do it. One by one we had to follow some very hesitant people among us! I have always had a fear of heights. In our Sleaford days I dare not move from the top of our bay window onto the ladder until Mike Smith came to ensure my safety. I took a stand and refused to go over the edge. "We are all individuals with different fears. I am not afraid to take a stand and refuse to do this" I said as I looked over the edge. "It takes as much courage to take a stand and be the odd man out as it does to be herded over the edge. I am not going over."

Then Chris Fullwood who was Roland's secretary and part of the team spoke to me, "David, you have made no secret of the fact that you are scared. Now, we will all think more of you if you overcome your fear and go over the edge. I know you, you can do it and then you will glad that you did" she smiled reassuringly.

"OK "I shouted, "here I come" and within a few minutes I was at the bottom being congratulated by Roland. I am so glad that I listened to Chris.

Half way through our stay at Eagles Nest we were joined by a member of the Nottingham Divisional Office staff, he had some involvement in Human Resources, and being called Richard we always referred to him behind his back as "Tricky Dicky"

He brought his own clip board and stop watch and made his own notes as the exercises rolled out. He had a turbo charged Renault car and one evening decided to go to a little pub he knew in Hawkshead. Knowing that I did not touch alcohol he invited me to go along with him so that he could have a drink in the assurance that I would drive back. It was difficult for me to exploit the turbo in the dark on unfamiliar winding roads, but I could have enjoyed a spin in daylight!

It was Roland's turn to lead and direct one the tasks. He was good at recognising people's strengths and delegating suitable parts of the exercise to them. So he was not rushing to begin, he was choosing very carefully which of us would do what. Things were not moving quickly enough for the colleague who had stripped to his underpants and plunged into the icy water. He began shaking his head and striding round the room "NO. No No, we don't want to do it that way, listen to me you guys."

Roland continued gently selecting his key players, but our vociferous friend was holding his own little meetings with various members and shaking his head at Roland's suggestions. The assessor, and Tricky Dicky were there with their stop watches and clip boards, time was slipping by and already ten minutes had passed and we were nowhere. Uncharacteristically I shouted, "Will you shut your gob and let Roland get on with this. He is leading this not you" then regretting what I had said I felt embarrassed and said very little for the rest of the session. At the conclusion of the exercise we gathered round the assessor for the customary feedback.

"For the first ten minutes you ran round like headless chickens until one of you demanded that someone should shut his gob. That came eight minutes too late and should have come from you Roland." I still felt embarrassed as in some way I could not get of my mind the feeling that I had undermined our District Manager. That, coupled with my outburst during the very first task that it was impossible, made me anxious about what may have been written about me on the clipboard!

The few days at Eagles Nest did seem to pass quickly and as a team building exercise it was successful. I think too that it had a far reaching effect upon our future prospects with the Company, although I am not sure that we sensed that at the time. Our time there ended after breakfast on the Friday and we were all eager to get back to our families. We were enjoying a relaxing breakfast now that all the tensions were over, when we were galvanised into action by one of the staff.

"If you guys don't set off immediately you will be cut off as Lake Windermere is about to flood over onto the main road." Fortunately our cases were already in the cars, so still munching our food we took our leave of Eagles Nest and its memories. Roland was a good driver, but the lake was already lapping across the road as he edged his Ford Granada gently through the threatening water. Once clear of Windermere we had a good journey home, reminiscing and laughing at some of the escapades we had got ourselves into during the last few days.

I was so tired that I slept most of the weekend, but on Monday it was business as usual, but more tests were to follow. Roland and I were called to Nottingham to undergo a psychometric test. On the way home he told me that he expected the result within a few days and that he would call me in to discuss the result with me. I don't think that either of us had thought very seriously about the accuracy of this type of test. When I sat in Roland's office to receive my feedback, he told me that he had already had his own feedback and that it was incredible how accurate he felt the assessment of his character was.

"David, they can tell from this test how likely it is that you will put your hands in the till."

I listened eagerly as my Manager took me through the feedback. I felt naked and exposed as though someone who had been watching me every moment of my life was telling someone what I was like.

So a long period of challenge and assessment had come to an end. I would know soon whether I still had a job, and if so in what capacity. Within a few months I was sitting once again in the District Manager's office to be told my fate.

"Congratulations David, I am pleased to inform you that I want you on my team. When S3 rolls out you will be one of the two Customer Services Managers. The whole District will be divided between the two of you. By the way I have decided to give you the better of the two areas"

This meant leaving the area I had looked after for about eighteen years. My area had covered the villages and homes from Tetney and Northcotes taking in Holton Le Clay, Humberston and almost all of Cleethorpes right up to its boundary with Grimsby. My new area would start there, and extend almost to the Humber Bridge and across to Caistor. The new area would come to me with two vacant agencies including the Caistor agency, which was the largest and busiest, dark nights, a temporary six months probationary period, and a brand new dark blue turbo charged Volvo 440 which somewhat sweetened the probation period pill!

Six months after roll, out, I was out of my probationary period and signed my permanent contract.  Little did I imagine that quite soon I would be sitting in Roland's office confiding in him that I needed to leave the Prudential Assurance Company after almost 30 years, fifteen of which I had worked for him.

# Tommy

There are few places more depressing than a night club on a cold dismal morning. However much life and atmosphere had been abundant last night, this morning was the complete opposite. Lifeless, no atmosphere, lingering odours of stale tobacco and beer. On the still uncleared tables were glasses and beer mugs, ash trays still spilled their contents over onto the table tops. One or two dim lights were struggling to illuminate the scene as a couple of staff were wearily clearing and cleaning the table tops and lazily hoovering the floor with uncoordinated and haphazard sweeps of the vacuum cleaner. I wondered whether they had been working until very late the previous evening.

It was ten o'clock in the morning and I was in the Victor's Club on Oxford Street in Grimsby. The only uplifting image in the building was the beaming face of Tommy Lee the proprietor. He was speaking with me whilst he tidied up the bar, at first I struggled to hear him as the sonorous tone of the vacuum cleaner droned on.

Traditionally most of my sales appointments seemed to fall in the evening. I understood that as those who worked nine to five were only available then. However there were a great many shift workers in the area who with forethought and planning could be seen in the daytime. Young Rob had arranged for me to see Tommy mid-morning, and I welcomed the opportunity. The subject in hand was one of Tommy's policies and I think he welcomed the opportunity of seeing me when he was working rather than sacrificing some of his leisure time.

The Victor's Club was not a huge building but it was planned so that a large audience could be accommodated in ampi-theatre style. It had its own car park in which my own car had only one or two companions. I guessed that the majority of its clients would walk there as the area was quite densely populated and was one of the neediest parts of the area with high unemployment, high teenage pregnancy rates, low literacy rates and high premature death rates. Tommy was the ideal host to bring the community together on an evening and he had a loyal faithful clientele.

We had finished our pleasantries and I was just about to get down to business when the phone rang. Tommy smiled at me as he asked,

"Do you mind if I answer this."

As he slid a glass of Coca Cola towards me across the bar, he mouthed that his phone call was not private, so I sipped my drink as I heard snatches of the conversation. The call ended and Tommy replaced the receiver as he smiled at me,

"That was Ken Dodd."

"Really Tommy, he sounded very friendly "

"Yes he is, its always good to talk with him. He has just lost his little dog which he has owned for years. He is a bit down and out of sorts."

"Ken Dodd is one man I could not imagine being depressed Tommy."

"He says he needs the uplift he gets from a Grimsby audience, He wants to come to the Victors Club and do an evening performance. He likes appearing here. He says there is a warmth and welcome here which is sincere and he needs to have a good dose of it, it will be like a tonic for him."

Tommy explained to me that his diary was at his home, so he would be ringing Ken Dodd back later that day to make a firm booking.

"Yes, Ken has appeared here several times. He is not rude and crude, children can enjoy his performance as they understand most of his jokes." Then Tommy laughed as he added,

"The only problem with Ken's evening show is that it never finishes on the same day it started!"

I laughed as Tommy continued,

"Oh he does not just believe in giving good value for money, Ken loves performing for a live audience, when he gets warmed up there is no stopping him. I have threatened to put all the lights out at midnight when he has still been going strong."

Tommy shared some of his stories concerning Ken Dodd. Apparently Ken Dodd's drummer was not able to play for him during one of his visits to the Victor's Club. He rang Tommy to ask whether their resident drummer would drum for him. "I'll pay him the going rate" promised Mr Dodd.

The local drummer was thrilled to be playing for the great Ken Dodd and the going rate for a nationally known star would be a welcome payment. Ken came to the Victor's, performed and the Grimsby drummer boy supported him for almost five hours. As Ken Dodd left the club for his car he popped an envelope into the drummer's hand and thanked him for a job well done. The envelope contained five pounds! Even that was more generous than on a previous occasion when as a reward for services rendered Ken Dodd popped a tea bag into his helper's pocket, as with a smile he said "Have a drink on me'"

I had met Tommy and his lovely wife Joan two or three times before, but we had met in their home just a stone's throw from the sea front in Cleethorpes. I had been impressed then by the warmth of their welcome and their genuineness.

Their love story began in 1951 at the YMCA in Heneage Road Grimsby. Tommy was there to play sport and Joan was taking a secretarial course. When Tommy first saw Joan she was fifteen. He said to a colleague,

"I will marry Joan one day."

True to his word, romance blossomed and when Joan was twenty years old, they were married in a lovely old church, thus began over 50 years of married happiness. They never left the area they grew up in.

Tommy had trained as a plumber and gas fitter, and just three years after their wedding, was called to a house on Park Street in Cleethorpes on an urgent emergency call. Contractors working there had fractured a gas pipe in the road and a major gas leak was threatening the house. Showing exemplary bravery, Tommy managed to get the four occupants out of the house to a place of safety before the house exploded. He and his apprentice were injured as he carried him to safety. Then Tommy collapsed and was in hospital for some time. He was awarded the British Empire Medal for bravery and a commendation from the Carnegie Hero Trust for Bravery. He was only 23 years old.

Tommy and Joan had three daughters, Tracey became a published author, and her book "The Variety girls" by Tracey Baines was set in Cleethorpes. Dianne Elizabeth became a Counsellor and therapist, and Taryn Jane became a barrister qualifying as a QC.

Tommy's first vision had been to marry Joan, now he had another vision, he wanted to run a pub. So as thorough as ever, he trained in pub management and took over the running of a Cleethorpes pub, well known as The Submarine. He realised that the clients wanted entertainment and so he provided this every night of the week.

Ready for a change, Tommy and Joan took over a large fish and chip restaurant on the promenade turning it into a night club which they called The Sands Club. It was there that an impressive line up of musicians performed to support the many famous cabaret artists.

But Tommy and Joan thought of others less fortunate than themselves and became keen philanthropists. The beneficiaries of many special charity nights were local children with special needs and physical disabilities.

It was from here, The Sands Club that Tommy and Joan took over the Victor's Club and eventually renamed it The Casablanca Club. Here they arranged well known acts such as Ken Dodd, The Supremes, Bernard Manning and a host of others. Some became part of the family as they chose to stay with Tommy and Joan rather than checking into a local hotel.

Unfortunately, in February 2012 Tommy passed away just one month before they were to celebrate their 55th wedding anniversary. A local journalist wrote,

"Tommy reached out to everyone as he was a very sociable and kind individual, a true "Mine host". He continued with his charity work by organising a mini olympics and pool tournament at the Casablanca, ably supported by Joan and the family. When he retired he did voluntary work helping young people wherever he could, with the same goals as the YMCA where Joan and Tommy met all those years before."

Tommy was so self effacing that none of this was apparent when speaking with him. I retired from the Prudential Assurance Company in 1992 and several years later decided to sell my Volvo privately, so I drove round with a For Sale notice in the window. One day I returned to my parked car which was on a street just off the sea front. A note was secured under the windscreen wiper.

"I am interested in buying your car, please knock at number ten."

I happened to be parked right outside number ten, but had forgotten who lived there. In response to me knocking on the door, it opened and a smiling Tommy Lee greeted me. I sat in the passenger seat as he had a test drive, I wanted to show him where I lived so that he could contact me, on the way there, and quite close to our home, Tommy pointed out a large detached house which I walked past every day whilst dog walking.

"One of our daughters lives there, she is a barrister". Tommy said proudly.

Tommy bought my car, and for the next few years, each time I saw a bright red Volvo S40 I looked to see whether Tommy was driving!

I never imagined when chatting with Tommy in the Victors Club that morning, that the same Club would host a significant event which had a huge bearing on mine and Edith's lives. The venue had been booked by Grimsby New Life Church for a mid week evening event. This was a brave and adventurous initiative which reminded me in many ways of those Holmfirth days when we visited the working men's clubs with a Gospel singer or musician.

The church in which we were members, Cleethorpes New Life church had been born out of a church plant into Cleethorpes by Grimsby New Life church, and we were keen to support the event.

The building was packed and many of the people were not church attenders. The evening was structured to allow a man and wife team, Charles and Paula Slagle who were visiting from America. There was little traditional preaching, Charles played the guitar whilst he and Paula sang some traditional and lesser known Christian songs. I think that if we had branded their performance with a name, it possibly would have been "The Singing prophets."

However the Slagles present website describes them as "people who listen to God" before imparting to individuals what they feel God has said about them.

I was very busy at the Prudential but had managed to take an evening off and was sitting there feeling so relaxed when Charles Slagle pointed directly at me and asked me to stand. He told me that I reminded him of his doctor back in America, before continuing with what he sensed that God had told him about me.

"You know what it is to restore an old motor car. You know that the most important thing is to ensure that the frame underneath is strong and capable of carrying the restored car safely. There is no point repairing all the paintwork and the engine and the upholstery unless the frame is strong enough to ensure that the car can enjoy its new lease of life. God is putting a new frame into you which will be strong enough to carry something new which He is going to do. Oh, and that which you have decided to build will come together very quickly. You will live a very long life and will feed a lot of people"

There was an incredible accuracy in his reference to car restoration. When I was at grammar school in Wakefield, my dad bought a 1948 Volkswagen Beetle. It was left hand drive, it did not have the modern synchromesh gear box, it had a split rear screen which was the mark of the very early models. It had been hand painted a horrible rusty-red colour. I learned to drive in it. Dad decided to restore it to make it look new. He attended to the mechanical work rebuilding the engine and gear box etc. He thoroughly checked the frame or chassis. My job was to scrape off every inch of paint down to the bare metal and rub the whole car down with fine sandpaper. It took all my spare time. The carpets and seats were removed, new carpets were made and the seats were reupholstered. Whilst this was being done the car was professionally resprayed a lovely ivory colour. After months of work it was completed. Resplendent with its new paintwork, its new seats and carpets and all its mechanical parts rebuilt. All safe on a secure frame!.

So I knew exactly what Charles Slagle had been referring to. But how did this affect me? It was at that time a mystery. Equally a mystery was the reference to building something which would soon come together. It was comforting to hear that I would live a very long life, but what did the promise that I would feed a lot of people mean? I was doing a little bit of preaching and teaching and I thought that Charles Slagel's words may refer to an increase in this Christian ministry. I ought to have begun to wonder what God was up to. But I didn't.

At the end of the meeting we were quickly surrounded by friends who knew us well asking what we had decided to build.

"Are you going to build a new house?"

"No."

"What have you decided to build then?"

"Nothing really!"

"Have you had plans drawn up for something?"

"No!"

"What is Charles Slagle referring to then?"

"No idea at all."

Edith and I speaking about it later could only think of one thing we had decided to build. That was our pension! We had waited until we could afford it before deciding to pay extra into the Prudential Pension Scheme through Additional Voluntary Contributions hopefully to build up the size of our pension pot in case I wanted to retire early.

Yes! That is the only thing we had decided to build!

I am grateful to the YMCA RICH HISTORY for some of the information about Tommy.

# Life Inspectors

As Section Superintendent I was programmed to work with each member of my team on a regular basis and my expectation of them was that they arrange a full session of sales appointments. I never expected the icing on the cake I was happy to have a go at the more difficult sales interviews or the selling of more complicated products which they were not licensed to sell. I did expect though that they did not leave all the selling to me. I expected them to successfully prospect for business in an attempt to be self-sufficient. This, in an ideal world, meant that sales I obtained when accompanying them added to their success and was not the sole reason for their success.

Each of my staff had a different outlook and this was evidenced by the quality of the sales appointments they took me on. I light heartedly referred to one of my staff as "the geriatric specialist" as he only seemed to have a rapport with his older clients and many of the prospects he took me to see were retired with health issues but my colleague thought that they may be in the market for "a bit of a top up" to their life cover.

I had one agent who seemed to think that he had to protect his clients from "thinking big" He took me one afternoon to meet Mr. and Mrs. Church, self-employed shop owners to discuss topping up the  small pension policy they were  paying into. Their large detached bungalow bore the proud name sign "Green Pastures" and was surrounded by extensive lush lawns. The superb bungalow and its tasteful furnishings shouted at me that here there was no shortage of money. They had a pension policy with the Prudential into which they paid such a tiny amount of contributions that the final payout would be ludicrously small. They had held this small premium for years, and it was due for payment. The agent had called to collect the £250 and had suggested that he took me along to discuss a "bit of a top up."

Much to the embarrassment of my colleague I asked our clients whether they were both salaried out of their business and upon finding that they were asked whether they would mind telling me what their taxable income was.

"You don't need to tell him" chipped in their local Man from the

Prudential, "What you both earn is private and you don't need to tell us."

I kicked him gently on the ankle as I continued,

"Yes that's right, you don't need to tell me how much you earn, but if I am going to offer you the best advice I really do need to know. I also need to know whether you are paying into any other pension policies in addition to the one you have with the Prudential."

"Mr. Robinson, we trust you and have no problem sharing information with you. The £250 per year which we pay into our pension plan with you is the only pension plan we have, and are taxable earnings are…"

I wrote down on my pad the figures he had shared with me and asked that they allow me a few minutes for me to work out some figures.

"Well, the present income tax regulations allow you to pay up to a certain percentage of your taxable income into providing for your retirement pension.

Your current earnings allow you to invest just over £6000 a year in pension contributions, and you are presently paying the grand total of £250 a year. You are losing out on valuable tax relief and you are not making adequate provision for retirement, I recommend that you top up your pension contribution by £6000 per year, and these are the benefits you will receive at retirement age"

"Mm!" said Mr. Church.

Their local agent coughed, went red in the face, and shuffled uncomfortably on the settee. I knew what he was going to say and tried to prevent him by gently tapping him on the ankle again. It was too late.

"Oh there is no need to pay all that. Mr. Robinson has just made a suggestion, not many people pay as much as that. You can pay anything you are comfortable with a modest top up will be fine by us."

Mr. Church abruptly interrupted his agent's apologetic interjection as he looked me in the eye,

"Mr. Robinson, if a job is worth doing it is worth doing well. We will contribute an extra £6000 a year into our pension plan."

"Thank you sir, you are doing the right thing, can I suggest that you pay by direct debit at £500 per month."

So we left our client's bungalow with a cheque for £500 and a direct debit and a proposal form for £500 a month in premiums. We had not even reached my car parked on the avenue before the local agent began bending my ear.

"David, they will change their mind, as soon as they realise how much they have signed up for they will change their mind. You will have a phone call to cancel or I will eat my hat. You should not have aimed so high. Little fish are sweet you know."

"Yes Bert, but little fish don't give you enough to live on during retirement. I did the right thing, the advice I gave was sound and professional. You are thinking too small."

I dropped Bert off at his own bungalow less than a mile away and drove home to have an early tea before going out on my evening appointments. Before I had finished my tea I had a phone call from Mr. Church.

"Mr. Robinson, you have been to see us this afternoon and we gave you a cheque for £500 and signed a direct debit. We have been thinking and would rather pay the £6000 once a year by cash or cheque. Would it be asking too much of you to call back and we will give you another cheque for £5500 and you can then cancel the direct debit."

Later that evening I called at Bert's home. He answered the door with a guilty look as though he had been caught out at home when he should have been working.

"Bert, I have had a phone call from Mr. and Mrs. Church about their pension plan."

"I knew it, I knew that you had gone in too heavy, I just knew they would cancel, I told you that they would change their mind" there was by now a hint of smugness in Bert's face.

"Yes Bert, they have changed their mind. They have decided to pay the premium yearly so here is their additional cheque for £5500 pounds which you need to pay in with the £500 cheque you already have."

I drove away from Bert's home wondering what the outcome would have been had Bert visited Mr and Mrs Church on his own. Would he have recommended that they doubled their pension contribution from £250 to £500? It would have been a marvelous achievement to have got Mr. and Mrs. Church to double their pension contribution, or would it? It depends on your perspective! But I wondered how much business we had lost over the years by small thinking and not offering what hard working clients really deserve, realistic advice which they can take seriously. It was in the 1980's when I met Mr. and Mrs. Church with Bert and £6000 was a lot of money. Within a few years the Financial Services Act made it compulsory to complete a Personal Performance Review form (PFR) with each client before beginning to advise them. The PFR included full details of their income, assets, liabilities, existing insurances and savings, their hobbies and interests, hopes for the future and their aversion to risk etc. The client had to sign the Review which was sent into the Companies Chief Office attached to the proposal forms for any new business recommended. Any bad advice was likely to come back and bite you in years to come. Many of the staff greeted the introduction of the PFR with doom and gloom. They thought that it would make it almost impossible to continue to sell our products. This was largely due to the fear of risking losing clients by asking them personal questions. It quickly became a valuable tool to help ensure that we recommended only the products which were suitable and necessary, and also ensured that we did not undersell or oversell. We were often surprised to discover that our clients had policies with other companies with much larger premiums than similar ones with Prudential. I did notice a pattern, policies sold by home service insurance companies, i.e. those who visited the clients in their own homes month by month tended to be smaller than those sold by companies which had not built up a close family relationship. Could it be that the desire to protect clients in order to safeguard friendship was actually working against our clients' interests.

My agents worked with me in turn on a Rota, possibly averaging once in every ten working days. I too had the services of the Life Inspector allocated to my team once each week. His only responsibility was sales. He did not have to manage a team, do audits, carry vacant agencies etc. etc. He was gloriously free to do nothing but sell life assurance pensions, mortgages and investments. He had to be prepared for all eventualities as he had no idea of the type of client he would be taken to. Therefore his product knowledge had always to be up to date. his understanding of taxation had to be current, and when licensing was introduced, he had to ensure that he had the license to sell every product in the Companies portfolio. We certainly would not be using him to the full advantage if we took him to prospects only wanting to invest two or three pounds a month.

When the Life Inspector was allocated to work on my section it was up to me whether I accompanied him personally or whether I chose one of my team to work with him. Although I really enjoyed working with the Life Inspector I often asked one of my team to accompany him, when they would be personally responsible for providing the programme of sales appointments. In reality though, the responsibility was a shared one and other agents would chip in with a prospect and if there were insufficient appointments, I could normally generate one or two from my own lists. On the rare occasions when there were more appointments than could be coped with, I would take some of them and so together we got through the workload. We sometimes had a joyful reunion at a local hostelry to savour our joint successes.

I always looked forward to working with the Life Inspector as on such occasions the pressure to perform was on him and not on myself. More importantly though, it was always good fun. Some of my happiest moments were those spent with John Spink, our Life Inspector supreme, or with Bill Belshaw during my 18 years in the Grimsby District. Edith always knew when John Spink and I had had a successful evening, if John was chuckling as we walked in through our front door she knew that we had done well. John could be trusted with any client, he never upset them, never pressured them, always had their best interests at heart and he never descended into the abyss of belittling another company to try and score points over them. I have to admit though that more than once I nodded off and fell asleep whilst John was in the middle of his sales presentation. It was our practice to go to Ernie Beckets or Steele's fish and chip shop, in Cleethorpes Market Place for tea, and working on a hot sultry evening, with a fish that size feeling heavy within, coupled with John's familiar voice had a soporific effect.

John and I were out together one evening and for some reason we were using my car. I ran out of petrol as I drove along Grimsby Road Cleethorpes and the car chugged to a complete halt.

"Don't worry John, I will walk back to the Esso Station on the corner of Daubney Street and get some petrol, they will lend me a can."

"I'll go with you David and stretch my legs."

We were soon in the kiosk but the lady informed me that they did not have a can to lend me. John noticed that they had some green plastic petrol cans for sale, and picking one up he said,

"Yes you do have a can, here is one. Why can't David borrow this one?"

"They are five pounds each, how do I know he will bring it back if I lend it to him."

Quick as a flash, I took the can from John and as I exited the kiosk said to the attendant,

"You can be sure I will bring it back, I will leave John as deposit on the can"

John patiently waited in the kiosk until I had filled up the can, walked back to the car, emptied the fuel into the car and driven back to the garage and filled up to the brim. John was not at all offended by all this, when I returned he was cheerfully engaged in conversation with the lady attendant who just as cheerfully "released" him when I had paid and returned her can. Years later, John was promoted to Chesterfield branch as District Manager. Grimsby District had a farewell meal and presentation to say goodbye to him. In his speech he said that he had enjoyed his time in Grimsby but the lowest depth he had sunk to was when David Robinson left him as deposit on a petrol can.

So in February 1985 John took up his duties as District Manager in Chesterfield. I still treasure a letter he sent me dated 3rd February 1985,

Dear David,

I would like to thank you for the wonderful support and warm friendship over the last nine years whilst we both worked together

It was always a pleasure to work with you-even when the business would not come! I hope David that I can generate in Chesterfield the example that you set in teamwork and in sincerity.

I suppose that when I walk into the Chesterfield Office tomorrow, I will realise that I am no longer the Life Inspector for Grimsby.

Please convey to Edith and to your family my very best wishes for a happy and contented future. I do hope that you will take the opportunity to come and see us when you are in our neck of the woods.

Once again David, many many thanks for all your help and support.

Best wishes

John.

I owe my love of pens to the years I worked with John Spink. John liked good quality pens and often had a new fountain pen. He spent many hours completing forms and writing up reports, so I guess that he regarded his pens as the tools of his trade. He was not a disposable biro man, His pens were quality articles of craftsmanship. He used a solid silver Yard O Led pencil too. I can remember John rubbing his pen with a yellow duster to keep it pristine. His love of fine writing instruments was passed on to me and very many years later, well into my retirement, I am a collector of good quality pens, preferring a good fountain pen to a ballpoint. John did not realize that he would be responsible for stimulating me to begin collecting pens. My collection is now around seventy pens including several solid silver Yard O Led's.

Many people assume that fountain pens are things of the past, but they have a cult following. Fountain pens play a very interesting traditional role when the American President signs an Executive Order or a Bill. As a way of thanking those who have done a lot of behind the scenes work in preparing the Order or Bill, the President donates the pen he has signed it with to them as a personal memento. That is easy if there is only one person to thank. When Barack Obama famously signed The Health Care Bill he used twenty two pens, jotting down one tiny portion of each of the eleven letters of his name as a time. He was heard to apologise in advance, "This is going to take a little while." Then the twenty two pens were given as souvenirs, many of them to legislators who had steered the bill through. This tradition goes back as far as President Roosevelt. These Presidential pens are made by A T Cross the pen maker of Rhode Island USA. From George W Bush to Barack Obama the Cross Townsend pen was the favourite due to its metal construction, deep black lacquer and real gold plated tip. President Obama switched the choice of presidential pen to the Cross Century 11 pen. The pens have a hefty price tag of about 120 dollars but can be worth five hundred dollars once used by the president. The quick drying ink which writes on most surfaces was important to most presidents.

Good quality fountain pens have a cult following worldwide. Some brands have top of the range models costing several thousand pounds and some vintage pens are highly sought after and are worth many times more than they cost when they were new. This reminds me that I do not have a Cross Presidential Pen in my collection-yet!

Bill Belshaw took over from John after his promotion. Had I been a Life Inspector I would not have wanted to be John Spink's successor. However Bill transitioned well and proved himself a worthy successor to John. Bill, a likeable Yorkshire man from Doncaster was so different in style and temperament to John. John had previously worked in a bank and his father, John Spink senior, who lived opposite us was a retired Prudential District Manager. Bill had been an electrician with Pilkington's Glass Company and was an intensely practical man who would tackle anything, John would rather pay a professional to do what was necessary. Bill was popular with the staff and did well for them when he was working on their behalf.    He built his own house just outside Scunthorpe and it was his pride and joy. It was a timber framed kit house, and in Bill's own words, "it came on the back of a lorry." I visited there frequently and he had a home to be proud of.

Bill took up oil painting whilst working in Grimsby. He was very enthusiastic and produced still life paintings at an alarming rate. Each time we worked together he seemed to have more new paintings in his car boot ready to be dropped off at the picture framers. He confided in me that when he was painting he was completely relaxed and de-stressed and he needed that kind of therapy as his job was so intense. I did not have a great knowledge of painting, but I did feel that Bill was creating a style of his own. He was not a copier of other people's style, he was developing that almost undefinable something, which enabled you to say "That's a Bill Belshaw painting" when you saw one.

Bill and I continued the trend of eating tea at Beckets or Steele's. The favourite place was Beckets as it was quicker than Steeles and cheaper.

One evening we went to Steele's and enjoyed the more leisurely meal, so we went back there the next week and the next and the next. When we walked into Ernie Beckets again, Joan, the lady who usually served us almost accosted us with the greeting,

"I have seen you going over the road into Steele's these last few weeks. Aren't we good enough for you? Why did you desert us for them?"

Jokingly I responded,

"It's nothing personal Joan, we went there the first week because you were full up, and then when we saw how big their fish are compared to yours, we just went back again"

Becket's fish were legendary. They were huge, they hung over the sides of the plate, and it was a brave man who could tackle one of Becket's fish. Joan fixed me with a look which seemed to threaten revenge before stomping off to get our order.

She stomped her way back, almost making the floor shake. She slammed our plates down on the table challenging us,

"You will eat all of those if you know what's good for you."

Bill and I were dumfounded, not only were our fish the biggest we had ever seen, they far exceeded the normal size, but there was a fish and a half on each of our plates, a slag heap sized pile of chips topped off with a huge mountain of mushy peas and a pile of bread and butter.

Joan shouted from the till,

"If you don't eat all that you are in trouble, I'll give you "Steele's fish are bigger than yours."

Half an hour later Bill and I managed to leave our empty plates behind and clutching our stomachs we paid and walked uncomfortably to Bill's car to drive to our next appointment. We both made some comment about going back to Steele's the following week, but we returned to Beckets next week and the next and the next! We dare not expose ourselves to Joan's all seeing eye.

Bill was not quite as well organized as John Spink, it was not unknown for him to lose paperwork and the occasional cheque. Possibly it was because he often threw paperwork onto the back seat of his car and then drove with the window open. A local milkman was delivering on one of the streets in Cleethorpes when he saw a plastic carrier bag in the gutter. Assuming that it could be a bag of empty beer bottles he decided to remove it. He was amazed to find that the bag contained ten thousand pounds. He handed the money in at the Police Station but no one claimed it. The newspaper published the story that no one had come forward to claim the money. Bill's reputation for misplacing things caused a humorous response amongst the Prudential staff who wondered how long it would take Bill to discover that he had lost ten thousand pounds. Cruel but in the spirit of fun.

Bill and I had just finished our working day together when he said,

"Next week when we work together David, it will be your birthday. So if you can fix up appointments for daytime we can finish by four o'clock."

"Why is that Bill what have you in mind?"

"Your uncle Bill has a birthday present for you, but we will need to be leaving Grimsby by teatime. The surprise will keep until next week."

I was able to plan so that we could finish work in good time, and just after four o'clock we were back at my home where we both changed into casual clothes. Within half an hour we were heading across the Humber Bridge towards the North Bank which seemed to beckon us towards its soft sunlit greenery.

"We are going fly fishing" said Bill, "to Driffield Beck. It's one of the most northerly chalk streams in the UK and Driffield Anglers club only allow their members to fish the beck." Bill explained that his brother in law was the water bailiff and it was he who would take us under his wing, teach us to cast a fly and ensure that we caught fish.

Nationally, Driffield is probably best known amongst the angling fraternity. In 1806 a leading angler said that he had fished in many parts of Scotland and England, but of all the places he had fished, he preferred the delightful river at Driffield.

The gin clear chalk –bed streams of the Wolds provide the perfect habitat for trout, and Driffield's Beck is renowned for its grayling, chub, dace and especially wild trout. The same water flow which once drove Driffield's two largest watermills now draws game anglers from all over the country. Driffield Anglers Club was established in 1883 and is an exclusive club controlling over six miles of pristine chalk stream water in and around Driffield. We met up with Bill's brother in law and he took us to see the members club house which spoke of affluence. When he told us the cost of a year's membership we knew that there was no way we would be able to even consider membership. There was a large highly polished oak table in the club house and each member had his own name plate with his name in gold leaf to mark his place at the table. Beside the name plate was a leather bound blotting pad, a fly tying vice, club notepaper and a pen.

This was going to be a birthday present which probably would never be repeated. Then a walk along the river bank, there was no difficulty spotting the huge trout as the water was gin clear. I had never tried to cast a fly before but as the river was not wide and we could see the trout facing upstream, I soon was casting quite well and hooked my first fish. It weighed about three pounds and I was delighted until Bill's brother in law hit it on the head with a priest and soon it was motionless in my hands.

"Oh, I wanted to put it back in the river" I said sadly.

"Sorry my friend, all fish have to be killed and removed if they are above a certain size." For that reason I only continued to fish for a short time as when I was responsible for the deaths of three lovely fish I felt guilty. Bill too had success and by nine o'clock we were on our way home, the golden sun setting on a wonderful day, only marred by the thought of the beautiful fish lying dead in the car boot. My three fish went into our freezer and were cooked when special guests visited us shortly afterwards. Needless to say I could not eat any. I looked at them lying in the dish telling myself that had it not been for me, they probably would have still been swimming wild and free

This is one of my lasting memories of Bill and is still fresh very many years later. Another abiding memory of Bill concerns the night he split his trousers.

It was half past eight on a dark cold winter night and we had the claim form with us for a Prudential Plan which was maturing with a payout of ten thousand pounds. I had sold the plan ten years previously and I knew that the lady was elderly and that by this time her door would be fastened for the night.  Bill thought that it was worth knocking on the door and against my better judgement I fell in with this.

The curtain inside moved and a pink face appeared near the window in the door.

"Yes who is it"

"Billy Belshaw and David Robinson from the Prudential."

"What! At this time of night?"

"Yes, it's important you have some money due and there is a form to sign."

"Does it have to be done tonight?"

"Whilst we are here we may as well do it, aren't you going to ask us in?"

"Do I really have to?"

"Yes if you want your money."  Bill's attempt to make light work of it was not working. We heard the key turn and heard the bolt sliding back before the door opened just a few inches.

"I would rather see Mr. Robinson on his own in the daytime. He is the gentleman I always deal with. Why do you have to be involved?"

"Because I am helping him tonight."

"He does not need help from you, he set me the investment up ten years ago and knows what he is doing."

"Can we come in?" Bill almost begged.

"If you have to."

Within a few more seconds we were standing in the warm entrance hall.

"Can we come right in" asked Bill.

Nodding towards the front room door she snapped "If you have to."

This was progress by degrees.  We were in but not right in.  We entered the front room, and Bill said "Can I sit down?"

"If you have to."

Bill dropped from a standing position with some force onto the settee. As his rear extremity hit the cushion there was an ominous tearing noise. He put his hand between his bum cheeks and the cushion exclaiming,

"Oh dear."

"You have not split my cushion please tell me you have not torn my suite"

"No it's worse than that."

"What can be worse than that?"

"I have split my trousers."

"Good"

Bill stood and bent towards us. His trousers seam had opened up from where the belt at the back to where the zip started at the front.

"Have you a needle and cotton?" Bill requested bashfully.

"Yes but you are not taking your trousers off in here."

"I don't intend to take them off, I will stitch them whilst I am wearing them."

Soon our hostess, much to the amusement of her husband who had not said a word, appeared with needle and cotton.

"If you do it yourself you will be here all night, bend over the settee arm."

"OK but you will be careful where you put the needle won't you."

"Don't tempt me."

Soon the temporary repair was done, Bill had his form signed, and the hostess, who I think was by now enjoying the light entertainment was leading us back to the front door. I was about to open the door when Bill prevented me,

"I am sorry but I need the loo and I have to drive back home to Scunthorpe. Can I borrow your toilet?"

"If you have to, it's at the top of the stairs look, that's the door there.

Bill proceeded up the stairs hoping that the stitching would hold and disappeared into the loo. I stood with our hostess at the foot of the stairs waiting, waiting until the Niagara Falls ceased to flow.

"Does he have to wee like a donkey" she said with a twinkle in her eye.

Yes, working for the Prudential has its ups and downs. But even some of the downs are ups- depending on your viewpoint.

# A New Challenge

Bill Belshaw was appointed the sales manager within the restructured Grimsby District of the Prudential Assurance Company and following his retirement he became a professional artist and art teacher. This was typical of Bill, he was a man of vision, single minded and would pursue his vision tenaciously.

We continued to work together until I took early retirement at the age of fifty and enjoyed frequent and welcome refreshment breaks at Ernie Beckets our favourite fish and chip eating place.

Ernie Becket the owner of Beckets Fish and Chip Restaurant was also a man of single minded vision. I met him several times professionally at his shop in Cleethorpes Market Place, and we usually dealt with our business in the preparation room at the rear. He enjoyed relating to me one day how he set up in business. He worked on Grimsby Fish Docks for a fish merchant, but his vision was to open his own fish and chip shop. This proved incredibly difficult as he had no capital and in those days none of the banks were prepared to back him. He shared his vision and his frustrations with his employer who offered to lend him the capital needed to set up his business provided Ernie bought all his fish from him. That was a deal, and with that backing Ernie found an empty shop on a back street parallel with St Peter's Avenue, the main shopping thoroughfare. One major frustration was the high cost of a sufficiently large advertisement in the Grimsby Telegraph. Ernie told me,

"I wanted a half page advert, but would have needed a mortgage to pay for it. I wanted to get my shop noticed."

He decided to publicize his new venture in an unusual way. He had a poster printed which he placed in the shop window. It offered a free fish and chip take away meal on his opening day to the first hundred pensioners who produced evidence of their age.

Mrs. Becket advised him against this as did other colleagues. It will cost you a lot of money and you have no guarantee that any of those benefiting from a free meal will ever come back again.

"Ah but they will come back "predicted Ernie confidently, "I will give them such huge fish and such a large portion of chips that they will be back for more." That was the founding ethos of the small business which would soon become the "go to" place to eat for many thousands of Cleethorpes holiday makers and locals who appreciated excellent value when they saw it.

On the morning Ernie was due to open his fish and chip shop, he was working in the preparation room when he had an inspired idea.

He rang Grimsby Telegraph and spoke with the News Desk.

"Are you interested in a newsworthy story" he asked. "There is a new fish and chip shop opening in Cleethorpes and the public spirited owner is giving away one hundred free fish and chip meals to the first hundred pensioners to visit his shop. I think that's a very praiseworthy thing to do and the owner deserves to get on."

"Really, where is this new fish and chip shop?"

Ernie told them exactly where the shop was, but then began to play hard to get.

"Can we have your name Sir, we can feature you in our article."

"Oh no I don't want you to mention my name."

"Fine but do you know the name of the man who is opening the shop?"

"I did hear that it's a Mr. Becket, yes that's it. Mr. Ernie Becket. I have just walked past the shop and he seems to be in there working now."

"Thank you sir, leave it with us"

Half an hour later there was a knock on the shop door. There stood a young lady accompanied by a photographer. Mr. Becket opened the door,

"I am very busy but can I help you."

"Are you Ernie Becket the proprietor?"

"Yes that's me."

"We are from the Telegraph and we have heard about your grand opening with a hundred free fish and chip meals. We would like to feature it in the local paper."

"Oh I am not sure about that, would it mean that you would print a picture of me and a story."

"Yes that's what we have in mind."

"But I am a very shy person and don't like a fuss, I don't think that I would like to be featured in the newspaper"

Ernie related to me how he let them talk him into posing for a photograph and giving them an exclusive interview with pictures of his shop and details of its opening hours etc. Ernie could not wait to see the next edition. He had a half page feature, far more advertising than he could have ever afforded to pay for, all completely free.

When we ate there many years later, Ernie was still faithful to his founding vision of giving such large portions of fish and chips that his customers returned again and again. Of course he also had the skill to cook his meals exactly right, but the main ingredient in his success was his singleness of vision, his entrepreneurialism, and his dedication to his original ethos of giving such good measure that the customers will come back.

In the late 1970s there was a serious shortage of potatoes, and those which were available cost an arm and a leg. Other fish and chip shops reduced the size of their portion of chips and some also charged more for their smaller portions. Mr Becket did not falter from his original vision of generosity. He gave the same generous sized portion of chips at the normal price even though every portion of chips he sold represented a loss which had to be subsidized out of the profit he made on his fish. So in that particular trading year, his taxable profits were well down.

The Tax Inspector queried his Tax Return but was assured that it was correct but was reluctant to accept Mr. Becket's explanation and began an investigation. Then in August, in the peak of the busy season, two well-dressed pin stripe suited men appeared in the restaurant. They chose the table which was closest to the cash register and ordered their meal. They had a note book and wrote down the amount of every transaction entered into the cash register. They also kept a total of how many customers came into the restaurant. They repeated this for two whole weeks. Ernie realized who they were and what they were doing and as they approached the till to pay, he took over from the lady who was waiting to take their money.

"Can I ask you whether you are paying for all your meals out of your own pocket or are you charging it up to expenses?"

"We don't know what you mean.. How much do we owe?"

"Of course you know what I mean! You are spies from Inland Revenue.

Why have you chosen to spy on me in August, the busiest month of the year? If you come back again in February I will pay for your meals myself"

Every time I was enjoying my meal at Beckets, I admired him for pursuing his vision of generosity even at a time of great challenge. I did not realise then that the time would come when I would need to take a stand in supporting my own vision, even in times of severe challenge.

Rob, my youngest agent who did so well for me and attended the Star Dinner in London as a reward for his success one year was also prepared to pay the price to support his vision. Due to changes in his circumstances he found himself questioning his purpose and ambitions in life. He felt the challenge to start a new life by going to university and retraining for a new career. He had a hard time, he was so well liked by his policyholders that a great many of them almost pleaded with him to stay with the Prudential. Others encouraged him to make changes whilst he was still young and adaptable. He had to make a tough decision. Should he stay in a well-paid job which he enjoyed and which certainly held out promotion prospects in the future, or should he pursue his vision, even though it incurred a high cost. After a real struggle Rob chose to pursue his dream and I was sorry to lose him.

On our last working day together, Rob gave me a Thank You Card which I have to this day, he wrote in his unique way,


When the business failed to come,
We would laugh and not be glum.
We'd just work and not be sad,
Saying things aren't really bad.

And of course our spirits were high
Because in the end we could not deny
That in a call it would be funny
To listen to the sounds from my boss's tummy.

When a client offered a drink,
We would have to sit and soberly think,
Just how much noise can they stand
From that gastronomic band?

And the Prudential should pay expenses for irresistible Mars Bar frenzies,
Cups of coffee by the score.
Who cares about calories? More and more!

But I'd like to sincerely say
That through my happy and pleasant stay
You've been not just a boss but a friend
And to you my thanks I humbly extend.

During my time as Superintendent in Grimsby, I heard through the Prudential Staff Magazine that Dennis Carolan, who had been my superintendent in my Sleaford days and followed his dream and had taken early retirement. I heard that he was not well and wrote him an encouraging letter. Dennis replied from his home in Great Gonerby, Grantham,

Dear David,

Many thanks for the wonderful letter you wrote to me. The sentiments you expressed therein gave me enormous pleasure and will, I am certain, sustain me during my retirement.

I too remember our Sleaford days with fond affection, and deeply appreciate the warmth and friendship shown to me by yourself and Edith when I arrived from Nottingham.

If I have played some small part in the success you have had so far in your career David, then I am delighted, but I am also very conscious of the fact, having worked a good many years for the Company, that you could not have attained your managerial status without having an abundance of natural talent and a capacity for hard work, which time and time again you demonstrated when we worked together in Sleaford. I sincerely hope that your career spirals ever onwards and upwards David.

Thanks once again for your most kind letter and please give my warmest regards to Edith and the children

Yours sincerely,

Dennis Carolan.

Sadly Dennis's hopes of a long and happy retirement were brought to a premature end when he passed away due to leukaemia.

I had no ambition for further promotion and never sought it. I enjoyed what I was doing so much that I had every intention of continuing until normal retirement age, in the hope that Edith and I would be healthy and strong enough to enjoy those golden years. I was reckoning without the life changing effect of what happened to me during a normal church service one Sunday morning in the autumn of 1991.

I was part of the leadership team of Cleethorpes New Life Christian Fellowship, and we held our Sunday morning services in a local school off Middlethorpe Road in Cleethorpes.

The far reaching changes with the Prudential structure and operations meant that I was busier than ever, and Sunday was a chance to relax and recharge my batteries ready for Monday.

Dennis Brown, our pastor was preaching and was coming to the end of his address when he realized that he needed a few more minutes in order to round off to a good conclusion. He smiled at the congregation as he said,

"I know that your chicken is in the oven folks, but just give me five more minutes."

As soon as he had spoken those words, I heard some unspoken words which did not come from him. They did not come via my ears, or through any of the five human senses. There was no audible voice, but it was no less real because of that. Deep in my spirit I heard the challenge,

"What about those who have no chicken to put in the oven? What about those who have no oven to put a chicken in? What about those who have no home, who have nowhere to live!? What have you done in your Christian life for those who have nothing?"

The challenge hit me right between the eyes. I sensed that those moments were especially sacred and I promised there and then that I would respond to the challenge which had dropped on me from a great height that Sunday morning.

The next few months would be very interesting and very challenging.

# The Green Light

It was during the autumn of 1991 when I had those uncomfortable moments of challenge towards the end of Sunday morning service in Lindsey School Cleethorpes. I was not looking for extra work to do as my workload with Prudential had never been so acute. Yet I could not shrug off the experience which had affected me deeply as I felt that it was a personal challenge to me, but not to myself alone, but to involve the church in pursuing the heart of God for the poor and disadvantaged, many of whom who would never consider going anywhere near a church.

I spoke with Dennis Brown our Pastor, he knew me well enough to sense that this had affected me too deeply to be just a passing phase. Understanding how stressed my secular work situation was, he suggested that I took a six months holiday from church leadership responsibilities and duties. During this break I would have time and space to work through what I sensed God was saying, and plan a strategy. I welcomed the opportunity and in later years was thankful for Dennis's thoughtful and sensible stance. Whilst I was taking a six months break from church leadership Alec Depledge who had lead the Immingham Assembly of God Church for many years, and was currently leading a church in Brigg came in at Dennis's request to serve our church until I was able to resume duties.

My decision was not to seek out any advice or ideas from colleagues. I took the view that if God had begun something with that Sunday morning challenge to me, then He was more than capable and willing to lead further step by step. It was down to me to listen, sense and validate what He was leading me into. The time would come when I had a fully formed vision and strategy which could be shared with suitable people but before that day there was much personal and private preparation to pursue.

There are people who claim to have heard from God but in reality it has been the result of too much cheese for supper the night before! Sometimes is has been the leading of a personal hobby horse! If my challenge really came from God then it would be confirmed as I spent time trying to listen to God and especially through the Bible which is God's living Word.

As far as the Bible was concerned it was incredible how passages which were familiar suddenly spoke to me powerfully. Even when I opened the Bible at random and began to read, the page had opened where the needs of the poor and disadvantaged were prioritized. I worked on the premise that God would never lead the church into actions and strategy which were contrary to the general teaching and ethos of the Bible. By the time a few months had passed I was in no doubt at all that what I had sensed God was calling me to do had been undoubtedly validated and confirmed by Scriptures. I am so glad that this was an important stage in developing the vision because when my strategy was eventually shared and made public, a lady who was a member of our church was openly antagonistic. She said that local church should not be involving itself in social work, adding "Where is that in the Bible?" I knew where it was in the Bible! Years later she came to see me as I was leading and heading up the resultant Charity and apologized for her earlier attitude. She said "I think that I may have cursed the charity through my attitude to it and the things I have said publicly about it." I smiled at her and said "Well, if you have cursed us maybe you should curse some more because all we have sensed is God's blessing!"

Scripture spoke to me powerfully confirming the challenge and directing my thoughts. Time and space prevents a full commentary, but here are some examples of the Biblical landscape I travelled.

Amos, one of the so called "minor" prophets had some stinging criticism of how poor and underprivileged people had been treated. In the fifth chapter of his prophecy he laments,

*You who turn justice into bitterness and cast righteousness to the ground... you hate the one who reproves in court and despise him who tells the truth. You trample on the poor and force him to give you corn...I know how many are your offences and how great your sins. You oppress the righteous and take bribes and you deprive the poor of justice in the courts. Therefore the prudent man keeps quiet in such times for the times are evil. Hate evil, love good, maintain justice in the courts. I hate, I despise your religious feasts, I cannot stand your assemblies, even though you bring me burnt offerings and grain offerings, I will not accept them. Though you bring me choice fellowship offerings I will have no regard for them. Away with the noise of your songs, I will not listen to the music of your harps, but let justice roll on like a river, righteousness like a never failing stream.*

Years later I became friends with a social worker who warned me that she was "up to the eyes" with Christianity and had no time for it. She said "You and I will get on fine provided you don't try to talk to me about Christianity." I discovered that she had a brother-in-law who was a full time minister of an evangelical church. He saw her as the black sheep of the family and to use her own words, he tried to convert her.

She summed up her brother-in-law in these words, "All he is concerned about, Sunday after Sunday, is perfection in the pulpit. The sermon, the singing, the church building, everything has to be perfect and look right. But he has no thought whatsoever for the poor, the hurting, the needy, the homeless the destitute."

She was offended by his emphasis, or by his lack of emphasis on the needs of the poor. Although she was not a Christian believer, she thought that her brother-in-law's faith was flawed and had an underlying hypocrisy in it. His lack of interest in the needy and underprivileged presented a brand of Christianity which she wanted no part of. If she found Christianity which did not care for the poor to be abhorrent, how does Almighty God feel!

That surely is what Amos is speaking of here. Although the words came out of Amos's mouth we must not lose sight of the fact that God was telling him how He felt about worship when there was no concern for the poor and the needy.

Strong language, so challenging, and we cannot water it down!

*I hate, I despise your religious feasts. I cannot stand your assemblies. Even though you bring me burnt offerings I will not accept them. Away with the noise of your songs! I will not listen to the music of your harps, but let justice roll on like a river, righteousness like a never failing stream.*

Is God really saying "Put down the guitars, switch off the keyboard," Tell the singers to stop singing. I will not listen, unless you are serving the poor, righting wrongs, overturning poverty and injustice."

Is the Amos passage saying that whilst we were singing our Christian worship songs in Lindsey School that Sunday morning, God's heart was being stirred and moved by the plight of those outside of the church who could not afford a chicken to put in the oven, and those who had no oven or home of their own?    I believe so.  His words which were a blistering attack upon the hypocrisy of Israel, came to me as a reminder that God demands more from professing Christians than what goes on in church on a Sunday.

Then the familiar words of Jesus from Matthew chapter 25 began to speak to me powerfully.   It is amazing enough to realise that God has a heart of concern for the disadvantaged, but it is even more amazing to understand that just as He feels their hurts, he also feels relief when their needs are met.

The words of Jesus from Matthew 25 can have no other interpretation.

*When the Son of Man comes in His glory, and all the angels with Him, He will sit on His throne in heavenly glory.  All the nations will be gathered before Him and he will separate the people one from another as a shepherd separates the sheep from the goats…..then the King will say to those on His right, "Come you who are blessed by my Father, take your inheritance, the kingdom prepared for you since the creation of the world. For I was hungry and you gave me something to eat, I was thirsty and you gave me something to drink, I was a stranger and you invited me in. I needed clothes and you clothed me.  I was sick and you looked after me, I was in prison and you came to visit me.   Then the righteous will answer Him, Lord when did we see you hungry and feed you, or thirsty and gave you something to drink.  When did we see you a stranger and invited you in or needing clothes and clothe you. When did we see you sick or in prison and go to visit you.*

*The King will reply I tell you the truth, whatever you did for one of the least of these brothers of mine you did for me.   And some will answer, Lord when did we see you hungry, or thirsty or a stranger or needing clothes or sick or in prison and did not help you.  He will reply, I tell you the truth, whatever you did not do for one of the least of these, you did not do for me*

Is the Bible teaching us that God vicariously feels the emotions and pains of those who are hurting?  I believe so, and if God feels the hurts how much more does he feel the relief and release when help comes.

The charity which was formed following this period of challenge had a strap line "Touching lives with hope." I took this as my theme when invited to give a talk at a professional women's society meeting held in a local golf club, I had been retired from General Management of the Charity for a number of years but on occasions still gave talks about the Charity…  I spoke on the theme "Touching lives with hope" and noticed during my address that a lady was looking at me intently as though she was trying to draw more out of me. I had completed my contribution and retired into the bar to have a coffee and this lady followed me and sat beside me.

"You have just spoken to us about "touching lives with hope", and I want you to know that is exactly what you did for our daughter all those years ago. She never forgot how you brought hope to her"

She mentioned her daughter's Christian name and I immediately remembered her. She had been stabbed multiple times and left for dead. She recovered but there were mental scars and she became homeless. We housed her in a flat and provided her with a Christian support worker who befriended her and provided pastoral care and help.

"Yes" the lady continued, "I am pleased that you remember my daughter. Your charity was the only organization which offered her help and support. No-one else was interested. The talk you have given tonight is all true. That is what your charity does, they touch lives with hope. You touched my daughter's life with hope, but I want you to know that in touching her with hope, you touched me too. My daughter died recently but she never forgot what your charity did for her. You certainly touched her with hope."

Those words made my whole evening worthwhile. "In touching her you touched me too" I quietly thanked God for the privilege of touching this lady with hope simply by touching her daughter's life.

Is it too incredible to think that when a life without hope is touched God feels that touch too! I don't think so. That is surely what Jesus is saying here in Matthew's Gospel. *"What you did for these you did for me."*

I saw from this that ministering to the hurting and needy is in some remarkable way also ministering to the God who feels what we feel. It is a valid part of our Christian worship and service. There were other Biblical passages which intensified the challenge I had felt that Sunday and the vision grew stronger.

There had to be a starting point, and I felt very strongly that the starting point would be the giving away of essential furniture etc to those who were in the various poverty traps

But what were we to give out of? Most churches had enough of a struggle to maintain their own overheads and had very little spare resources to give from.

I felt the challenge to build a RESOURCE so that there would always be a supply of good quality furniture etc. which we could give out of. Being a resource to the community was the key. We should build something which was significant enough to be missed if it was no longer there. As a CHRISTIAN I needed to take ACTION and be ENTERPRISING to build such a RESOURCE.

Re-arranging the sequence slightly gave me CHRISTIAN ACTION RESOURCE ENTERPRISE. This would be the name of the proposed registered charity. The initial letters spell CARE so our RESOURCE would be a charity shop called CARE SHOP. This should be opened as a Christian witness which would receive donated goods and give a considerable amount of the goods away free of charge to people in the various poverty traps. The goods we sold would cover overheads and enable us to provide financial help to people where necessary.

This was a pioneering concept in the early 1990s. There were numerous charity shops in our community but none of them gave away goods. . Their priority was to sell goods given to them by the public to raise money to sustain their charitable activities. A little later when one of them did begin to donate items to needy people it was obvious that they chose the goods which not many people would want to buy as items with which to "bless the poor".

I felt that once the charity was up and running, I would not wish to give an item of furniture to a needy person unless I would be personally happy to use that item myself. Why should someone be expected to sleep on a mattress which I would shrink from? When we began to function, we would not select the inferior goods to donate to people. We would treat people with dignity. If God is in the business, why not give them the good quality stuff. In so doing we would be treating them with dignity and planting seeds which we trusted God would bless and produce a harvest from so that we in turn could bless others.

I felt that we would not wait until we had accumulated resources before beginning to give out, we would do it immediately.

We would not do things in a corner, hoping that people would not hear about us. As soon as the charity shop was open, we would write to our local Social Services to let them know that we are available to try and help needy people with free items of essential furniture.

But there was another vital principle which I felt God was stressing through a New Testament event. A principle which would have a far reaching impact and would give us a distinctive ethos and hopefully demonstrate to people just how much God loves them.

In Acts chapter three Peter and John were going up to the temple at three o'clock in the afternoon which was the time for prayer. As they passed through the Beautiful Gate they passed a man who had been born a cripple, he was sitting begging for money. When he saw Peter and John he asked them for money. Peter and John looked straight at him saying "Look at us" The man gave them his full attention expecting to receive some money. What happened next is amazing and deeply thought provoking and became a principle which we proved time and time again in the CARE charity. Peter addressed the man with the disappointing words, "Silver or gold I do not have." In other words, his purse was empty! "But what I have I give you, in the Name of Jesus Christ of Nazareth, rise up and walk." Then taking him by the right hand he helped him up and instantly the man's feet and ankles became strong. The former cripple began to walk, then he went into the temple courts walking, jumping and praising God.

How Peter dealt with the man's request for money is very powerful. What Peter established that day, as he stepped out in faith, was that as committed Christians we are not without resource just because our purse is empty. "Silver or gold we do not have, BUT WHAT WE HAVE IN THE NAME OF JESUS WE GIVE YOU....RISE UP AND WALK." This was the first time Peter reached into his second purse! The purse which contained all that he had in the Name of Jesus.

I remember saying to Dennis Brown after the launch of the CARE Charity that I felt that God wanted to remind us that not having the resources was not a valid reason for not giving. We need to reach into the second purse in faith, believing that in the Name of Jesus God would underwrite what we asked for.

This had an immensely practical edge to it. Someone had a desperate need for something we did not have, we would reach into the second purse by asking God to supply it. We would expect answers, we received answers!

It was so vital for the success of Christian Action and Resource Enterprise that we had staff and volunteers who had the discernment to know when it was time to reach into the second purse and enough faith to believe that God would answer our prayer on behalf of a needy person. Yet it could be so easy to lose sight of this supernatural resource and become ordinarily secular.

So after a break from church leadership, my vision now had the arms and legs of a workable strategy. As CHRISTIANS we needed to take ACTION to become a RESOURCE and be people of ENTERPRISE to explore ways of ministering to the needy. The first outlet for all this would be a charity shop called the CARE SHOP. We would generously give away essential furniture and household goods, and we would be people of Christian faith, knowing when to reach into the second purse of prayer to see needs met.

I shared all this with Dennis Brown our pastor and the church leadership team. It is fair to say that one of the leaders wrote all this off as a stupid idea and treated it somewhat scornfully. Dennis arranged for me to meet with several local church leaders to share the vision. A few weeks later, a group of these leaders met in Dave Kitchen's home on Weelsby Road Grimsby. Dave was the senior leader of Grimsby New Life Christian Fellowship. Also present were   Colin Wilson, Ray Lewis and Doctor Bob Duerden all elders of Grimsby New Life Christian Fellowship, Alec Depledge leader of Brigg Christian Fellowship, Dennis Brown and myself. I shared the vision fully and the assembled team all sensed that God was in it and prayed for success and future direction.

The green light seemed to be well and truly on!

# The Care Shop

We had gone through far-reaching organizational changes at Prudential Assurance Company. I was fortunate in retaining my position, had had to successfully transition from Section Superintendent into Customer Services Manager. Although grateful that I was one of the successful staff members who were retained, I had been offered my new role on a six months' probation. This seemed to be the norm and I and other affected colleagues were not happy that after very many years of unblemished service we found ourselves on probation. The workload and the pressures were severe but I was glad that at the end of the six months I was able to sign my permanent contract. So here I was, in my 49th year with reasonable assurance of full time employment until I retired, in a job I had previously always enjoyed, and now with the added bonus of a turbo charged Volvo company car.

Permanence had a sweet savour after so much uncertainty!

Cleethorpes New Life Christian Fellowship, our local church had been striving to present a permanent image to the community. Since inception in the mid nineteen eighties we had met on a Sunday in hired school halls. This had severe disadvantages. One pressure was that the public address system, keyboard etc etc had to be transported to the venue each Sunday and set up and taken down. This soon became routine but a church who rented a building for public worship was not as highly regarded as the local church with their own building, as they seemed to be regarded as a permanent part of the community. Dennis Brown our pastor continued to rent office accommodation within the Grimsby New Life Christian Fellowship complex on Freeman Street in Grimsby, we were looking for a more permanent base even though initially that base may just be our registered office, with a facility in Cleethorpes where people could visit.

Whilst I was "enjoying" my six month's break from church leadership, premises became available at 46 Alexandra Road Cleethorpes which would make an ideal office base. With some stud walls and partitioning suitable premises were constructed with a private office for Dennis accessed from a reception area with sufficient room for a desk and workstation for his secretary. At the rear was a meeting room which would accommodate thirty people and which would be ideal for mid-week prayer meetings etc.  At the front, looking out onto The Pier Gardens on Alexandra Road was a small retail area.

It was this small retail area which Dennis offered to make available for use as the possible CARE SHOP.  I went to see the area on offer and immediately knew that it was far too small.  It would be ideal for a small second hand clothes shop but there was no room for furniture items.  I felt that this room was not ambitious enough and that it would severely restrict what the CARE SHOP could do.

Dennis had a good relationship with Rev John Fenner a local minister who was heavily involved with The Heifer Project.   The Heifer Project was an excellent charity which raised money to pay for the supply of a cow to be given to poor villages in countries facing poverty. The local people could then produce their own milk and they were helped towards self-sufficiency.  John thought that the retail area which had been offered to me was ideal to use as a second hand clothes shop to support The Heifer Project, and he began to rent the area from the church.  John called the shop "The Sunshine Shop" and it was amazing how much difficulty some people had in pronouncing the name.  It was frequently referred to as "The Shunsine Sop" and other derivatives!  John appointed Geoff Robinson as the Manager whose role was to elicit donations of clothes from the public and sell them, to raise funds for The Heifer Project.

The next unit to 46 Alexandra Road, number 47, was in use as a charity shop known as Project 85 and was run by Peter Stacey.  Numbers 46 and 47 were owned by the same landlady, and spanning the two downstairs properties were seven flats also owned by the same landlady.

Pete Stacey only had one arm, and seeing how he coped with this disability was amazing. A friend bought a wardrobe from him at Project 85 and Pete offered to put it onto her car roof rack for her.  Her protests that he would not be able to manage it were completely ignored.  Pete hugged the wardrobe to his chest with his one arm and lifted it up enough to get his foot underneath the bottom.  Then he "walked" it down the shop lifting it with his foot whilst hugging it as though dancing with it.   He crossed the busy pavement with it and suddenly it miraculously was on top of the lady's car nestled safely on the roof rack.  Pete went back to attend to the shop leaving her to tie it securely to the rack.

Pete was a very sociable person, and soon after our church had moved into its new office at number 46, he popped in to introduce himself to Dennis and to enquire what plans the church had for the premises. Dennis mentioned to Pete that we would like to start a charity shop to help the local needy and needed quite large premises Pete confided that he had been running Project 85 for six or seven years and he was sensing that it was time to draw it to a conclusion hinting that there may be a chance we could take over his lease. Dennis arranged that I meet with him and Peter Stacey so that I could share with Peter my vision for the CARE SHOP, and we had a very profitable time together.

Pete shared with us why he launched the Project 85 shop. He had been attending a funeral in the chapel in Cleethorpes Cemetery and was rather dismayed at the poor condition of the chapel. He spoke to one of the staff who explained that the Council did not have the funds to renovate the building. Peter decided to rent an empty shop, receive and sell donated items to raise money to refurbish the chapel. He named the shop Project 85. Once he had raised money for the chapel, he went on to support other local projects but now he had had enough and wanted to retire. Being very impressed by what we wished to achieve through CARE SHOP he said that he would be delighted if we could take over the his lease of number 47 Alexandra Road. He added that one of his lady volunteers was keen to take over his lease and that he did not want her to have it. "It will not be a proper charity if she gets her hands on it" he confided. Peter offered to speak to his landlady and recommend us to take over his lease. She was happy to accept us, so now we had a fifteen hundred square feet retail shop in which to launch the CARE SHOP and it was next door to Cleethorpes New Life Christian Fellowship's office.

Pete was a well-known local character and although he did much good for the community he was misaligned and treated with suspicion in some quarters. Due to his incapacity he became known as One Armed Pete, a name which I don't think would have offended him, but he was a sensitive man and I think the name One Armed Bandit must have hurt him. He could be very brash and when he was economizing by having the heating on very low in Project 85, one of his volunteers complained that she was cold. "Well move about then and get some work done that will warm you up" chided Pete. I must confess that I tried this ploy once we had opened the CARE SHOP but I obviously did not have Pete's accomplished way of saying it!

Pete's disability occurred during childhood but it had not prevented him succeeding where others dare not even try. He had many years' experience in selling second hand furniture and antiques and I asked him how he originally started in business.

Many years ago, Pete had watched a Council lorry loaded with old furniture as it pulled up beside some lock up garages on Poplar Road Cleethorpes. He watched as the workmen began carrying the furniture into an almost full garage before asking them,

"What are you going to do with all this stuff?"

"It's all been left in empty council houses we have been told to clear, so we are filling these empty garages with it for now."

"But then what will you do with it all, how long will you leave it in these garages?"

"It will have to stay here until we have time to get rid of it."

"How will you get rid of it?"

"Probably need to have several large bonfires."

"Would you like me to get rid of it all for you? I will do it for nothing. Think of the time it will save you!"

So Pete was allowed access to the garages, he rented an empty shop and using a handcart transported all the furniture laboriously to his shop. There he repaired, cleaned, polished and valued it all before putting it on sale as GOOD QUALITY USED FURNITURE. He had a unique advantage, he got all his stock for free so his profit margin was significant. He was able to buy better stock out of his profits and so began the story of One Armed Pete the second hand dealer. There were a lot of lessons to be learned from Pete's success, he was an opportunist, an entrepreneur, and he was cheeky, not afraid to ask. When he began buying second hand furniture he had access into hundreds of people's homes where he always had his eyes open for that special item of value. Maybe this earned him the name the One Armed Bandit! Pete admitted to me that he made his money in young adulthood.

He like his public profile and was very adept at generating free publicity.

When we took over Pete's empty shop, he gave me a five pound note as an "investment" into the future of care. There was a small underfloor safe in one part of the shop and I secreted the five pound note in there. Sadly we lost the key and were never able to obtain a replacement. Almost thirty years later the five pounds note is still in the safe and sadly Pete is no longer with us. If Pete was still alive he would be asking "How much is that five pounds worth now then?"

I had no intention of leaving the Prudential, it was my intention to stay in secular work until retirement age, and I would get the CARE SHOP off the ground staffing it initially with volunteers, give it some direction and keep a careful hand on it as it developed.

Dennis had other ideas. He called to see Edith one afternoon to test the water,

"How do you think David would feel about leaving The Prudential and getting CARE SHOP off the ground?" Then having taken soundings he approached me,

"Unless the man who has the vision for it does it full time it will never get off the ground. Why don't you put your money where your mouth is, leave the Prudential and get CARE of the ground?"

This was another challenge I had not been prepared for!

Dennis kindly said that I would obviously be paid for working for CARE and offered me a salary which was almost exactly a third of my current one.

CARE had no money to pay me out of. CARE was only alive in my heart. The Prudential had plenty of money and I had a secure well paid permanent job there which would take me through the next fifteen years to retirement with a great pension. I also had a company Volvo for which I paid a nominal amount for private use, I did not have to pay for road tax, insurance, repairs etc. Leaving that secure job after almost 30 years was a major decision. I was sure that God would bless CARE but should I be leading it full time. I agreed to write to the Prudential Staff Pension Scheme Trustees to obtain a quotation of how much my pension would be if I retired 15 years early.

The accurate pension details came back. It was unthinkable. Taking retirement there and then, at the age of fifty was a no brainer. The pension was greatly reduced and, and however long I lived, I would be receiving a pension based on a greatly discounted amount.

I knew that I could trust Roland Huitson my Prudential Manager so I approached him. It was only recently that I had sat with him at his desk signing my permanent contract with the Company. I was not sure how he would react.

"Roland, I feel as though I am pregnant and need to give birth to something."

"I have often looked at you David and wondered when your baby was due!"

"I know that I can trust you Roland and that you won't take advantage of me if I share this with you."

Roland's smile invited me to continue. I told him about the challenge I was facing and my desire to set up the CARE charity. I explained what I hoped the charity would achieve.

"Do you think that the Company would release me Roland?"

"I think that Company will probably take the view that you could just leave and set up the charity."

"I have thought of that and have even got a figure from staff pensions. If I retire now my pension will be hugely discounted. I just cannot afford to take such a reduced amount."

"Would you like me to contact Divisional Office and put your case to them telling them why you feel the need to leave the Company?"

"Yes please Roland"

The interview was over in a few minutes. Now it was a waiting game to see what would happen. Not easy to focus on the job with such distractions at the back of my mind.

It was several weeks before Roland rang me one morning,

"Hi David, when you have got your stall set out, pop down and see me in my office please."

I took my coffee down with me into Roland's office, he said gently,

"David, do you still want to leave?"

A couple of hours later I had returned home for lunch. Edith said that I was as white as a sheet when I came into the house.

"I have seen Roland this morning. The Company have agreed that I can leave on the 12th May on my 50th birthday. That's several weeks away, and I am not allowed to tell my team until the Company says so, otherwise it will be difficult to maintain morale. Oh and my pension will be enhanced, it will be three times greater than the amount quoted by staff pensions."

Neither of us remembered the prophecy spoken over me by Charles Slagel in the Victors Club a few years previously. He had said that God was putting a new frame within me which would support something new, and almost as an afterthought he had added that which we had decided to build would suddenly come together,. The only thing we had decided to build was our pension!

Edith said that when she saw my white face she wondered what was wrong. It was clearly decision time. Supported by Edith, who was feeling very unsteady, I decided to leave the Prudential on my 50th birthday to pursue the vision for CARE.

Dennis was delighted. He had been busy negotiating the lease with the landlady which had taken several weeks. We needed to set up a limited company and a registered charity for CARE to trade. Trustees needed to be appointed, a suitable bank account had to be opened and we needed to plan for some kind of special opening with all the publicity that would bring.

Whilst I served my several weeks' notice with Prudential, Dennis began advertising for donated goods and there was a response from the public and from the churches. As we did not have access to the large shop next door to the church centre, we were able to store the donated goods in what was the church mid-week meeting room as a temporary measure.

I was fifty years old on Tuesday the 12th May 1992 and the Prudential arranged for me to retire on Friday the 8th. Our official opening was scheduled for the last Saturday of May, which was Bank Holiday Saturday. Councilor Keith Brookes, the Conservative Mayor of Cleethorpes accepted our invitation to perform the opening ceremony. There was so much to do before then.

# Stepping Forwards

When I commenced working for the Prudential on Friday 3rd December 1965, I was met by a welcoming party of one man, Walter Slater my superintendent. When I left the company on Friday the 8th May 1992, just a few days before my 50th birthday, I was "seen off" by a party of one person! Roland Huitson had forgotten that it was my last day but as he was in Nottingham at meetings he could not be available. When I left the office at lunch time, Chris Fullwood, Roland's PA and myself were the only staff in the office. It was around 12-30 pm, my desk was cleared, I had no outstanding work. Roland would not be in the office until the Monday, so I said to Chris,

"My desk is cleared Chris. No work outstanding, so that's me done now. There is no point in me coming back this afternoon"

Chris was visibly uncomfortable, she said,

"This does not feel right David. It's just as though you are going home for lunch and will be back in an hour. But you will not be coming back after lunch, you are never coming back again. There should have been something arranged to give you a proper send off, but you know how things are, you understand the workload."

She gave me a kiss and made some amusing comment which I have often recollected with a smile,

"Good bye Arkright, come back and see us won't you"

Chris was referring of course to Arkright the lead character in Open All Hours, I think she had difficulty imagining me in a brown smock selling second hand goods in a charity shop. I never actually wore a brown smock or an apron in the shop and think that I always managed to look fairly tidy and clean in casual clothes. One morning I was on my knees on the shop floor cleaning and polishing a second hand wardrobe which had been donated to us. A leader in a local church who was aware of my career with Prudential was looking round the shop when he saw me with cleaning cloths and polish. In a loud haughty voice he exclaimed,

"Oh dear, you have come down to this have you!"

I looked him straight in the eye as I responded,

"Actually I have stepped up to this thank you!" He understood my message and was embarrassed by his thoughtless and arrogant comment. I was certain then that God had called me to do this, and as I write this almost 30 years later that conviction has not changed!

So I walked out of the Prudential Office that Friday lunch time, I knew that I would miss my colleagues, but I also knew that I would be fully occupied learning new skills and facing new challenges. I had been retired from the Prudential several months before Edith and I were invited to a presentation lunch at the Coach House in Cleethorpes, where there were suitable speeches and goodbyes and I was presented with two nice reclining patio chairs. Sometime after that occasion I was invited to Nottinghham Office to be presented with my carriage clock to celebrate 25 years' service. The special presentation also included being taken to the Theatre Royal in Nottingham to see Nicholas Lyndhurst as the lead character in Barnum. The workload at Prudential due to all the dramatic changes was so intense that many routine things were put on hold until quieter times.

I handed my office keys and night safe keys to Chris Fullwood together with my Prudential licenses for all the products I was qualified to sell, and said "Goodbye"

On the way home for lunch I picked up the Care Shop keys from Dennis Brown. I had refused to have keys whilst I was still employed by Prudential so that there could be no suspicion that I was not fully committed to my Prudential work.   As I walked into the 1500 square feet of retail space, echoingly and mockingly empty, I realized what I had done. Voices began attacking my brain, "What if this does not work out, you will look like an idiot!

I was beginning to feel very insecure, a report in the local newspaper had disturbed me and filled me with doubts.  When Peter Stacey had met with Dennis and me, he warned us that if one of the volunteers he had at Project 85 offered her services as a volunteer in the Care Shop, we should not accept her. He explained that once she knew that he was considering closing the shop, she had immediately expressed an interest in taking over his lease and keeping Project 85 running but in her own name. For some reason Peters words had stuck in my mind, "It will not be a proper charity if she gets her hands on it."

There had appeared to be very little chance that she would get her hands on it, as Peter had advised the landlady not to allow this lady to take over his lease. Peter had wholeheartedly recommended us as being eminently suitable to take over his lease. Furthermore he had promised to leave for us all his unsold stock to give us a start, together with all his contacts. There was something reassuring in all this.

But then the local paper shouted out the great news that Project 85 was not closing, it was transferring to another shop two or three doors away and would continue to trade under its new name,

Project 92. It would be run by the very lady Peter had warned us about. She took all the unsold stock, she retained all the contacts.

To be honest this news affected me deeply. I had given up a secure and well paid job to take the uncertain step of opening a new charity shop. There would be enough obstacles to contend with without this lady trading in opposition to us just a few yards away.

Peter came to see me and tried to explain whilst at the same time trying to encourage me. I was grateful for his concerns, but I was already receiving greater encouragement from the One I believed had called me to set up the charity. I had my eyes opened to what I saw as the truth. What we were about to do was so important that it needed contending for. This was to be our first battle. The overwhelming sense that it would work out and be successful came back to me. . The words of a well-known Christian came to mind! He famously said, "God does not sponsor flops!"

A few years later I gave a short talk at the Town Hall about the work of CARE. The local police chief superintendent was there. He came to me after my talk saying that he had enjoyed it very much, but that I had omitted to say one thing which was vitally important.

"Really Sir, what did I omit to say?"

"David, you should have told the audience that CARE has no connection whatsoever with Project 92."

"I could not say that in a meeting such as this."

"This is exactly the right place to make such a statement as that. Please make an appointment to come and see me and together we will look at ways of closing Project 92 down."

I felt that here was a friend who knew us and who knew who was in opposition against us, but I had to answer him,

"I am sorry sir, I can't be a party to what you suggest. There is a greater power than the police and I am content to leave this in His hands"

Within a few years Project 92 had gone whilst almost thirty years later Christian Action and Resource Enterprise is still serving the community with integrity and compassion. God does not sponsor flops!

So I pressed on cheerfully with our plans to open the Care Shop. I knew nothing about dealing in second hand goods but realized that there were strict regulations to be complied with. I contacted Trading Standards and Barry Chambers, their local officer came to see me at our home. I familiarized him with our vision for the Care Shop and he took me through all the regulations, especially those concerning gas and electrical products and fire regulations for furnishings. Barry became a regular visitor in the Care Shop and his friendly professionalism kept us on the right path.

Dennis Brown and myself drew up a business plan with what we felt were fair predictions for the development of the Charity. We presented this to Leslie Jones the Enterprise Manager at Midland Bank in Grimsby. He expressed surprise that I had given up a management job with Prudential in order to set up a small charity.

"It looks as though you will need a three and a half thousand pounds overdraft facility at the end of your first three months of trading. That is no problem, I will open an account for you. I know that this will work because you have done your homework, I have every confidence in you." Ten years later Les Jones was a guest when CARE celebrated its tenth anniversary at the Ice House in Grimsby. We never needed the overdraft which was canceled after about two years of trading.

Edith and I made a cash donation of £1500 to the charity to help prime the pump. I worked long hours cleaning, preparing and pricing furniture ready for the official opening. Any gas and electrical goods had to be checked and all soft furniture needed to be fire retardant. I looked around some second hand shops to get some idea of prices. Our family were a brilliant support and helped out with the cleaning and the polishing.

By the day of the official opening, 31st May 1992 we had paid out £650 in rent for the shop. Following the opening ceremony, the shop was open for the rest of the day. When I cashed up at five pm we had taken over £640 on our first day of trading. The six hundred and fifty pounds paid out in rent almost recovered in full. We took this as another sign that God was with us!

The opening day dawned with heavy rain and strong winds. I had to take our little doggy out for her walk, and when I returned Edith greeted me,

"I had a phone call just after you had set out. A man said he was Keith and wanted to know where he would get changed because of the bad weather"

Edith had sounded puzzled until Keith reminded her that he was the mayor and would be opening the Care Shop. He needed to know where he could go to put on his chain of office!

We decided to have a very brief outdoor ceremony when the Major would cut the ribbon and declare the charity open. Then we would move inside into the meeting room used by New Life Christian Fellowship. We would have the formal speeches in there and have official photographs taken.

Our Mayor wished the charity great success and I in turn promised that we would serve our community with integrity and compassion. Then we all moved into the Care Shop to browse the goods and set the cash register ringing. At this stage the shop doors were open to the public. The bad weather helped us somewhat. It was too nasty to walk along the promenade so people came into the shop instead and many of them spent money.

Late in the afternoon on the opening day, a lady expressed an interest in buying a gold dralon three piece suite from us. She was a very refined lady and not the type of person I would have expected to buy a second hand three piece suite. It was priced at £90 and she made no attempt to barter with us for a cheaper price.

"I would like this three piece suite but can you deliver it to my home in Gainsborough. I will of course pay delivery."

Gainsborough is just over 40 miles away, and I was unsure whether Steve Brown our self-employed driver would be happy to travel so far, so I phoned him at his home to check.

"Yes that's fine David, I will be glad to do it but will have to charge £25."

The lady was delighted to hear this and gave me a cheque for the purchase price and the delivery.

"I will be looking forward to getting my new suite but I must insist that you do not deliver it until you have cleared my cheque. Here is my phone number and address. Please ring me to arrange delivery."

I protested that there was no need to wait for her cheque to clear but she was insistent. A few days had passed before I phoned her to arrange delivery.

"Thank you Mr Robinson I will be ready for when your driver arrives. By the way would you accept my old suite as a donation to the charity.? You will be able to sell it I am sure."

"That's so kind of you and your donation is greatly appreciated. Steve Brown our driver will bring it back with him when he returns to Cleethorpes."

Steve and his assistant loaded the gold suite into his van and I waved them off for Gainsborough. They had not been gone long when the lady rang me to check that they were on their way.

"I will have hot coffee and cakes ready for them when they arrive and they can have a short rest before they put my old suite into the van."

I found myself wondering what condition this "old "suite would be in. Logically, if its replacement was seven or eight years old it could be assumed that it would be much older, and I was beginning to wonder whether it would be nice enough to sell or whether it was an item which we would have to take to the tip.

My mind was set at rest when Steve Brown rang me on his mobile phone.

"Hi David, we are just setting off back to Cleethorpes. We are bringing the ladies old three piece suite with us. We can't understand it. It is brand new, only three months old. It had hardly been sat in and is a lovely suite. It is a super red colour and the lady gave us the receipt she was given when she bought it, it cost £400 three months ago."

A mystery was beginning to develop, but my thoughts were interrupted when a shopper asked me,

"Have you any other three piece suites or are these the only ones you have? I am looking for something a bit newer than these."

"You could not have come to us at a better time. Our driver is at this moment bringing a red dralon suite into the CARE SHOP. It is only three months old and looks as though it has never been sat in"

"It will be £275 Sir."

"How much? That's a lot of money for a charity shop"

"But it cost £400 only three months ago and is indistinguishable from new. If you don't buy it someone else will snap it up Sir"

The man and his wife said they would go and have a coffee and would return. They returned several times at five minute intervals! He stuck his head in at the shop door and shouted,

"Has it come yet?"

When it did finally arrive someone else was eyeing it up and sitting in it when our eager friend returned for about the ninth time.

Seeing that he had a rival, he declared,

"That suites mine. Here is £10 deposit. I'm off to the hole in the wall for the rest of the money"

Steve Brown quoted £5 to deliver the suite to a small bungalow in the resort, and before the suite had been in the shop half an hour it was back in Steve's van on the way to its new home. The bungalow had new UPVC front and back doors and it proved impossible to get the settee into the bungalow through either door. Steve explained that the suite would have to go back to the Care Shop who would refund the money, but our customer was not going to agree to that. He had a bargain and he was not going to part with it.

"Can't you take the window out and bring it in that way?"

"I could" replied Steve, but I can't do all that for the £5 I quoted you. It will take quite a while, I will have to charge you £25"

"That's fine just get on with it."

Steve returned to the shop without the suite which had been safely delivered, but he was angry.

"The chap agreed to pay me £25 for delivery provided I took the window out and replaced it. I went to all that trouble and then he would not pay me anything. He said he had no intention of paying delivery when he had paid £275 for a suite which the charity shop had got for nowt. Told me I could whistle for my money"

I was sorely disappointed to hear this and decided that the Care Shop would pay the £25 so that Steve was not unrewarded for his efforts I was still puzzled why a lady would want to replace a brand new suite with an ageing one, so decided to ring her.

"I am just ringing to thank you for looking after our driver and his mate so well. I understand that the coffee and cakes were delicious. I must thank you too for the lovely suite you gave to us which we have already sold. It is a very generous donation and we are very grateful."

"No, thank you Mr Robinson. Did you think it strange that I gave you a brand new suite and bought a second hand one?"

"Yes, it did puzzle me, but it seems to me that you are happy and we are so happy that you have helped us."

"It's like this Mr Robinson. I was a nurse at Grimsby hospital during the war and I nursed a German pilot who had been shot down over Grimsby. He recovered and on the day he was discharged he thanked me for caring for him and asked whether my conscience would allow me to accept an invitation from him to have a nice meal in a restaurant. Of course I had no problem with that, he had only been fighting for his country in the same way that our own young men fought for theirs. I had a meal with him, and we began dating."

"That's a lovely story, so pleased to hear it"

"Yes Mr. Robinson, we used to go to a hotel on Cleethorpes sea front for a meal, and it there that he asked me to marry him and I accepted.

That hotel is now the CARE SHOP. Every year on the anniversary of our engagement we returned to Cleethorpes and bought something to commemorate our engagement. We tried to buy from a shop as close as possible to where we became engaged. We married of course, and a few months ago my husband died suddenly. I came to Cleethorpes on the anniversary of our engagement planning to buy something to celebrate the happy evening when we got engaged. Now Mr Robinson, the last thing my husband bought was the three piece suite I gave to the CARE SHOP. We had only had it a few weeks when he complained of feeling unwell, he sat on the settee and died. Every time I looked at the settee I could see him there and decided that it must go. Then I saw three piece suites for sale in the same building in which we got engaged all those years ago and knew what I had to do."

I was very moved by her story and grateful for the way in which she had blessed us with her generosity.

A year later, the man who had bought her suite from us came blustering into the CARE SHOP. Seeing me at the till he accosted me from several yards away,

"Hey, that suite I bought from you twelve months ago, that lovely bargain suite! Well it has completely fell to bits. Have had to get rid of it. I am not very happy."

Before I could think of a suitable reply, one of our volunteers spoke up

"It's your fault. God has punished you for not paying the delivery money you promised to pay."

The man obviously did not expect us to do anything about it, he just wanted to give vent to his feelings. He marched out of the shop. An elderly gentleman came up to me and said,

"Don't worry about him. I live opposite him and I know what goes on in his front room. His grandkids jump up and down on his three piece suite, up and down for hours on end, treat it like a trampoline they do, so don't worry about him"

I had thought that I would miss some of the colourful characters from my Prudential days. I soon learned that there would be others who would brighten our path as we served our community with integrity and compassion.

Our new journey had begun. We had little idea where it would lead us.

# Foundations

So the CARE SHOP had opened its doors for the first time. Ahead of us lay a blank sheet of paper, our journey had begun but we had no preconceived plans other than that we would give away generously. We would sell goods to raise money to cover overheads and would respond to financial needs in the community which fitted our charitable criteria. Our Trust Deed stated that we would address poverty and homelessness in the local community. Church was not really known for being a generous resource of help for people in need. If we are honest, most churches were better known by their appeals for money, mainly to keep the roof over their heads and only necessary because the members failed in their obligations to support their church financially in a sound Biblical way. We wanted to reverse this concept, and as a charity representing the Christian church, we wanted to stand with open arms saying "Come to us if you are in need."

We saw ourselves as representatives of Jesus Christ, whose invitation to the masses is still, "Come unto me all you who are weary and heavy laden, and I will give you rest." People in our community were weary of life with insufficient resources. Weary of the constant battle of wits to keep out of debt. Weary of the constant fear that should their State Benefits be arbitrarily sanctioned they would not have the money to keep their home warm and feed their children. To many of us, these fears seem overdrawn and over emphasized, sadly, to a large section of the community it was a daily reality. There were other voices in the community, crying "Come to us if you need a new cooker or a bed for your child. We are here to help you. We will lend you the money" So many who had no other resource entered the trap. Some of these loans were at a rate of interest approaching 1000 % and once you were in their grip there could be a long and degrading struggle ahead. Before long, there would be threatening visits from debt collectors, sleepless nights, uncertainty and fear.

We saw it is our mission to be there for people in poverty traps. If we could give them a decent cooker, decent beds, comfortable three piece suites, clean and serviceable furniture and pots and pans, we could hopefully stop them getting into debt.

Our simple message was therefore "Come to us." We backed this up by writing to Social Services to let them know that we were available to help families in need. We needed a strict criteria to ensure that we gave only to the neediest, that criteria worked. I personally paid a visit to everyone who completed an application form for help. I discovered a staggering fact. Not many people were trying to take advantage of us. In fact most applicants had asked us for less than they actually needed. It was as though they had self-prioritized their need.

We found that the people of Cleethorpes and Grimsby responded well to our appeals for goods and the shop was generally well stocked.

We knew that it was important that the Charity was well managed, and my accountability was to a Board of excellent Trustees. Over the years Christian Action and Resource Enterprise has been blessed by the support and commitment of a first class team of Trustee –Directors, all unpaid volunteers.

Dennis Brown, Leader of Cleethorpes New Life Christian Fellowship, Dave Kitchen, leader of Grimsby New Life Christian Fellowship, Ray Lewis, the business manager of the Ice House Grimsby, Howard Field, head of family law at John Barkers Solicitors Grimsby, Keith Tondeur, founder of a leading national debt relief charity, Credit Action, Rev Alun Taylor, Leader of Grimsby Elim Church, Philip Wooffindin Cleethorpes Assembly of God leader and member of the Executive Council of Assemblies of God in Great Britain and Ireland, David Jones, leader of the Grimsby Assemblies of God church, Rev David Peacock, Vicar of St Peters Parish Church in Cleethorpes, Stephen Franklin, leader of the Marshes Christian Fellowship and a chartered accountant with his own practice, Deborah Linford, local solicitor, Richard Keeble, Pastor of the Willows Church Grimsby, Paul Brown a local business man, Rev John Ellis Vicar of St John and St Stephens Anglican church in Grimsby, Dave Postle who held a senior post in local government, Tony Jewitt, the Fisherman's Mission director for the Grimsby area, all these were assets to the charity and brought their own unique gifts and perspectives. I was to join them later as a Trustee when I ceased to be employed by the charity, and thus I was able to be involved with CARE for a considerable number of years.

Obviously not all these trustees served at the same time! It was my privilege to be accountable to them and to be guided by their wisdom and spiritual prayerful discernment.

Smethurst and Buckton accountants of Grimsby became our auditors and accountants and CARE have enjoyed a long professional relationship with them. Their Paul Gallant was always a treasured source of wisdom and advice and saw first-hand how the charity developed and grew over the years,

In order to ensure that the Care Shop was successful we needed procedures and working practices and I drafted these and developed them into working models, they in turn were approved by our Trustees. We needed a stock control policy so that we could account for everything which was donated to the shop. The local Community Police Officer was impressed by the lengths we went to ensure that there was an audit trail for all the goods coming into the shop. We had to ensure safety of all electrical items and so we employed Gerry Hebdon and Geoff Robinson to safety check all electrical goods, often replacing faulty parts to ensure that the item worked well and gave satisfaction.

I also made an induction programme for volunteers and staff. This covered the Biblical concept of giving, the heart and compassion of God, and our Christian ethos.

I had no experience of valuing second hand furniture but travelled to Horncastle, the antiques centre of Lincolnshire to seek advice from Claire Boam the owner of two antique shops. She freely gave advice and helped get us onto a good foundation.

Whilst we were preparing the shop and its stock for the opening day, our family were a great help. Often there until late evening they washed crockery and china, cleaned and polished furniture and spruced up three piece suites ready for the big day.

However, there was one aspect of running the shop which I had not thought about. How would I run the shop on my own? There would be so many jobs to do, many of them at the same time! How could one man cope? Needy people were approaching me for help, the phone was ringing, and the driver was bringing goods into the shop which needed signing in and checking. Customers were waiting to be served, someone who looked as though he could be a shop lifter needed watching, a lady needed a heavy object taking out to her car boot, and I needed to spend a penny. Then there were home visits to do. I coped and I loved it, even then, when the shop was functioning, my family came into the shop in the evening to clean and prepare goods. They were a massive help.

Soon after our opening day, a rather nervous looking lady came into the shop. I formed the opinion that she was wishing to speak with me but lacked the confidence. I assumed that possibly she needed some help. I was wrong. She wanted to help me.

"I have been in the shop a few times and have noticed that you are always on your own. It can't be easy as it gets so busy. Could I come in as a volunteer and help?"

Her name was Marie Bloomfield. I interviewed her and took up a reference from her GP. It all looked good so I invited her to start work. She was an absolute gem, she was the first volunteer we had and in a way paved the way for others to follow. Before long she was answering the phone, serving at the till, polishing and cleaning, helping to check the goods into the shop. Helping to cash up and go to the bank to pay in. And, she was making tea and coffee. Marie was a quick learner and was always accountable. Anything she was not sure about, she asked. Before long I could leave her alone for short periods if necessary.

I salute Marie Bloomfield and all the other charity volunteers like her, who really have no idea how important their role is in the charity sector.

Marie soon picked up the principle that when we give to others we are really sowing seeds. We will be rewarded according to the measure in which we give. I remember her saying one day,

"Nobody is spending any money today, there is hardly any money in the till. We need to make a good donation out so that money will come in."

Not many minutes later someone came into the shop needing help. I vetted her quite easily as I could check with her social worker. We sent the van to her home loaded with goodies to alleviate her needs. Within a few minutes of the goods leaving our premises, people began spending money and we had an excellent day for sales.

Marie grinned,

"I told you that we needed to make a good donation to someone to bring the money in"

I was so glad that she understood that Biblical principle. We just dare not withhold from people in genuine need. The Bible says that there is a withholding which tends to bring poverty and a giving away which leads to prosperity. I have lost count of the number of times we proved that to be a practical reality.

The Care Shop was a Christian initiative and I felt that it was very important that in sensitive ways we did all we could to present the Christian distinctiveness. One way in which we could do this was to play Christian music whilst the shop was open. Someone had given us a lovely music center with radio, record deck and cassette tape deck. We had it plugged in near the till where I could easily control the volume which was kept as a background level of sound. Loud enough to be heard clearly but not so loud that it dominated and prevented conversation. I made up some cassette tapes of Christian music, hymns with sound theology, songs sung by Graham Kendrick and Chis Bowater, and every forty five minutes or so, a recording of Graham Kendrick singing The Apostles Creed. It was all played at a sensitive level, if someone wanted to listen to its message they could do so, but it was not loud enough to make it impossible to ignore. It created an atmosphere in the shop. Several times people asked,

"Is this a Christian charity?" And we had the opportunity to express who we were and why we were there.

Marie seemed to enjoy the music as she was always keen to switch it on in the morning, however, one day a shopper asked me,

"Is this music center for sale?"

"It certainly is" I replied, it is a really good one as you can hear. It is a Panasonic and everything works as it should."

"How much do you want for it?"

Taking a deep breath, I said "It's a bargain at fifty pounds"

A few minutes later I had fifty more pounds in the till and there was an empty space where the music center had been.

Marie seemed amazed that I had sold it,

"Now what are we going to play our music on!"

I grinned at her,

"The Lord will provide Marie, The Lord will provide."

I was dusting where the music center had been when Marie exclaimed,

"Look"

I turned and approaching till were two ladies, Shirley Hardy and Carol Wilson, both from Grimsby New Life Christian Centre. Carol was carrying a music center and Shirley was following with a speaker under each arm."

Shirley smiled,

"I have just upgraded my music system and have brought you these. Can you use them?"

We shared what had just happened with Shirley and Carol, and within a few minutes Graham Kendrick was singing the Apostles Creed again and Marie and I were smiling again.

It was important that we tried to use the Care Shop as a Christian witness. We did not preach at people or hand Christian literature to them. We tried to create an atmosphere in which people could sense the peace of God and on occasions touch the miraculous power of God.

A young man came into the shop on behalf of his sister Cathy. Cathy lived in a council house in Grimsby and her rooms were not carpeted. Her children were crawling and playing on a bare concrete floor and this was a concern to local social services who suggested that we may be able to supply carpets. So her brother, who used to be a carpet fitter called in to see us. He could not have chosen a worse day to enquire as we did not have a single carpet in the shop.

I completed an application form with him on his sister's behalf and indicated the size of the room.

"The first carpet which comes into the shop is your sister's. I will promise you that."

"But what if the first carpet which comes in is too small?"

"It won't be too small. God knows the size of the room, your sister needs a carpet, and we are the only hope, so the first carpet which comes in will fit."

"Wow" responded her brother.

I was just stooping at the counter putting the finishing touches to the application form when he exclaimed,

""Wow, look at this!"

I looked up and there was a well-dressed man in a long Macintosh walking down the aisle of the shop towards the till. On his shoulder was a rolled up carpet which he laid at my feet with a flourish,

"I know that you will be able to find a good home for this, there is nothing wrong with it, we just wanted a change so have bought a new one."

"Thank you Sir, we already have a good home for it, you are going to tell me now that it is thirteen foot square I am sure."

"Actually it is twelve foot square."

"Thank you Sir, you have just answered someone's prayers."

Within a few minutes the carpet was loaded into the back of my car and Cathy's brother and I were on our way to Wirral Avenue Grimsby to deliver the carpet which he would fit.

Cathy came to the door and her brother said,

"We are bringing you a nice carpet"

"I don't have any money for a carpet."

I responded,

"You don't need any money Cathy, it is a gift from the Care Shop"

Her brother immediately recounted the story of how the carpet "miraculously" came into the shop and she was amazed.

I glanced round the room and saw that the metal springs were protruding from the three piece suite. This was far from ideal for young children to sit and play on.

"How would you like a nice three piece suite to go with your new carpet Cathy? I can take you back to the Care Shop and you can choose one, it will be a gift"

I took Cathy back to the Care Shop leaving her brother to begin fitting the carpet. We had several three piece suites in stock and I immediately showed her the best one. It was an Ercol wooden cottage suite with red cushions and was in immaculate condition. It was the most expensive suite we had in the shop but I offered it to Cathy. We needed to raise as much money as we could from selling goods as we supported local charitable projects with cash donations where appropriate but I needed to role model the principle of sowing and reaping to the staff.

Cathy replied,

"I can't accept this suite, its lovely but it's the best one in the shop. You are giving me one, so why can't I have the cheapest one?"

"Because if you like the Ercol suite, we would like to bless you with it. It will last a long time and you need one which will last. Would you like it Cathy?

Amazed at the way we did business, she accepted the Ercol cottage suite with the red cushions and a few minutes later our delivery driver was on his way to Cathy's home with the three piece suite safely in the van and Cathy safely in the passenger seat.

It was lunch time so I popped home for lunch. I only lived a short distance away on Cromwell Road Cleethorpes and could be home in two or three minutes. Often I enjoyed curry and chips behind the till in the Care Shop but it was good just to get away for a short while. About an hour later I was back at the Care Shop and the first thing I noticed as I walked in was a lovely immaculate Ercol wooden cottage suite with red cushions. My first thought was that Cathy had not accepted the suite we had given her and had sent it back.

John O'Neil was now a staunch volunteer at the shop, and we owe a great debt of gratitude to him for his hard work and commitment.

"John" I quizzed, "what's the story about the Ercol three piece suite, has Cathy sent it back?"

"No, you won't believe it, about five minutes after you had left for lunch a man came into the shop. He had just bought a new three piece suite and he had brought his old one to give to us. It was on a trailer attached to his Land Rover parked outside the shop. I thanked him and said that I would help him carry it in. I could not believe my eyes when I saw it. It was identical to the one we had just given to Cathy a few minutes before."

I silently thanked God for proving to us that we cannot out give Him. Biblical principles really do work when applied in simple faith.

The next day Cathy's brother returned to the shop, he had brought a thank you card from Cathy.

"Cathy knows that this is a Christian charity and wanted to give you a musical card which played a hymn tune but she could only find a card which plays Scotland the Brave. She hopes that it will be OK she is so grateful."

The card was pinned in a prominent position on the notice board in my office. Each time my door opened and there was a draft, the card blew open and played "Scotland the Brave." As I closed it I saw Cathy's message, with grateful thanks from Cathy, Wirral Avenue" The card was still there when I retired years later but by then the battery had run out. But Cathy's message was still powerfully moving.

After giving me the thank you card, Cathy's brother remarked about the Ercol three piece suite and asked why Cathy had sent it back.

"She hasn't" I replied, and continued to tell him the story of how we had acquired it... He shook his head in disbelief before continuing,

"Cathy is ever so grateful for the lovely carpet, and keeps going into the room just to look at it and admire it. She never ever thought she could own a carpet of such quality. She has not asked me to make another request and does not know I am asking on her behalf, but do you think that you could help her again.

"What's the problem, we can certainly try."

"Well as you know Cathy's front room is really two rooms knocked into one and the carpet you gave her only covers half of the floor. The other half is still; bare concrete. Do you think that you could help her with a carpet for the other half of the room please?"

I once again found myself saying "We don't have a carpet in the place, but the next one that comes in is Cathy's, I promise you that."

I had hardly got the words out of my mouth when the telephone rang. I answered "Hello thank you for ringing The Care Shop"

"Hello, we have just had a new carpet fitted and would like to offer you the old one. We bought this house a year ago and the carpet was already fitted and was only about a year old. We were not keen on the colours so have replaced it. If you would like it it is rolled up in our hall ready for collection."

I knew without asking that this would fit Cathy's room and thanked the donor, adding that they were the answer to someone's prayers.

Five minutes later Cathy's brother was a passenger in my car and we set off to a large house quite near Grimsby Hospital to collect the carpet. We knocked on Cathy's door again and she was so grateful and amazed that another carpet was hers. The carpet was the right size and although not an exact match, it blended well with the carpet we had given her a couple of days before.

On the way back to the Care Shop Cathy's brother kept putting his hand above my head as though feeling for something.

"What are you up to" I smiled.

"I am feeling for the halo, you must be an angel or something. Things are happening in the Care Shop which I can't get my head round it is amazing."

I explained that I was no angel, just an ordinary Christian trying his best to serve God by helping look after the local needy people. Moments like this have a powerful impact and are very thought provoking to the beholder. Very often the Care Shop proved to be a very special place where events made it so easy to share the Christian faith.

A professional lady began visiting the shop. She worked with disadvantaged families and soon discovered that we could help her by supplying necessary items to some of the hard pressed families she worked with. One day she left the shop by the back entrance as her car was parked on Dolphin Street just at the rear. I walked with her back to her car and said "Goodbye"

As I walked back towards the shop I was conscious of a feeling of unease and anxiety. I felt as though someone had just said to me "You had better sit down I have some bad news for you."

It was almost as though a physical weight had been dropped onto me. I walked back to the shop thinking "Why do I feel like this?"

The same inner voice which had challenged me to set up the Care Shop spoke silently.

"That's how she feels all the time. Get praying for her."

This lady had already told me that she had a bad experience of someone who professed to be a Christian and let us know that she was not interested in the Christian faith but was grateful for the help she could obtain from us for her clients.

She was on my mind a great deal and there were not many days when she did not visit the Care Shop. I said to her one day,

"Why do you always dress in dark colours? It is because you don't want to be noticed or is it because you are sad?"

To be perfectly honest I had no recollection of saying those words to her and was amazed when she rang me one morning,

"I am afraid that you gave me a sleepless night last night."

"Oh, I am sorry about that, but how did I give you a sleepless night?"

"It was something you said to me when I was in the Care Shop yesterday. You asked me why I always wore dark colours and enquired whether it was because I was sad inside.

"Really, I can't remember saying that to you and I am sorry if it hurt you."

"But you know nothing about me do you, how do you know that I am sad? I have no emotions, I can't cry, I can't be happy, I am frozen inside but how do you know?"

"Why not pop in and we can have a chat, I will be pleased to talk with you."

When the lady came in to see me, I told her how I had felt when I waved her off a few days previously. I explained the weight, the unease, the burden I had experienced. I explained my thoughts "Why do I feel like this?" I told her about the silent voice which responded with "That's how she feels all the time so get praying for her."

This lady who had said that she had no interest in Christianity sat in my office and said simply,

"You had better get praying for me then" and she told me her life story culminating in her marriage to a foreigner, her journeying with him to his homeland, his father spitting in her face when he met her and exclaimed" we don't want any western sluts in this house, you should have had one of your own kind". But she was trapped, trapped in her marriage to a man who turned out to be a womanizer and a wife beater.

Four children later she had had enough. A member of her husband's family told her to go back to England before he killed her. She took the four children intending escaping with them. Her husband sent a man to intercept her at the airport, he seized the children and she had to make a decision. Should she turn her back on her children and board the plane, or should she return and risked being killed. The last image she had of her children was of them reaching out to her as she turned her back on them to make her escape back to England.

Now she was tormented. What kind of mother am I, what will the children think of me. Will I ever see them again?

The dear lady accepted my invitation to do the Alpha Course and I went along with her each week. She professed faith in Christ and joined our local church. She became part of the home group led by Edith and I and it was there that one of our group prophecied over her that "God would call her children from afar"

Soon her youngest daughter arrived in Cleethorpes and became my personal assistant, soon all four of her children were reunited with her. She said to me one day,

"During my time at church I have experienced a time of great healing."

We became friends and were friends for many years. Touching lives in this way by the grace of God is very humbling and we are so privileged to have the opportunity to serve in this way.

One day this lady rang me to enquire,

"What are you doing at lunch time? If I bring some fish and chips in and come with a colleague from work will you talk to her about Christianity?"

True to her word she came arm in arm with a young lady bearing fish and chips. I shared the Christian faith and the young lady also completed the Alpha Course. She came to faith in Christ and years later she and her husband are worship leaders in a local church.

Whilst we were available to touch lives in this way, we continued donating good quality furniture to needy families and raising money for worthwhile local causes. These included one thousand pounds towards the MRI scanner for the local hospital, cash donations to a local homeless charity and lots of others. We were giving away furniture with a retail value of approximately two months cash sales.

Then, the scenario changed when we began to launch projects of our own which needed sustaining.

# Growth

The CARE SHOP at 47 Alexandra Road Cleethorpes was situated next door to the unit used by Cleethorpes New Life Christian Fellowship at 46 Alexandra Road. This was a most convenient arrangement as Dennis Brown, the church's leader had become the first chairman of the CARE Charity and ease of access to him was a great blessing. The Heifer Project, a charity supporting third world countries, rented the small retail area from the church, trading as a second hand clothes shop. I am not sure who decided what to call the shop, but the Sunshine Shop did not slip off the tongue too easily. If you did not have the right teeth in it was so easy to say The Shunshine Sop, which is what I heard it called several times. Funds raised helped to pay to supply a cow to poor villages in impoverished countries, thus helping to provide milk to needy people, which was a great step towards self-sufficiency.

Not wishing to adversely affect their trade, we did not sell second hand clothes from the Care Shop, choosing to pass them on to the Sunshine Shop to assist them.

Dennis was involved in overseeing the Sunshine Shop, and it became apparent to him that it was not viable. Eventually the Care Shop took over the retail space which had been used by the Heifer Project thus extending our retail area. This became our second hand clothes department, and under the umbrella of Care Shop it began to generate well needed income.

Within a short while we were able to take over the lease of number 46 Alexandra Road, but Dennis continued to have his office there and the church paid a rent to Care Shop. So within a few short years we had almost doubled our retail space, and of course our rent. It was a step of faith but it worked well. We had an understanding landlady in Elaine Price, who live with her husband in the three bedroomed flat immediately above the Care Shop.

Within a few short years of Care Shop simply being a vision to strive after, we were in a double fronted retail area in a prime location on the sea front where the footfall, especially in the summer, was absolutely huge.

Our main activity in those early years was donating decent furniture to families who were in poverty traps, and raising money to help other local charities as and when we were able.

Every family who requested free furniture from us was visited by me in order to assess their needs. It was whilst carrying out these essential and profitable visits that we sensed that our attention was being drawn to a huge local need.

Within the space of a few weeks, whilst I was sitting in a home sorting out what help we could provide, I witnessed a disturbing event at least half a dozen times.

There was threatening knock on the door, the lady of the house asked me to excuse her whilst she answered the door. I could not avoid hearing the conversation which went on at the doorstep. The unwelcome visitor was a debt collector and their language was intimidating and threatening. There were no pleasantries, no allowances for the fact that the family were in dire straits, just horrible threats of what was likely to happen next time the visitor returned, unless they paid some money today.   I felt a great sense of unease.

These were not debts incurred by buying some unaffordable luxury, these were debts incurred by taking out loans in order to survive, in order to provide a home for the children, keep food on the table and keep the home warm. This kind of threatening attitude could be enough to push a fearful young mother over the edge. I could understand the sleepless nights and the havoc this issue had on normal family life. But it did not happen only once, at least half a dozen times within a few weeks I was witness to the same scenario.

I thought about my many years with the Prudential Assurance Company and about the thousands of home visits I had carried out. In almost thirty years I had not witnessed one event when a debt collector had come to the door.

I sensed a great pressure to try and do something to help local people who were crippled by debt. The events of the past few weeks made me wonder just how big the debt problem was in our locality.  We were a small charity, still in our infancy with no huge resources behind us.  But we had a big heart and wanted to be open to where we sensed that God was leading us.  I shared my heart with Care's Trustees by placing my concerns on our agenda. The Trustees gave approval for me to do local research before providing them with a full report.

My enquiries led me to the Citizen's Advice Bureau on Town Hall Street in Grimsby. I had no appointment but I asked to see their manager I sat in the crowded waiting room. As I looked at the people sitting around me, I began to wonder how many of them were there to seek debt advice. There were so many people there that I expected a long tedious wait. It was not long though before the receptionist beamed at me,

"Mr. Smith will see you now sir. Just go straight up the stairs, he will be waiting on the landing for you."

I felt guilty as I left the waiting room, would these longsuffering people think that I had jumped the queue and feel irritated with me. I smiled at them as I left the waiting area.

Mr. Smith was waiting for me outside his office door. My first glance of him reminded me of Walter Slater my first boss at The Prudential Assurance Company. Mr. Smith was quite tall, bespectacled, and balding, with a welcoming gentle expression. I guessed that he was about retiring age. He looked tired and stressed, but I thought that I sensed in his manner almost a sigh of relief that my visit would give him some relief from whatever he was doing. He led me into his office which was not luxuriously furnished, it was plain and functional. His desk was extremely tidy, he sat at his desk and invited me to sit opposite him.

I quickly explained the reason for my visit and my sense of concern for those fighting the burden of debt. I outlined the events which had troubled me over the previous few weeks. I explained that CARE was a new charity, still in its infancy, and that we were researching the severity of local debt and whether there was anything we could do to help break its debilitating hold upon families.

"Please Mr. Smith, can you at the Citizens Advice Bureau give me some idea of the severity of the problem?"

Mr. Smith examined my business card before looking me in the eye and saying,

"So you work for a local charity. Could you not get a proper job? In my experience people who end up in charity work only do it because they can't get a proper job."

I felt a righteous anger stirring, yet there was something in his eyes which indicated that possibly he was just being mischievous. I ought to have responded by saying,

"Oh, isn't the Citizen's Advice Bureau a charity? Are you the manager here because you can't get a proper job?" but I didn't!

His gentleness shaped my response,

"Sir, for almost thirty years I worked for the country's largest insurance company, the Prudential. I served almost 20 years on the management team here in Grimsby before applying for early retirement so that I could start the Care Charity. I assure you that I gave up a proper job to do charity work."

"Oh, I see, do you know Roland Huitson?" he smiled.

"Certainly, I worked for him for about 18 years, he was my manager. How do you know him?"

"I serve on the Crime Prevention Committee with Roland. I am a retired detective chief superintendent, I know Roland well. By the way, call me Ron."

There must be a core of steel in a man who was the Police Detective Chief Superintendent, but there was also a softness, in fact tears were not far from his eyes

"People come in here with a carrier bag full of papers. As they put it on the desk they burst into tears as they inform us that the bag is full of bills, bills they just cannot pay. There are final demands, threatening letters, County Court Judgements. They put the bag down as though it was a huge burden and say "Can you help me please? I don't know where to turn." Then they often burst into tears.

There was a tear in Ron's eyes as he continued,

"If someone comes in here today with such a carrier bag full of unpaid bills, we cannot give them an appointment for at least a month. That is not acceptable, it won't be long before someone gets pushed over the edge and our help will be too late."

"Ron, there is no point CARE trying to reinvent the wheel. You are past masters in helping people in debt, what is the most effective way we can help and what would it cost?"

I invited Ron to prepare a report on the severity of local debt, backed up by statistics, together with proposals for ways in which CARE and Citizens Advice Bureau could work together to tackle the problem. We would need exact costings before being able to consider what part, if any, we could play."

I left Ron's office knowing that he would be checking me out with Roland Huitson before investing any time on my behalf which could be wasted.

What I did not know though, was that on two occasions in the next few years, Ron would ask me to seriously consider training as a Citizens Advice Bureau debt advisor.

He informed me, "When you came into my office that day doing your research I could have done without seeing you. I was so busy and was totally stressed. As I was talking with you though, I was aware of a huge peace washing over me. I would like to think that people harassed and stressed by debt could be exposed to that sense of peace."

I also had no idea that when Ron was made a Freeman of Grimsby, he would choose me as his guest to be present whilst he was honored. I also had no idea that within a few years, Ron would be calling me his boss, as he joined the payroll of the Care Charity. As they say, God moves in mysterious ways.

Ron attended our next Trustee's meeting and addressed us all giving a well-documented and presented resume of the severity of local debt. He told us how acute the issues were, how short of funds the CAB were. He informed us that 14 years ago the Bureau had offered debt advice in Cleethorpes but the center had to be closed due to lack of funding.

What was needed was the opening of a new debt advice center in the Resort. If CARE could provide office facilities with access to photocopying and fax and phone, a private office for counselling plus a waiting room area a lot could be done.  Oh, and CARE would need to pay the salaries for two days of debt counselling per week.  And then there was the added cost of providing the extensive "library" of information needed by their workers. In addition to the initial cost of this library, there was the ongoing cost of keeping it up to date as all the amendments are issued.  To a small charity like CARE, the cost seemed huge.  We had a relatively small income but we believed that we had a big God.  We took another step of faith and committed to pay these ongoing costs so that we could be part of the battle of setting free those who are bound by debt.

Within a short time, Citizens Advice Bureau were offering full debt counselling for two full days each week in the office at the CARE SHOP. Within a short while the service was extended to include a third day when general advice was given.  Many more people began to beat a path to our door as they sought help from CAB.  Very many of them shopped in the CARE SHOP and donated goods to us from time to time.  The facility stretched us financially, but we were able to continue our support in this way for seven to eight years.  It was a privilege in this time to get to know Barbara Scaife and Susan Hailes, who according to Ron Smith, were "the best two debt counsellors in the country.

Within a very short time over two million pounds worth of debt was being handled each year by CAB through our support, and that figure, though large, did not include mortgages.

Our involvement with Citizens Advice Bureau opened our eyes to other needs in the community.  Needs which needed a response.  But that is another story.

# Care Rent Scheme

The link we forged with Grimsby Citizens Advice Bureau led to several golden years of partnership which helped a considerable number of local people into freedom from debt.

We were determined that our new financial commitment to support the CAB would not adversely affect our ongoing work of supporting the community with free furniture and cash grants. I am pleased to say that the amount of furniture and cash donated to people during our first year of operation continued successfully. The Grimsby Telegraph published this report at the end of our first year of trading as the Care Shop

"Cleethorpes Care Shop has handed out more than £13,000 to local needy people in its first year in business. Organisers are keen to thank all those who have donated goods to the Alexandra Road shop. Donations to local people include a cooker for a disabled gentleman, installing a telephone for a lady who is sick, as well as cheques and goods to other local charities such as Grimsby's Doorstep organisation and a Catholic Charity. Lists of all goods and money handed out during the year can be obtained from the Care Shop or by telephoning Grimsby 291629"

Then the same newspaper reported on our first two and a half years of operation, as follows.

"The Care Shop was opened as a registered charity in Cleethorpes, as a resource centre for the community in 1992. It began with no money and no resources. The Care Shop has received no grant help, the only income being that raised by selling donated goods and furniture. In two and a half years CARE has ploughed back into the local community about £38,000 which has been almost a 50 per cent mix of cash help and goods."

Looking back on our years of supporting the CAB with finance and resources it can be concluded that the CARE charity was not impoverished but blessed as we helped them. The Bible teaches that there is a withholding which tends to produce poverty, and there is a giving away which leads to prosperity.

As a Christian charity we firmly believed in the Biblical principles of sowing and reaping and never knowingly missed an opportunity to sow seed generously.

One way in which we were blessed by our links with the CAB was that our reputation was enhanced. The local newspaper published a photograph and report of the official opening of the Debt Advice Centre. The report explained that the new centre would reduce the current four weeks wait to obtain a debt counselling appointment. The centre was officially opened by Councillor Kelly Bradley, (Mayor of Cleethorpes) Pictured was Ron Smith, the CAB manager, holding aloft the banner displaying the CAB Charter. Looking on are Dennis Brown, Ray Lewis and Philip Wooffindin, all Trustees of the CARE Charity, Joy Thompson, CAB receptionist, David Nicholson Chair of the CAB management committee, Susan Hayles, debt advisor and myself, the general manager of CARE. Immediately after the launch, the official party together with the newspaper reporter and photographer popped into the Care Shop next door to meet the staff and volunteers. We did not want to leave them out as without them we would be like a man with no arms! The Mayor and the Chief Executive of Cleethorpes Borough Council met and thanked the shop staff. Dennis Brown chair of Care Trustees and David Nicholson, Chair of CAB Management Committee, Ron Smith the CAB Manager and Susan Hales, one of the debt advisors met and thanked David Fountain, John O'Neil, Peggy and Sandy, staff and volunteers at the Care Shop. Ron Smith posed with a toy he had taken a liking to! This publicity raised our profile immensely.

The fact that CARE were thanked for their support in the CAB annual report certainly added to our credibility in the area. I think it is true to say that there is usually a suspicion of new charities when they start up. Our links with the Citizens Advice Bureau, a solid National Charity gave a huge boost to our credibility in those early days

Of course the more people knew about us, the more goods came into the Care Shop.

Then there was our friendship with Susan Hayles and Barbara Scaife, the two CAB debt advisors who worked from the Care Shop base. They sang our praises at every opportunity. I was totally impressed at the huge dedication to their work, their professionalism and compassion. Although they saw hundreds of clients in our premises, they maintained a strict policy of confidentiality. I often saw people sitting in their waiting room and saw clients coming and going, but I never knew who they were or what their issues were. In fact if one of the debt advisors happened to see a client in the street, they were forbidden to greet them in case a spectator could be given the impression that they were greeting a debt client. Of course if the client made the first move in acknowledging the CAB staff member, then there was a warm greeting

One sad and lingering memory from those days concerns a young man whose wife had left him. The debt advisor sensed that he needed someone to befriend him and take him for a coffee and be there for him as he seemed to be friendless. I was not told his name or address, just that the advisor had asked him if he was happy for me to take him for a coffee and be there as a friend. It appears that he was eager to do this. However I was never introduced to him. He did not keep his next appointment to see the debt advisor. I had been asked to be on standby to see him after his appointment and had ensured that I was accessible. When the advisor told me that he had failed to keep his appointment and that she was anxious about him as he was very low and depressed, I suggested that she phone him to check whether he had forgotten. It appeared that this was against regulations. It could only be hoped that he would arrive late or get in touch.

We heard a few days later that he had gone into his garden shed, doused himself with petrol and set fire to himself. He did not survive. Ron Smith's words came back to me forcefully,

"If we don't get to people quickly enough, one day one will be pushed over the edge and it will be too late"

This extremely tragic event made us realise just how vital was our supporting of the CAB debt advice service.

As our profile lifted, there was an increase in people beating a path to our door to ask for help. There was a pattern emerging. Several people requesting free furniture items had no money because they had spent every penny to secure a rented property for themselves. Landlords were reluctant to accept tenants who were "on benefit". In fact some advertised properties clearly stated "NO DSS" It was possible for a DSS benefit family to obtain a rented house, but it was so difficult to raise the money required. This could be £1000 as landlords required a month's advance rent and a deposit which would hopefully be returned when the tenancy ended, provided there was no damage or rent arrears. Some landlords exploited the situation and found dubious reasons for withholding the deposit. This made it even harder to move on into another and perhaps necessarily larger property.

There were many good landlords though and we got to know who they were and who the others were!

So people needed free furniture because they had spent all in securing the property. Others had provided furniture for themselves but had no money left for landlords deposits and advance rent. Such people asked us for financial assistance. We responded whenever we could, but I had what I thought was a good idea. Our profile in the town was now established, we had a fair measure of credibility. Instead of lending someone money to be used as deposit for a property, I would ask the landlord if he would accept a written guarantee from us enabling him to call upon us for up to £300 if the tenant damaged the property. To my surprise every time I requested this of a landlord, we were accepted as a guarantor. I soon realised that if we continued this practice we would build up a huge liability which could wipe us out if there was a high default rate.

It became obvious to me that what was needed was a local scheme with its own ring fenced funds to act as guarantors to landlords and to offer four weeks advance rent on the same day the tenant moved in. If the Housing Benefit was paid direct to the Scheme, we could pass it on to the landlord preventing tenants with little in the way of budgeting skills spending the money on other things. The Scheme would take up references and vet the tenants, complete all the necessary paperwork etc.

I shared my "vision" for this kind of scheme with our Trustees and they gave their backing for me to do research locally. They were interested in knowing whether the area really needed such a facility and if so, what would it cost to run.

I wrote to several local organisations who had some involvement in housing and homeless issues. I asked them, among other things, "Does our area need such a scheme?" If so what is the likely demand? What do you see are the pitfalls?

Ron Smith was still the Citizens Advice Bureau manager but was close to retirement. I obviously wrote to him for his feedback. Although an incredibly busy man he took the trouble to respond with nine hand written

A4 sheets of observations, suggestions and assessment. His report began "God bless you for your vision for the homeless" He pointed out the pitfalls but said that we should be aware of them but not frightened off by them. He added that if we spent too much time looking at possible problems we would not get anything off the ground.

My face to face research took me to Cleethorpes Borough Council offices where I asked to see the Director of Housing. After a brief wait I was ushered into the office of Colin Kitt and quickly explained my mission. The look in his eyes said it all, here was a man who cared deeply about those needing decent housing. With a pained look he said,

"If we close our housing waiting list today and don't add another name to it, it would take eighteen years to house everyone on the list. Some people have no hope at all" he added that the situation was similar in Grimsby the adjoining Borough.

When I had sketchily outlined what we would like to do to help local homeless, he smiled and said"

"If you can get this Scheme off the ground I will give you £2500 out of my budget to prime the pump. Go and see David Hopwood, he is my counterpart in Grimsby Borough Council, tell him what you have told me and that I have promised you £2500. He will not want to appear ungenerous!"

I tried to see David Hopwood but he was on holiday but his deputy, Richard Boxall listened to my story. He asked a little about my background. I mentioned my long years with the Prudential Assurance Company. In reply he asked,

"Do you know Adrian Smart?"

"Yes I certainly do, he is a lovely guy, and I was his line manager at the Prudential until I retired."

"That's interesting, I play cricket for the same team as Adrian, and I will be seeing him tomorrow night."

I knew that he would be checking me out with Adrian, but I had no worries on that front. Within a few days I received a phone call from Grimsby Borough Council,

"If you can get that Scheme off the ground we will give you £2500 to prime the pump."

We did get the Scheme off the ground and for many years we received £5000 per year from the local authority to help with its running costs.

I advised our Trustees that if we could raise £10,000 which we would ring-fence for the homeless scheme, we would be able to make a start. They authorised me to put some flesh on the ideas and come up with a workable model. I was fortunate in that Ron Smith had retired from the CAB and was doing quite a menial filing job locally.

"I am a project man" he said.

"I am frustrated doing what I do all day. Can you find me a desk and a quiet corner? If you take me on as a volunteer I will take your outline vision for the Scheme and develop it into a workable model with proper policies and procedures. If you trust me to do that, you will have more time to raise the funds to do it."

So we found Ron a desk and he worked in a corner of the room used by the Citizens Advice Bureau Debt advice centre waiting room. He was in his element. He was back with people he had worked with for many years and the pleasure was mutual. Ron had been a very popular manager and still had a great deal to offer even though he was at the CAB compulsory retiring age. His staff sent a petition to their head office, they made strong representations for the Bureau allowing Ron to postpone his retirement. Their rock solid case for allowing Ron to stay longer fell on deaf ears. They would not bend the rules, so they had said their goodbyes very reluctantly. Now they had the opportunity to share the same office and they were delighted. One day Ron seemed to forget that he was no longer employed by CAB. Their volunteer receptionist was sitting close by and every time she answered the phone she said loudly in a brassy northern accent,

"CAB"

Ron could stand it no more, he stepped across to her, smiled gently and corrected her,

"Madam, you are not employed by a taxi office. You represent the Citizens

Advice Bureau. When you answer the phone you must say clearly, Good morning Citizens Advice Bureau, how can I help you"

The blousy receptionist nodded just as her phone began to ring again.

Smiling at Ron, she picked up the receiver with the greeting,

"Good morning CAB how I may help you."

If I was the visionary behind what became known as Care Rent Scheme, Ron was the architect and builder. He invested so much in considering every angle ensuring that the pitfalls were anticipated but were mitigated as much as possible. He could pick up the phone and speak to the Grimsby MP Austin Mitchell, he had trodden the corridors of power in the local authority and knew who to speak to and what to ask. After weeks of work he had produced a blueprint which would stand the test of time.

I had been busy fund raising and we were almost at our target of £10,000, when Colin Kitt rang me to offer Cleethorpes Town Hall free of charge to host a public meeting. The Council would write to every landlord on their list inviting them to a special meeting where we would explain the considerable benefits of the Care Rent Scheme and give them the opportunity to place their properties under our management.

Ron and I and the Chair of CARE's Trustees spoke at the meeting attended by about thirty local landlords. Quite a large proportion indicated a willingness to sign up with CARE.

The Scheme offered a £300 guarantee bond to cover the first six months of the tenancy, it also paid four weeks rent in advance to the landlord as soon as the tenant moved in (it was sometimes taking up to eight or ten weeks before the landlord received the first Housing Benefit payment) The Housing Benefit would be paid direct to CARE who would pass this on to the landlord. All attendant paperwork would be completed including thorough references, tenancy agreement, Housing Benefit Application forms etc. etc. recoup the four weeks advance rent.

Care Rent Scheme went live in August 1995 with Ron as its first paid manager. He took to the role like a duck to water. His shrewdness and intuitions gained over many years as a senior detective were an asset, it was not easy to fool Ron. I think that the fact that Ron was working for us also did something to enhance our credibility. I heard someone comment,

"CARE can't have anything to hide or they would not have a retired detective chief superintendent poking his nose everywhere."

Care Rent Scheme had already launched when I applied for funding to Tear Fund, a leading Christian Charity who work through churches and Christian charities. I received a phone call from their Grant Assessment Officer, David Greaves. He was keen to meet with me and see for himself just how we were operating. David was based in Teddington and promised to be with me by eleven am next morning. He had a request,

"Please ensure that I leave you in time to get to my next appointment by two pm."

"Certainly Mr Greaves, but where is your next appointment?"

"It's in Edinburgh."

"Edinburgh! Are you travelling in a jet plane?"

"No, a Ford Escort."

"Have you looked on the map to see where Edinburgh and Cleethorpes are?"

"No not yet"

Needless to say the Edinburgh visit took place on another day. David Greaves spent two or three hours with me and also met some of our staff and volunteers. He saw Care Rent Scheme in operation and was able to meet Ron and see him in action. He commented that it was the most exciting project he had heard about.

When David left me he promised that he would be recommending that Tear Fund offer us a grant. Within a few months we had received £10,000 from them. David also recommended that if possible the Care Rent Scheme office should be relocated into a local church building where it can become part of the life flow of a local church. Within a few months we had re-located the Scheme into the offices of New Life Christian Centre, Freeman Street Grimsby.

David recommended that CARE should have a Patron.

"Cliff Richard is Tearfund's Patron, do you know anyone with a high profile who would become the Patron of CARE?"

Within a few months I had invited The Right Rev. David Rossdale, the Bishop of Grimsby out for lunch. It was the first time we had met, he showed a great interest in our work, as he was getting into his car on Alexandra Road Cleethorpes, I said,

"Bishop David, Tearfund have suggested that CARE should have a Patron, a good Christian with a high profile. Do you know anyone who ticks those boxes?"

Bishop David looked me in the eye, and said,

"Wont I do.?"

"Yes but we have only just met, you don't know a great deal about us Bishop."

"I know enough, if you will have me, get on with it" was his parting remark.

Our Trustees were delighted, and soon, we did not just have a new office and £10,000 of extra funding in the bank, we had our first Patron.

We were able to add to our official letter heading,

"Patron, the Bishop of Grimsby, the Rt Rev David Rossdale.

Bishop David proved to be a good friend and a great supporter of CARE for several years. He spoke at our 10th Anniversary and paid a lovely tribute to me when I retired. He is now living in semi-retirement and has moved out of our area. We miss him. His place has been taken by the Rt Rev David Court, the Bishop of Grimsby.

I am writing this in 2021. Care Rent Scheme is still in operation. I served long enough as Care's General Manager to see our local newspaper report on the occasion when Care Rent Scheme housed the 500th person, the 1500th person and the 2000th person. More evidence that the fruit God gives remains.

# Ron Moves On

Ron Smith, to use his own words, was a "project man" He proved that many times over as he took the raw material of my vision for Care Rent Scheme and skillfully transformed it into a working and often life transforming force. Ron was so pleased when we housed the first homeless or badly housed person. It made all the long hours of planning worthwhile. He was a skilled interviewer, none threatening, and none judgmental, caring and compassionate. He soon put people at ease, and there was no suggestion during an interview that he was a retired long standing senior police officer. Except when the interviewee was not being cooperative and was obviously trying to hide something. Then it was likely that Ron would gently ask the unexpected question "Have I ever arrested you in my days as a cop?" this usually flushed out the truth. We took our responsibilities to our landlords very seriously. I heard Ron say on more than one occasion "I am not risking placing a possible arsonist or a rapist in a property which has been entrusted to us."

A local young man with learning difficulties approached Care Rent Scheme for help. He had lived with his parents who had both died. With support from Social Services he had continued to live in the same rented house and had fallen in love with a homeless dog which he had adopted. His landlord would not let him have the dog in the house overnight, so the answer was a kennel. He was so proud of his doggy friend but shocked when he discovered the cost of a new kennel. In his simple naivety he thought "Care Rent Scheme will help me." Ron listened to the young man's request for help to buy a dog kennel. He did not embarrass the young man in any way, he treated him with the respect and dignity for which Ron had become known. Then he popped down to see me in my private office. We had relocated the Care Rent Scheme base into Grimsby New Life Centre offices, and I split my time between a compact little office on the ground floor and my main office in the Care Shop premises. Ron had the large open plan space upstairs sitting at the head of the staff and volunteers

"David, I have a young man upstairs who, following his parents' death has rescued an abandoned dog and given it a good home. The little dog has brought warmth love and purpose into his life, but his landlord will not allow the dog to sleep in the house. He is asking if we can lend him £100 to buy a new kennel. I have looked at his finances and he can afford to pay it back over six months..."

"The young man has made an impression on you hasn't he Ron?"

"He certainly has, I am impressed with him. I know that what he is asking does not fit our criteria, but there is merit in helping him. He needs to know that he has people who believe in him, he needs protecting from possible eviction if he lets the dog sleep in the house at night. And he needs protecting from the temptation to get the money from a loan shark."

"I agree with you Ron, and am happy to support you in it."

"He can afford to pay £5 back each week and has promised to come into the office on the same day each week with his £5"

The young man got his £100 and the little dog got his kennel. Care rent Scheme got £5 back each week without fail. When there was only £10 still outstanding, Ron said to the young man,

"You have kept your word to us. You have never missed a payment so as a reward I am letting you off the outstanding £10. You are welcome to pop in and see us anytime but you don't owe us anything. Thank you so much."

Ron was going to put his hand in his own pocket for £10 to clear the account. I prevented him. I felt that we had invested £10 into a young man who tended to be marginalized because of his learning difficulties. We had built bridges with him and I was certain that if any housing difficulties arose he would come to us for help. Our name was CARE and that is what we had extended to this young man.

There was a lot of demand for help from Care Rent Scheme, and in a way I think that Ron felt that his work was done now that the Scheme was operating successfully. He was now about 70 years old and although still very capable he needed a gentler way of life. We were immensely privileged that not only had he got the Scheme off the ground, but he had become its first manager, and proved that it worked well.

Ron retired and we all missed him. I had recommended to our Trustees that we approach John Games and invite him to apply for the forthcoming vacant position. John was a former hospital manager within the NHS and was currently working for our local authority in charge of the letting out of our schools for private use but was on the verge of leaving. He was a committed Christian, a gifted administrator, and a man who upheld the ethos of CARE completely. John had good news and bad news for us. The good news was that he would love to manage Care Rent Scheme, the bad news was that he had committed himself to work on a voluntary basis for eighteen months as the local administrator for the forthcoming Luis Palau evangelistic mission this was to be held at the Ice House in Grimsby in 1998. We sensed that having John as the Care Rent Scheme manager was a coup, our Trustees asked me if I would manage the Scheme in the interim in addition to all my other duties. I knew that we had some excellent volunteers and agreed wholeheartedly. The fact that we were not paying out a manager's salary for that period helped the Care Rent Scheme to build up its ring fenced funds.

When Ron was with us, I was always fully conversant with what was happening within the Scheme and I stood in for Ron on his days off or when he needed to be out of the office to inspect properties etc. Now I was to be fully immersed in the day to day management of the Scheme. I got to know its volunteers really well and was grateful for the great honour of working with them.

I was also conscious that however good the Care Rent Scheme was, and however excellent the planning which had gone into it was, the vision for it was something which God birthed in me. It was now my privilege and priority to build upon Ron's foundation, by ensuring that the Scheme very clearly had the heart of God and carried the Christian ethos in a powerful but none threatening way. Care Rent Scheme would be prayerfully run, and we expected to see some of those coincidences which only seemed to happen because we were prayerful.

If I was to manage the Care Rent Scheme well and not allow all my other duties to suffer, it was very important to be disciplined and well organized. My office as General Manager was situated within the Care Charity Shop building, but my responsibilities as Care Rent Scheme Manager meant that I needed to be at the Freeman Street office in Grimsby for much of the week.

We had a lot of applications from homeless and badly housed people who needed decent affordable accommodation. We also had a filing tray with details of properties which local landlords had made available to the Scheme.

Landlords do not want their properties to be vacant for longer than necessary, and we made it a matter of priority to find a suitable tenant quickly for each property which had been offered to us.

I decided that to ensure smooth running, all applicants for housing would be interviewed on the same day if that was possible. This meant that one day was designated as "interview "day. We often interviewed eight or ten people in the day. I also took up telephone references from the referees prior to the interview. If we were completely happy with the verbal references, we did not always wait for the written ones, but often offered a property to the applicant immediately after the interview. This created much goodwill with the public who were impressed with the speed at which we worked, and of course with our landlords as very often their property was filled very quickly.

We were flexible enough to be able to interview on other days if necessary, but dealing with 95% of them in one day was our aim.

Before a vacant property found its way into our filing tray, I always carried out a personal inspection to ensure that it was suitable and that it would provide a really good home for its new tenant. We had a very important checklist to work through. Electrical safety, gas safety, quality of the heating and insulation were all important issues. Adequate work tops in the kitchen, room sizes to ensure that there was no overcrowding, quality of the decorations were important too.

It was vital that a full inventory of the condition of the property was completed before the tenant moved in, often we took photographs. This ensured that neither landlord nor tenant could be wrongly blamed for damage or unfair wear and tear which was brought to our attention later. Credit for designing the relevant check lists for all these items must go to Ron Smith who thoughtfully covered every possible contingency.

There was a lot of paperwork to complete including Housing Benefit application, transferring the utilities into the name of the new tenant, ensuring that water, gas and electricity were all connected prior to them moving in. Sometimes but not often, a dispute arose between the landlord and the tenant and we had to mediate. Infrequently a landlord claimed against the Scheme for damage caused by his tenant, and we had to ensure fair and speedy recompense. So there was always a hefty workload. Then news of Care Rent Scheme travelled and we had parties of people from churches in other towns or cities seeking our advice on setting up and running a similar scheme in their community. This was heartwarming and fulfilling. Then of course there was the whole business of making grant applications to charitable trusts, this was very demanding work and very often very many hours of tedious work proved nonproductive. There was a real thrill when a charitable trust decided that they liked CARE and wished to grant fund a part of our work.

It was obvious that some of our tenants needed practical support if we were not setting them up to fail. Part of my vision was that we would have a team of support workers, not just befrienders! Who would visit the tenant in their new home and help them through any practical and emotional difficulties. In those early days we had a small but vitally important team of volunteer workers who met with me one evening each month so that they could be allocated families to support and feed back to me their activities of the last few weeks. They were our eyes and ears and they all had quick access to the team in the Care Rent Scheme office should there be urgent issues. It was an exciting day when we appointed Pauline from Louth as our first salaried support worker. Pauline was the type of lady anyone would gladly open their door to! Friendly, warm, approachable, she empathized with our tenants and was very popular. We had no designated funding to pay Pauline, but we took a step of faith. It was a few years before our floating support work was grant funded by the Government's Supporting People fund. Later we were successful in obtaining funding from the National Lottery. Whatever people think about the Lottery, they ensure that charities they are funding are completely accountable to them in how they manage and achieve the required outputs. The Lottery really ensures that every penny of grant funding they invest is spent exactly as it is designated, and we welcomed and appreciated the strict discipline this involved. As grant funding became available we were able to employ full time, trained and experienced support workers. They are greatly appreciated by our tenants, and are a vital part of the reason for our continued success.

The birth of our successful support programme goes back to those monthly meetings I held in my office with a handful of committed volunteers who probably had no real concept of how vital their work was. David and Linda Coates, Michael Gray and Don Fortune from Grimsby New Life Christian

Fellowship, and Marilyn England from Grimsby Celebration Church were the committed core in those formative years. They were the seeds from which our larger support team blossomed. We are truly grateful to them.

The happiest time of my eleven years setting up and managing the CARE CHARITY was the very special period when I acted as Care Rent Scheme Manager. This brought me face to face in a relevant way with the people the charity was set up to help. Hearing their stories, empathizing with their situation, bringing some light into their darkness and hope into their hopelessness was a huge privilege. We were unashamedly a Christian charity with the simple believe that God loves and cares for individuals and that we were there to show His love to them at their time of need. We were blessed with volunteers who shared that passion and we knew instinctively when it was appropriate to offer to pray for an applicant. We saw answers to prayer which some people would write off as mere coincidences. We knew differently! A leading Christian who pastored the world's largest church once said "When I pray coincidences happen, when I don't pray coincidences don't happen. That is why I pray." We found that to be true.

A lady approached us in the hope that we could find accommodation for her disabled grandson. He and his wife had been managing a public house in Leicester where he had fallen down the stairs and broken his back in several places. He was restricted to a wheel chair and would never walk unaided again. His "loving" wife told him that he was no longer any good to her and sent him to Grimsby to be cared for by his grandma. Before he could be laid in the back of an estate car to make the journey to Grimsby he had to receive pain killing injections from his general practitioner.

Grandma lived in a little terraced house off Boulevard Avenue in Grimsby, it was completely unsuitable for a severely disabled person, so she approached us for help. She had a friend who owned an old peoples home, and this friend had kindly agreed to look after the young man until suitable accommodation could be found for him. I agreed that we would try to help but suggested that she also contact the homeless team at the local council. Within a few hours had a phone call from Marion Killick who was a local council homeless officer.

"David, I am going to the old people's home to interview this disabled young man. He will be in bed and the interview could be stressful to him.

I know his grandma has applied to CARE for help. Why don't you come along with me and we can interview him together. That will make it a lot easier for him."

So the next day, Marion and I were sitting by his bedside gently assessing his situation and need. It was obvious that he needed a property which had been completely adapted for a severely disabled person.

Marion told him gently,

"I am so sorry but the council do not have any properties vacant which are suitable for you, but the CARE charity are involved, and when they get involved we know that things happen! "

I added,

"Yes that's true, when CARE become involved things do happen. It does not really matter whether the Council or Care manages to offer you a suitable place to live. I will pray that one of us will be able to do it quickly"

Having given the young man some hope, Marion and I left. I had only been back at my desk a couple of hours when I took a phone call from a gentleman who had a property to offer to us.

"My mother has died and she left me her ground floor flat. She was disabled and the flat has been completely adapted for a disabled person with a sit in shower, wide access doors for a wheel chair and every other thing necessary to enable a disabled person to live comfortable. I was thinking of having it converted back into a normal flat, but would like to offer it to CARE first. I don't suppose you need a ground floor flat for a disabled person, by the way the flat is quite close to Boulevard Avenue Grimsby."

I assured his that his flat was needed, and that it was needed urgently. I rang Marion Killick and reported the "coincidence" to her. She was quite matter of fact in her response,

"I knew that something would happen once CARE became involved."

It was not just the type of flat which had been offered to us which was amazing, but its location could not have been better. It was only a few hundred yards from grandma's house, it would be so easy for her, along with the necessary carers to be on hand for her grandson. Within a few days our disabled young man proudly took possession of his new home and began a new life, assisted by his gran and his carers. We felt privileged and proud that we had been instrumental in helping him.

At a time when we did not have any vacant properties awaiting tenants, I was approached by Janey, a local social worker who needed to find accommodation quickly for a young lady and her son. Her partner had become increasingly violent and it was only likely to be a short time before his aggression was turned onto the little lad. Social Services had intervened and would take the boy into Care unless his mum left her violent partner and moved into a home where she and her son were safe from him. This was a priority need and we were anxious to help but we were helpless as we had no properties to offer. Whilst Janey sat in my office, I rang every landlord we knew to enquire whether they had a vacant property. None of them had.

It is a frustrating situation knowing that someone has a desperate need for help which we cannot respond to. I sensed that I needed to reach into the second purse which I have previously alluded to. I found myself saying to Janey,

"Please come back at 12 noon tomorrow. We will have a suitable house for the young lady and her son."

Lying in bed that night I did begin to have some uneasy thoughts. What if when Janey comes back at 12 noon tomorrow we still have nothing to offer? Suddenly I felt at peace. I discovered that God is never late! He may sometimes keep us hanging on in faith, but never beyond the deadline. It was eleven forty five am next day when I took a phone call from a perfect stranger.

"Good morning, is that Care Rent Scheme?"

"Yes Sir it certainly is, how can we help you?"

"Well, I am hoping that I may be able to help you. I have a two bedroomed house available in Immingham. It is vacant and will be ideal for a single parent or a couple with one child."

"That's good timing Sir, we need such a house urgently and in fifteen minutes time a young lady and her Social Worker are coming to our office because I have promised them a house by twelve noon today. When can we see it?"

"I will be there just before one o'clock and will look forward to meeting you all."

On the stroke of noon, Janey and the young mum and her son arrived... They had expectant looks on their faces. . As they stepped into my office I said cheeringly,

"Your house has come. It's in Immingham and we are viewing it at one o'clock today."

Janey's friendly eyes met mine,

"But you must have known yesterday that you were expecting a house to be offered to you this morning."

"No I had no prior knowledge. I made that promise in faith trusting that God would not let us down."

I drove us all out to Imminghham in my car, and on the journey Janey explained how suitable Immingham was, as it was as far away from the violent partner as it was possible to be without leaving this area. So it was looking good! The smiles were soon to be wiped from our faces when we saw the condition of the house. The accommodation was ideal, but it was filthy. The previous tenant had left it in a mess and it was not fit to move into unless a lot of work was done.

"Don't worry" beamed the landlord. "You can have the keys and move in on Friday, it will be shining like a new pin long before then. During the next two days, before I go to France on holiday, no effort will be spared to have the place fit for a queen."

I discovered on the next day that the landlord had already gone to France and the house had not been touched. Myself and John O'Neill one of the Care Shop staff committed to work like Trojans for two days and make the house suitable for the young lady and her son. Janey passed the house and saw that my car was parked outside so she called in. John was on his knees in the back garden getting rid of all the dog excrement and broken glass before he could cut the grass. I was on my knees in the bathroom trying to unblock the stinking toilet. Our Social Worker friend was extremely quiet. She told me later that seeing John and I on our knees tackling dirt and filth for a young lady we hardly knew, and who could do nothing to pay us back, broke her!

She said "I had seen a demonstration of Christianity I had never seen before and it broke me." It was not long before she enrolled on an Alpha Course which is a great course for those wishing to explore the Christian faith and life. She embraced the Christian faith and became a member of our church and for quite a while was part of the Home Group run by Edith and me. The young lady and her son were able to move into the peace and security of their new home.

We quietly thanked God for using Care Rent Scheme as a vehicle to bring His help to someone in desperate need.

They were exhilarating days, the Care Charity and Care Rent Scheme were in their infancy and it was a learning curve for all us. We were given to understand when we launched Care Rent Scheme that it was so innovative that there was nothing else quite like it. A member of the local council homeless team said that the Scheme could not possibly last more than six months, but as I write these precious memoirs, the Scheme is now in its 25th year of operation. One colleague, referring to Care Rent Scheme, said clumsily but with deep conviction,

"God does not sponsor flops."

We did have a strong sense that the presence of God was with us. People frequently said that they could feel the presence of God in our rooms. Whatever was happening, the inexplicable could not be written off as coincidences.

Colin and Samantha (not their real names) approached Care Rent Scheme for help. They had two young toddlers who had been taken into social services care because of the chaotic lifestyle of their parents. There had been a drugs problem which they were still trying to address, and they had become homeless. Social Services would not consider returning their children until they obtained and made a success of a suitable home. A suitable home was obviously one large enough for the family of four. They were disadvantaged from the start however as the Housing Benefit would only pay for a house with one bedroom. If they took a larger house they would have to contribute quite a large amount towards the rent. As money was also needed for furnishings etc etc, such a step would set them up to fail. So they came to us. At the time they were sleeping rough in Grimsby Hospital grounds, and it was not the ideal time of year not to have a roof over their heads. The nights were longer than the days, and the weather was cold and hostile. We interviewed them late on a Tuesday afternoon, and on Tuesday evening we held the Alpha Course in the church premises on Freeman Street in Grimsby. The Alpha evening always commenced with a hot meal where there was a relaxed none threatening atmosphere. We thought it a good idea to invite Colin and Samantha along to enjoy the free hot meal and made sure that they understood that there was no expectation that they stay for the whole evening. But here was a couple for whom the welcome mat was never out, until tonight. They felt so welcome and at home that they decided to stay for the whole evening.

They were amazed to see their doctor and his wife in attendance, and were overcome by the warmth they showed them. Doctor Rob and his wife Joan were members of another church in Grimsby who were considering doing their own Alpha Course and so they sat in for the eight weeks of our course to gain a good working knowledge of how to run the course.

Normally we watched a video after the meal before diving into small groups to discuss it. Nicky Gumbel, the Anglican Vicar from Holy Trinity Church, Brompton, London gave the recorded address, but tonight we had a live speaker. Chris Lewis preached a simple gospel message of forgiveness through Christ for the mess we have made, power through Christ to make a new start, and the opportunity to serve God's kingdom as disciples in the church family.

The love of God had been pulling on Colin and Samantha's heart strings all evening, and at the close of Chris's address they went to the front for prayer. Doctor Rob and his wife asked me if they could be allowed to pray with Colin and Samantha, as they were aware of their problems and were praying for them personally. So we witnessed the unusual scene, doctor and his wife embracing Rob's patients and praying with them with faith, compassion and tenderness.

The evening drew to a close and I shared my heart with Doctor Rob,

"Rob, I know where Colin and Samantha are going when they leave here. They are going to sleep in the hospital grounds and I don't feel comfortable in allowing them to do that."

Rob smiled at me,

"We can't let them do that, I will pay for them to stay in a hotel."

We shared this proposal with Colin and Samantha but the idea did not sit comfortably with them and I could understand why. The suggestion of staying in a bed and breakfast also seemed to be a cringe factor. Then I had an idea.

"Colin, Samantha, would you like to sleep in the Citizens Advice Bureau waiting room at the rear of the Care Shop in Cleethorpes. There are electric heaters in the room, there is a kitchenette with fridge, milk, tea coffee and there is a decent toilet. The room will be set out with a circle of chairs, but I can soon find a decent bed and some bedding in the Care Shop and make it up for you.

You will have to vacate the room by 9-00am in the morning, but I will be there then and will put the bed and bedding away and arrange the waiting room ready for use. I will be happy to meet you there every night and do the same thing until Care Rent Scheme can offer you a permanent place of your own."

They were really happy with this idea, and soon they had said goodbye to the Alpha colleagues they were getting to know, and we were in my car heading for the Care Shop.

It was a dark unwelcoming night when I parked on Dolphin Street at the rear of the Care Shop. We all walked down the yard towards the back door, I asked them to wait outside for a few seconds until I had killed the burglar alarm and put the lights on. As we walked in out of the darkness, we all blinked in the bright fluorescent lights. None of us was prepared for the sight which greeted us.

All the waiting room chairs were stacked neatly at one end of the room, which was no longer a sparsely furnished waiting room, but an inviting, tasteful well-furnished bedroom.

There was the beautiful double bed complete with spotless bedding, pillows and a tasteful headboard. There was a bedside cabinet at each side of the bed complete with bedside lamps. And there against the wall, a nice wardrobe.

I was taken completely by surprise, but not Colin and Samantha, they beamed at me,

"You rang someone and asked them to get it ready for us, someone knew we were coming!"

"No I didn't ask anyone to get it ready for you, I have not spoken to anyone..."

Then pointing upwards, I continued,

"You are right though, someone knew you were coming."

As I left Colin and Samantha for their first night in their proper bedroom, the following words came into my mind very powerfully.

"Thou prepares a table before me in the presence of my enemies,

Thou anointest my head with oil, my cup runneth over" Psalm 23

This was a young couple who never trod the welcome mat, tonight had been one continuous welcome mat. The effect upon them cannot be quantified.

I asked the Care Shop staff next morning what had been going on in the little waiting room

"Oh Alan Bray the driver brought the bed, bedding, bedside tables, lamps wardrobe etc into the shop just before closing time last night. There was not much room to put it all in the shop, so we arranged it all as a bedroom in the waiting room as a joke  to give you a surprise when you arrived at work this morning.."

God is not short of ways to demonstrate His love. Within a few days we were able to move Colin and Samantha into a suitable flat on Hainton Avenue, Grimsby.  Sadly the court decided not to return their children to them, and they were placed up for adoption.  The judge's decision was based of his assessment that Colin and Samantha had done too little and too late.

I am sure that the "guest chamber" prepared for them would serve for a long time as a reminder that God loves them, whatever they are going through.

It certainly reminds me that God loves to bless us in unexpected ways.

One morning there was a nervous knock on our office door, I opened the door to find a young lady who felt compelled to come to us for help as all other avenues had proved to be blind alleys.

She was quite tearful as she explained her unusual circumstances.

"I live in a council house with my children, it is a lovely house, ideal in every way, but we cannot possible stay there any longer as we are all frightened."

"Really" I responded, "I am so sorry to hear that, are you suffering anti-social behavior or bad neighbour issues?"

"No, it's worse than that, our house is haunted, I and the children have seen very frightening things and our health is suffering. We have applied to the council for a move to another house, but because we are adequately housed we are very low priority."

I questioned the lady carefully and sensitively. There was no doubt in my mind, she was seriously frightened. Between tears she explained some of the experiences they were having to endure.

It was not easy for me to tell her that she had little or no priority with us as she was not homeless and was more than adequately housed. She began to cry again.

"If anybody is going to do a runner, let it not be you but let us make sure that what is causing your problems does a runner."

"Do you mean that my home needs an exorcism?"

"I would not go as far as that, but your home could benefit from Christians praying the peace and blessing of God into it."

"Really, do you know someone who will do that for me?"

"I certainly do, our church minister is in the building in his office. I will pop through and ask him if you wish."

"Oh yes, most definitely and thank you."

I popped through to Dave Kitchen's office, Dave was our church leader and also a Trustee of the CARE charity. A few words of explanation from me were all that was necessary before Dave grinned at me,

"She is your contact mate, you go and do it but take someone with you."

Colin Wilson, one of the church elders, and John Games our church administrator were in the building so I had a word with them and we made an appointment to visit the troubled home on Carnforth Crescent, Grimsby.

So on the Monday morning, Colin and John joined me in my car as I drove out to Carnforth Crescent on Grimsby's Grange estate.

The house was spotless, tidy, well cared for and was a credit to the family. The lady described to my companions some of the things which were happening to disturb the peace and tranquility of their home. With her permission we all entered every room in the house and as we did so I read Psalm 91 as a powerful proclamation of the protecting presence of God. One of us prayed in each room, just simple prayers asking the Holy Spirit to bring peace and wellbeing into the home. The lady seemed a little disappointed, I think that she was expecting some sort of conflict with evil powers! She thanked us asking,

"What happens next?"

"Just wait and see" we encouraged as we left.

I had not been back at my desk more than a couple of hours when I accepted a phone call from the homeless team at our local council.

"Hello, John Collins here from the homeless team. I understand that you and some colleagues have performed an exorcism in a council property."

I wrongly assumed that I was being reprimanded,

"On no John, nothing as heavy as that. We just read a psalm from the Bible and prayed that the peace of God would fill each room, we did not do anything drastic" I was beginning to babble, but John cut in,

"Oh don't apologise. I have worked for the council for eighteen years and there has been problems in that house all that time. We don't tell the tenants when they move in, but they soon discover what is going on and leave. By the way, what happens next, are you going to find the family another home?"

"Sorry John, but we can't do that. She is not homeless, in fact she has a very nice home. We will just have to see what happens."

I heard no more from the lady and as the weeks passed I had forgotten our excursion to her home on the Grange estate, but I had another surprise phone call which reminded me of the episode.

"Hello, John Collins here from the homeless team. Do you remember praying in a house on Carnforth Crescent"

"Oh yes John, I certainly do."

"Well, are you aware of what has happened since your visit?"

"No I am afraid I have not had any more contact with the lady. She has not been back to see us."

"Well, since you and your colleagues visited her, the house has been lovely and peaceful, all the strange goings on have stopped and the family are really happy there. In fact they like it so much that they have withdrawn their application for a move to another house."

"Oh that's just great John."

"But surely you must have known about all this."

"No, I have not contacted the lady, I suppose I was a bit scared of feeling a fool if she told me that nothing had changed since our visit."

John responded quickly,

"Oh ye of little faith! By the way, we have other houses owned by the council where strange things are happening, I don't suppose we could get you to…."

"Certainly not John, we are happy to deal with it if it pops up in our line of duty but we are not going looking for it."

"Yes, I understand, but what was in the house, how did it get there, what did you do to get rid of it?"

"John, if you believe that there is a personification of good, then logically there must be a personification of evil…"

"I have no problem with that view ."

So for forty five minutes we had an interesting discussion and I was pleasantly surprised by John's openness.

At the next Care Rent Scheme Advisory Panel meeting I shared this little story.

The council representative on the panel commented,

"Oh, that story has been reverberating along the corridors of power in the council offices. People are saying that there must be some power in Christianity."

It was our privilege to be experiencing that power on a regular basis!

# Fund Raising - The sweet and sour

Grant making trusts seem to be more interested in helping a relatively new charity to get established than in helping sustain an existing charity. This is partly the reason for so many charities departing from their initial vision and launching into something new. They hope that the "newness" of the project will make it easier to obtain financial grants.

Some charities are tempted to compromise their ethos if there is financial reward for doing so. We, at CARE always refused to sell our soul for money, and it was local need in its varying ways which directed and shaped our steps and not the pot of gold promised if we chased after a new rainbow.

Grant making trusts had their own constitution to adhere to. Some had committed their funding to tackle health related issues, some to address racial issues, some to improve social mobility, some were committed to helping the homeless. So before applying to a Trust it was important to do research in order to understand whether their heart was beating to the same rhythm as ours.

It was inevitable that entrepreneurs could see the potential to earn a lot of money by facilitating fund raising courses. I am not sure how many of the so called "trainers" had ever actually made successful fund raising applications themselves! However I found myself on a fund raising course in Grimsby scheduled to last half a day a week for eight weeks.

In reality, all the trainer was able to do was instruct the candidates in how to tick all the right boxes. They could not instill passion, enthusiasm, integrity, all qualities which I am sure prospective funders look for first of all when they receive an application.

Some of the people on the course had actually founded the charity they were working for, and it showed. Those who were there simply because it was part of their job to raise money seemed to lack some vital dynamic, and it showed. I realized first hand on that course that professional fundraisers often do not carry the heart and the ethos of the charity they are fundraising for. Rightly or wrongly, since I attended that course I have never been enthusiastic about using professional fundraisers on behalf of the CARE charity.

The trainer certainly told us how to tick the right boxes. If the Application Form states that it must be completed in BLACK ink, then there is no point using BLUE ink as this would automatically cause it to be rejected. Another piece of valueless advice was "Think carefully before you decide whether to send the Application using first class or second class stamps."

Apparently some Trusts would see the first class stamps and immediately think "if they can waste money on first class stamps then we are not prepared to let them waste our money."

But, some Trusts would notice that your Application bore second class stamps, and they would conclude, "If raising money is of so little importance that it only deserves second class stamps, then we will not invest our money into them."

Having worked through some of the confusion I came to the conclusion that the person attempting to raise funds must carry the strong vision of the charity, he or she must be able to transmit to the Trust a belief in and an enthusiasm for the charity, and convince them that any money invested in them will bring them the kudos of being part of a life changing local initiative.

My early attempts at fund raising had been successful because I was able to sit down face to face with someone in authority, and enthuse them for our cause.

Our application to Tear Fund had resulted in a face to face meeting, and we had obtained £10,000 from them and entered into a working relationship with them. After face to face sessions with the Housing Managers of Cleethorpes and Grimsby Councils, we obtained funding from them. I tried to transmit our enthusiasm and relevance through the words I wrote in our funding applications. Such applications could take hours of work and I entered into this knowing that it was likely that most applications would not be successful due to the great demand. We regarded the process as sowing the seed, and we prayerfully expected a return.

It was always a relief to be able to be happy enough with a fund raising application to actually post it off to the Trust. We always prayed before sending the application, not that we would be successful, but that if it was right to receive money from that source we would be successful.

I was relieved to put two applications in the post. One to Lloyds TSB Foundation requesting £12,000 to help with core costs. The other to Crisis requesting £40,000 which would enable us to widen our age criteria for Care Rent Scheme and enable us to house a wider range of needy people.

The first reply was from Crisis. They would like to meet me and gave me a choice of appointments. Our quick reply secured an early appointment and their assessor came to discuss our application. I asked Rev. Alun Taylor, one of our Trustees if he would like to be present at the interview and I was pleased that he was able to support.

Very often the first question a stranger asks you shows where their heart is. I was entirely unprepared for the first question..

"Before we get down to business I need to ask you, How Christian is this organization?"

"Perhaps I can ask you a question in response."

"Yes certainly."

"Then my question is this, How human are you?"

"What kind of question is that, you are either human or not, there is no middle ground?"

"Exactly, CARE is a Christian organization through and through. But if you think that we exploit vulnerable people by dragging them to church and pushing the Bible at them you are quite wrong. You need to realise that the local council homeless team refer lots of people to us. The Women's Refuge refer lots of ladies to us, as do the Salvation Army Hostel, the Citizens Advice Bureau and many other local organisations. Do you think they would send so many people to us if we took advantage of the vulnerable?"

"Well I only have your word for that. But I could take you to a "Christian" housing project in Edinburgh who are only interested in helping people if they promise to go to church. That is not acceptable."

"I completely agree with you, but we do not work like that."

"Maybe you don't work like that but there are things here which concern me and will have to be dealt with if we are to give you a grant."

"Really, what kind of things."

"Well, for a start the word CHRISTIAN will have to be removed from your letter heading."

"Why is that?"

"Because it is an overt symbol of Christianity."

"But it is our official name, we are registered with the Charity Commission and with Companies House as CHRISTIAN ACTION AND RESOURCE ENTERPRISE and the word CHRISTIAN is not a problem to any other organization."

"Nevertheless, it is not acceptable to us. Also unacceptable to us is the fact that the cross is part of your logo."

"I see, and is there anything else you object to?

"Yes, on your notice board is a poster stating that you hold a weekly staff prayer meeting."

"Yes that's correct, what is wrong with that?"

"Well the poster invites any one to request if they have any issue they would like prayer for. We can't have that as we have to protect the vulnerable."

As far as I was concerned the sooner this meeting was over the better. The man's pompous attitude was intolerable and I was already deciding that we did not wish to work with him or the charity he represented, CRISIS.

As he left us, he suggested that we pay a visit to a homeless charity in Hull which they were partly funding,

"You will be able to chat with them and get the feel for how we work."

A few weeks later, John Games and I drove over the Humber Bridge to Hull to spend an hour with the manager homeless charity who were receiving grant funding from Crisis.

John immediately drew my attention to the notice board on the office wall.

There were several posters advertising New Age and very questionable activities. Psychic Art sessions, Fortune Telling, Seances, Palm Reading, crystal therapy. You name it, it was there, prominently displayed to entrap the vulnerable. The sheer hypocrisy of Crisis's stance almost overwhelmed us.

When we returned to Grimsby I was in a fighting mood. A few days later the letter came from CRISIS the homeless charity. We had applied to them for about £42,000 to enable us to begin housing homeless people in the 16 to 25 years age group. Our criteria then was to concentrate on the over 25 years age group. The additional risk incurred by taking the younger people indicated that we would need much more funding.

According to the letter from CRISIS there was certainly the chance of receiving £40,000 from them, but it was conditional. The word CHRISTIAN and the CROSS would have to be removed from our letter heading. The poster adverting the weekly staff prayer meeting would have to be removed. In the view of CRISIS these were all overt symbols of Christianity. I noticed with interest a statement at the foot of their letterhead.

"PATRON OF CRISIS , The Most Rev and the Rt Hon, The Lord Archbishop of Canterbury, George Carey.".

Was this not an overt symbol of Christianity? Crisis were happy for the kudos and respectability of patronage from the highest Christian in the land, but it all appears to be lip service.

I did not even bother to consult our own Trustees as I knew their heart well. I wrote a polite letter to CRISIS informing them that we were not willing to work with them. I stated firmly that our "overt symbols of Christianity" would remain in place as we were not prepared to sell our soul for money. I drew their attention to the dangerous posters we had seen in the office of the charity which represented them in Hull. I asked them to give the £42000 to some other organization as we no longer wanted it.

Then I wrote to the Archbishop of Canterbury in his capacity as Patron of CRISIS. I explained their anti-Christian attitude, I also explained the posters we had seen in Hull. I expressed the feeling that I thought he would want to know what was going on in his name.

I did receive a reply of sorts. Written and signed by a secretary, it simply thanked me for taking the trouble to write to His Grace and informed me that the Archbishop did not personally involve himself in any matters concerning CRISIS.

I had lost the chance of around £40,000 in grant funding. I had seen first-hand an unacceptable hostility towards a Christian organization, I had seen blatant hypocrisy and it seemed that CRISIS were free to just get on with it without even being accountable to their Patron. This was a sour experience of fundraising! However it was to be more than balanced out by a very sweet experience.

I was still waiting to hear from Lloyds TSB Foundation, and I was not kept waiting for long. Their Stephen Robinson made an appointment to visit me to discuss my application, and we were soon sitting together in my little office in the CARE SHOP. Introductions over, Stephen asked me his first question. I have previously said that very often the first question lays bare the enquirer's heart. I was not prepared for that first question from CRISIS. Neither was I anticipating that first enquiry from LLOYDS TSB FOUNDATION.

"Do you have a shredder?"

"Yes I do Stephen but why?"

"Here is the Application we received from you, I would like you to shred it please."

"Is it not filled in correctly Stephen?"

"Oh yes, it's a good application but you have sold yourself short. You have only asked for £12,000 we are looking to give you about £70,000"

There was no inquisition, no anti-Christian attitude. Our achievements shown in our latest published accounts were our credentials. Very soon we had confirmation that LLOYDS TSB FOUNDATION would be giving us £72,000 spread over three years. When the three years had expired we were offered more funding from them. Stephen and LLOYDS TSB FOUNDATION became great friends and supporters of CARE.

I am convinced that God had a hand in all this. He does not hide behind the phrase, "He does not involve Himself personally in individual affairs."

The Bible encourages us to "Cast all our cares upon Him because we are His special concern."

God honoured us and blessed us because we did the right thing. Elsewhere the Bible says "Them that honour me, I will honour."

I believe that had we accepted the money from CRISIS and honoured their conditions then that would have been the first step of a downward spiral.

It was recorded of Samson, "He did not know that the Spirit of the Lord had left him."

How sad for history to have recorded "CARE did not know that the Spirit of the Lord had left them"

God is so faithful. We proved it time and time again.

# Even in Africa

At critical times in our Christian experience, God has clearly spoken to Edith and I through what the New Testament describes as "a word of prophecy. "

The modern role of Christian prophecy is not primarily a predictive one. It is not fortune telling, a gift very often claimed by fraudsters. The New Testament prophetic gift is primarily to encourage and build up Christians in their faith, it is inspired by God and is not of natural origin. It can be a few words of encouragement at a time when this is sorely needed. It can be a confirmation that a path we are considering taking is the right one. We do not "swallow" every prophetic word which is given to us. Rather we weigh it and consider it taking into account the character and reputation of the speaker, we consider whether it is consistent with the teaching of Scripture, and we look for confirmation in the fact that the same message has come to us through other sources. Very often there is a strong feeling that the inspiration and authority of God is the primal force behind the prophetic words. Does the message have the "ring of truth"?

Sometimes God speaks to us directly through the Bible without human agency. A particular verse or passage suddenly seems to be "lit up" to us with a powerful radiance. This will be confirmed later through other channels.

Edith and I have been blessed on occasions when someone has imparted a prophetic word to us, or a passage of Scripture has spoken powerfully to us. When Edith and I moved to live in Cleethorpes one of our first priorities was to find and settle into a local church. I have previously described how we settled in the local church which met on Seaview Street in Cleethorpes later buying the disused fisherman's Bethel on Tiverton Street. I have not yet shared that when we had been members of this local church family for several years, we began to feel that is was no longer the church where God wanted us to be. How wrong to be impulsive and leave a church at the drop of a hat just because the grass looks greener elsewhere! Believing that local church is the spiritual family which God has planted us into creates strong bonds and loyalties with our fellow members. Just as it would be unthinkable for a person to decide that he no longer wishes to remain in the family into which he was born, it is an equally serious decision that you no longer should remain in the church of which you are a part. Leaving a church family causes hurt, it is unavoidable. Other members who have a concern and love for you will miss you and probably not understand the reasons. The Christian leaders who have the responsibility for your care will feel hurt, and will begin to examine whether they have let you down. The Apostle Paul likens this kind of separation as being the spiritual equivalent to the breakage of a bone in the human body.

So leaving the church in which you are a committed and loved member is never to be a flippant trivial hasty decision. It is important to have the mind of God, because there are occasions when it is in God's will to move on.

So Edith and I were unhappy, remaining in the local church becoming very difficult but we knew that if we resigned there could be a lot of hurt. We were living in the hard grip of a dilemma. We were hurting where we were, but knew beyond doubt that we would hurt others if we left.

It was into this situation that God spoke. A few verses in my daily Bible reading suddenly leapt of the page and I knew that God was using a passage from the Bible to give us the direction we so badly needed. The passage was in Genesis chapter thirteen,

And quarrelling arose between Abram's herders and Lot's. So Abram said to Lot, "Let's not have any quarrelling between you and me or between your herders and mine, for we are close relatives. Is not the whole land before you? Let's part company. If you go to the left, I'll go to the right, if you go to the right I'll go to the left. The two men parted company.

I wrote our resignation letter and sat with our pastor on the platform at the end of the Sunday morning service, reading our resignation letter to him. It contained the words quoted above from Genesis chapter thirteen. That was our last Sunday worshipping with that local church.

The big question though was whether we had done the right thing. Again God spoke to us in an incredible way. The following weekend we went to stay with Christian friends in Luton. Their pastor knew nothing about our situation, but beginning his sermon on the Sunday morning, he read his text,

Let's not have any quarrelling between you and me or between your herders and mine, for we are close relatives. Is not the whole land before you? Let's part company….the two men parted.

The following week we were back in Cleethorpes and went to the mid-week meeting of a Grimsby church. They had a visiting preacher and his text?

Let's not have any quarrelling between you and me for we are close relatives. Is not the whole land before you, lets part company. If you go to the left I'll go to the right. The two men parted.

When God has graciously spoken and confirmed His word in that way, a great peace descends, God had given us direction and then had confirmed that we had taken the right step.

I remember passing through the hardest days of my life in my work with the Prudential Assurance Co. I was driving three friends to a Men's Christian meeting in Leicester. One of my friends enquired how things were at work.

"It's dreadful, people are having nervous breakdowns all over the place. I feel like a piece of elastic being pulled at both ends and wondering how much I can take before something snaps."

We arrived at the De Montfort Hall and the preacher rose to address the audience. Pausing, he looked across the congregation before passing on a prophetic word God had just given him,

"You have said that you feel like a piece of elastic being pulled at both ends. You question how much more stretching you can take before something breaks. Know this, God is in control and He will not allow you to be stretched beyond that which you can stand. Know this also, that when the stretching process is ended, you will not shrink back to what you were before the stretching began."

Coincidence! I don't think so for a moment. God is interested in the circumstances we have to cope with and when we need encouragement He will find a mouthpiece through which to bring it.

When the Prudential were promoting me to section superintendent in Grimsby, we travelled from Sleaford to Cleethorpes one Saturday to meet my future District Manager and his wife. He intimidated me to the degree of making me frightened of accepting the promotion to work under him. He caused me to seriously doubt whether I could do the job and that night I could not sleep. I made the decision to let the Company know that I had changed my mind and that I would be cancelling my acceptance of the promotion I had already accepted.

God had other ideas! We had a visiting preacher that morning at Sleaford Assembly of God Church. Pastor Michael Smith invited him to read from the Scriptures during the service. Our preacher friend was not expecting this, and as he walked to the lectern opened his Bible at random and read the passage it opened at, which was Psalm 75.

He read,

"For promotion cometh neither from the east, not from the west nor from the south. But God is the judge, He putteth one down and setteth up another."

Edith, knowing how I was feeling, nudged me meaningfully. I knew that God had spoken. I did not change my mind. We went to face the challenges of my new job in Grimsby knowing that God had ordained it. That is a very precious experience.

God does promise to lead and guide those He loves. Normally all the guidance and leading we need comes to us through our Bible reading and through time spent in prayer. But at crucial times God does show impeccable timing and perfect care by releasing a prophetic word through someone of good Christian character.

When I applied to leave the Prudential Assurance Company after almost thirty years to follow what I believed was the will of God for my life, it is natural that I had times of doubt and insecurity and uncertainty. Was I doing the right thing? Am I being fair to Edith and to our dependent children?

Within an hour of leaving the Prudential Office for the last time I had picked up the keys for the vacant shop we were renting. Its fifteen hundred square feet of emptiness seemed to be filled only with voices. Voices shrieking at me "What if this does not work?" "You are a fool to give up what you had for this."

"What do you know about charity shops and selling second hand goods?"
"If this does not work you will look a complete fool."

Maybe I did not share my feelings, but God knew how I was feeling. In those early days after launching the CARE Charity, God spoke prophetically, words of great encouragement, of confirmation and even of direction. When God speaks into a situation there is always a sense of peace and wellbeing. Prophetic words are to build up and encourage. If someone claims to speak the counsel of God to you, and you are left feeling wretched and sucked dry, then those words have not come from God.

So prophetic words soon began to flow, personal prophecies for me and prophecies for the CARE charity when it was in its infancy...

There was a striking prophecy from Denny Cramer, visiting from America. We had never met but he asked me to stand in a packed church meeting and spoke to me,

"The Lord would say David, I have given you a pastor's heart. You've known it for some time but have not known what to do with it. I have brought you here this weekend to activate you. I am giving you definition now. I have called you to love my sheep, I have called you to feed my sheep, and I have called you to guard my sheep. Oh but dear God, I'm too busy. I have got too much going on. I've got to go here and I've got to go there. I've made you a successful man, I've given you the ability to put your hands to so much and see it blessed. This is a day of activation I am stirring you and stimulating you. I have anointed you with a spirit of counsel and you are going to begin to counsel my people, and I want to say something to you my brother. I see people coming to you wounded and bleeding and just struggling. God says that you are going to nurse them and love them and father them and mother them for the Lord would say that the gift of mercy shall increase in you and on you and you are going to have encounters with me. You are going to say "God you know it was good when you met with me, you changed my life and took me down a new course." So get ready for all kinds of neat stuff to happen. Get ready for all kinds of new direction. Get ready for door after door to open."

And another prophetic word from a gifted servant of God who did not know us. He asked Edith and I to stand in a well-attended church meeting and spoke over us,

The Lord shows me that you have been pillars, pillars, pillars, pillars in the house of God and both of you have been burden bearers. You have borne the burden of others faithfully and with much mercy, sympathy and compassion.

"God says Man of God, I've made you a strong man, strong strong strong in my Word. Oh a man that will now begin to view the Word of God as literally as lifesaving and life sustaining. You will draw upon the Word of God for what it is, even my word, says The Lord. You have always held my Word in high esteem and you have lived your life both in integrity and character and you have been a witness, good job says God, you have been a witness to me, you let your light shine in your own way. A relational man, a man that people have come to who have needed counsel and you have spoken and brought people through even devastating and life altering situations, because God would say that when others turned away you have turned towards the need. You turned towards people and said "I'll not run like they did, no I'm not a false shepherd, I'm a true one. You said "Lord I'll lay down my life for the sheep you have given me" so man of God, listen to me, even though others have seemed to succeed more in many ways and have seemed to ride the waves of success and popularity, you were not interested in those things and neither was I. I've seen your faithfulness my son of your life and ministry and I commend you this night for doing what I told you to do. You have been an obedient man, you have walked in my will, counsel and way, therefore you have seen the blessing and even the safety and the intervention of angelic beings in your life. They have come alongside you and you need to know this, man of God. I'm going to watch out for you and your wife. I'm going to make a way, I'm going to plot and plan a course for both of you so get ready for doors to open, get ready for some things to shake you to your core, good things. Oh God, I never thought I would do that! Well, God says "Son I never asked you what you thought. I've asked you to obey me and God says get ready for new and exciting doors to open for The Lord says "I am activating this couple, I am prophesying activation over you, and I am prophesying activation over you sweetheart and activation over you my brother. God says that your lives will never be the same. The Lord says "I am destroying the status quo, I am destroying the routine mundane regularity of your lives, and God says that the two of you will be taken to the next level activity, the next level of ministry. The Lord says that it is not over, it has only begun This creative, powerful prophetic word is going to begin to work in you and in you and on you and on you. Get ready to mother and father my children, for many shall call you mum and many shall call you dad says the Lord"

These are awesome things to hear following taking a step into the relatively unknown. How gracious of our loving God to confirm that we were walking in the path He had called us into and that He was doing things in us and with us which would facilitate us for the journey. With that sort of confirmation and encouragement from God, I felt that I could drive along the road, wherever it may lead, with the impregnable course of a great steam roller allowing no bumps in the road to be a problem. These are some of the encouraging words, inspired by God which were passed on to Edith and me when we needed to hear.

There were prophetic words too relating to the CARE charity. Words usually came from strangers I had not met but they all had the common thread.

"In beginning the work you are involved in, you have thrown a pebble into the water. You can only see those ripples close to you, you have no idea how far those ripples will spread."

"Do not think only in local terms. I am going to enlarge your heart, extend your boundaries and increase your influence."

"This is what the Lord says, I will make CARE the head and not the tail."

There were many other encouragements like these. If someone began a new business today in uncertain times, how special it would be to hear such assuring confirmations as these. We were so privileged that God directed, guided, encouraged and confirmed us in those early days. The ethos of CARE was to run towards people in need, especially those from whom others had turned away. To guard them, love and protect them became our priorities.

We recognised that there is no guarantee that a particular prophetic word will come to pass. Fulfilment is conditional, obedience to God is always the key. Following His leading, displaying His heart, maintaining a true servant spirit, and having Christ and His will at the centre. I believe that these are prerequisites if God's full potential is to be achieved. There is great encouragement when God speaks in these ways.

When the CARE charity was in its infancy I went with several local church leaders to a day long Christian conference in Milton Keynes. The sessions were held in a sports centre and there were several hundred in attendance from all over the country.

It was quite a rush to be there in time for the first session, but we managed it, and after a welcome cup of coffee took our seats with the rest of the large congregation. The chairman invited a gentleman onto the stage whilst he introduced him to us all. He was Bryn , and was introduced as a "Christian leader with a strong prophetic gift." We were told that Bryn was not one of the speakers at the conference but that he had been given the authority to step to the lectern at any time during the conference and share any prophetic word he felt God had given him. I never saw Bryn again until the closing session which was scheduled for 4 pm until 5 pm. The preacher at this last session was a cousin of Nelson Mandela, and I believe his name was Rev Joseph Cobbo. After an inspiring closing address, he took his seat. The applause was beginning to die away, but before the chairman could get to his feet to close the conference, Bryn with the prophetic gift was standing at the lectern. This was a man I had never seen before or since. We clearly did not know each other. He looked in my direction and said that he had a prophetic word for the gentleman wearing the navy blue blazer. I was wearing a navy blue blazer but was so certain that he did not mean me that I looked behind me to see whether someone else fitted his description.

"No, please don't turn round. Yes I am talking to you, the gentleman wearing spectacles and the navy blue blazer."

I looked at him in uncertainty pointing at my chest.

"Yes sir, God has given me a word for you."

By now every pair of eyes seemed to be on me but I did not have any fears over what he may say, just a sense of excitement and privilege.

Bryn told me he felt sure that I was not a pastor but that I headed up some kind of Christian ministry which was relatively new. He said that he could visualise me sitting with a group of men and sharing with them. He urged me to keep good communication with these men and be accountable to them as they were my safeguard. We said that I had thrown a pebble in the water and had no idea how far the ripples would spread. He also said that in the short time the Christian ministry had been in operation, I had been digging the ground with a garden hoe, this would change and I would begin to dig the ground with a large garden spade and we would see lots of fruit. He told me that it had been in my heart to head up something with a local emphasis, and urged me not to think only in local terms. He said that what I was doing would have a huge impact on the local community, that we would impact the nation and that that we would have an impact upon Africa.

I was sitting between two of CARE's trustees, Dennis Brown and Stephen Franklin and they both elbowed me as the prophetic words were flowing. Dennis's wife, Linda approached me and said,

"You had better have your passport ready if you are going to Africa."

"Going to Africa" was unthinkable. We were a small local charity running on a shoe string financially. We knew that we had a big God and that if He had work for us to do in Africa it would come to pass. What possible impact could we have all those thousands of miles away. I felt that God had called me to be a kind of missionary into my own community and my vision was focussed there.

How spot on though were the words Bryn had spoken. I was regarded by the charity trustees as the visionary behind the CARE charity and we all met regularly in the Ice House in Grimsby where I reported on progress, finance, staff and personnel issues, and more importantly my vision for the future. I never pursued any aspect of future vision until I had the endorsement of the trustees. There was a total security in that relationship, I could follow my vision responsibly and they could act as charity trustees with the correct diligence and authority. I do believe that here was one of the keys to the reason for God blessing the charity so much. We had strong vision, strong trustees and strong lines of accountability between them and me. They were not afraid to challenge me if necessary.

So Bryn's prophetic encouragement was significant. He had confirmed, as others had before him, that we had no idea how far the ripples would spread. He had referred to the small beginning as though we were trying to dig with a garden hoe. He emphasised that we would dig with larger implements and that there would be fruitfulness. He also promised that we would impact our community, the nation and Africa. There was much encouraging food for thought here!

A local social worker who often asked the CARE Shop for help for families she was supporting warned me that the Director of Social Services had issued a directive requesting that social workers did not ask the CARE Charity for help. Although the directive did not give specific reasons, it was felt that there was much suspicion of us because we had strong Christian roots. My first inclination was to ask for a meeting with the Director of Social Services but I felt it right just to continue our work into the community without presenting a challenge to him. It was only a matter of time before I received a letter from the Director. Although we had not met, he addressed me as "Dear Dave" and went on to say that he viewed CARE as a partner with Social Services as we had done a great deal to help some of their most vulnerable clients. Because of the help and support we had given I was invited to take part in one or two case conferences where the help and support we promised was recorded as part of the Care Plan. So here was a way in which digging with a hoe was giving way to digging with a spade!

Bryn's prophecy that we would impact the local community took shape. Through the support and finance we made available to Citizen's Advice Bureau over two million pounds worth of debt was handled each year for several years at the CARE Shop offices. Since 1992 we have given away a considerable amount of free furniture. This is still ongoing after almost thirty years and I believe that an average annual value of the goods we have given away is between £14,000 and £15,000. A considerable amount of goods when considering the relatively low value of the used but quality items. Shortly before my retirement we began the Daily Bread Food Larder in conjunction with the local churches. David Swannack my successor had a great vision for this and developed this valuable programme. It became the main "growth area" of the charity and the demand for food parcels increased year on year. It was only when the food larder began to hinder our core business that we stopped handing out individual food parcels. However we still collected food and donated it to some of the other food banks which did not exist when we began donating food. Another valuable programme which David Swannack had the vision to set up was known as the Routes Programme. David sensed that residents in hostel type accommodation were likely to struggle to maintain independent living when they left the hostel. They needed something in between the hostel and their own tenancy of a flat. So in conjunction with the Salvation Army Hostel David set up the Routes Programme. The CARE charity provided accommodation in shared houses overseen by support workers. The experience was designed to enable young men to make the transition from institutionalised living to complete independence. Young men were helped and we had successes. Sadly the cost of running the programme was extremely high, too high for a small charity to bear, so the programme was brought to a conclusion.

Providing floating support to many vulnerable tenants we had housed through our housing and support scheme also became a major part of our work. For some it made the difference between failure and success in their new tenancy.

Whilst doing this we touched the need for the impartation of parenting skills, and Di Briggs joined us and for as long as we could get the funding, Di presented excellent parenting courses which enriched the lives of many.

Then of course our rehousing badly housed and homeless people became a major contribution to the community. Since the initiative began in 1996 we have housed and supported approaching 5000 people. We have certainly impacted the community.

Bryn prophesied that we would impact the nation. How could this happen?!

Our Scheme to enable struggling tenants to obtain a decent tenancy without the burden of finding a huge amount of money for advance rent and security bond had a major facility. Because we were a registered charity, we could ensure that the Housing Benefit was paid direct to us and not to the tenant. This meant that we could immediately pay the rent over to the landlord. There was no risk that a cash strapped tenant could use the Housing Benefit to pay other commitments, so the landlords felt secure in letting CARE have their properties. It was crucial to the continued success of CARE Rent Scheme that we could receive Housing Benefit direct from the local authority.

However all this was set to change. In its wisdom the government decided that those in receipt of housing benefit should receive the money personally in order that they exercise their own management of the money. As soon as it was obvious that this change was imminent, one local letting agency boasted at a meeting that they had issued 57 eviction notices so that they could get rid of Housing Benefit tenants before the new payment system began.  Some local authorities were chosen as "Pathfinder" areas where the new arrangements could be rolled out first and tested for problems. Grimsby was such an area.

Local landlords did not like this and they held meetings to lobby the government in their efforts to stop it. The government sent a representative from the Department of Works and Pensions, Mr David Barr, who addressed local landlords at a public meeting in the town hall. He was trying to allay their fears but they savaged him.  Soon after this I received a phone call from Austin Mitchell our MP.  He asked whether I was prepared to travel to Westminster to meet with a senior civil servant to discuss the forthcoming Pathfinder Scheme.

Two other areas were going live as Pathfinder projects around the same time as we were, and they too would have a representative invited to attend the same meeting.  I agreed to be part of this important meeting and it was not long before I received a hefty briefing pack giving all the proposed details and fine print associated with the proposed Pathfinder roll out.  I made it my priority to study the briefing pack and was pleased to see that there were circumstances when the Housing Benefit could be paid to the landlord direct, or to CARE direct. This depended on whether the tenant was considered to be vulnerable. There needed to be a past history of vulnerability and there was little recognition that a sudden change in circumstances could make a person vulnerable for the first time. I studied carefully the DWP definitions of vulnerability and personally was unhappy with them. I did not feel that they were broad enough and if applied rigidly they would be very restrictive.

The meeting was to be held at the Waldorf Hotel situated just off the Strand in Westminster. I was glad to stretch my legs after leaving the train and there was time for a quick walk along The Strand. I came upon a shop selling Barbour clothing and decided to have a look inside.  After browsing for a few minutes I thought that I should find the Waldorf Hotel but before I could leave the shop, the owner asked whether he could help me.  He gave me directions to the hotel and I told him that I would return when my meeting there had finished and try some coats on.

After the meeting with the DWP I returned and decided to buy a Barbour coat and wrote out a cheque.  As I went into my pocket for my wallet, the Chinese shop owner asked "What are you looking for?"

"I am just getting my cheque guarantee card out of my wallet, you will need that."

"No, no need of your cheque guarantee card, you have an honest face. You promised to come back after your meeting and I knew that you would come back. Put your cheque guarantee card away it is not needed, I know that your cheque will be fine. Thank you for buying from me." I still have that coat many years later and it reminds me of the day when someone who had never seen me before trusted me, and it brings back memories of my incursion into the corridors of power in Westminster.

I found the Waldorf Hotel and felt a little intimidated by the opulence of the reception area I quickly found that the DWP were renting the entire top floor as offices, and it was there that my meeting would take place. I was asked to sit and wait until someone came down to escort me to the meeting place. As I was waiting, a lady came in and approached the reception desk. She was a brassy blond, was chewing gum and seemed to be draped in expensive jewellery. She was there for the same meeting as I was and she managed a homeless scheme in a Yorkshire city who were also destined to be a Pathfinder area. We were conducted together into the lift and soon were crossing the large open plan office which was a hive of industry. We were taken into a glass fronted private office and introduced to Mr David Barr. He exchanged pleasantries for a short while until the third invitee to the meeting joined us. She was a middle aged West Indian lady involved in helping homeless people in a Devonshire city.

We sat facing David Barr across his desk. Behind him I could see the London Eye lazily revolving like a large cycle wheel.

I asked Mr Barr if he would accept my apologies for the way he had been received at his meeting with the Grimsby landlords. He smiled as he replied,

"Don't worry it goes with the territory. It was the day of our son's birthday though and I would much rather have been at home with him."

Then we were down to business. The government wanted the Pathfinder projects to work. They were keen to educate people to budget sensibly and be responsible for their own money. That would never happen whilst they had their rents paid direct to their landlord. He needed our input and insights as he recognised that we were working at the sharp end. He wanted to listen to us.

Our West Indian lady friend interjected,

"Are you suggesting that Housing Benefit could soon be paid direct to the tenants?"

Recognising that she was out of touch and had not read her briefing pack, Mr Barr smiled and said to her,

"Just sit and listen my dear. You may soon catch up."

Then he turned to our jewel decked friend and I asking,

"If the roll out of the Pathfinder Scheme makes it difficult to recruit landlords for your homeless projects, what would you do?"

The Yorkshire lady, still chewing her gum responded with very little feeling,

"Oh I don't really need the job I would just jack it in and go and live on my boat."

So for the remainder of the meeting the conversation was between David Barr and myself. I challenged the proposed definitions of vulnerability. They were deeply flawed because to be classed as vulnerable there had to be a past history of vulnerability. A past history of rent arrears, a past history of not sustaining a tenancy. I explained scenarios which would suddenly make a person vulnerable who had never trodden that path before. He began to see my point and asked me to go back to Grimsby and draw up what I considered to be a fair criteria for measuring vulnerability. Smiling he asked

"Do you think that you can do all that and let me have it in ten days?"

Within the allotted time frame I had submitted detailed definitions of how I would measure vulnerability. Included in my submissions was the position that if someone had to approach a homeless charity for help then by definition they were vulnerable, in spite of their past history. Hence homeless charities should automatically be entitled to have their tenants Housing Benefit paid direct to the charity. Mr Barr accepted our proposals and the concessions introduced were a valuable advantage to homeless charities enabling them to continue helping our vulnerable people who were homeless or badly housed.

I remembered Bryn's prophecy that CARE would have an impact on the nation and felt so privileged that in a small way I had seen this happen.

Bryn had referred to the community, the nation and to Africa. I think that subconsciously I had forgotten about Africa as there was no way it could appear on our map or agenda.

However I was invited to be interviewed at the Grapevine Christian Festival held on the Lincolnshire Showground each August. The interview took place in the Big Top on August Bank Holiday evening. There were several thousand people in attendance. I remember that the preacher that evening was Gerald Coates and he was sitting close behind me on the platform. The interview was designed to feature the work of the CARE charity and lasted about twenty minutes when I had the opportunity of sharing some special stories about CARE.

I was back at my desk next day re-running the interview in my mind and wondering whether I had made the most of the opportunity given. I was so grateful for the publicity CARE had enjoyed through the interview as Grapevine was attended by Christians from all over the country and the meetings were available on video. Again there was a sense that we had in another way been able to impact the nation.

Imagine my surprise when a few days later I received a phone call from The God Channel, the Christian TV company based in Sunderland. The gentleman ringing me had been in the audience during my Grapevine interview and was keen to invite me to be a studio guest in one of their TV programmes. He wanted me to share more about the work of CARE and what we sensed was the call of God to begin the work.

I immediately agreed and then wondered what I was letting myself in for! During the few weeks whilst I was waiting to be given a date for the interview I alternated between excitement and fear. Eventually I had a firm date and I would be the studio guest from 11-00pm until midnight. During that hour the interviewer would return to me three or four times and music would be played between my slots. I rang them the day before the interview to check up on the dress code. Having been assured that "smartly casual" was fine I made the observation,

"Eleven o'clock at night is rather late and possibly there will not be a large audience at that time. I hope that when the programme is transmitted it will be at a more suitable time."

"What do you mean David? It will not be a recorded interview it will be a live transmission. Eleven o'clock in the UK is prime time in America there will be a vast audience."

"America! It will be broadcast live to America?"

"It most certainly will, and when you are being interviewed in our Sunderland studio you will be seen live in fifty seven nations. EVEN IN AFRICA."

I quietly thanked God that we were following a prophetic pathway. The pathway God had laid out for us.

# Why Another Book?

This little book should be in the Guinness Book of Records as a recognition of the length of time it has taken to write it! I began recording my experiences as The Man from the Prudential in the early 1990's and today in the first week of 2022 I am at last putting the concluding remarks together. Had I depended on my literary output for my income I regret that my wife and family would be in a sorry state by now!.

I had devoured all the vet books by James Herriot (The pen name of James Alfred Wight) I thought of the pleasure he had brought to himself and his family by setting down on paper the stories of his interaction with the colourful and memorable Yorkshire characters he rubbed shoulders with as the Yorkshire Vet. I don't think he had any intention of becoming a published author when he began writing. It was a way of unwinding after a challenging day's work and of making sure that his memories were preserved to be enjoyed later. Later in life he remarked that his memories were a safe place to return to.

We were able spend a family holiday on more than one occasion in a little holiday cottage in Thirsk known as " Sunnyside. " In James Herriot's early days in Thirsk, Sunnyside was the home of the local midwife and local ladies gave birth in the spare bedroom which was equipped as a delivery room. James Herriot's children were born there and the same bright yellow door which shone out across The Green when the Herriot children were born was still radiantly smiling at us as it welcomed us for our holidays there.

It was during one of those holidays that I saw a poster announcing that every Wednesday afternoon at 2-00pm, James Herriot welcomed visitors at the Vets Surgery. He looked forward to meeting the public, chatting with them as he gave a conducted tour round "Skeldale House". He would also talk about his experiences, answer questions and have his photograph taken with his guests.

I did not miss this opportunity, and promptly at 2-00pm the large heavy door opened and there stood the man himself beaming a welcome, resplendent in a spotlessly white coat and looking every bit like a refined school headmaster.

He was at ease and put everyone at ease. With great charm he accommodated the wishes of the gushing American lady who insisted on having her photograph taken with him. He apologised for the fact that he would not be able to sign autographs. He explained that as a vet for very many years he had of necessity had to push his hands into uninviting places and then dip them into a bucket of ice cold water to clean them. This had caused arthritis and signing his name was now a slow and painful process. However, as he was watching TV in the evenings he was unhurriedly able to sign his name on sticky book labels which he was happy to hand out to us... He gave one to me which I stuck onto the fly leaf of one of his books.

There was no edge to him, he was a very humble self-effacing man and we all warmed to him. As we listened to some of his stories I found myself thinking that I had met many unusual and amusing characters in my years working as the Man from The Prudential and I felt sure that in my own way I could write down some of my experiences and decided to have a go.

So in February 1991, having written seven short chapters, I sent them to James Herriot at the surgery, explaining that I had met him recently and become motivated by him to write something for myself. I simply asked that if he had the time to look at them, I would welcome his opinion whether I was wasting my time or not.

On 20th February 1991 he replied with a typewritten letter on his personal headed paper bearing his home address and phone number. He had enjoyed the chapters and encouraged me to keep going. It was signed JAMES HERRIOT and knowing how difficult it was for him to sign his name I was especially grateful. So early in 1991 I decided to "keep going" but so much has got in the way since.

A year later I retired from the Pru and launched the charity Christian Action and Resource Enterprise and that took up much time. There was always so much to do with priorities and deadlines. An occasional new chapter saw the light of day, but it was not until the Covid 19 lockdown that I found the time to really concentrate on chronicling some of my experiences.

The content and style of this little book changed once I began writing about that organisation which is special to me and close to my heart, CARE or CHRISTIAN ACTION AND RESOURCE ENTERPRISE.

When I retired from paid employment with CARE I was appointed to its board of Trustees a position I still enjoy today. I realise that I am the only person involved with the Charity who has been intimately associated with it since its birth in May 1992 and earlier than that. My involvement began when it was just a challenge from God to do something for the local needy and vulnerable. I felt a sense of urgency, an urge to set down in writing a record of how CARE began and what is was like in those early days. I did not want to leave this life until I had left a permanent record which hopefully will uplift and inspire with a sense of hope.

Then I realised that May 2022 is a very significant month. It marks the time when I will have drawn my Prudential staff pension for longer than I worked for the Company. I wonder how many people reach that milestone! In May 2022 it will be 30 years since I walked out of the Prudential offices in Grimsby for the last time, free to pursue my vision of setting up a local Christian charity. May 2022 is the month when the CARE charity celebrates 30 years of local Christian service. At that time I will also celebrate 30 years of personal involvement with CARE. This coincides with my 80th birthday on the 12th May 2022. Suddenly there was a new urgency to get this little book finished in time for May 2022 so that it could be a part of CARE's 30th anniversary celebrations.

I previously had no thought of trying to publish this personal record which was just my private store of memories and my "safe place to be." It became my intention to dedicate this book to the CARE charity who would be the sole beneficiary from any proceeds.

I also wish to celebrate the personal privilege of being able, supported by others, to plough the first furrows of CARE and, to change the metaphor, lay foundations which are still holding firm after thirty years.

Looking back after thirty years I am more certain than ever that God called me to launch CARE, and Edith and I are so grateful that God has rewarded us in excess of the sacrifices made when I left the Pru and stepped into the unknown.

I do sometimes ponder over the question whether or not I was God's first choice. Rheinard Bonke the late great German evangelist had a humbling experience. He had a powerful call from God to produce a Gospel leaflet which he called "From Minus to Plus" he knew that he had to get a copy of this booklet into every house in Europe. A massive step of faith. Anxious to know that his theology expressed in the booklet was sound, he submitted it to three evangelical theologians for their comments. God challenged him in his private prayer time "Rheinard, why have you submitted your booklet to the three people who were my first, second and third choice of people to produce it and get it into every house in Europe. They all turned me down!"

Knowing that he was not God's first choice was humbling experience for Rheinard.

I cannot imagine that I would have been God's first choice of person to set up the CARE Christian Charity, but who knows!   If the first, second and third choices are out there somewhere, thank you for allowing me the opportunity!

I also wish to celebrate the strong presence of God throughout the work of CARE in those formative years. There was a distinctive ethos which lifted us into something very special.

I also wish to celebrate the support of all our Christian Trustees from the first day until now. Dennis Brown, Dave Kitchen Philip Wooffindin and David Jones have given great support as Chairs of the Trustees.  David Jones, who is my Pastor is CARE's present Chair of Trustees, and I have asked David to write an introduction to this book.  Sincere thanks for the tireless labours of all staff, paid and volunteers, you have made such a difference. Thanks too to individual supporters who have donated money to us over the years, some on a regular monthly basis.  Grateful thanks too to the philanthropic organisations who have made grants to us over the years.  Thanks to the Midland Bank (HSBC) who have been our bankers for thirty years and have supported us well. Thanks to TRIODOS ethical bank who advanced the mortgage to enable us to buy the CARE SHOP building with the seven flats above it.  Heartfelt thanks to Rev David Swannack who succeeded me as General Manager.  David brought his own vision which was true to our original ethos.  Then Sarah Taylor took the reins from Dave Swannack, our time with Sarah at the helm was very special. Latterly, Stephen Durkin, who after commencing work with CARE as the CARE RENT SCHEME manager became General Manager, a position Steve still holds.  Steve has worked for CARE for 17 years.  I have asked Steve to contribute to this little book by writing the closing chapter. I am sure that Steve will remind us all of the lives touched by CARE over the years and of course the incredible work still going on today. It is so sad that the malaise of poverty and hardship is still with us, this should not be a surprise as Jesus warned that we would always have the poor with us. I wish to celebrate our journey as it took in Holmfirth, Sleaford, Grimsby and Cleethorpes as the Man from The Pru. Looking back I believe that is was all a preparation for what was to come in 1992 when CARE was birthed. Throughout our journeys there has been the presence of the still small voice, preparing, shaping and positioning.

We celebrate and thank God for all those who helped Edith and I to hear and follow the still small voice.

A great thank you to all who have prayed for us over the years I believe that your prayers have helped keep us on course under the mantle of God's blessing.

Please recommend this little book, this will be a great help to CARE who is the sole beneficiary of any proceeds generated. . You can find further details of CARE on its web site. CHRISTIAN ACTION AND RESOURCE ENTERPRISE.


God bless you

David.

rdavid481@btinternet.com

# Epilogue by Stephen Durkin

As you will know by now, having read so far into this book, CARE came into being as one Christian's response to what he saw at the time as being such need in the area of North East Lincolnshire. It was his response to the poverty, hardship and distress that he saw daily as he went about his business. He saw that people who were already down in the gutter of life, whose self-esteem and self-worth were at rock bottom, kept on being knocked, battered, as officialdom seemed not to offer much help to them. They did not want much at all: just a place to live, a bed to sleep on, food to feed themselves and their families, and to enjoy themselves. He saw this, I am sure, as being far from the "abundant Life" that his Lord and Master, Jesus the Christ, came to earth to bring us (John 10:10). So, he hatched his plan to set up a charity that would be an organisation that would put people first, that would recognise people who were made in God's image and likeness and understand that everyone has an innate dignity and value due to this.

From that time back in 1992 we continue to carry out this work in our local community. In May of this year we will have achieved thirty years. I wonder if David Robinson ever thought that after starting CARE there would still be the need for its services some thirty years later, I doubt it; but the fact is that the need has gone up exponentially in this time. That which started as a way for David to show his Christian faith in a practical way, rolling up his sleeves, literally, to scrub and clean everyday household items to give them by way of a blessing to individuals that often lacked basic items, that you and I can take for granted, was as incredible then as it is today. Yet, with the help of too many people and organisations to be able to name and credit here, we keep CARE's light shining here in North East Lincolnshire, in the darkness of poverty, hardship and distress.

I am currently the fourth General Manager, including David himself; there were David Swannack and Sarah Taylor, and to each of them I pay tribute to their effort and achievements. During this time we have continued to bring God's love to the people of our community in much the same way as we always have, being God's hands and feet, and eyes and ears, bringing care and support to many thousands of people that have come to us for our help. None of this could have been done without the support of large numbers of volunteers, who over the years have given us their unselfish and unflinching amounts of their time, care and attention. The eponymous care that has enabled us, as a small local charity, to help so many people. We are a small charity with a mighty heart.

Just to give you a flavour of what we have been able to do over these years, whilst not condemning you to death by statistics; over thirty years we have:

- helped over 60,000 people with housing, support and donations

- Given out over £807,000 of help and assistance (averaging £26-27,000 per year).

So I am sure that you can see that CARE is like the parable of the mustard seed, that we read in the Bible (Matthew 13:31-32). From the smallest of seeds it becomes a massive tree, in which "the birds come and perch in its branches."

And we carry on finding housing, donating furniture and other household goods, supporting people, being an emergency food provider through our Empty Chair Appeal, and also help with fuel poverty by making utility donations.

And now, here in 2022 we find ourselves at a crossroads in the life of CARE. It costs a considerable amount of money to be able to operate our housing and community support work to the standard that our clients deserve. Consequently, as a small local charity we are very reliant on grant funding. For the last six years we have worked in partnership with the National Lottery Community Fund (NLCF) which gives grants to organisations to enable them to carry out their critical work across the country. This is made available from the money that is set aside by the National Lottery from the 'Good Causes' monies that is raised by the players of the lottery; and I want to say a very big thank you to all of them.

The National Lottery Community Fund now finds itself to be very oversubscribed and that means that in a two-stage application process a first stage application only has a 20% chance of going through to the second and last stage; so that means a failure rate of 80% at the first hurdle. In addition to this, it is unlikely that they would fund us for a third time to the same extent as previously, so this time it will involve us applying to two or three grant funders. That is the process that we are in at the moment. So if you are one to pray, please pray for us this year. Failing this, your very best wishes would not go amiss either.

This process of applying for grants will, in fact, be the last major contribution that I will make for CARE because I will retire at the end of 2022 after eighteen years of working for the charity. I applied for the position of Housing and Community Support Manager at the end of 2004, was made the Retail and Development Manager in 2015 and then was asked to step into the breach, as it were, in December 2018 after the departure of Sarah Taylor. Well, I suppose it served me right for being the only man standing at that time. I am sure that if circumstances had been different I would not have been the Board of Trustees' choice. So I see myself as a reliable, steady hand on the tiller at a time when stability was needed – therefore, very much a Caretaker General Manager.

When I was asked to contribute something to this book it was suggested to me that I could give an operational perspective with a flavour of what my vision for CARE was. Whilst I was happy to make this little contribution, I have to admit that my visionary days are further back in the past, than they are in the future, and that is why I have said that CARE now finds itself at a crossroads. It is now, and going forward, that my 'vision' for the future is that the Board of Trustees should set themselves the task of succession planning with a view to bringing in someone with an energy and a vision for where he or she wants to take CARE into its fourth decade of being a small, local charity with a massive heart for the people of North East Lincolnshire.

During my time I have always thought, and my prayer has been, that we would see the day when there was no longer a need for CARE to exist. What a thought! Wanting to see a day when there was no need, no poverty, hardship and distress in the area where we live. Sadly, I am confident that that day is nowhere to be seen, nowhere coming up in the days, weeks, years and decades ahead. Society today, as we sit here in a pre-post pandemic age, where the lockdowns and restrictions have been endured for so long, where government spending and support has been enormous and the cost of which now has been reckoned and we now require plans to pay it all back, leaves welfare and benefits a poor relation. Those of us who read the bible should not be surprised. When Jesus walked on the earth he told those who would listen to him that the poor will always be with you (Matthew 26:11). The need for CARE has never been greater!

Finally, my 'vision' for CARE is that another person, someone with a heart for people like David Robinson will appear and gather around them others who want to carry out God's work to the vulnerable and needy people of our area; to bring them dignity and respect, care, love and support, so that they too may have life and have it abundantly.

Stephen Durkin

General Manager

February 2022

Printed in Great Britain
by Amazon